Fodor's 98

Hong Kong

The complete guide, thoroughly up-to-date

Packed with details that will make your trip

The must-see sights, off and on the beaten path

What to see, what to skip

Vacation itineraries, walking tours, day trips

Smart lodging and dining options

Essential local do's and taboos

Transportation tips

Key contacts, savvy travel advice

When to go, what to pack

Clear, accurate, easy-to-use maps

Books to read, background essays

Fodor's Travel Publications, Inc.
New York • Toronto • London • Sydney • Auckland
www.fodors.com/

Fodor's Hong Kong

EDITORS: Christina Knight, Chelsea Mauldin

Editorial Contributors: Jan Alexander, Rob Andrews, David Brown, Denise Cheung, Eva Chui, Shann Davies, Heidi Sarna, Helayne Schiff, M. T. Schwartzman (Gold Guide editor), Joanne Shen, Dinah A. Spritzer
Editorial Production: Linda K. Schmidt
Maps: David Lindroth, *cartographer*; Steven Amsterdam, *map editor*
Design: Fabrizio La Rocca, *creative director*; Guido Caroti, *associate art director*; Jolie Novak, *photo editor*
Production/Manufacturing: Robert B. Shields
Cover Photograph: Jeffrey Aaronson/Network Aspen

Copyright

Special Sales

PRINTED IN THE UNITED STATES OF AMERICA

10 9 8 7 6 5 4 3 2 1

CONTENTS

Maps

ON THE ROAD WITH FODOR'S

WE'RE ALWAYS THRILLED to get letters from readers, especially one like this:

It took us an hour to decide what book to buy and we now know we picked the best one. Your book was wonderful, easy to follow, very accurate, and good on pointing out eating places, informal as well as formal. When we saw other people using your book, we would look at each other and smile.

Our editors and writers are deeply committed to making every Fodor's guide "the best one"—not only accurate but always charming, brimming with sound recommendations and solid ideas, right on the mark in describing restaurants and hotels, and full of fascinating facts that make you view what you've traveled to see in a rich new light.

About Our Writers

Our success in achieving our goals—and in helping to make your trip the best of all possible vacations—is a credit to the hard work of our extraordinary writers.

Jan Alexander is a journalist who has lived on and off in Hong Kong since 1992. She has written about the region for *Newsweek,* the *Wall Street Journal, Far Eastern Economic Review,* and *Money Magazine.* She is also the author of *Getting to Lamma,* a novel inspired by her travels in China and Hong Kong, published by Asia 2000, Hong Kong.

Denise Cheung, the food and style editor of *HK Magazine,* was born and raised in Hong Kong and is intimately familiar with her city, from its world-renowned hotels to its street-side eateries. She covers the scene with restaurant reviews, features, and articles on food and shopping. She has also written about travel, food, and entertainment for local publications.

A Hong Kong native who grew up in Melbourne, Australia, **Eva Chui** returned to her hometown three years ago to scoop the territory's art and nightlife scene as entertainment editor of *HK Magazine* (work and play blurred many a time). Eva assures us that nightlife in Hong Kong is continuing at its blistering pace, this time led by young locals rather than expats. She's now working at Channel [V], the leading Asian music channel.

Shann Davies is a British-born travel writer who has lived and worked in 15 countries around the world but always comes back to Asia. She first visited Macau in 1960 and has since made it her spiritual home, although for the past few years she's been based in Hong Kong.

Since graduating from Princeton University, freelance writer **Joanne Shen** has worked and traveled widely throughout Asia, using Hong Kong as her base. Besides teaching for a year in Guangzhou and working for two at *HK Magazine* as an editor and staff writer, she has been an editor for *The Chinese,* a new Mandarin monthly.

New This Year

We've added walking tours of Hong Kong and Macau that will lead you through the best of the exploring sights, taking into consideration the time you have to spend.

And this year, Fodor's joins Rand McNally, the world's largest commercial mapmaker to bring you a detailed color map of Hong Kong. Just detach it along the perforation and drop it in your tote bag.

We're also proud to announce that the American Society of Travel Agents has endorsed Fodor's as its guidebook of choice. ASTA is the world's largest and most influential travel trade association, operating in more than 170 countries, with 27,000 members pledged to adhere to a strict code of ethics reflecting the Society's motto, "Integrity in Travel." ASTA shares Fodor's devotion to providing smart, honest travel information and advice to travelers, and we've long recommended that our readers consult ASTA member agents for the experience and professionalism they bring to the table.

On the Web, check out Fodor's site (www.fodors.com/) for information on major destinations around the world and travel-savvy interactive features. The Web site also lists the 85-plus stations nationwide that carry *Fodor's Travel Show,* a live call-in program that airs every weekend. Tune in to hear guests discuss their wonderful adventures—or call in to get answers for your most pressing travel questions.

How to Use This Book

Organization

Up front is the **Gold Guide,** an easy-to-use section divided alphabetically by topic. Under each listing you'll find tips and information that will help you accomplish what you need to in Hong Kong. You'll also find addresses and telephone numbers of organizations and companies that offer destination-related services and detailed information and publications.

The first chapter in the guide, Destination: Hong Kong, helps get you in the mood for your trip. New and Noteworthy cues you in on trends and happenings, What's Where gets you oriented, Pleasures and Pastimes describes the activities and sights that really make Hong Kong unique, Fodor's Choice showcases our top picks, and Festivals and Seasonal Events alerts you to special events you'll want to seek out.

The Exploring chapter is subdivided by neighborhood; each subsection recommends a walking or driving tour and lists neighborhood sights alphabetically, including sights that are off the beaten path. The remaining chapters are arranged in alphabetical order by subject (dining, lodging, nightlife and the arts, outdoor activities and sports, shopping, and side trips).

At the end of the book you'll find Portraits, wonderful essays about ever-changing Hong Kong and its cuisine, business customs, and shopping, followed by suggestions for any pretrip research you want to do, from recommended novels to nonfiction and reference reading.

Note

Floor numbers in Hong Kong are indicated by the letter F and follow the British system, in which the first floor is what Americans would call the second.

Some street and site names and colonial monikers may revert to their Chinese names or be renamed to honor events or people of mainland China. At press time Hong Kong was just beginning its new status as a Special Administrative Region, and no name changes were planned.

Icons and Symbols

★ Our special recommendations
✕ Restaurant
🏨 Lodging establishment
🐣 Good for kids (rubber duckie)
☞ Sends you to another section of the guide for more information
✉ Address
☎ Telephone number
☉ Opening and closing times
💰 Admission prices (those we give apply to adults; substantially reduced fees are almost always available for children, students, and senior citizens)

Numbers in white and black circles that appear on the maps, in the margins, and within the tours correspond to one another.

Credit Cards

The following abbreviations are used: **AE,** American Express; **DC,** Diners Club; **MC,** MasterCard; and **V,** Visa.

Don't Forget to Write

You can use this book in the confidence that all prices and opening times are based on information supplied to us at press time; Fodor's cannot accept responsibility for any errors. Time inevitably brings changes, so always confirm information when it matters—especially if you're making a detour to visit a specific place. In addition, when making reservations be sure to mention if you have a disability or are traveling with children, if you prefer a private bath or a certain type of bed, or if you have specific dietary needs or other concerns.

Were the restaurants we recommended as described? Did our hotel picks exceed your expectations? Did you find a museum we recommended a waste of time? If you have complaints, we'll look into them and revise our entries when the facts warrant it. If you've discovered a special place that we haven't included, we'll pass the information along to our correspondents and have them check it out. So send us your feedback, positive *and* negative: email us at editors@fodors.com (specifying the name of the book on the subject line) or write the Hong Kong editor at Fodor's, 201 East 50th Street, New York, New York 10022. Have a wonderful trip!

Karen Cure
Editorial Director

Hong Kong

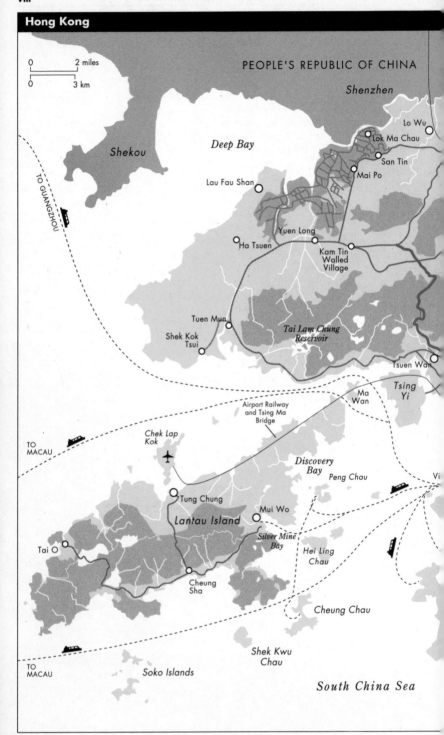

PEOPLE'S REPUBLIC OF CHINA

Shenzhen

Lo Wu

Lok Ma Chau

San Tin

Mai Po

Shekou

Deep Bay

Lau Fau Shan

Yuen Long

Ha Tsuen

Kam Tin Walled Village

TO GUANGZHOU

Tuen Mun

Shek Kok Tsui

Tai Lam Chung Reservoir

Tsuen Wan

Ma Wan

Tsing Yi

Airport Railway and Tsing Ma Bridge

Chek Lap Kok

TO MACAU

Discovery Bay

Peng Chau

Vi

Tung Chung

Lantau Island

Mui Wo

Silver Mine Bay

Tai O

Hei Ling Chau

Cheung Sha

Cheung Chau

TO MACAU

Soko Islands

Shek Kwu Chau

South China Sea

0   2 miles

0   3 km

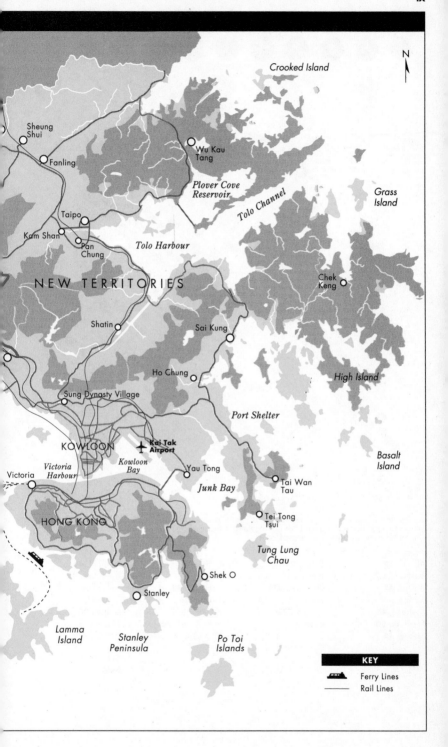

World Time Zones

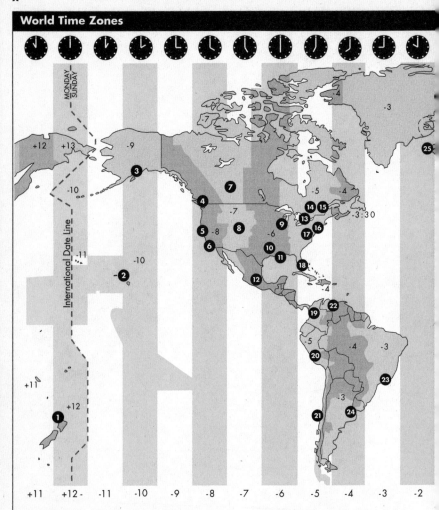

MONDAY
SUNDAY

International Date Line

+12 +13 -9 -4 -3 25

3 -7 7 -5 -4 -3:30

4 -7 14 15

-8 8 9 13

5 -6 17 16

6 10 11 18

-10 -11 2 -10 12

19 22

-11 -5 -4 -3

+11 20 -4 -3

+12 -3 23

1 21 24

+11   +12 -   -11   -10   -9   -8   -7   -6   -5   -4   -3   -2

Numbers below vertical bands relate each zone to Greenwich Mean Time (0 hrs.).
Local times frequently differ from these general indications,
as indicated by light-face numbers on map.

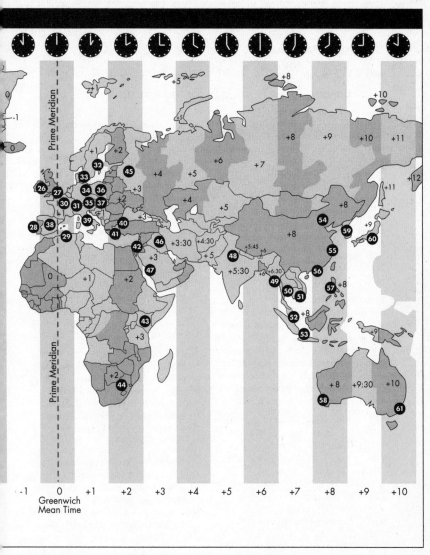

SMART TRAVEL TIPS / THE GOLD GUIDE

SMART TRAVEL TIPS A TO Z

Basic Information on Traveling in Hong Kong, Savvy Tips to Make Your Trip a Breeze, and Companies and Organizations to Contact

A

AIR TRAVEL

Most people choose a flight based on price, but because of the time and distance involved in traveling to Hong Kong, there are other issues to consider. These include smooth connections, the number of departures available, and a carrier's frequent-flyer partners, which allow you to credit mileage earned on one airline to your account with another.

Non-stop flights from the United States to Hong Kong are rare. Either a direct flight, which requires at least one stop, or a connecting flight, which requires a change of airplanes (and sometimes airline), will often be your only choice. Some flights, especially nonstops, may be scheduled only on certain days of the week.

➤ To Hong Kong: **Asiana** (☎ 800/ 227–4262). **Canadian** (☎ 800/426– 7000). **Cathay Pacific Airways** (☎ 800/233–2742 in the U.S.; 800/268– 6868 in Canada). **China Airlines** (☎ 800/227–5118). **Continental** (☎ 800/ 231–0856). **Korean Air** (☎ 800/ 438–5000). **Northwest** (☎ 800/447– 4747). **Singapore Airlines** (☎ 800/ 742–3333). **United Airlines** (☎ 800/ 241–6522). **Virgin Atlantic** (☎ 800/ 862–8621).

➤ To Macau: **Asiana** (☎ 800/227– 4262). **Korean Air** (☎ 800/438– 5000). **Northwest** (☎ 800/447– 4747).

➤ From the U.K.: **Cathay Pacific Airways** (☎ 0171/747-8888). **Virgin Atlantic** (☎ 01293/747747). **British Airways** (☎ 0345/222111).

GET THE LOWEST FARE

Shop around, since you never know who may have the best deal. Make sure to call the airlines directly, get price quotes from a travel agent or tour operator who is experienced in booking travel to Hong Kong, and contact a few consolidators. The

Sunday travel section of most newspapers is a good place to look for deals.

Usually, you must **book in advance** and meet certain restrictions, such as minimum stay requirements, to get cheaper fares. However, even the least-expensive airfares from the major airlines are often refundable. Also **check different routings,** and if you are making several stops, try not to backtrack in order to make connections. The lowest fares require a confirmed flight; however, you can often leave your return open or change your plans for a $50–$100 fee. Fares are generally comparable whether you are flying transpacific or transatlantic.

To save money on round-trip flights from the United Kingdom, **look into an APEX or Super-PEX ticket.** APEX tickets must be booked in advance and have certain restrictions. Super-PEX tickets can be purchased at the airport on the day of departure—subject to availability.

Try to **avoid connecting flights,** which require a change of plane. Two airlines may jointly operate a connecting flight, so ask if your airline operates every segment—you may find that your preferred carrier flies you only part of the way.

USE AN AGENT

Travel agents, especially those who specialize in finding the lowest fares (☞ Discounts & Deals, *below*), can be especially helpful when booking a plane ticket. When you're quoted a price, **ask your agent if the price is likely to get any lower.** Good agents know the seasonal fluctuations of airfares and can usually anticipate a sale or fare war. However, waiting can be risky: The fare could go *up* as seats become scarce, and you may wait so long that your preferred flight sells out. A wait-and-see strategy works best if your plans are flexible, but if you must arrive and depart on certain dates, don't delay.

CHECK WITH CONSOLIDATORS

Consolidators buy tickets for scheduled flights at reduced rates from the airlines then sell them at prices that beat the best fare available directly from the airlines, usually without advance restrictions. Sometimes you can even get your money back if you need to return the ticket. Carefully read the fine print detailing penalties for changes and cancellations, and **confirm your consolidator reservation with the airline.**

➤ CONSOLIDATORS: **United States Air Consolidators Association** (✉ 925 L St., Suite 220, Sacramento, CA 95814, ☎ 916/441–4166, FAX 916/441–3520).

AVOID GETTING BUMPED

Airlines routinely overbook planes, knowing that not everyone with a ticket will show up, but sometimes everyone does. When that happens, airlines ask for volunteers to give up their seats. In return these volunteers usually get a certificate for a free flight and are rebooked on the next flight out. If there are not enough volunteers the airline must choose who will be denied boarding. The first to get bumped are passengers who checked in late and those flying on discounted tickets, **so get to the gate and check in as early as possible,** especially during peak periods.

Always **bring a photo ID to the airport.** You may be asked to show it before you are allowed to check in.

ENJOY THE FLIGHT

For more legroom, **request an emergency-aisle seat;** don't however, sit in the row in front of the emergency aisle or in front of a bulkhead, where seats may not recline.

Some carriers have prohibited smoking throughout their systems, so **contact your carrier regarding its smoking policy.**

To avoid jet lag, which occurs when travel disrupts your body's natural cycles, try to maintain a normal routine. At night, **get some sleep.** By day, move about the cabin to **stretch your legs, eat light meals, and drink water—not alcohol.**

COMPLAIN IF NECESSARY

If your baggage goes astray or your flight goes awry, complain right away. Most carriers require that you file a claim immediately.

➤ AIRLINE COMPLAINTS: U.S. Department of Transportation **Aviation Consumer Protection Division** (✉ C-75, Room 4107, Washington, DC 20590, ☎ 202/366–2220). **Federal Aviation Administration (FAA) Consumer Hotline** (☎ 800/322–7873).

The gateway to Hong Kong, at least until April 1998, is **Kai Tak International Airport,** also known as Hong Kong International Airport. The new airport (unnamed at press time) at **Chek Lap Kok** is scheduled to open in April and will handle all flights to and from Hong Kong 24 hours a day. Nearby **Macau International Airport** allows travelers to fly directly into the neighboring island.

Flying time to Hong Kong is between 17 and 20 hours from New York or Chicago, via Vancouver or Honolulu, and 13 hours direct from Los Angeles or San Francisco. Macau is a 20-minute flight from Hong Kong.

➤ AIRPORT INFORMATION: **Kai Tak International Airport** (☎ 011–852/2769–7531). **Macau International Airport** (☎ 011–853/785–448).

TRANSFERS TO AND FROM CHEK LAP KOK AIRPORT

Starting in June 1998, a high-speed, high-frequency railway will whisk you via the Tsing Ma Bridge from the airport to Tsim Sha Tsui in Kowloon in 18 minutes, and to Central on Hong Kong Island in 23 minutes. The airport railway station will have platforms connected to the arrival and departure levels.

In Central, the terminus will connect to the existing transportation infrastructure. In Kowloon, the terminus will connect to the West Kowloon Expressway and other transportation links.

During the interim between the airport's opening in April and the railway's completion in June, shuttle buses will serve you, also via the Tsing Ma Bridge.

THE GOLD GUIDE / SMART TRAVEL TIPS

TRANSFERS TO AND FROM KAI TAK AIRPORT

A fast and efficient way to get to and from Kai Tak Airport is to use the **Airbus** (☎ 2745–4466), which runs every 10 to 20 minutes from 7 AM to midnight. Route A1 (HK$12) runs through the Kowloon tourist area and serves the Ambassador, Empress, Grand, Holiday Inn Golden Mile, Hyatt Regency, Imperial, International, Kowloon, Miramar, New World, Park, Peninsula, Regent, Shangri-La, and Sheraton hotels, plus the YMCA and the Star Ferry. Routes A2 and A3 (HK$19) go to Hong Kong Island. A2 serves the Harbour View International House, Furama, Hilton, Mandarin, and Victoria hotels. A3 serves the Causeway Bay hotels: Caravelle, Excelsior, and Park Lane Radisson.

You can also follow signs to the area where hotel limousines wait. For normal taxi service, expect to pay HK$50 to HK$60 for Kowloon destinations and up to HK$120 for Hong Kong Island destinations, which includes the two-way toll for either cross-harbor tunnel. Drivers add a luggage-handling charge of HK$5 per piece.

➤ SHUTTLES: **Airbus** (☎ 2745–4466).

B

BUS TRAVEL

Double-decker buses have extensive routes and you can pick up a route map at any HKTA office and also at some gift shops. Drop your exact change into the box by the driver when you get on (no change is given out). Fares range from HK$1.10 to HK$32.

Minibuses, 14- to 16-seat yellow vehicles with single red stripes, travel all over Hong Kong and stop almost anywhere on request; **look for a minibus for quick transportation.** They are, however, slightly more expensive than ordinary buses. Their destination is written on the front, but the English-language characters are small. **Wave the minibus down when you see the one you want.** Since fares are adjusted throughout the journey, you could pay as little as HK$2 or as much as HK$7 (pay as you exit).

Maxicabs look the same as minibuses but have single green stripes and run fixed routes. Rates run from HK$1.50 to HK$18 (pay as you enter).

➤ SCHEDULES & INFORMATION: **Hong Kong Tourist Association** (☎ 2807–6177).

BUSINESS & TRADE SERVICES & CONTACTS

BUSINESS CENTERS

There are many business centers outside the hotels; some are considerably cheaper than hotel facilities. Others cost about the same but offer private desks (from HK$250 per hour for desk space to HK$8,000 a month and up for a private office).

Amenities include a private address and phone answering and forwarding services. Many centers are affiliated with accountants and lawyers who can speed company registration. Some will even process visas and wrap gifts for you.

Harbour International Business Centre (✉ 2802 Admiralty Centre Tower I, 18 Harcourt Rd., ☎ 2529–0356, FAX 2861–3420) provides typing, secretarial support, and office rentals. Reservations are not required.

The **American Chamber of Commerce** (✉ Room 1904, Bank of America Tower, 12 Harcourt Rd., Central, Hong Kong Island ☎ 2526–0165, FAX 2810–1289) can arrange a Breakfast Briefing Program at your hotel for a fee that is negotiable according to the size of the group. The chamber hosts many luncheons and seminars, and the Young Professionals Committee holds cocktail parties at least once a month. There is also a library and a China trade services section.

Other business organizations of note are **AMS Management Service Ltd.** (✉ 18th floor, Wilson House, 19–27 Wyndham St., Central, ☎ 2846–3100, FAX 2810-7002), **Brauner's Business Centre** (✉ Room 903–5, 9th floor, Kowloon Centre, 29–43 Ashley Rd., Tsim Sha Tsui, ☎ 2376–2855, FAX 2376–3360), **Business Executive Centre** (✉ Room 3715, Sun Hung Kai Centre, 30 Harbour Rd., Wanchai, ☎ 2827–7322, FAX 2827–4227), **Business Station** (✉ 5th floor, East Wing Duke Wellington

House, 14–24 Wellington St., Central, ☎ 2521–0630, FAX 2521–7601), and 6th floor, Cosmos Bldg., 8–11 Lan Kwai Fong; Central, ☎ 2523–6810, FAX 2530–5071), **Central Executive Business Centre** (✉ 11th floor, Central Bldg., 1 Pedder St., Central, ☎ 2841–7888, FAX 2810–1868), and **United Network Business Centre** (✉ 4th floor, Albion Plaza, 2–6 Granville Rd., Tsim Sha Tsui, ☎ 2734–4888, FAX 2367–2151).

CELLULAR PHONES

Hongkong Telecom International (HKTI) rents cellular phones and has offices throughout the territory. The 24-hour office is at Hermes House, 10 Middle Road, in Tsim Sha Tsui (☎ 2888–7184 and 2888–7185); another main office is at 1 D'Aguilar St., Central (☎ 2810–0660).

CHAMBERS OF COMMERCE

American Chamber of Commerce in Hong Kong (✉ Room 1904, Bank of America Tower, 12 Harcourt Rd., Central, Hong Kong Island, ☎ 2526–0165, FAX 2810–1289).

British Chamber of Commerce (✉ Room 1401–2, Tung Wai Commercial Building, 109–111 Gloucester Rd., Wanchai, Hong Kong Island, ☎ 2824–2211, FAX 2824–1333).

Chinese Manufacturers' Association (✉ 5th floor, CMA Bldg., 64–66 Connaught Rd., Central, Hong Kong Island, ☎ 2542–8600, FAX 2541–4541.

Federation of H.K. Industries (✉ 407 Hankow Centre, 5–15 Hankow Rd., Kowloon, ☎ 2732–3188, FAX 2721–3494.

Hong Kong General Chamber of Commerce (✉ United Centre, 22nd floor, Queensway, Hong Kong Island, ☎ 2529–9229, FAX 2527–9843).

Hong Kong Japanese Chamber of Commerce and Industry (✉ Hennessy Centre, 38th floor, 500 Hennessy Rd., Hong Kong Island, ☎ 2577–6129, FAX 2577–0525).

Hong Kong Productivity Council (✉ HKPC Bldg., 78 Tat Chee Ave., Kowloon Tong, ☎ 2788–5678, FAX 2788–5900).

Indian Chamber of Commerce Hong Kong (✉ Hoseinee House, 2nd floor,

69 Wyndham St., Central, Hong Kong Island, ☎ 2523–3877, FAX 2845–0300).

Swedish Chamber of Commerce (✉ Shun Ho Tower, 24–30 Ice House St., Central, Hong Kong Island, ☎ 2525–0349, FAX 2537–1843).

CONVENTION CENTER

The **Hong Kong Convention and Exhibition Centre** (✉ Harbour Rd., Wanchai, Hong Kong Island, ☎ 2582–8888, FAX 2582–8828) is a state-of-the-art 693,000-square-ft complex on the Wanchai waterfront, capable of handling 140,000 visitors a day. There are five exhibition halls, and two main convention halls; the new addition jutting into the harbor doubled the center's size and hosted the 1997 handover ceremony. The complex, Asia's largest, houses two hotels, the 600-room Grand Hyatt and the 900-room New World, an apartment block, and a 54-story trade center/office building.

COPY SERVICES

All hotels and business centers have photocopy machines, as do many stores scattered throughout the territory. For heavy-duty, oversize, and color copying, try **Xerox** (✉ Central: New Henry House, 10 Ice House St., ☎ 2524–9799, FAX 2845–9271; Admiralty: United Centre, Unit 34, 95 Queensway, ☎ 2527–6162, FAX 2529–5416; Wanchai: Shanghai Ind. Investment Bldg., 48–66 Hennessy Rd., ☎ 2528–0761, FAX 2865–0799; Tsim Sha Tsui: China Hong Kong City, Shop 3, 4 Canton Rd., ☎ 2736–6011, FAX 2736–6278).

FACSIMILE

The Post Office and Hong Kong Telecom International (HKTI) offer a joint service called "Postfax." Check the **General Post Office** (✉ Next to Star Ferry Terminal, Central, Hong Kong, ☎ 2921–2222) to find out which post offices have the service. Postfax is available at Hong Kong Telecom's 24-hour office (✉ Hermes House, 10 Middle Road, Tsim Sha Tsui, Kowloon, ☎ 2843–9466).

MESSENGERS

Deliveries can sometimes be arranged through your hotel concierge. Most business centers offer delivery service, too. However, there is a good chance

THE GOLD GUIDE / SMART TRAVEL TIPS

that both of them will contact DHL's local courier service, run simultaneously with their international one. There are numerous **DHL Express Centres** (☎ 2765–8111) in major buildings and at various Mass Transit Railway stations. DHL will also pick up from your hotel. Weight and distance determine exact price. If your timing is right at the Express Centre, you should be able to get same-day delivery.

OVERNIGHT MAIL

The post office has an overnight express service called Speedpost. Large international couriers, including **DHL** (☎ 2765–8111, FAX 2764–0641), **Federal Express** (☎ 2730–3333, FAX 2730–6588), and **UPS** (☎ 2735–3535, FAX 2738–5070) have Hong Kong offices.

TELEX

If you want to avoid the hotel surcharge or your business center is closed, the public telex for sending is at **Hong Kong Telecom International (HKTI)** offices. There are many offices throughout the territory; the 24-hour office is at Hermes House, 10 Middle Road (across the street from the Sheraton), in Tsim Sha Tsui, Kowloon (☎ 2888–7184 or 2888–7185).

TRADE INFORMATION

Hong Kong Trade Development Council (✉ 38th floor, Office Tower Convention Plaza, 1 Harbour Rd., Hong Kong Island, ☎ 2584–4333, FAX 2824–0249). The TDC has 51 overseas offices, including 12 in the United States and one in the United Kingdom.

Trade Department (✉ Trade Department Tower, 700 Nathan Rd., Kowloon, ☎ 2789–7444, FAX 2789–2491).

Industry Department (✉ Ocean Centre, 14th floor, 5 Canton Rd., Kowloon, ☎ 2737–2573, FAX 2730–4633).

BUSINESS HOURS

Most banks are open 9 AM to 4:30 PM, but some open in the evening, and major ones are open 9 AM to 12:30 PM on Saturday, and even on Sundays for special purposes. There is 24-hour automated banking in most branches.

Office hours are more or less the same as in the West, 9 AM–5 or 6 PM, but shops usually open about 10 AM and stay open until 9 or 9:30 PM, especially in the tourist and residential areas.

Although there are no hard and fast rules about hours, shops in Hong Kong tend to open and close late. On Hong Kong Island, the Central area is open from 10 AM to 6 PM; Causeway Bay and Wanchai from 10 AM to 9:30 PM. Kowloon's Tsim Sha Tsui East is open from 10 AM to 7:30 PM; Tsim Sha Tsui, Yau Ma Tei, and Mong Kok from 10 AM to 9 PM.

C

CAMERAS, CAMCORDERS, & COMPUTERS

Always **keep your film, tape, or computer disks out of the sun.** Carry an extra supply of batteries, and **be prepared to turn on your camera, camcorder, or laptop** to prove to security personnel that the device is real. Always **ask for hand inspection of film,** which becomes clouded after successive exposure to airport x-ray machines, and **keep videotapes and computer disks away from metal detectors.**

➤ PHOTO HELP: Kodak Information Center (☎ 800/242–2424). *Kodak Guide to Shooting Great Travel Pictures,* available in bookstores or from Fodor's Travel Publications (☎ 800/533–6478; $16.50 plus $4 shipping).

CUSTOMS

Before departing, **register your foreign-made camera or laptop with U.S. Customs** (☞ Customs & Duties, *below*). If your equipment is U.S.-made, call the consulate of the country you'll be visiting to find out whether the device should be registered with local customs upon arrival.

CAR RENTAL

Because of difficult driving conditions, traffic jams, and parking problems, you should **avoid renting a car in Hong Kong.** Public transportation is excellent and taxis are inexpensive. If you do decide to rent a car, it is advisable to take one *with* a driver. Several operators offer such services, which can be arranged through your hotel. Charges are HK$800–

HK$1200 for the first four hours (depending on car model) and HK$200–HK$300 for each subsequent hour.

The only major agency renting in Hong Kong is Avis. Rates begin at $90 a day and $372 a week for an economy car with air conditioning, an automatic transmission, and unlimited mileage.

➤ MAJOR AGENCIES: **Avis** (☎ 800/ 331–1084, 800/879–2847 in Canada).

➤ LOCAL AGENCIES: **Ace Hire Car** (✉ 16 Min Fat St., Happy Valley, ☎ 2893–0541; turn left at the Hong Kong Bank). **Fung Hing Hire Co.** (☎ 2572–0333) rents chauffeured cars only.

CHILDREN & TRAVEL

CHILDREN IN HONG KONG

Be sure to plan ahead and **involve your youngsters** as you outline your trip. When packing, include things to keep them busy en route. On sightseeing days try to schedule activities of special interest to your children. If you are renting a car don't forget to **arrange for a car seat** when you reserve. Most hotels Hong Kong allow children under a certain age to stay in their parents' room at no extra charge, but others charge them as extra adults; be sure to **ask about the cutoff age for children's discounts.**

➤ LOCAL INFORMATION: *The Great Hong Kong Dragon Adventure,* published by the Hong Kong Tourist Association (HKTA; ☞ Visitor Information, *below*), is a story about a dragon that flies children from place to place. The HKTA also offers maps, brochures, and leaflets of activities sure to enthrall young visitors.

FLYING

As a general rule, infants under two not occupying a seat fly at greatly reduced fares and occasionally for free. If your children are two or older **ask about children's airfares.**

In general the adult baggage allowance applies to children paying half or more of the adult fare. When booking, **ask about carry-on allowances for those traveling with infants.** In general, for babies charged 10% of the adult fare you are allowed one carry-on bag and a collapsible stroller, which may have to be checked; you may be limited to less if the flight is full.

According to the FAA it's a good idea to use safety seats aloft for children weighing less than 40 pounds. Airlines, however, can set their own policies: U.S. carriers allow FAA-approved models but usually require that you buy a ticket, even if your child would otherwise ride free, since the seats must be strapped into regular seats. Airline rules vary regarding their use, so it's important to **check your airline's policy about using safety seats during takeoff and landing.** Safety seats cannot obstruct any of the other passengers in the row, so get an appropriate seat assignment as early as possible.

When making your reservation, **request children's meals or a free-standing bassinet** if you need them; the latter are available only to those seated at the bulkhead, where there's enough legroom. Remember, however, that bulkhead seats may not have their own overhead bins, and there's no storage space in front of you—a major inconvenience.

CONSUMER PROTECTION

Whenever possible, **pay with a major credit card** so you can cancel payment if there's a problem, provided that you can provide documentation. This is a good practice whether you're buying travel arrangements before your trip or shopping at your destination.

If you're doing business with a particular company for the first time, **contact your local Better Business Bureau and the attorney general's offices** in your state and the company's home state, as well. Have any complaints been filed?

Finally, if you're buying a package or tour, always **consider travel insurance** that includes default coverage (☞ Insurance, *above*).

➤ LOCAL BBBs: **Council of Better Business Bureaus** (✉ 4200 Wilson Blvd., Suite 800, Arlington, VA 22203, ☎ 703/276–0100, FAX 703/ 525–8277).

THE GOLD GUIDE / SMART TRAVEL TIPS

CUSTOMS & DUTIES

When shopping, **keep receipts** for all of your purchases. Upon reentering the country, **be ready to show customs officials what you've bought.** If you feel a duty is incorrect, appeal the assessment. If you object to the way your clearance was handled, get the inspector's badge number. In either case, first ask to see a supervisor, then write to the port director at the address listed on your receipt. Send a copy of the receipt and other appropriate documentation. If you still don't get satisfaction you can take your case to customs headquarters in Washington.

ENTERING HONG KONG

Except for the usual prohibitions against narcotics, explosives, firearms, and ammunition (all of which must be declared upon arrival and handed over for safekeeping until departure), and modest limits on alcohol, tobacco products, and perfume, you can bring anything you want into Hong Kong, including an unlimited amount of money.

Nonresident visitors may bring in, duty-free, 200 cigarettes or 50 cigars or 250 grams of tobacco, and 1 liter of alcohol.

ENTERING THE U.S.

You may bring home $400 worth of foreign goods duty-free if you've been out of the country for at least 48 hours and haven't already used the $400 allowance or any part of it in the past 30 days.

Travelers 21 and older may bring back 1 liter of alcohol duty-free. In addition, regardless of your age, you are allowed 200 cigarettes and 100 non-Cuban cigars. (At press time, a federal rule restricting tobacco access to persons 18 years and older did not apply to importation.) Antiques, which the U.S. Customs Service defines as objects more than 100 years old, enter duty-free, as do original works of art done entirely by hand, including paintings, drawings, and sculptures.

You may also send packages home duty-free: up to $200 worth of goods for personal use, with a limit of one parcel per addressee per day (and no alcohol or tobacco products or perfume worth more than $5); label the package PERSONAL USE, and attach a list of its contents and their retail value. Do not label the package UNSOLICITED GIFT, or your duty-free exemption will drop to $100. Mailed items do not affect your duty-free allowance on your return.

➤ INFORMATION: **U.S. Customs Service** (Inquiries, ✉ Box 7407, Washington, DC 20044, ☎ 202/927–6724; complaints, Office of Regulations and Rulings, 1301 Constitution Ave. NW, Washington, DC 20229; registration of equipment, ✉ Resource Management, 1301 Constitution Ave. NW, Washington DC, 20229, ☎ 202/927–0540).

ENTERING CANADA

If you've been out of Canada for at least seven days you may bring in C$500 worth of goods duty-free. If you've been away for fewer than seven days but more than 48 hours, the duty-free allowance drops to C$200; if your trip lasts 24–48 hours, the allowance is C$50. You may not pool allowances with family members. Goods claimed under the C$500 exemption may follow you by mail; those claimed under the lesser exemptions must accompany you.

Alcohol and tobacco products may be included in the seven-day and 48-hour exemptions but not in the 24-hour exemption. If you meet the age requirements of the province or territory through which you reenter Canada you may bring in, duty-free, 1.14 liters (40 imperial ounces) of wine or liquor *or* 24 12-ounce cans or bottles of beer or ale. If you are 16 or older you may bring in, duty-free, 200 cigarettes and 50 cigars; these items must accompany you.

You may send an unlimited number of gifts worth up to C$60 each duty-free to Canada. Label the package UNSOLICITED GIFT—VALUE UNDER $60. Alcohol and tobacco are excluded.

➤ INFORMATION: **Revenue Canada** (✉ 2265 St. Laurent Blvd. S, Ottawa, Ontario K1G 4K3, ☎ 613/993–0534, 800/461–9999 in Canada).

ENTERING THE U.K.

From countries outside the EU, including Hong Kong, you may import, duty-free, 200 cigarettes or 50 cigars; 1 liter of spirits or 2 liters of fortified or sparkling wine or liqueurs; 2 liters of still table wine; 60 milliliters of perfume; 250 milliliters of toilet water; plus £136 worth of other goods, including gifts and souvenirs.

➤ INFORMATION: **HM Customs and Excise** (✉ Dorset House, Stamford St., London SE1 9NG, ☎ 0171/202–4227).

D
DISABILITIES & ACCESSIBILITY

ACCESS IN HONG KONG

Hong Kong is not the easiest of cities for people in wheelchairs; there are few ramps or other provisions for access. Progress is being made, however; the airports, City Hall, the Academy for Performing Arts, and the Hong Kong Arts Centre have made efforts to assist people in wheelchairs. For more information, get a copy of the local guide to accessibility, *A Guide for Physically Handicapped Visitors in Hong Kong*, available from the Hong Kong Tourist Association (HKTA). The guide lists the rare places that have special facilities for people with disabilities, in addition to the best access to hotels, shopping centers, government offices, consulates, restaurants, and churches.

TIPS AND HINTS

When discussing accessibility with an operator or reservationist, **ask hard questions.** Are there any stairs, inside *or* out? Are there grab bars next to the toilet *and* in the shower/tub? How wide is the doorway to the room? To the bathroom? For the most extensive facilities meeting the latest legal specifications, **opt for newer accommodations,** which are more likely to have been designed with access in mind. Older buildings may offer more limited facilities. Be sure to **discuss your needs before booking.**

➤ COMPLAINTS: **Disability Rights Section** (✉ U.S. Department of Justice, Box 66738, Washington, DC 20035–6738, ☎ 202/514–0301 or 800/514–0301, FAX 202/307–1198, TTY 202/514–0383 or 800/514–0383) for general complaints. **Aviation Consumer Protection Division** (☞ Air Travel, *above*) for airline-related problems. **Civil Rights Office** (✉ U.S. Department of Transportation, Departmental Office of Civil Rights, S-30, 400 7th St. SW, Room 10215, Washington, DC, 20590, ☎ 202/366–4648) for problems with surface transportation.

TRAVEL AGENCIES & TOUR OPERATORS

The Americans with Disabilities Act requires that travel firms serve the needs of all travelers. That said, you should note that some agencies and operators specialize in making travel arrangements for individuals and groups with disabilities.

➤ TRAVELERS WITH MOBILITY PROBLEMS: **Access Adventures** (✉ 206 Chestnut Ridge Rd., Rochester, NY 14624, ☎ 716/889–9096), run by a former physical-rehabilitation counselor. **Accessible Journeys** (✉ 35 W. Sellers Ave., Ridley Park, PA 19078, ☎ 610/521–0339 or 800/846–4537, FAX 610/521–6959), for escorted tours exclusively for travelers with mobility impairments. **CareVacations** (✉ 5019 49th Ave., Suite 102, Leduc, Alberta T9E 6T5, ☎ 403/986–6404, 800/648–1116 in Canada) has group tours and is especially helpful with cruise vacations. **Hinsdale Travel Service** (✉ 201 E. Ogden Ave., Suite 100, Hinsdale, IL 60521, ☎ 630/325–1335), a travel agency that benefits from the advice of wheelchair traveler Janice Perkins. **Wheelchair Journeys** (✉ 16979 Redmond Way, Redmond, WA 98052, ☎ 206/425–2210 or 800/313–4751), for general travel arrangements.

DISCOUNTS & DEALS

Be a smart shopper and **compare all your options before making a choice.** A plane ticket bought with a promotional coupon may not be cheaper than the least expensive fare from a discount ticket agency. For high-price travel purchases, such as packages or tours, keep in mind that what you get is just as important as what you save. Just because something is cheap doesn't mean it's a bargain.

LOOK IN YOUR WALLET

When you use your credit card to make travel purchases you may get free travel-accident insurance, collision-damage insurance, and medical or legal assistance, depending on the card and the bank that issued it. American Express, MasterCard, and Visa provide one or more of these services, so **get a copy of your credit card's travel-benefits policy.** If you are a member of the American Automobile Association (AAA) or an oil-company-sponsored road-assistance plan, always **ask hotel or car-rental reservationists about auto-club discounts.** Some clubs offer additional discounts on tours, cruises, or admission to attractions. And don't forget that auto-club membership entitles you to free maps and trip-planning services.

DIAL FOR DOLLARS

To save money, **look into "1-800" discount reservations services,** which use their buying power to get a better price on hotels, airline tickets, even car rentals. When booking a room, always **call the hotel's local toll-free number** (if one is available) rather than the central reservations number—you'll often get a better price. Always ask about special packages or corporate rates.

➤ AIRLINE TICKETS: ☎ 800/FLY-4-LESS.

➤ HOTEL ROOMS: **Steigenberger Reservation Service** (☎ 800/223-5652). **Travel Interlink** (☎ 800/888-5898).

SAVE ON COMBOS

Packages and guided tours can both save you money, but don't confuse the two. When you buy a package your travel remains independent, just as though you had planned and booked the trip yourself. Fly/drive packages, which combine airfare and car rental, are often a good deal. In cities, ask the local visitors bureau about hotel packages. These often include tickets to major museum exhibits and other special events.

JOIN A CLUB?

Many companies sell discounts in the form of travel clubs and coupon books, but these cost money. You must use participating advertisers to get a deal, and only after you recoup the initial membership cost or book price do you begin to save. If you plan to use the club or coupons frequently you may save considerably. Before signing up, find out what discounts you get for free.

➤ DISCOUNT CLUBS: **Entertainment Travel Editions** (✉ 2125 Butterfield Rd., Troy, MI 48084, ☎ 800/445-4137; $23-$48, depending on destination). **Great American Traveler** (✉ Box 27965, Salt Lake City, UT 84127, ☎ 800/548-2812; $49.95 per year). **Moment's Notice Discount Travel Club** (✉ 7301 New Utrecht Ave., Brooklyn, NY 11204, ☎ 718/234-6295; $25 per year, single or family). **Privilege Card International** (✉ 237 E. Front St., Youngstown, OH 44503, ☎ 330/746-5211 or 800/236-9732; $74.95 per year). **Sears's Mature Outlook** (✉ Box 9390, Des Moines, IA 50306, ☎ 800/336-6330; $14.95 per year). **Travelers Advantage** (✉ CUC Travel Service, 3033 S. Parker Rd., Suite 1000, Aurora, CO 80014, ☎ 800/548-1116 or 800/648-4037; $49 per year, single or family). **Worldwide Discount Travel Club** (✉ 1674 Meridian Ave., Miami Beach, FL 33139, ☎ 305/534-2082; $50 per year family, $40 single).

E

ELECTRICITY

To use your U.S.-purchased electric-powered equipment, **bring a converter and adapter.** The electrical current in Hong Kong is 200 volts, 50 cycles alternating current (AC); in Macau it is 220 volts, 50 cycles. Some outlets in Hong Kong take plugs with three round prongs, while others use plugs with two square prongs. There is no standard plug size in Macau; check with your hotel regarding their setup.

If your appliances are dual-voltage, you'll need only an adapter. Don't use 110-volt outlets, marked FOR SHAVERS ONLY, for high-wattage appliances such as blow-dryers. Most laptops operate equally well on 110 and 220 volts and so require only an adapter.

EMBASSIES & EMERGENCIES

Police, fire, or ambulance, ☎ 999.

Hong Kong Police Visitor Hot Line (☎ 2527-7177). English-speaking police wear a red shoulder tab.

➤ CONSULATES & COMMISSIONS: **U.S. Consulate** (✉ 26 Garden Rd., Hong Kong Island, ☎ 2523-9011, FAX 2845-0735). **Canadian Commission** (✉ Tower 1, Exchange Sq., 11th-

14th floors, 8 Connaught Pl., Hong Kong Island, ☎ 2810–4321, FAX 2810–8736). **British Trade Commission** (✉ Visa Section, 3rd floor, 1 Supreme Court Rd., Hong Kong Island, ☎ 2901–3111.

➤ HOSPITALS: **Queen Mary Hospital** (✉ 102 Pok Fu Lam Rd., Hong Kong, ☎ 2855–3111), the **Queen Elizabeth Hospital** (✉ 30 Gascoigne Rd., Kowloon, ☎ 2958–8888), the **Tang Shiu Kin Hospital** (✉ 284 Queen's Rd. East, Hong Kong, ☎ 2831–6800), the **Princess Margaret Hospital** (✉ 2-10 Princess Margaret Hospital Rd.; Laichikok, Kowloon, ☎ 2990–3200), and the **Prince of Wales Hospital** (✉ 30–32 Ngan Shing St., Shatin, New Territories, ☎ 2636–2211).

F

FERRY TRAVEL

The **Star Ferry Harbour Cruises** is one of Hong Kong's landmarks. Double-bowed, green-and-white vessels connect Hong Kong Island with the Kowloon Peninsula. The cost for the seven-minute ride is HK$2.20 upper deck and HK$1.90 lower deck. The Star Ferry also runs a service to Hunghom for HK$1.70–HK$2 and between Wanchai and Tsim Sha Tsui (HK$2).

The ferries of the **Hong Kong & Yau Ma Tei Ferry Company** (HKF) go to Hong Kong's beautiful outer islands. Call for ferry schedules and departure points; you can also contact the HKTA (☞ Visitor Information, *below*). Return fares vary from HK$15 to HK$50. Hover-ferries, operated by the same organization, travel from Central to Tsuen Wan for HK$6–HK$7.50 and to Tsim Sha Tsui East for HK$4.

Ferries are extremely crowded and noisy on weekends. If you have to go to the more distant parts of Hong Kong, **choose a linking ferry service to beat surface traffic and save time.**

➤ SCHEDULES & INFORMATION: Contact the HKTA (☎ 2807–6543 or hot line 2807–6177), **Star Ferry Harbour Cruises** (☎ 2366–2576 or 2845–2324), and the **Hong Kong and Yau Ma Tei Ferry Company** (☎ 2542–3081). For information about ferry service to Macau and locations in China, *see* South China A to Z *in* Chapter 9 *and* Macau A to Z *in* Chapter 8.

G

GAY & LESBIAN TRAVEL

Criminal sanctions on homosexual relations between consenting adults were lifted in Hong Kong in 1991.

➤ LOCAL RESOURCES: *Contacts,* a magazine covering the local gay scene, is available for HK$35 at the boutique **Fetish Fashion** (✉ Basement, 29 Hollywood Rd., Central, ☎ 2544-1155). Among popular nightspots are **Petticoat Lane** (✉ 2 Tun Wo La., Mid-Levels, ☎ 2973–0642), and **Propaganda** (✉ 30–32 Wyndham St., Central, ☎ 2868–1316), the largest gay and lesbian bar in Hong Kong. Meeting spots include **Middle Bay Beach** (a 10-minute walk from Repulse Bay along South Bay Rd. toward South Bay), **South Bay Beach**, the **Morrison Hill Swimming Bath** (✉ Oi Kwan Rd., Wanchai), and **Tom Turk's Fitness Club** (✉ Citibank Tower, Citibank Plaza, 3 Garden Rd., 3rd floor, Central, ☎ 2521–4541).

Hong Kong's **AIDS Hotline** can be reached at 2780–2211.

➤ GAY- AND LESBIAN-FRIENDLY TRAVEL AGENCIES: **Advance Damron** (✉ 1 Greenway Plaza, Suite 800, Houston, TX 77046, ☎ 713/850–1140 or 800/695–0880, FAX 713/888–1010). **Club Travel** (✉ 8739 Santa Monica Blvd., West Hollywood, CA 90069, ☎ 310/358–2200 or 800/429–8747, FAX 310/358–2222). **Islanders/Kennedy Travel** (✉ 183 W. 10th St., New York, NY 10014, ☎ 212/242–3222 or 800/988–1181, FAX 212/929–8530). **Now Voyager** (✉ 4406 18th St., San Francisco, CA 94114, ☎ 415/626–1169 or 800/255–6951, FAX 415/626–8626). **Yellowbrick Road** (✉ 1500 W. Balmoral Ave., Chicago, IL 60640, ☎ 773/561–1800 or 800/642–2488, FAX 773/561–4497). **Skylink Women's Travel** (✉ 3577 Moorland Ave., Santa Rosa, CA 95407, ☎ 707/585–8355 or 800/225–5759, FAX 707/584–5637), serving lesbian travelers.

H

HEALTH

MEDICAL PLANS

No one plans to get sick while traveling, but it happens, so **consider signing up with a medical-assistance company.** Members get doctor referrals, emergency evacuation or repatriation, 24-hour telephone hot lines for medical consultation, cash for emergencies, and other personal and legal assistance. Coverage varies by plan, so **review the benefits carefully.**

➤ MEDICAL-ASSISTANCE COMPANIES: **International SOS Assistance** (✉ Box 11568, Philadelphia, PA 19116, ☎ 215/244–1500 or 800/523–8930; ✉ 1255 University St., Suite 420, Montréal, Québec H3B 3B6, ☎ 514/874–7674 or 800/363–0263; ✉ 7 Old Lodge Pl., St. Margarets, Twickenham TW1 1RQ, England, ☎ 0181/744–0033). **MEDEX Assistance Corporation** (✉ Box 5375, Timonium, MD 21094-5375, ☎ 410/453–6300 or 800/537–2029). **Traveler's Emergency Network** (✉ 3100 Tower Blvd., Suite 1000B, Durham, NC 27707, ☎ 919/490–6055 or 800/275–4836, FAX 919/493–8262). **TravMed** (✉ Box 5375, Timonium, MD 21094, ☎ 410/453–6380 or 800/732–5309). **Worldwide Assistance Services** (✉ 1133 15th St. NW, Suite 400, Washington, DC 20005, ☎ 202/331–1609 or 800/821–2828, FAX 202/828–5896).

I

INSURANCE

Travel insurance is the best way to **protect yourself against financial loss.** The most useful policies are trip-cancellation-and-interruption, default, medical, and comprehensive insurance.

Without insurance you will lose all or most of your money if you cancel your trip, regardless of the reason. It's essential that you **buy trip-cancellation-and-interruption insurance,** particularly if your airline ticket, cruise, or package tour is nonrefundable and cannot be changed. When considering how much coverage you need, look for a policy that will cover the cost of your trip plus the nondiscounted price of a one-way airline

ticket, should you need to return home early. Also **consider default or bankruptcy insurance,** which protects you against a supplier's failure to deliver.

Medicare generally does not cover health-care costs outside the United States, nor do many privately issued policies. If your own policy does not cover you outside the United States, **consider buying supplemental medical coverage.** Remember that travel health insurance is different from a medical-assistance plan (☞ Health, *above*).

Citizens of the United Kingdom can buy an annual travel-insurance policy valid for most vacations during the year in which it's purchased. If you are pregnant or have a preexisting medical condition, make sure you're covered.

If you have purchased an expensive vacation, particularly one that involves travel abroad, comprehensive insurance is a must. **Look for comprehensive policies that include trip-delay insurance,** which will protect you in the event that weather problems cause you to miss your flight, tour, or cruise. A few insurers sell waivers for preexisting medical conditions. Companies that offer both features include Access America, Carefree Travel, Travel Insured International, and Travel Guard (☞ *below*).

Always **buy travel insurance directly from the insurance company;** if you buy it from a travel agency or tour operator that goes out of business you probably will not be covered for the agency or operator's default, a major risk. Before you make any purchase, **review your existing health and home-owner's policies** to find out whether they cover expenses incurred while traveling.

➤ TRAVEL INSURERS: In the U.S., **Access America** (✉ 6600 W. Broad St., Richmond, VA 23230, ☎ 804/285–3300 or 800/284–8300), **Carefree Travel Insurance** (✉ Box 9366, 100 Garden City Plaza, Garden City, NY 11530, ☎ 516/294–0220 or 800/323–3149), **Near Travel Services** (✉ Box 1339, Calumet City, IL 60409, ☎ 708/868–6700 or 800/654–6700), **Travel Guard International** (✉ 1145 Clark St., Stevens Point, WI

54481, ☎ 715/345–0505 or 800/826–1300), **Travel Insured International** (✉ Box 280568, East Hartford, CT 06128–0568, ☎ 860/528–7663 or 800/243–3174), **Travelex Insurance Services** (✉ 11717 Burt St., Suite 202, Omaha, NE 68154-1500, ☎ 402/445–8637 or 800/228–9792, ✆ 800/867–9531), **Wallach & Company** (✉ 107 W. Federal St., Box 480, Middleburg, VA 20118, ☎ 540/687–3166 or 800/237–6615). In Canada, **Mutual of Omaha** (✉ Travel Division, 500 University Ave., Toronto, Ontario M5G 1V8, ☎ 416/598–4083, 800/268–8825 in Canada). In the U.K., **Association of British Insurers** (✉ 51 Gresham St., London EC2V 7HQ, ☎ 0171/600–3333).

L

LANGUAGE

The official languages of Hong Kong are English and Chinese. The most commonly spoken Chinese dialect is Cantonese, but Mandarin is gaining popularity because it is the official language of China. In Macau, the official languages are Portuguese and Chinese, but many people speak some English.

In hotels, major restaurants, shops, and tourist centers, almost everyone speaks fluent English. However, this is not the case with taxi drivers, bus drivers, and workers in small shops, cafés and market stalls.

The HKTA has introduced a color-coded badge system for their information officers. **Look for badges or window stickers that show which languages are spoken by staff members** (in *addition* to English): a red stripe indicates Japanese; a green stripe, Mandarin; purple, German; and blue, French.

M

MAIL

RECEIVING MAIL

The **General Post Office** (✉ next to the Star Ferry Concourse in Central, ☎ 2921–2222, or at Hermes House, 100 Middle Rd. in Kowloon, ☎ 2366–4111 or 2843–9466 for addressee information) is speedy and efficient, with deliveries twice daily,

six days a week, and overnight delivery in main business areas.

Travelers can receive mail at the **American Express** office (✉ 16–18 Queen's Rd., Central; Ground floor, New World Tower, Central, ☎ 2801–7300). This service is available only for AMEX cardholders or traveler's check holders. Mail should be addressed c/o Client Mail Service at the office listed above.

MONEY

The units of currency in Hong Kong are the Hong Kong dollar ($) and the cent. There are bills of 1,000, 500, 100, 50, 20, and 10 dollars. Coins are 10, 5, 2, and 1 dollar and 50, 20, and 10 cents. At press time the Hong Kong dollar was fixed at approximately 8 dollars to the U.S. dollar, 6.52 to the Canadian dollar, and 12.5 to the pound sterling. The image of the Queen will no longer appear on coins, but the old ones in circulation are still valid.

There are no currency restrictions in Hong Kong. Money-changing facilities are available at the airport, in hotels, in banks, and at private money changers scattered through the tourist areas. You will get better rates from a bank or money changer than from a hotel. However, **be aware of money changers who advertise "no selling commission"** and do not mention the "buying commission" you must pay when you exchange foreign currency or traveler's checks for Hong Kong dollars.

The official currency unit in Macau is the pataca, which is divided into 100 avos. Bank notes come in five denominations: 500, 100, 50, 10, and 5 patacas; coins are 5 and 1 patacas and 50, 20, and 10 avos. The pataca is pegged to the Hong Kong dollar (within a few cents). At press time there were 8 patacas to the Hong Kong dollar. Hong Kong currency circulates freely in Macau but not vice versa, so remember to change your patacas before you return to Hong Kong.

ATMS

Before leaving home, **make sure that your credit cards have been programmed for ATM use in Hong Kong.**

Note that Discover is accepted mostly in the United States. Local bank cards often do not work overseas or may access only your checking account; **ask your bank about a MasterCard/Cirrus or Visa debit card,** which works like a bank card but can be used at any ATM displaying a MasterCard/Cirrus or Visa logo. These cards, too, may tap only your checking account; check with your bank about their policy.

➤ ATM LOCATIONS: **Cirrus** (☎ 800/424–7787). A list of **Plus** locations is available at your local bank.

CURRENCY EXCHANGE

For the most favorable rates, **change money at banks.** Although fees charged for ATM transactions may be higher abroad than at home, Cirrus and Plus exchange rates are excellent, because they are based on wholesale rates offered only by major banks. You won't do as well at exchange booths in airports or rail and bus stations, in hotels, in restaurants, or in stores, although you may find their hours more convenient. To avoid lines at airport exchange booths, **get a small amount of local currency before you leave home.**

➤ EXCHANGE SERVICES: **International Currency Express** (☎ 888/842–0880 on the East Coast or 888/278–6628 on the West Coast for telephone orders). **Thomas Cook Currency Services** (☎ 800/287–7362 for telephone orders and retail locations).

TRAVELER'S CHECKS

Whether or not to buy traveler's checks depends on where you are headed. **Take cash if your trip includes rural areas** and small towns, traveler's checks to urban areas. If your checks are lost or stolen, they can usually be replaced within 24 hours. To ensure a speedy refund, buy your checks yourself (don't ask someone else to make the purchase). When making a claim for stolen or lost checks, the person who bought the checks should make the call.

P

PACKING FOR HONG KONG

From May to September, high humidity warrants light clothing. However, air-conditioning in hotels and restaurants can be glacial, so bring a sweater or shawl for evening use indoors. Don't forget your swimsuit and high-protection suntan lotion; several hotels have pools, and you may want to spend some time on one of the many beaches. Dress in Hong Kong is fairly informal, but a few hotels and restaurants do insist on a jacket and tie for men in the evenings.

In October, November, March, and April, a jacket or sweater should suffice, but from December through February bring a raincoat or a light overcoat. Whatever the time of year, it is wise to **pack a folding umbrella.**

Bring an extra pair of eyeglasses or contact lenses in your carry-on luggage, and if you have a health problem, **pack enough medication** to last the entire trip or have your doctor write you a prescription using the drug's generic name, because brand names vary from country to country. It's important that you **don't put prescription drugs or valuables in luggage to be checked**: it might go astray. To avoid problems with customs officials, carry medications in the original packaging. Also, don't forget the addresses of offices that handle refunds of lost traveler's checks.

LUGGAGE

In general, you are entitled to check two bags on flights within the United States and on international flights leaving the United States. A third piece may be brought on board, but it must fit easily under the seat in front of you or in the overhead compartment.

If you are flying between two foreign destinations, note that baggage allowances may be determined not by piece but by weight—generally 88 pounds (40 kilograms) in first class, 66 pounds (30 kilograms) in business class, and 44 pounds (20 kilograms) in economy. If your flight between two cities abroad *connects* with your transatlantic or transpacific flight, the piece method still applies.

Airline liability for baggage is limited to $1,250 per person on flights within the United States. On international flights it amounts to $9.07 per pound or $20 per kilogram for checked baggage (roughly $640 per 70-pound bag) and $400 per passenger for unchecked baggage. Insurance for losses exceeding these amounts can be bought from the airline at check-in for about $10 per $1,000 of coverage; note that this coverage excludes a rather extensive list of items, which is shown on your airline ticket.

Before departure, **itemize your bags' contents** and their worth, and label the bags with your name, address, and phone number. (If you use your home address, cover it so that potential thieves can't see it readily.) Inside each bag, **pack a copy of your itinerary.** At check-in, **make sure that each bag is correctly tagged** with the destination airport's three-letter code. If your bags arrive damaged or fail to arrive at all, file a written report with the airline before leaving the airport.

PASSPORTS & VISAS

Once your travel plans are confirmed, **check the expiration date of your passport. Your passport must be valid for another six months from the date you arrive in Hong Kong.** It's also a good idea to **make photocopies of the data page**; leave one copy with someone at home and keep another with you, separated from your passport. If you lose your passport, promptly call the nearest embassy or consulate and the local police; having a copy of the data page can speed replacement.

U.S. CITIZENS

All U.S. citizens, even infants, need only a valid passport to enter Hong Kong for stays of up to 30 days.

➤ INFORMATION: **Office of Passport Services** (☎ 202/647–0518).

CANADIANS

You need only a valid passport to enter Hong Kong for stays of up to 3 months.

➤ INFORMATION: **Passport Office** (☎ 819/994–3500 or 800/567–6868).

U.K. CITIZENS

Citizens of the United Kingdom need only a valid passport to enter Hong Kong for stays of up to 30 days.

➤ INFORMATION: **London Passport Office** (☎ 0990/21010) for fees and documentation requirements and to request an emergency passport.

R
RICKSHAWS

Because rickshaws are a tourist attraction rather than a common mode of transportation, prices run high. Rates are supposed to be around HK$50 for a five-minute ride, but rickshaw operators are merciless. A posed snapshot can cost from HK$10 to HK$20. When you hire a rickshaw or take an operator's picture, **agree on the price in advance.**

S
SENIOR-CITIZEN TRAVEL

To qualify for age-related discounts, **mention your senior-citizen status up front** when booking hotel reservations (not when checking out).

➤ ADVENTURE TRAVEL: **Overseas Adventure Travel** (✉ Grand Circle Corporation, 625 Mt. Auburn St., Cambridge, MA 02138, ☎ 617/876–0533 or 800/221–0814, FAX 617/876–0455).

➤ EDUCATIONAL TRAVEL PROGRAMS: **Elderhostel** (✉ 75 Federal St., 3rd floor, Boston, MA 02110, ☎ 617/426–8056). **Folkways Institute** (✉ 14600 Southeast Aldridge Rd., Portland, OR 97236-6518, ☎ 503/658–6600, FAX 503/658–8672).

SHOPPING

If you buy Chinese lacquer or other breakable keepsakes, **buy an all-risks insurance policy for any delicate purchases that you ship home.** Ivory has long been a prized souvenir of trips to the Orient. However, in 1990 the Hong Kong government imposed a stringent policy on the import and export of this bone derivative. As a result, you must **get an import license from your country of residence, as well as an export license to take ivory out of Hong Kong.** Failure to comply may result in a fine and forfeiture of the purchase. Remember that all goods, with the exception of alcohol, tobacco, petroleum, perfume, cosmetics, and soft drinks, are duty-free everywhere in Hong Kong, not just in "duty-free" stores. Bargaining, even at street markets, has become increasingly rare in Hong Kong. **Beware of merchants who claim to be giving you a "special" price;** you may not be getting what you're paying for.

If you are considering the purchase of ivory products, check with the **Hong Kong Department of Agriculture and Fisheries** (☎ 2733–2283), as well as your home consulate or trade commission.

SIGHTSEEING

ORIENTATION TOURS

The **Hong Kong Island Tour** is a three- to four-hour bus tour that departs from all major hotels daily in the mornings and afternoons. Routes vary, but the following areas are generally covered: Victoria Peak, Wanchai, Aw Boon Haw Gardens, Repulse Bay and Deep Water Bay, Aberdeen, the University of Hong Kong, and Western and Central districts.

The **Kowloon and New Territories Tour** takes in sights as varied as Kwai Chung Container Terminal, the Castle Peak fishing village, a Taoist temple, the town of Yuen Long, the Chinese border at Lokmachau, and the Royal Hong Kong Golf Club at Fanling. The six-hour "Land Between Tour" offers a glimpse of rural Hong Kong. Tours can be booked through the Hong Kong Tourist Association (☞ Visitor Information, *below*).

Harbour and Islands, Watertours of Hong Kong Ltd., (☎ 2739–3302 or 2724–2856) and the **Seaview Harbour Tour Co. Ltd.** (☎ 2561–5033) operate a variety of tours that cover the Inner Harbour and outer islands via junks and cruisers. Tours can be booked through the Hong Kong Tourist Association (☞ Visitor Information, *below*).

Star Ferry Harbour Cruises (☎ 2366–9885 or 2345–2324) offers sundown cruises and a late-night "Harbour Lights" cruise that enjoys the romantic view from the water.

SPECIAL-INTEREST TOURS

➤ DOLPHIN WATCH: The Chinese white dolphin is on its way to extinction in the South China sea (the massive land reclamation for the new airport may have further threatened the dolphins' breeding grounds). **Hong Kong Dolphin Watch** (✉ GPO Box 4102, Central, ☎ 2984–1414, FAX 2984–1414) sponsors tours, by junk, to dolphin habitats around Lantau Island and beyond.

➤ HELICOPTER: **Heliservices Hong Kong Limited** (✉ Helipad, Fenwick Pier, Wanchai, ☎ 2802–0200 for reservations, 2523–6407 main office) offers helicopter tours around the territory; the chopper seats up to five passengers.

➤ HERITAGE: The **HKTA** (☎ 2807–6390 for tour department, 2807–6177) offers a four-hour "Heritage Tour" that takes in the Lei Cheng Uk tomb, Sam Tunk Uk Folk Museum, Tai Fu Tai mansion, and Man Shek Tong ancestral hall.

➤ HORSE RACING: The HKTA runs a tour to both Shatin and Happy Valley tracks during the September–May season. This tour is for nonresidents only, so bring your passport.

➤ HOUSING: The HKTA's **Family Insight Tour** gives you a glimpse of the way ordinary people live in Hong Kong. It takes you inside a huge public housing estate—apartments designed in the early 1990s to give lower- and middle-income families the chance to own their homes. This kind of aid may contradict Hong Kong's laissez-faire system, but in fact 50% of the population live in subsidized housing and the government does its best to provide temporary shelters to people who lose their homes. You can also visit a senior citizens center or kindergarten in Kowloon. The tour culminates at Wong Tai Sin Temple. Make reservations at the HKTA Information Center at Star Ferry Concourse in Tsim Sha Tsui, or Shop 8, Basement, Jardine House in Central. For information, call 2807–6390 or 2807–6177. Cost: HK$275 adults, HK$235 children under 16 and senior citizens. Tour departs Thurs. from the Excelsior Hotel on Hong Kong Island at 9 AM and the Kowloon Hotel on Kowloon at 9:30 AM.

➤ MACAU: The **Macau Tourist Bureau** (☎ 2540–8180) offers day and night sightseeing tours of this nearby Portuguese territory. Included in the package are embarkation taxes, lunch, and transfers.

➤ NIGHTLIFE: The "Hong Kong Night Tour" offers a Chinese dinner at the

Jumbo floating restaurant in Aberdeen, followed by a visit to a Chinese night market. Contact the **Watertours** (☎ 2739–3302).

Open Top Tram Tours (☎ 2801–7430) offers open-air cocktail rides atop a tram and a four-hour night tour that includes dinner in a luxe restaurant and a night-owl tour of the city.

➤ SAILING: **B. Tours** (☎ 2851–9601) operates pleasure cruises for private parties on its sailing junk, the Duk Ling. The vessel accommodates up to 35 people.

Contact the **HKTA** (☎ 2807–6390) for a list of other boat tours, including their *Harbour Junk and Sung Dynasty Tour,* an all-day event consisting of a sail on one of those fabled junks, followed by a coach trip to a living-history, 1,000-year-old-village for lunch and a traditional cultural performance.

➤ SHOPPING: There are a number of private shopping tour operators. Non-Stop Shoppers (☎ 2523–3850, FAX 2868–1164) charters a bus once a week to visit factory outlets, mostly in Kowloon and the New Territories. The itinerary, which varies from week to week, takes in outlets for cookware, towels, brass ware, porcelain, furniture, and carpets. Cost is HK$280 per person. Call or fax for current schedule.

At the high end of the shopping spectrum, **Asian Cajun Ltd.** (⊠ 12 Scenic Village Drive, 4th floor, Pokfulam, ☎ 2817–3687, FAX 2855–9571) offers customized shopping tours for visitors looking for good buys in antiques, art, jewelry, designer clothes and specialty items. Escorted tours are US$80 per hour, with a three-hour minimum. There is an extra hourly charge for a car and driver.

STUDENTS

To save money, **look into deals available through student-oriented travel agencies.** To qualify you'll need a bona fide student ID card. Members of international student groups are also eligible.

➤ STUDENT IDS AND SERVICES: **Council on International Educational Exchange** (⊠ CIEE, 205 E. 42nd St., 14th floor, New York, NY 10017, ☎

212/822–2600 or 888/268–6245, FAX 212/822–2699), for mail orders only, in the United States. **Travel Cuts** (⊠ 187 College St., Toronto, Ontario M5T 1P7, ☎ 416/979–2406 or 800/667–2887) in Canada.

➤ HOSTELING: **Hostelling International—American Youth Hostels** (⊠ 733 15th St. NW, Suite 840, Washington, DC 20005, ☎ 202/783–6161, FAX 202/783–6171). **Hostelling International—Canada** (⊠ 400-205 Catherine St., Ottawa, Ontario K2P 1C3, ☎ 613/237–7884, FAX 613/237–7868). **Youth Hostel Association of England and Wales** (⊠ Trevelyan House, 8 St. Stephen's Hill, St. Albans, Hertfordshire AL1 2DY, ☎ 01727/855215 or 01727/845047, FAX 01727/844126). Membership in the U.S., $25; in Canada, C$26.75; in the U.K., £9.30).

➤ LODGING: Bargain lodging has become increasingly rare in Hong Kong. For moderate prices by Hong Kong standards, see the **Booth Lodge, Garden View International House,** or the **YMCA** in Chapter 4. You can also try the **STB Hostel** (⊠ HK Ltd., 1st floor, Great Eastern Mansion, 255–261 Reclamation St., Mong Kok, Kowloon, ☎ 2710–9199, FAX 2385–0153), which has dormitory-style sleeping quarters or the **YMCA International House** (⊠ 23 Waterloo Rd., Yau Ma Tei, Kowloon, ☎ 2771–9111, FAX 2771–5238).

SUBWAY TRAVEL

The Mass Transit Railway (MTR) links Hong Kong Island to the shopping area of Tsim Sha Tsui and to parts of the New Territories. Trains run frequently, and are safe and easy to use (there are only four lines). Station entrances are marked with a simple line symbol resembling a man with arms and legs outstretched. There are clearly marked ticket machines inside the station; change is available at the Hang Seng Bank counters inside the stations. Fares range from HK$4 to HK$12.50.

➤ SCHEDULES & INFORMATION: **Mass Transit Railway (MTR,** ☎ 2750–0170) or the **Hong Kong Tourist Association information service** (HKTA, ☎ 2807–6177).

TRAVEL CARD

The electronic Octopus Card (HK$100) is accepted on the MTR, Kowloon Canton Railway (KCR), Kowloon Motor Bus (KMB), and Citybus cross-harbor routes. A refundable deposit of HK$50 must be placed on the card, which is on sale at ticket offices and HKTA information counters. Cards can also be reloaded in HK$100 increments at AddValue machines.

T

TAXES

➤ HOTEL: Hong Kong levies a 10% tax on hotel rooms.

TAXIS

Taxis in Hong Kong are usually red and have a roof sign that lights up when the taxi is available. Fares in the urban areas are HK$14 for the first 2 km (1.2 mi) and HK$1.20 for each additional .2 km (.12 mi). There is a surcharge of HK$5 per large piece of baggage and a HK$20 surcharge for driving through the Cross-Harbour Tunnel or Eastern Harbour Crossing. Aberdeen Tunnel carries a surcharge of HK$5, and the Lion Rock Tunnel toll is HK$6. Taxis cannot pick up passengers where there is a solid yellow line painted on the road.

It is difficult to find taxis from 3:30 to 6 PM. Most taxi drivers speak some English, but to avoid problems, **get someone at your hotel to write out your destination in Chinese.**

Outside the urban areas taxis are mainly green and white (blue on Lantau Island). New Territories taxis cost less than urban red taxis, with fares of HK$11.80 for the first 2 km (1.2 mi), and HK$1.10 every .2 km (.12 mi). Urban taxis may travel into rural zones, but rural taxis must not cross into the urban zones. There are no interchange facilities for these taxis, so **do not try to reach the urban area using a green taxi.**

COMPLAINTS

Taxis are usually reliable in Hong Kong, but just in case, **get the taxi's license number,** which is usually on the dashboard. The police hot line for complaints is ☎ 2527–7177. Your complaint will not be investigated without the license number.

TELEPHONES

The country code for Hong Kong is 852. When dialing a Hong Kong number from abroad, drop the initial 0 from the local area code.

To make a local call from a pay phone, use a HK$1 coin. Although pay phones are not hard to find, the tradition is to pop into any store and ask to use the telephone. Many small stores keep their telephone on the counter facing the street. Local calls are free on residence and business lines.

CALLING HOME

Before you go, **find out the local access codes** for your destinations. AT&T, MCI, and Sprint long-distance services make calling home relatively convenient, but you may find the local access number blocked in many hotel rooms. First ask the hotel operator to connect you. If the hotel operator balks, ask for an international operator, or dial the international operator yourself. One way to improve your odds of getting connected to your long-distance carrier is to travel with more than one company's calling card (a hotel may block Sprint, for example, but not MCI). If all else fails, call your phone company collect in the United States or call from a pay phone in the hotel lobby.

Many hotels offer direct dial, as do many business centers, but always with a hefty surcharge. Call 013 for international inquiries and for assistance with direct dialing. Call 010 for operator-assisted calls to most countries, including the United States, Canada, and the United Kingdom. Dial 011 for international conference calls or outgoing collect calls. Long-distance calls can also be made from Hong Kong Telecom International (✉ Century Square, 1 D'Aguilar St., Central, ☎ 2810–0660, and TST Hermes House, Kowloon, ☎ 2888–7184 or 2888–7185). You can dial direct from specially marked silver-color phone booths that take phone cards, available from the Hong Kong Telephone Companies retail shops and Seven Eleven convenience stores located throughout the island. The cards come in values of HK$25, 50, and 100 and have no expiration date. Multilingual instructions are posted in the phone booths.

➤ To Obtain Access Codes: **AT&T USADirect** (☎ 800/874–4000). **MCI Call USA** (☎ 800/444–4444). **Sprint Express** (☎ 800/793–1153).

OPERATORS & INFORMATION

Dial 1081 for directory assistance from English-speaking operators. If a number is constantly busy and you think it might be out of order, call 109 and the operator will check the line.

TIPPING

Hotels and major restaurants add a 10% service charge. In the more traditional Chinese restaurants, a waiter will bring small snacks at the beginning of the meal and charge them to you, even if you did not order them. This money is in lieu of a service charge. It is customary to leave an additional 10% tip in all restaurants, and in taxis and beauty salons.

TOUR OPERATORS

Buying a prepackaged tour or independent vacation can make your trip to Hong Kong less expensive and more hassle-free. Because everything is prearranged you'll spend less time planning.

Operators that handle several hundred thousand travelers per year can use their purchasing power to give you a good price. Their high volume may also indicate financial stability. But some small companies provide more personalized service; because they tend to specialize, they may also be more knowledgeable about a given area.

A GOOD DEAL?

The more your package or tour includes, the better you can predict the ultimate cost of your vacation. Make sure you know exactly what is covered, and **beware of hidden costs.** Are taxes, tips, and service charges included? Transfers and baggage handling? Entertainment and excursions? These can add up.

If the package or tour you are considering is priced lower than in your wildest dreams, **be skeptical.** Also, **make sure your travel agent knows the accommodations** and other services. Ask about the hotel's location, room size, beds, and whether it has a pool, room service, or programs for children, if you care about these. Has your agent been there in person or sent others you can contact?

BUYER BEWARE

Each year consumers are stranded or lose their money when tour operators—even very large ones with excellent reputations—go out of business. So **check out the operator.** Find out how long the company has been in business, and ask several agents about its reputation. **Don't book unless the firm has a consumer-protection program.**

Members of the National Tour Association and United States Tour Operators Association are required to set aside funds to cover your payments and travel arrangements in case the company defaults. Nonmembers may carry insurance instead. Look for the details, and for the name of an underwriter with a solid reputation, in the operator's brochure. Note: When it comes to tour operators, **don't trust escrow accounts.** Although the Department of Transportation watches over charterflight operators, no regulatory body prevents tour operators from raiding the till. You may want to protect yourself by buying travel insurance that includes a tour-operator default provision. For more information, *see* Consumer Protection, *above.*

It's also a good idea to choose a company that participates in the American Society of Travel Agents Tour Operator Program (TOP). This gives you a forum if there are any disputes between you and your tour operator; ASTA will act as mediator.

➤ Tour-Operator Recommendations: **National Tour Association** (✉ NTA, 546 E. Main St., Lexington, KY 40508, ☎ 606/226–4444 or 800/755–8687). **United States Tour Operators Association** (✉ USTOA, 342 Madison Ave., Suite 1522, New York, NY 10173, ☎ 212/599–6599, FAX 212/599–6744). **American Society of Travel Agents** (☞ *below*).

USING AN AGENT

Travel agents are excellent resources. In fact, large operators accept bookings made only through travel agents. But it's a good idea to **collect brochures from several agencies,** because some agents' suggestions may be influenced by relationships with tour and package firms that reward them for volume sales. If you have a special interest, **find an agent with expertise in that area;** ASTA (☞ Travel Agencies, *below*) has a database of specialists worldwide. Do some homework on your own, too: Local tourism boards can provide information about lesser-known and small-niche operators, some of which may sell only direct.

SINGLE TRAVELERS

Prices for packages and tours are usually quoted per person, based on two sharing a room. If traveling solo, you may be required to pay the full double-occupancy rate. Some operators eliminate this surcharge if you agree to be matched with a roommate of the same sex, even if one is not found by departure time.

GROUP TOURS

Among companies that sell tours to Hong Kong, the following are nationally known, have a proven reputation, and offer plenty of options. The classifications used below represent different price categories, and you'll probably encounter these terms when talking to a travel agent or tour operator. The key difference is usually in accommodations, which run from budget to better, and better-yet to best.

➤ SUPER-DELUXE: **Abercrombie & Kent** (✉ 1520 Kensington Rd., Oak Brook, IL 60521-2141, ☎ 630/954–2944 or 800/323–7308, FAX 630/954–3324). **Travcoa** (✉ Box 2630, 2350 S.E. Bristol St., Newport Beach, CA 92660, ☎ 714/476–2800 or 800/992–2003, FAX 714/476–2538).

➤ DELUXE: **Globus** (✉ 5301 S. Federal Circle, Littleton, CO 80123-2980, ☎ 303/797–2800 or 800/221–0090, FAX 303/347–2080). **Maupintour** (✉ 1515 St. Andrews Dr., Lawrence, KS 66047, ☎ 913/843–1211 or 800/255–4266, FAX 913/843–8351). **Tauck Tours** (✉

Box 5027, 276 Post Rd. W, Westport, CT 06881-5027, ☎ 203/226–6911 or 800/468–2825, FAX 203/221–6828).

➤ FIRST-CLASS: **Collette Tours** (✉ 162 Middle St., Pawtucket, RI 02860, ☎ 401/728–3805 or 800/832–4656, FAX 401/728–1380). **Orient Flexi-Pax Tours** (✉ 630 Third Ave., New York, NY 10017, ☎ 212/692–9550 or 800/545–5540, FAX 212/661–1618). **Pacific Bestour** (✉ 228 Rivervale Rd., River Vale, NJ 07675, ☎ 201/664–8778 or 800/688–3288, FAX 201/722–0829). **Pacific Delight Tours** (✉ 132 Madison Ave., New York, NY 10016, ☎ 212/684–7707 or 800/221–7179, FAX 212/532–3406). **United Vacations** (☎ 800/328–6877).

➤ BUDGET: **Cosmos** (☞ Globus, *above*).

PACKAGES

Like group tours, independent vacation packages are available from major tour operators and airlines. The companies listed below offer vacation packages in a broad price range.

➤ AIR/HOTEL: **Brendan Tours** (✉ 15137 Califa St., Van Nuys, CA 91411, ☎ 818/785–9696 or 800/421–8446, FAX 818/902–9876). **DER Tours** (✉ 9501 W. Devon St., Rosemont, IL 60018, ☎ 800/937–1235, FAX 800/282–7474; FAX 800/860–9944, for brochures). **Orient Flexi-Pax Tours** (☞ Groups, *above*). **Pacific Bestour** (☞ Groups, *above*). **Pacific Delight Tours** (☞ Groups, *above*). **United Vacations** (☞ Groups, *above*).

➤ IN THE U.K.: Contact **British Airways Holidays** (✉ Astral Towers, Betts Way, London Rd., Crawley, West Sussex RH10 2XA, ☎ 01293/723–171). **Kuoni Travel** (✉ Kuoni House, Dorking, Surrey RH5 4AZ, ☎ 01306/740–500). **Tradewinds** (✉ Helmshore, Rossendale, Lancashire BE4 4NB, ☎ 01706/219–111).

THEME TRIPS

➤ CUSTOMIZED PACKAGES: **Pacific Experience** (✉ 185 Spring St., Newport, RI 02840, ☎ 800/279–3639, FAX 203/618-0121).

➤ JEWISH CULTURE: **American Jewish Congress** (✉ 15 E. 84th St., New

York, NY 10028, ☎ 212/879–4588 or 800/221–4694).

➤ LEARNING VACATIONS: **Smithsonian Study Tours and Seminars** (✉ 1100 Jefferson Dr. SW, Room 3045, MRC 702, Washington, DC 20560, ☎ 202/357–4700, FAX 202/633–9250).

TRAIN TRAVEL

The **Kowloon-Canton Railway** (KCR) has 13 commuter stops on its 22-mi (34-km) journey through urban Kowloon (from Kowloon to Lo Wu) and the new cities of Shatin and Taipo on its way to the Chinese border. The main station is at Hung Hom, Kowloon, where you can catch express trains to China. Fares range from HK$7.50 to HK$40. The crossover point with the MTR is at Kowloon Tong Station (☎ 2602–7799). The **Light Rail Transit** runs between Tuen Mun and Yuen Long in the New Territories (☎ 2468–7788).

TRAMS

For schedules, call the Hong Kong Tourist Association information service (☎ (2807–6177).

STREET TRAMS

Trams run along Hong Kong Island's north shore from Kennedy Town in the west all the way through Central, Wanchai, Causeway Bay, North Point, and Quarry Bay, ending in the former fishing village of Shaukiwan. There is also a branch line that turns off in Wanchai toward Happy Valley, where horse races are held during the season. Destinations are marked on the front; the fare is HK$1.60. Avoid them at rush hours which are generally 7:30 AM to 9:00 AM and 5:00 PM to 7:00 PM, Monday through Friday.

PEAK TRAMS

This funicular railway dates back to 1888 and rises from ground level to Victoria Peak (1,305 ft), offering a panoramic view of Hong Kong. Both residents and tourists use the tram, which has five stations, although most passengers get on at the terminus between Garden Road and Cotton Tree Drive. The fare is HK$15 one way or HK$23 round-trip. The tram runs every 10–15 minutes daily from 7 AM to midnight. There is a free shuttle bus to and from the Star Ferry.

TRANSLATION SERVICES

CIAP Hong Kong (✉ Flat 15, 7F, Mt. Nicholson Gap, 103 Mt. Nicholson Rd., Happy Valley, ☎ 2838–5852), **Translanguage-IRH Ltd.** (✉ Room 1003, Working Field Commercial Bldg., 408–412 Jaffe Rd., Wanchai, ☎ 2893–5000), or **Polyglot Translations** (✉ Time Centre, 53 Hollywood Rd., Central, ☎ 2851–7232).

TRANSPORTATION

Being a collection of islands scattered in the South China Sea, along with a chunk of the Chinese mainland, Hong Kong has more types of transportation than probably any other city in the world. Ferries (☞ Ferry Travel, *above*) and a subway system (☞ Subways, *above*) connect Hong Kong Island with the Kowloon peninsula and the Outer Islands. Buses (☞ Bus Travel, *above*) run throughout Hong Kong Island, Kowloon, and the New Territories, and along a number of routes linking the two sides of the harbor. On Hong Kong Island are two kinds of trams (☞ Trams, *below*): a street-level tram that runs across the north shore of the island, and the Peak Tram, a funicular railway that climbs Victoria Peak. Trains (☞ Trains, *above*) travel north from Kowloon serving cities all the way to the Chinese border. Choose, as well, from limousines (the Mandarin and the Peninsula hotels have chauffeur-driven Rolls-Royces for rent), and the touristy rickshaws (☞ Rickshaws, *below*). You can also rent cars with drivers (☞ Car Rental, *above*).

TRAVEL AGENCIES

A good travel agent puts your needs first. Look for an agency that has been in business at least five years, emphasizes customer service, and has someone on staff who specializes in your destination. In addition, **make sure the agency belongs to the American Society of Travel Agents** (ASTA). If your travel agency is also acting as your tour operator, *see* Payments *and* Tour Operators, *above*.

➤ LOCAL AGENT REFERRALS: **American Society of Travel Agents** (ASTA, ☎ 800/965–2782, 24-hr hot line, FAX 703/684–8319). **Alliance of Canadian Travel Associations** (✉ Suite 201, 1729 Bank St., Ottawa, Ontario K1V 7Z5, ☎ 613/521–0474, FAX 613/

THE GOLD GUIDE / SMART TRAVEL TIPS

521–0805). **Association of British Travel Agents** (⊠ 55–57 Newman St., London W1P 4AH, ☎ 0171/637–2444, ℻ 0171/637–0713).

TRAVEL GEAR

Travel catalogs specialize in useful items, such as compact alarm clocks and travel irons, that can **save space when packing.** They also offer dual-voltage appliances, currency converters, and foreign-language phrase books.

➤ MAIL-ORDER CATALOGS: **Magellan's** (☎ 800/962–4943, ℻ 805/568–5406). **Orvis Travel** (☎ 800/541–3541, ℻ 540/343–7053). **TravelSmith** (☎ 800/950–1600, ℻ 800/950–1656).

U

U.S. GOVERNMENT

The U.S. government can be an excellent source of inexpensive travel information. When planning your trip, **find out what government materials are available.**

➤ ADVISORIES: **U.S. Department of State** (⊠ Overseas Citizens Services Office, Room 4811 N.S., Washington, DC 20520); enclose a self-addresses, stamped envelope. Interactive hot line (☎ 202/647–5225, ℻ 202/647–3000). Computer bulletin board (☎ 301/946–4400).

➤ PAMPHLETS: Contact the **Consumer Information Center** (⊠ Consumer Information Catalogue, Pueblo, CO 81009, ☎ 719/948–3334) for a free catalog that includes travel titles.

V

VISITOR INFORMATION

For general Hong Kong and Macau information before you go, contact the **Hong Kong Tourist Association (HKTA)** and **Macau Government Tourist Office** locations below. When you arrive, stop by one of the information centers in Hong Kong.

➤ IN THE U.S.: **HKTA** (⊠ 590 5th Ave., Suite 590, New York, NY 10036, ☎ 212/869–5008, ℻ 212/730–2605; ⊠ 610 Enterprise Dr., Ste. 200, Oak Brook, IL 60521, ☎ 630/575–2828, ℻ 630/575–2829; ⊠ 10940 Wilshire Blvd., Ste. 1220, Los Angeles, CA 90024, ☎ 310/208–

4582, ℻ 310/208–1869). **Macau Government Tourist Office** (⊠ Box 350, Kenilworth, IL 60043, ☎ 847/251–6421 or 800/331–7150, ℻ 847/256–5601).

➤ IN CANADA: **HKTA** (⊠ 9 Temperance St., 3rd floor, Toronto, Ontario M5H 1Y6, ☎ 416/366–2389, ℻ 416/366–1098).

➤ IN THE U.K.: **HKTA** (⊠ 125 Pall Mall, 3rd floor, London SW1Y 5EA, ☎ 0891/661–188 for brochures [calls are 50p per min] or 0171/930–4775 for all other information, ℻ 0171/930–4777). **Macau Government Tourist Office** (⊠ 1 Battersea Church Rd., London SW11 3LY, ☎ 0171/771–7006, ℻ 0171/771–7059).

➤ IN HONG KONG: **HKTA** (⊠ The Star Ferry Concourse, Kowloon; ⊠ Jardine House, Basement, Hong Kong Island; ⊠ Kai Tak International Airport. For help by phone, try the multilingual telephone information service (☎ 2807–6177). If you prefer to get help by fax, try the 24-hour facsimile information service (☎ 900–6077–1128).

W

WALKING

If you're not defeated by the heat, it is pleasant to stroll around Hong Kong. On Hong Kong Island you can enjoy a walk through the very traditional Western district, where life has not changed much over the years. If you are a very keen walker and relish the idea of a self-guided tour, you can **go for a long hike in the New Territories or on Lantau Island.** Contact the HKTA for walking-tour guides to these distinct areas of Hong Kong. Each includes a map and detailed instructions for getting from place to place.

WHEN TO GO

The high tourist season, October through late December, is popular for a reason: The weather is pleasant, with sunny days and comfortable, cool nights. January, February, and sometimes early March are cold and dank, with long periods of overcast skies and rain. March and April can be either cold and miserable or beautiful and sunny. By May the cold has broken and the temperature is warm and comfortable. The months of June through September are the typhoon season, when the weather is hot and sticky, with lots of rain. All visitors to Hong Kong should know in advance that typhoons (called hurricanes in the Atlantic) must be treated with respect. Fortunately, Hong Kong is prepared for these blustery assaults. If a storm is approaching, the airwaves will be crackling with information, and your hotel will make certain through postings in the lobby that you know the applicable signals. In addition, public places will have postings.

When a No. 8 signal is posted, Hong Kong and Macau close down com-pletely. Head immediately for your hotel, and stay put. This is serious business—bamboo scaffolding can come hurtling through the streets like spears, ships can be sunk in the harbor, and large areas of the territory are often flooded.

Macau's summers are slightly cooler and wetter than Hong Kong's.

The following are average daily maximum and minimum temperatures for Hong Kong.

➤ FORECASTS: **Weather Channel Connection** (☎ 900/932–8437), 95¢ per minute from a Touch-Tone phone.

Climate in Hong Kong

Jan.	64F	18C	May	82F	28C	Sept.	85F	29C
	56	13		74	23		77	25
Feb.	63F	17C	June	85F	29C	Oct.	81F	27C
	55	13		78	26		73	23
Mar.	67F	19C	July	87F	31C	Nov.	74F	23C
	60	16		78	26		65	18
Apr.	75F	24C	Aug.	87F	31C	Dec.	68F	20C
	67	19		78	26		59	15

THE GOLD GUIDE / SMART TRAVEL TIPS

1 Destination: Hong Kong

A BRIEF HISTORY

WHEN YOU FLY to Hong Kong, try to get a window seat on the aircraft; the landing will take your breath away.

When you hear the prelanding announcement, you will probably still be out over the gray South China Sea. As you approach the coast of China, you will spot a few small, rocky islands, tiny fishing boats, and sailboats in the channels leading into Hong Kong Harbour—the most spectacular harbor you will ever see.

If you arrive before April, when the new airport at Chek Lap Kok Island is scheduled to open, you'll get to experience the sudden, startling approach into Kai Tak Airport. If you come in over the sea, you follow the channel between Hong Kong Island and the mainland on wings that seem close enough to touch the boats or the windows of the skyscrapers rising above the hills. If you fly in over Kowloon, the plane will seem dangerously close to the scrub-covered hills, and you will see children playing in school grounds and perhaps even be able to read the advertisements on the sides of buses.

In Cantonese, Hong Kong means fragrant harbor, a name inspired either by the incense factories that once dotted Hong Kong Island or by the profusion of scented pink *Bauhinias,* the national flower (which has recently replaced colonial insignias). Under the modern veneer of skyscrapers and high fashion, Hong Kong is deeply rooted in ancient Chinese traditions—more so, in many ways, than China, which destroyed much of its heritage during the three decades following the Communist revolution. For these reasons, a mixture of pride and wariness is felt by the Hong Kong Chinese at unity with the mainland.

Hong Kong is on the southeast coast of China, at the mouth of the Pearl River, on the same latitude as Hawaii and Cuba. By air, it's 2¾ hours from Beijing, 20 hours from New York, 12¼ hours from San Francisco, and 13 hours from London. It consists of three parts: Hong Kong Island, roughly 32 square mi (82 square km); Kowloon, 3½ square mi (9 square km); and the New Territories, about 365 square mi (945 square km). Its land mass grows through land reclamation projects as Hong Kong Harbour narrows.

The name Hong Kong refers to the overall territory as well as to the main island, which is across the harbor from Kowloon. The island's principal business district is officially named Victoria, but everyone calls it Central. Also on the island are the districts of Wanchai, Causeway Bay, Repulse Bay, Stanley, and Aberdeen.

Kowloon includes Tsim Sha Tsui, Tsim Sha Tsui East, Hung Hom, Mong Kok/Yau Ma Tei, and the area north to Boundary Street. The New Territories begin at Boundary Street and extend north to the border with China, encompassing the container port, the Kai Tak airport, most of the major factories, and the outlying islands.

Hong Kong is 98% Chinese. Although the official languages are English and Cantonese, the use of Mandarin (or *Putonghua,* China's official language and the one spoken by most Chinese worldwide) is bound to rise. Many other languages and dialects are spoken here, including Hakka (the language of a group of early settlers from China), Tanka (the language of the original boat people who came here some 5,000 years ago), Shanghainese, and Chinglish (a mixture of Cantonese and English). Among the nationalities living in Hong Kong, some 30,000 Filipinos make up the largest foreign community. Most are women working as maids and nannies—called "amahs" in local parlance—many of whom socialize on their days off near the Star Ferry and at Statue Square park.

Buddhism, Taoism, ancestor worship, Christianity, and animism are the major religions, and you'll see signs of them everywhere. The distinctions between religions are often blurred because Chinese people tend to be eclectic in their beliefs. It is not uncommon for the same Hong Kong citizen to put out food and incense for his departed ancestors at Spring Festival time, invite a Taoist priest to his home to exorcise unhappy ghosts, pray in a Buddhist temple for fertility, and take communion in a Christian church.

Hong Kong's earliest visitors are believed to have been boat people of Malaysian-Oceanic origin who came here about 5,000 years ago. They left geometric-style drawings that are still visible on rocks in Big Wave Bay (on Hong Kong Island) and Po Toi Island. The earliest structure found so far is the 2,000-year-old Han Dynasty tomb at Lei Cheng Uk. More than 600 years later, the Tang Dynasty left lime kilns full of seashells—an archaeological mystery because there are no clues indicating how or why the lime was used.

There are also records from the 13th century, when Sung Dynasty loyalists fled China with their child-emperor to escape the invading Mongols. The last of the Sung Dynasty emperors, a 10-year-old boy, is said to have spent a night in the late 1270s near what is now the airport. One of his men is credited with naming Kowloon, which means "nine dragons" (he counted eight mountains that resembled dragons and added one for the emperor, who was also considered a dragon). The boy was the only Chinese emperor believed to have set foot in what is now Hong Kong. Many of his courtiers settled here. Today anyone visiting Po Lin monastery, high in the mountains of Lantau Island, will pass Shek Pik reservoir, where innumerable Sung Dynasty coins were found during the reservoir's excavation. You can also get a feel for life during the period by visiting Sung Dynasty Village, a reproduction of a Sung village, in an amusement park in Laichikok near Kowloon. The village is small, but it demonstrates the highly developed Sung civilization with spirit and charm and is well worth a visit.

Western traders first appeared in the Hong Kong area in 1513. The first were Portuguese, soon followed by the Spanish, Dutch, English, and French. All were bent either on making fortunes trading porcelain, tea, and silk, or on saving souls for their respective religions. Until 1757 the Chinese restricted all foreigners to neighboring Macau, the Portuguese territory 40 mi (64 km) across the Pearl River estuary. After 1757, traders—but not their families—were allowed to live just outside Canton for about eight months each year.

(Canton, now known by its Chinese pronunciation, Guangzhou, is only 20 minutes from Hong Kong by plane, or three hours by train or hovercraft.)

Trading in Canton was frustrating for the foreigners. It took at least 20 days for messages to be relayed to the emperor, local officials had to be bribed, and Chinese justice seemed unfair. The Chinese confined foreign traders to a small, restricted zone and forbade them to learn Chinese. The Chinese wanted nothing from the West except silver, until the foreigners, especially the British, started offering opium.

THE SPREAD OF the opium habit and the growing outflow of silver alarmed high Chinese officials as early as 1729. They issued edicts forbidding importation of the drug, but these were not strictly enforced until 1839. Then a heroic and somewhat fanatical imperial commissioner, Lin Ze-xu (Lin Tse-hsu), laid siege to the foreign factories in Canton and detained the traders until they surrendered more than 20,000 chests of the drug, almost a year's worth of trade. The foreigners also signed bonds promising to desist from dealing opium forever, upon threat of death. The opium was destroyed. The resulting tension between the government and foreign traders led to the Opium Wars and a succession of unequal treaties forced by superior British firepower. The most important of these treaties required China to cede the island of Hong Kong to Britain; later, another treaty added Kowloon. Finally, in 1898, China leased the New Territories to Britain for 99 years.

British-ruled Hong Kong flourished from the start of trade, especially the trade in opium, which was not outlawed in Hong Kong until after World War II. The population grew quickly, from 4,000 in 1841 to more than 23,000 in 1847, as Hong Kong attracted anyone anxious to make money or escape the fetters of feudalism and family.

Each convulsion on the Chinese mainland—the Taiping rebellion in the mid-1800s, the 1911 republican revolution, the rule of warlords of the 1920s, the 1937 Japanese invasion—pushed another group of refugees into Hong Kong. Then Japan invaded Hong Kong itself. The population, which was 1.4 million just before the Japanese arrived, dropped to a low of 600,000 by 1945. Many Hong Kong residents were forced to flee to Macau and the rural areas of China. The Japanese period is still remembered with bitterness by older local residents.

The largest group of Chinese refugees came as a result of the civil war in China between the Nationalists and Communists, which ended with a Communist victory in 1949. Many refugees, especially the Shanghainese (including the shipping family of Hong Kong's new chief executive, Tung Chee-hwa), brought capital and business skills. The population of Hong Kong was 1.8 million in 1947. By 1961 it stood at 3.7 million. For 25 days in 1962, when food was short in China, Chinese border guards allowed 70,000 Chinese to walk into Hong Kong.

DURING THE antilandlord, anticapitalist, and antirightist campaigns in China, and especially during the Cultural Revolution (1967–76), more and more refugees risked imprisonment and the sharks in Mirs Bay to reach Hong Kong. In 1967, inspired by the leftist fanaticism of the Red Guards in China, local sympathizers and activists in Hong Kong set off bombs, organized labor strikes, and demonstrated against the British rulers and Hong Kong's Chinese policemen. They taunted the latter by saying, "Will the British take you when they go?" But the revolutionaries did not have popular support, and the disruptions in Hong Kong lasted less than a year.

In the late 1970s, a half-million Chinese refugees came to Hong Kong, disillusioned with communism and eager for a better standard of living for themselves and their families.

Until October 1980 the Hong Kong government had a curious "touch-base" policy—a critical game of "hide-and-seek." Any Chinese who managed to get past the barbed wire, attack dogs, and tough border patrols to the urban areas was allowed to stay and work. Labor was needed for local industries then. At first, a similarly lenient policy was applied to Vietnamese boat people who arrived between 1975 and 1982. More than 100,000 of these refugees were allowed to work in Hong Kong pending transfer to permanent homes abroad, and 14,000 were given permanent resident status. As the number of countries willing to take the Vietnamese dwindled, Hong Kong detained the 20,000 most recently arrived refugees in closed camps, much like prisons, in the hope that no more boat people will come. All of the detained Vietnamese were returned to Vietnam before the handover.

In the early 1980s jobs became less plentiful as a result of worldwide recession. As the population continued to increase, the standard of services in Hong Kong began to deteriorate. After consulting China, the government decreed that everyone had to carry a Hong Kong identification card. Since the handover, mainlanders can apply to the Chinese government to request settlement in Hong Kong, but entries are restricted.

The future of Hong Kong after the expiration of the New Territories lease on June 30, 1997, was understandably the big question hanging over the colony from the moment Britain's then prime minister, Margaret Thatcher, set foot in Beijing in September 1982 to start talks with the late Deng Xiaoping. China stated from the beginning that it wanted to repossess all of Hong Kong. Officially, Britain was willing to return only the New Territories, but no one believed a Hong Kong without them would be economically viable: The New Territories consist of more than 97% of the land in Hong Kong and include most of the manufacturing facilities, the Kai Tak airport, and the container port. China proposed that Hong Kong become a Special Administrative Region (SAR) under the Chinese flag, with a Chinese governor. The Chinese added a 50-year guarantee of autonomy, effective July 1, 1997, labeling the deal "one country, two systems." Negotiations between China and Britain lasted for nearly two years, with China applying pressure by announcing that if a solution were not found by September 1984, it would declare one unilaterally. An agreement was inevitable.

Hong Kong's economy didn't react well to this political uncertainty. Land prices fell. The stock market plunged by as much as 50% from late 1981 to late 1983. The Hong Kong dollar careened to almost HK$10 to the U.S. dollar in September 1983, from HK$5.7 at the end of 1981.

This forced the government to intervene reluctantly by stabilizing the local unit at HK$7.80 to U.S.$1. Emigration reached record levels.

The Chinese government has dismantled certain civil-liberties provisions within the Hong Kong bill of rights. Meetings and political demonstrations may now be held only with permission from the police. China has also said it will not allow the press to publish certain opinions, such as "advocating" an independent Taiwan or Tibet. Formerly unabashed media are exercising caution. The Chinese appointed a provisional legislature, removing 20 elected legislative-council members from office. Elections were only recently introduced in Hong Kong, when the British allowed elected council members to join appointed ones. Free elections will be held again this spring, but carefully drafted election laws may prevent full participation of pro-democracy parties.

At press time, the stock market had recovered from initial political uncertainties. The main influences are the rise and fall of U.S. interest rates and the performance of the New York Stock Exchange. In the end the final agreement gives Hong Kong many safeguards and special freedoms that are not permitted in other regions of the People's Republic of China. Whether China lives up to guarantees in the agreement remains to be seen. However, Hong Kong's importance to China as a center for business and finance is unlikely to diminish, which gives hope to those who are destined to remain there.

A LOOK AT HONG KONG'S POSTCOLONIAL FUTURE

Nearly 150,000 visitors and journalists descended upon Hong Kong to witness the historic handover to China at midnight, June 30, 1997, but the real story is still in the making. The last British governor, Christopher Patten, sailed out at midnight with his family, after a ceremony in which his normal reserve almost gave way to tears. More than 4,000 People's Liberation Army troops moved over the border before dawn on July 1. The Union Jack, symbol of the colonial era, was replaced in government offices by the flag bearing the red star of the People's Republic of China and Hong Kong's own Bauhinia flower flag. Otherwise, Hong Kong looked much the same the next day. What happened in 1997 was not a revolution, but the start of a slow evolution from British colony into a Special Administrative Region (SAR) of China.

The official agreements between China and Britain over Hong Kong, known as the Joint Declaration and the Basic Law, state that Hong Kong will be an SAR for 50 years, belonging to China but functioning autonomously. China's policy is supposed to be "one country, two systems." The next few years will show us what these terms actually mean.

Curiousity will continue to drive tourism, and Hong Kong will still be a mecca for those who love shopping, Chinese culture, nightlife, sailing, hiking, horse racing, rugby, Asian cuisine, and cosmopolitan ambience. It will continue to be a duty-free port, with many goods available at bargain prices, and the excellent hotels, convention space, tourism assistance centers, and communications facilities will remain in place. Hong Kongers are great fans of the good life available here, and such colonial institutions as the Royal Hong Kong Yacht Club (which will probably drop the "Royal" in the near future) and the Hong Kong Jockey Club will retain their prestige.

Day-to-day life in Hong Kong is apt to be much as before, especially on the back streets, where small businesses thrive, laundry hangs from windows, outdoor market stalls serve noodles and congee, and incense from tiny makeshift altars curls into the air. Ordinary Hong Kong citizens will continue to work hard and invest their earnings, sweep their ancestors' graves on special holidays, and hope their children grow up to be prosperous. With China's growing market economy unlikely to reverse course, there may be a bright future ahead for Hong Kong's next generation.

The Hong Kong business community (both Chinese and ex-pat) feels very much a part of China, and is a beneficiary of the rapid economic growth there. Hong Kong accounts for more than two-thirds of

China's foreign investment, and has supplied most of the technical expertise that has helped China develop its industries and infrastructure. The business community maintains that the most important goal is to have a stable SAR, where business can flourish without intrusion from either the government or the demands of the people, thus keeping jobs abundant and the general public materially satisfied and content. Of course, the business leaders themselves will be the first to prosper and be content.

A great many of Hong Kong's six million people felt a tremendous sense of pride when the Chinese flag was raised after a 156-year absence. Many people were happy to see the British government go because they remembered—or at least had grandparents who did—when being Chinese in colonial Hong Kong meant being a second-class citizen. However, there were also Hong Kong residents who tempered their ethnic pride with a sense of foreboding, as well as those who felt that the handover to a government with such a dismal human rights record was no cause for celebration at all.

It is clear that the Beijing central government will not permit the civil liberties that the colonial government did. Hong Kong was never a democracy, but the British tradition of tolerance for a free press and free speech filtered into the colony. Just before the handover, China introduced amendments to Hong Kong's Public Order and Societies ordinances, spelling out a restriction on any activities or published statements that threaten "national security." Beijing made it clear that advocating independence for Taiwan, Tibet, or Hong Kong is a threat to national security.

Tung Chee-hwa, the new Chief Executive of Hong Kong, seems eager to reassure China that the SAR will not become a base for undermining Communist Party rule or defying its claim to sovereignty over Tibet and Taiwan. The local press, too, seems likely to suffer from restrictions on any statement that is unfavorable to Beijing. The Chinese language press may be more subject to scrutiny than the many English-language publications and broadcast stations in Hong Kong, but the English-language press is not immune. For one thing, media owners may not want

to alienate China with criticism. *The South China Morning Post,* the major English-language daily has as its majority owner Malaysian businessman Robert Kuok, who has many business interests in China. Last year the paper raised eyebrows when it brought in as a consultant Feng Xiliang, who was a founding editor of *China Daily,* China's official English language daily newspaper.

ON THE LEGISLATIVE front, there is a strong perception among Tung and his senior advisors that the democratic reforms that came to Hong Kong under Patten—one third of the 60-member Legislative Council (LegCo) was elected by universal suffrage, and the candidates advocating a more democratic system won by a wide margin—do not make for an efficiently functioning government. At the stroke of the handover, the Chinese government disbanded the old LegCo and replaced it with a provisional legislature, made up of 60 appointees favored by Beijing. Martin Lee and Emily Lau, two of the ousted democratic party leaders, hope to run for office again in the elections this spring. However, the election laws being drafted are expected to limit the participation of pro-democracy parties. Tung is a chairman of a corporation, as are most of his senior advisors, and they believe an oligarchy of the business elite is the best system for preserving Hong Kong's prosperity. Tung would like to have at least 40 seats selected almost entirely by the leaders of Hong Kong's business sector and the professions. The Beijing government, while not run by corporate leaders, seems to find this approach highly reassuring. Beijing considers Hong Kong an "economic" rather than a "political" city.

While the political future remains uncertain, there are also many "ifs" at work on the business front. True, tiny Hong Kong has shown miraculous economic growth in the second half of the 20th century, evolving from a center of manufacturing for export into a world financial capital. Today the multinational investment banks that line the streets of Central are there mostly to handle the flow of capital investment into China and other parts of Asia. Nearly half the direct investment into East Asia in recent years has been channeled through

Hong Kong because of its prominence as a regional financial center. Thus, economic growth in the region, especially in China, is important to Hong Kong's future.

The Basic Law, article 109, states that the government of the SAR will provide an economic environment that maintains Hong Kong's status as an international financial center and that encourages investment and trade. All of this was very important when the Basic Law was signed in 1990, when reform in China was in a precarious infant stage. Now that the giant next door is on the verge of becoming an economic superpower, Shanghai is beginning to rival Hong Kong as a financial capital. As the legal system and infrastructure of China develop, financial institutions that have based their China operations in Hong Kong simply because it was an easier place for the staff to live and conduct business, may start to find Shanghai equally attractive.

Many Hong Kong residents fear that the free-wheeling capitalism of colonial Hong Kong will become more like the multi-layered capitalism that exists in the urban areas of China today. There are opportunities to build factories, stores, and real estate developments in China, but for the most part only for those with either multinational clout or the ability to offer local officials special favors or equity in the business.

The future uncertainties, particularly in regards to human rights, have led all of the Hong Kong citizens who can to secure a means of leaving if life becomes difficult. Between January and July of 1996 nearly 400,000 Hong Kong citizens queued up to get British National Overseas passports, which, while not allowing them to emigrate to Britain, would enable them to travel more freely than on a Chinese passport. Some 364,000 such passports were granted. At the same time many Western expatriate residents applied for naturalization, so that they could remain in the territory as permanent residents. The expat community, some 60,000 strong before the takeover, includes many who have made their careers and homes in Hong Kong, and want the option of staying.

Indeed, the economy still thrives, the city is exciting, and there are other good reasons to stay. In the best case scenario, Hong Kong's vibrancy will influence China, rather than be squelched by her. Is this possible?

Culturally, the two systems couldn't be further apart. Hong Kong's language, Cantonese, is unintelligible to China's Mandarin speakers, who consider it an unrefined, harsh-sounding dialect. The Hong Kong Chinese have a religious tradition that was not interrupted by Maoism and revolutionary rhetoric, and is observed today in a mind-boggling number of holidays and rituals that involve ancestor worship, multiple deities, numerology, Buddhism, Taoism, Confucianism, and various forms of mysticism.

UNLIKE THE MAINLAND Chinese, the Hong Kong Chinese are accustomed to viewing movies from all over the world, dining on European cuisine, and seeing designer goods for sale on almost every corner. They have a palpable sense of confidence in the future: People start businesses at the drop of a hat, build buildings, and buy expensive things. Unlike the behemoth next door, Hong Kong has been a place where it is possible to achieve almost anything, with almost no bureaucratic or cultural barriers. Observers point out that the sense of abundance has produced a place where there is no envy. "In Hong Kong," noted an editorial in the *Far Eastern Economic Review,* "when people see a Rolls Royce there is not the resentment one finds in other places, because in Hong Kong they know it achieved on merit and not *guanxi,* or connections." Capitalism is only part of the reason for Hong Kong's success. Even though Hong Kong has not actually experienced democracy, it has had many of its benefits, including the rule of law and a free press. Its ambitious population has been able to focus on personal goals rather than on resentment of the system. *The Economist* pointed out just before the handover that "although the lack of freedom in mainland China has proved compatible with a manufacturing boom based on cheap labor, it is less likely to be compatible with (Hong Kong's) service and information based economy that relies on eduated and mobile professionals."

The credit for the free-wheeling meritocracy that Hong Kong has become rests particularly with the Hong Kong Chinese. They worked hard for their rights under colonial rule. At one time Chinese people were not allowed to live on Victoria Peak, the 1,805-ft high billionaire's paradise; the legislative and judicial positions in government used to be occupied strictly by British men. All of this changed well before the British government departed. Universities, corporations, and civil service branches in recent years began to favor hiring local Chinese men and women instead of expats, partly to save on relocation costs but also because of a growing nationalistic sentiment and an abundant pool of well-educated bilingual and multilingual professionals. Even Hong Kong's busy socialite scene of charity balls and exclusive parties is more than half Chinese these days. The citizens of Hong Kong will have to work even harder for human rights and democracy under Beijing's rule, and those who dedicate themselves to the effort will probably risk imprisonment or death.

Ultimately, it seems unlikely that Hong Kongers will take any more kindly to an authoritative hand from Beijing than to one from England. Though on the surface this appears to be a conciliatory society, concerned mostly with working, making money, and living well, there is a history of sympathetic activism on behalf of the mainland Chinese. In 1989, the citizens of Hong Kong raised millions of dollars in aid for the demonstrators in Tiananmen Square. Thousands more have attended annual candlelight vigils in memory of the victims of the June 4th massacre. (It is doubtful that organizers will be able to stage this event again without being accused of violating national security.)

The "one country, two systems" formula, guaranteed for only 50 years to begin with, is bound to come apart as the two systems become more intertwined through business deals and immigration in both directions. Hong Kong's system has a longer record for economic stability, and one can only hope that the Beijing government will ultimately recognize the foundations that made Hong Kong a cosmopolitan center and international financial capital. Hopefully, too, the people of Hong Kong will not be left alone in their efforts to show China a model for positive change. As long as the SAR remains open to foreign visitors, politicians, human rights activists, and media, the eyes of the world should be a monitoring force upon the Beijing government and the new Hong Kong leaders, sending a strong message that stifling the territory's individual freedoms or its laissez-faire business environment would backfire in the end.

— Jan Alexander

WHAT'S WHERE

Hong Kong Island

Hong Kong is a dazzling melée of human life and enterprise. From the harbor, the city's latest architectural wonders stand against a green mountainside backdrop, while on the other side of the island beaches and quieter villages slow the pace considerably. There is nearly everything in between. Moving clockwise, beginning with the harbor districts, Western and Central are two of the liveliest areas, full of markets, other shopping, restaurants, businesses—you name it. South of these, Mid-Levels, with its agglomeration of apartment towers, and Victoria Peak rise above the din of downtown. Wanchai is the next district east, formerly of ill repute but now the preferred locale for a night on the town. After that is Causeway Bay, another shopping haven. North Point is on the northeast corner; its principal tourist offerings are a market and a ferry pier. Shek O lies at a distant remove on the southeastern peninsula—a pleasant village with a beach for an afternoon's escape.

On the bottom of the Hong Kong Island, Stanley was a fishing village in the 19th century. Now mostly residential, it too has a pleasant beach, an interesting market, and restaurants that make a trip here worthwhile. Working your way back to the western part of the island, the amusements at Ocean Park and the large town of Aberdeen follow Repulse Bay, named for the HMS *Repulse*, which the British used to break the ring of pirates that occupied the area.

Kowloon

Occupying the tip of the peninsula across from Hong Kong Island, bustling Kowloon is where your airplane will actually land when you arrive in the area. Tsim Sha Tsui lies at the bottom of the peninsula, crammed full of shops, restaurants, and businesses. On the western side of Kowloon, Yau Ma Tei is noted for two temples, more practical shops, and great markets, such as the Jade Market and the Temple Street night market.

New Territories

Because of its distance, which in fact is not great, from the commercial hubs of Hong Kong Island and Kowloon, tourists often overlook the attractions of the New Territories. Parts of the area retain their isolated, rural character, even if to find them you must first make your way past massive housing developments (new towns built to house the burgeoning population). Shatin is one of these towns, with the ultra-modern Shatin Racecourse and the very old Temple of Ten Thousand Buddhas. Nonetheless the older character is what Hong Kong grew out of, and it is as interesting to see for its remaining traditional lifestyles as for its ancient temples and country parks. To the east, Sai Kung's country park is one of the most spectacular in the area.

Outlying Islands

As popular getaways for locals and tourists alike, the islands around Hong Kong in the South China Sea have unique charms of their own, from beaches and old fishing villages to hiking trails and remote, ancient Buddhist monasteries.

Macau

A tiny remnant of the 16th-century Portuguese spice trade, Macau provides a pleasant respite from the nonstop bustle of Hong Kong 40 mi (65 km) to the east. Construction on the island has taken away some of its quieter charms, but Portuguese influence—especially in the food—is yet another fascinating Eurasian variation played out in the South China Sea. Macau is the principal island of the territory, but the neighboring Taipa and Coloane islands are also worth visiting if you plan to spend a few days in Macau.

PLEASURES AND PASTIMES

Beaches

Surprising as it may seem, there are splendid beaches all over the area, some of which are well maintained by the government and served by lifeguards. **Repulse Bay** is a sort of Chinese Coney Island and around the corner is the smaller and less crowded **Deep Water Bay; Turtle Cove** is isolated and beautiful; Shek O's **Big Wave Bay** has a Mediterranean feel; and among New Territory and Outlying Island beaches, **Pak Sha Chau** has lovely golden sands, while **Lo Sho Ching** is a favorite of local families.

Chinese Culture

There are so many ways of taking in the phenomena of Asian life—at restaurants, in street markets where the very sense of an individual's space is so dramatically different than in the West, in ancient Chinese temples, in a karaoke bar, at the hands of a fortune teller, or in parks watching the morning t'ai chi ritual. Embrace as much of Hong Kong as you can. You'll never forget it.

Restaurants

No other city in the world, except New York, can match the distinct variety and integrity of cuisine found in Hong Kong. One of the most exciting aspects of dining on Chinese soil is the opportunity to eat truly authentic Chinese food. At the same time, at a cultural crossroads like Hong Kong, with all of its exotic connotations, the steamy, aromatic tastes of Pan-Asian cuisine are another unique culinary opportunity. All in all, there is enough to satisfy everyone, if not while sitting at the same table. If you approach this diversity with an open mind, try some things that you usually might shy away from, you may just leave Hong Kong wishing that you could take it all with you.

Shopping

Hong Kong has the best shopping in the world, if you work at it. Although the thought of crowded streets, mind-boggling choices, and endless haggling can be daunting, there is no place more conducive to big-time spending than this center of international commerce. Even nonshoppers get tempted to part with their money—and some have admitted to actually enjoying the experience.

The variety of goods is astonishing: everything from international designer products to intriguing treasures and handcrafted items from all over Asia. Just as remarkable is the fantastic choice of places to shop, which range from sophisticated boutique-lined malls to open-air markets and shadowy alleyways.

Walking

There is a wide range of pedestrian movement possible in Hong Kong—from the sort of sideways shuffling that one does in a street market to outstanding hiking on Hong Kong Island itself, in the New Territories, and on the Outlying Islands. The point is not how fast or far you go, but simply that you experience the area on foot. It is without question the most rewarding way to take in the sights, sounds, and smells of this astonishing territory.

NEW AND NOTEWORTHY

Nineteen ninety-seven was a year of great significance for Hong Kong, as sovereignty over the territory passed from Great Britain to China at midnight on June 30. For the next 50 years, Hong Kong will be a Special Administrative Region (SAR) before fully re-joining China. Under the Basic Law, Hong Kong's temporary constitution, Hong Kong will remain highly independent of China under the "one country, two systems" concept. Laws in place before the handover will remain basically unchanged, although some constraints have been placed on civil liberties such as the right to protest, and on speech promoting the independence of Taiwan or Tibet.

Hong Kongers, who have never experienced true democracy and are known more for their industriousness than political concerns, have reacted to the changeover with both unease and pride. Political scientists are waiting to see how Hong Kong will change China as well as vice versa, and the outcome of this historic event will shape the future of China's quest to regain Taiwan.

A walking trail of epic proportions. Even the territory's diehard hikers are still clocking in miles along the Wilson Trail, which opened in 1996. Named after a former governor who was a hiking enthusiast, the trail runs nearly 50 mi (80 km) from the steep hills of southern Hong Kong Island to Kowloon and the New Territories. It takes at least 31 hours to hike the entire trail, but the well-marked pathways are divided into 10 sections for day hikes. The least rigorous section will take you along a beautiful reservoir to the cliffs overlooking the tranquil Tolo Harbour. On other sections of the trail you'll see the fishing villages that dot the Sai Kung islands, tropical groves, incense-filled temples, sweeping panoramas of the sea islands, and of course, Hong Kong's majestic mountains.

The Airport Core Programme (ACP) Hong Kong is getting more than just a new 24-hour airport this April. The engineering feat on Chek Lap Kok island, which required mowing down a mountain to level the land for an airstrip and terminal, was just the beginning of a massive development project that will pave over the green hills of adjacent Lantau Island with highways, a subway line, and a long stretch of skyscrapers. The area of the airport itself is equal in size to the Kowloon Peninsula. A airport railway will speed to Tsim Sha Tsui and to Central over the world's longest road/rail suspension bridge, Tsing Ma Bridge. The Western Harbor Crossing tunnel connects the airport traffic between Western Kowloon and the Central District. This is all in keeping with explosive growth: Hong Kong's urban planning department expects the territory's population, currently 6.3 million, to triple within 30 years. You can see architectural models, videos, and photographs of what Hong Kong will look like when the 21st century dawns at the ACP Exhibition Centre. Call the Hong Kong Tourist Association (☎ 2807–6177) for information.

The **Sun Yat-sen walking trail** takes you by the sites where the Chinese doctor studied and plotted revolution. Sun (1866-1925), led the 1911 Revolution against the Qing dynasty, and became the first President of the short-lived Republic of China. He received his medical degree at Hong Kong College, where he was also inculcated with progressive ideas about reform and revolution. Dr. Sun's ghost wouldn't recognize much in Hong Kong, but the trail will take you on a nice, rambling stroll from Eastern Street in Western through the Mid-Levels and into Central. A map and detailed brochure, printed in English and Chinese, is available for purchase at the Central and Western District Board, across the street from the Sincere Department Store (⊠ Harbour Bldg., 38 Pier Rd., ground floor, Central, ☎ 2852–3549 or 2852–3477).

FODOR'S CHOICE

Dining

★ **Petrus.** A superb view, a fine selection of wine, and sumptuous dishes with artistic flair earn this French restaurant's prestigious reputation. $$$$

★ **Yü.** A creative East-and-West menu and posh decor make this not only the best seafood restaurant in town, but perhaps the best restaurant in Hong Kong altogether. $$$$

★ **Cafe Deco Bar and Grill.** Combining Hong Kong chic and Pan-Asian cuisine with panoramic views from atop Victoria Peak, this has become an Island favorite. $$$

★ **Yung Kee.** What you expect from Cantonese dining—lightning-fast preparations, high-energy service, and reasonable prices—is what you'll get at Yung Kee, which is why so many different kinds of people keep coming back. $$

★ **Wu Kong Shanghai Restaurant.** This simple Shanghaiese restaurant serves authentic northern Chinese cuisine with reasonable prices, and is very popular among local diners. $–$$

★ **Bela Vista, Macau.** In the landmark Bela Vista Hotel overlooking Praia Grande Bay, this romantic restaurant with veranda offers Portuguese seafood dishes, such as grilled *garoupa* (grouper) with mango. This is the place to come for a truly memorable Macanese dinner. $$$

★ **Afonso III, Macau.** For a wholly different experience of Portuguese cuisine, where the chef prepares food the way his grandmother did, try this simple café. $$

Excursions

★ The view of the coastline from the **Ocean Park cable car.** From here you'll think you're riding over the Mediterranean as you gaze down at a panorama of mountains, pastel villas, and the vast, blue sea.

★ Crossing the harbor on the **Star Ferry,** first class. Breathing the air of the South China Sea is vital to any experience of Hong Kong, whose very existence owes itself to the crossing of seas—not to mention today's stunning views.

★ A **tram ride** from Kennedy Town to North Point. Spare half of an afternoon to see Hong Kong at its bustling, crowded best. Find a spot on the upper deck for the ideal view of stores, office buildings, produce markets, traffic, and swarms of humanity, all with a uniquely Chinese flair.

★ A 30-minute **junk trip** through Macau's Inner Harbour, organized by the Maritime Museum, brings up close the life of the fishing population and the booming Chinese suburb on the opposite shore.

Lodging

★ **Island Shangri-La, Hong Kong Island.** This hotel, which towers above the Pacific Place complex, has spacious rooms and spectacular views of the Peak and Victoria Harbour. $$$$

★ **Mandarin Oriental, Hong Kong Island.** The Mandarin matches convenience with luxury, making it one of the world's great hotels. Celebrities and VIPs agree. $$$$

★ **Peninsula, Kowloon.** The "Pen" is the ultimate in colonial elegance with its mix of European elegance and Chinese details. $$$$

★ **Garden View International House, Hong Kong Island.** This small, attractive hotel overlooks the botanical gardens and the harbor. $

★ **Bela Vista, Macau.** Originally built in the 1880s and now a luxury all-suite inn, the Bela Vista retains its colonial ambience under the management of Mandarin Oriental Hotels. $$$$

★ **Pousada de São Tiago, Macau.** This traditional Portuguese inn is built into the ruins of a 17th-century fortress and incorporates ancient trees and natural springs into its design. The furnishings were custom made in Portugal and Hong Kong. $$$

Museums

★ **Hong Kong Museum of History.** See what Hong Kong looked like more than 6,000 years ago, when tigers and other animals ranged over the islands. Scenes of Neolithic life, life-size dioramas, military displays, and artifacts trace the territory's development up to the present.

★ **The Hong Kong Museum of Art.** This, of course, is the place in town to see ancient Chinese scrolls and sculpture along with the work of the territory's own contemporary masters.

★ **The Maritime Museum, Macau.** From its dragon boats to pirate-chasing *lorchas,* Portuguese voyage charts, and navigation equipment, the ship-shaped Maritime Museum provides a fascinating view of seagoing Macau.

Nightlife

★ **Temple Street Night Market.** After 8pm this stretch in Kowloon becomes an open-air market of food stalls, T-shirts and trinkets. The bilingual palm readers and informal Chinese opera performances are at the northern end of the street.

★ **Crazy Paris Show at Hotel Lisboa, Macau.** Girls, girls, girls (wait, was that a boy in there?)—if that's what you're after, this Paris/Vegas–style show is the best around.

Parks and Countryside Walks

★ **Dragon's Back in Shek O Country Park.** Bring your hiking boots and canteen and escape the urban madness on a moderately hilly trail where banana leaves grow to be 3 ft long and the view of the sea is nothing short of spectacular.

★ **Lantau Island, Shek Pik to Tai O.** If you're a seasoned hiker, try this wondrous all-day trek past the Shek Pik reservoir and a half-dozen tucked-away monasteries down to the picturesque seaside village of Tai O, still unmarred by serious development.

★ **Lou Lim Ieoc Garden, Macau.** For a lovely respite in Macau, stroll through this Soochow-style enclosed garden, a miniature landscape of bamboo, a lake, and a traditional nine-turn bridge.

★ **Coloane Park, Macau.** On the southernmost of Macau's three islands, Coloane Park has a remarkable walk-in aviary with more than 200 bird species (some quite rare), a nature trail, and a fascinating collection of exotic trees and shrubs.

Special Events

★ **Candlelight parades.** Two parades, one in honor of the mid-autumn moon and another at the Dragon Boat Festival in June, are both resplendent with traditional costumes, music, and general merrymaking.

★ **Bun Festival (May) on Cheung Chau.** The villagers still offer fresh-baked buns to placate vengeful spirits of the dead each year, with three 50-ft-high bun towers outside of the Pak Tai Temple. Bring a camera to catch the parade of elaborate floats and an altar of papier-mâché gods on film.

★ **Horse racing at Happy Valley track.** All of Hong Kong loves a gamble, and there's no better way to see a cross-section of the population, from the boxes to the bleachers, taking a chance on winning. Whether you win or not, you'll find the mood contagious.

★ **Fringe Festival.** Experience the best of Hong Kong's avant-garde theater, music, and art at the unique Fringe Club, housed in a historic building that used to be a dairy depot. The festival is held on various dates in January and February.

★ **The Good Friday Passion Parade, Macau.** In the first weekend of Lent, a statue of Christ is carried through the streets in procession, with stations of the cross erected along the way.

Street Markets

★ **Jade Market, Kansu Street, Kowloon.** Besides 10,000 jade bangles, baubles, and beads, this colorful open-air bazaar has Chinese-style jewelry galore, in every price range.

★ **Bird Market on Hong Lok Street, near Mong Kok MTR station Kowloon.** In an alleyway filled with the trill of songbirds, you might also hear a mynah cursing in Cantonese as old men feed grasshoppers to their prize songsters. Buy a beautiful handmade bamboo cage or win over a cockatoo by scratching its neck.

★ **Rua de Cinco de Outubro, Macau.** This is traditional Chinese Macau, with street markets offering incredible bargains in name brand clothing, made under licence in local factories.

Taste Treats

★ **Dim sum lunch** anywhere. Since you've come to the source, this is one tradition that you simply must not pass up.

★ A market-stall Chinese breakfast of **congee** (rice porridge) at Kowloon Park Road/Haiphong Road, Kowloon. There are plenty of tastes so exotic that we wouldn't recommend them, but this is a basic, quintessential experience of bustling Hong Kong culture.

★ **Afternoon tea** in the grand lobby of the Peninsula Hotel. Dignified and utterly civilized, this legacy of the British presence in Hong Kong can transport you beyond the elegance of the Peninsula to a wholly other era.

Temples and Shrines

★ **The Temple of 10,000 Buddhas, Shatin.** You will have to climb nearly 500 steps to reach this wonder, but with its 13,000 statues and gilded, mummified holy man, in addition to views of Amah Rock, the temple is worth the effort.

★ **Po Lin Buddhist Monastery, Lantau Island.** On a grander scale than most temple complexes in Hong Kong, Po Lin Monastery is home to Southeast Asia's tallest bronze Buddha, more than 100 ft high.

★ **A-Ma Temple, Macau.** Named for a sea goddess who, according to custom, saved a humble junk from a storm, A-Ma is the oldest and perhaps the most beautiful temple in Macau.

FESTIVALS AND SEASONAL EVENTS

Top seasonal events in Hong Kong include Chinese New Year, the Hong Kong Arts Festival, the Hong Kong Food Festival, and the Dragon Boat Festival. The most colorful festivals of all are the many lunar festivals celebrated throughout the year. For exact dates and further details about the following events, contact the HKTA (☞ Visitor Information *in* the Gold Guide).

WINTER

➤ LATE JAN.: Hong Kong Marathon is sponsored by the Hong Kong Distance Runner's Club.

➤ LATE JAN.–FEB.: Chinese New Year, a time to visit friends and relatives and wear new clothes, causes the city to come to a virtual standstill.

➤ FEB.: Spring Lantern Festival is on the last day of Chinese New Year celebrations; streets and homes are decorated with brightly colored lanterns.

➤ MID-FEB.–MAR.: Hong Kong Arts Festival takes place in venues throughout the territory.

➤ EARLY MAR.: Hong Kong Open Golf Championship, at the Royal Hong Kong Golf Club.

SPRING

➤ MID-MAR.: The annual Hong Kong Food Festival is more than two weeks of nonstop feasting and entertainment.

➤ LATE MAR. OR EARLY APR.: The Invitation Sevens is a premier rugby tournament.

➤ LATE MAR.: Hong Kong International Film Festival, featuring films from several countries, is a rewarding fortnight for film buffs.

➤ EARLY APR.: Ching Ming Festival is a time when families visit the burial plots of ancestors and departed relatives.

➤ LATE APR.: Birthday of Tin Hau, goddess of the sea. Fishermen decorate their boats and converge on seaside temples to honor her, especially around the Tin Hau Temple in Junk Bay.

➤ MAY: Birthday of Lord Buddha, when temples throughout the territory bathe the Buddha's statue.

➤ MAY: Bun Festival on Cheung Chau Island is a three-day spirit-placating rite, culminating in a grand procession that attracts thousands of people.

➤ JUNE: The Dragon Boat Festival pits long, many-oared dragon-head boats against one another in races to commemorate the hero Ch'u Yuen. International races follow a week later.

SUMMER

➤ JULY 1: Return to Motherland Day. This marks the day that Hong Kong reverted to Chinese sovereignty in 1997.

➤ MID-AUG.: Seven Sisters (Maiden) Festival is a celebration for lovers and a time when young girls pray for a good husband.

➤ AUG.: Hungry Ghosts Festival is a time when food is set out to placate roaming spirits.

AUTUMN

➤ SEPT.: Lantern Festival sees crowds with candle lanterns gather in parks and other open spaces.

➤ LATE SEPT. OR EARLY OCT.: Birthday of Confucius celebrates the revered philosopher.

➤ MID-OCT.: Chung Yeung Festival commemorates a Han Dynasty tale about a man taking his family to high ground to avoid disaster.

➤ LATE NOV.: The Macau Grand Prix takes over the city streets for a weekend.

➤ MID-DEC.: Hong Kong Judo Championship takes place at Queen Elizabeth Stadium.

2 Exploring

Hong Kong is one of the world's most compact, most intense travel experiences. The crowds can be overwhelming, but the city vibrates with life, energy, and the frantic quest for personal achievement and gain. This city is the very essence of Western capitalism, yet the soul of the place is truly Eastern—it is this blend and contrast that make exploring Hong Kong so fascinating.

Updated by
Jan Alexander

THERE IS SO MUCH TO SEE and do here, it's easy to be lured away from a hectic business schedule or a rigid sightseeing plan. Instead, you may find yourself heading down alleyways lined with shops selling everything from jewelry to sportswear and filled with the aroma from food stalls and some of the world's best Chinese restaurants. You won't find much ancient history, however. Hong Kong has existed as a city for little more than 150 years, and urban development has brought change even to old neighborhoods. The Chinese have been flocking to Hong Kong for decades, bringing with them their traditions as well as their energy and entrepreneurial spirit. Throughout its history Hong Kong has given full scope to that spirit, leaving it unhindered by political or social limitations. Today it is a Chinese city in flux, shedding its colonialist past and determining its new identity.

The island was officially ceded to Great Britain in 1841, at the end of the First Opium War with China. At that time it was hardly considered a valuable prize. It was a sparse little island, 30 sq mi (155 sq km) in size, with only one natural water source—a waterfall above what is now Aberdeen—and a mountainous center. The British military acknowledged its usefulness as an operational base or transshipping port, but was angry it wasn't offered a port on the mainland of China. The British foreign minister called Hong Kong "that barren rock," and Queen Victoria's consort (husband), Prince Albert, publicly laughed at this "jewel" in the British Crown. Except for the natural harbor, all its geographical, historical, and demographic factors should have guaranteed Hong Kong permanent obscurity.

Hardly an auspicious beginning for the island that author Han Su-Yin was to describe a century later as the "deep roaring bustling eternal market... in which life and love and souls and blood and all things made and grown under the sun are bought and sold and smuggled and squandered." Han's description is still the impression one gets when arriving on the island for the first time by the Star Ferry. (One of the unfortunate results of progress is that many visitors now get their initial view of Hong Kong Island as they emerge from the cavernous Cross-Harbour Tunnel or from the steps of the MTR, rather than from the legendary ferry.) Today, the "barren rock" contains some of the world's most expensive real estate and a skyline to rival that of any of the world's major cities.

The feeling of Hong Kong, what it is and why it exists, can best be discovered from the harbor. That body of water, chosen centuries ago by fishermen from China as a perfect shelter from the raging *tai'foos* ("big winds," the origin of the word *typhoon*), is still the island's centerpiece. Hong Kong began as a trading center and has grown into a bustling commercial capital largely because its harbor, emptying into the South China Sea, is a convenient gateway for traders from both East and West. Today, however, the harbor is almost as densely packed as the streets of Hong Kong's commercial districts. The Port of Hong Kong—the busiest on earth—barely has enough space left to accommodate the traffic in huge cargo ships from around the globe.

On either side of the harbor, the packed streets of Hong Kong Island and lower Kowloon Peninsula have the look of a futuristic metropolis, with skyscrapers built virtually on top of one another and hardly a green space in sight. Construction hasn't stopped just because there seems to be no visible patch of land left. Developers faced with a shortage of space on which to build are creating more land by dredg-

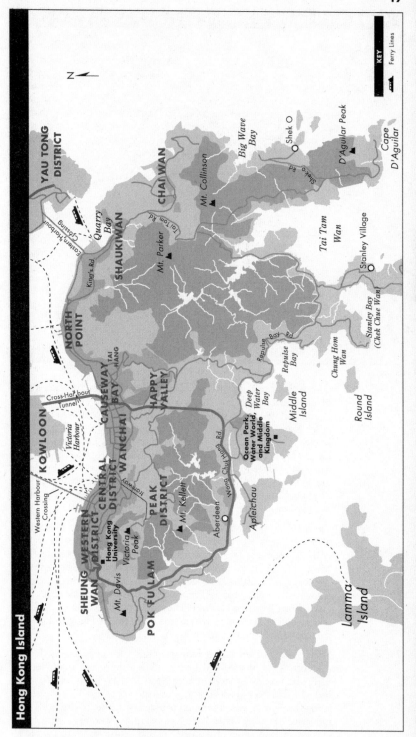

Hong Kong Island

YAU TONG DISTRICT

CHAI WAN

Big Wave Bay

Shek O

D'Aguilar Peak

Mt. Collinson

Cape D'Aguilar

Shek O Rd

Quarry Bay

King's Rd

SHAUKIWAN

Tai Tam Rd

Mt. Parker

Tai Tam Wan

Stanley Village

Eastern Harbour Crossing

NORTH POINT

Stanley Bay (Chek Chue Wan)

TAI HANG

Repulse Bay Rd

Chung Hom Wan

CAUSEWAY BAY

HAPPY VALLEY

Repulse Bay

Cross-Harbour Tunnel

WANCHAI

Deep Water Bay

Middle Island

Round Island

KOWLOON

Victoria Harbour

CENTRAL DISTRICT

Ocean Park, Water World, and Middle Kingdom

Wong Chuk Hang Rd

Western Harbour Crossing

PEAK DISTRICT

Tramway

Mt. Kellett

Aberdeen

Apleichau

SHEUNG WAN

WESTERN DISTRICT

Hong Kong University

Victoria Peak

Mt. Davis

POK FU LAM

Lamma Island

N

KEY

Ferry Lines

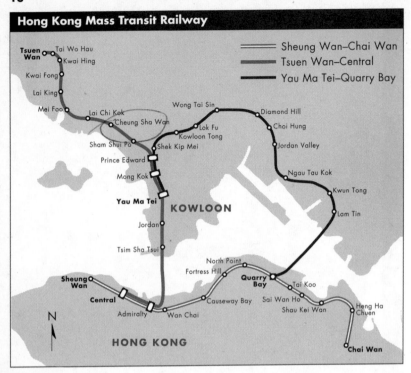

Hong Kong Mass Transit Railway

Sheung Wan–Chai Wan
Tsuen Wan–Central
Yau Ma Tei–Quarry Bay

Tsuen Wan
Tai Wo Hau
Kwai Hing
Kwai Fong
Lai King
Mei Foo
Lai Chi Kok
Cheung Sha Wan
Sham Shui Po
Prince Edward
Mong Kok
Yau Ma Tei
Jordan
Tsim Sha Tsui
Shek Kip Mei
Kowloon Tong
Lok Fu
Wong Tai Sin
Diamond Hill
Choi Hung
Jordan Valley
Ngau Tau Kok
Kwun Tong
Lam Tin

KOWLOON

Sheung Wan
Central
Admiralty
Wan Chai
Causeway Bay
North Point
Fortress Hill
Quarry Bay
Tai Koo
Sai Wan Ho
Shau Kei Wan
Heng Ha Chuen
Chai Wan

N

HONG KONG

ing it from beneath the harbor. The most ambitious reclamation scheme of all occurred just a few years ago with the leveling of Chek Lap Kok, an uninhabited island of rock and scrub that has been reshaped to fit Hong Kong's new state-of-the art international airport. The rock was leveled, and land was reclaimed to connect Chek Lap Kok to nearby Lantau Island, where farmers and fishermen whose families had lived in a small village for many generations were paid (not a great deal of money) to relocate. All along West Kowloon and the northwest shore of Hong Kong Island, additional land has been reclaimed to build a railway line running to and from the airport.

The intensely developed areas seen by most tourists belie the fact that about 75% of the territory is actually rural land. A bird's-eye view reveals the 236 islands that make up the lesser-known part of Hong Kong. Most of these undeveloped islands are nothing but jagged peaks and tropical scrub, just as Hong Kong Island itself once was. Others are throwbacks to an age of fishing villages and small vegetable farms. Even Hong Kong Island has vast stretches of green, with walking trails that take two days or more to cover. This other side of Hong Kong is easily accessible by boats and buses.

Hong Kong residents have a great fondness for open spaces. Indeed, the popularity of weekend hiking, junk sailing, and skydiving has reached almost manic levels in recent years. Perhaps this is because everyone who lives here knows nothing lasts forever, especially undeveloped land. The New Territories are full of industry instead of rice fields now; the farms of Lamma Island are disappearing as new apartment buildings go up; and many of the vast uninhabited stretches of Lantau Island, a favorite among hikers, will soon be filled with the offices and residential towers expected to spring up around the new airport. For now, Hong Kong's sudden economic boom has brought it into a sort of golden age, with a perfect balance of the old and the new, the dazzle of the city and the intrepid spirit of the outdoors. You can hike and camp in the woods, stroll through traditional Chinese villages, or spend the afternoon sailing, then via the city's mega-efficient highways and public transportation, arrive back in civilization in plenty of time for an evening of fine dining and glittering nightlife.

And what of Hong Kong's future? You can feel the change in the air. Street signs are still in English and traffic still flows British style, with steering wheels on the right, but there is less English spoken than a few years ago. At press time, the fate of a number of old colonial institutions, such as Government House, where the British governor lived, was yet to be determined. Although most major sites will remain in place, changes are bound to occur rapidly and many foreigners with business establishments in Hong Kong may be leaving. Think of visiting Hong Kong in 1998 as an opportunity to watch history in the making, and check with the Hong Kong Tourist Association information booth at the Star Ferry, Tsim Sha Tsui, or Jardine House for information about new sights and the status of old ones.

HONG KONG ISLAND

Many of the British who set up their trading warehouses on Hong Kong Island were of Scottish ancestry. They were among the most nationalistic (or homesick) in the Victorian era, and almost everything of importance was named after Queen Victoria. The central section was named Victoria City; the mountain peak, Victoria Peak; the military barracks, Victoria Barracks; and the prison, Victoria Prison. Victoria College and Victoria Park came later. Watch for changes in these names, since it's hard to believe the Chinese-appointed government will long abide these remnants of colonialism.

Before you head out to explore the island, take a moment to acquaint yourself with its many neighborhoods:

Central Hong Kong sits in the center of the north side of the island, a gleaming modern enclave that hums with life.

The **Western District** lies, as you might imagine, to the west of the Central District and is primarily an area of small shops and housing.

The **Midlevels** area, south of Central's business district, climbs out of the hills, with luxury skyscrapers growing right out of the tropical bush.

Victoria Peak, an exclusive residential area high above Midlevels, rises as high as 1,805 ft above sea level.

Wanchai, to the east of Central, was famed at one time for its nightlife, as immortalized in Richard Mason's novel *The World of Suzie Wong* and the movie it inspired.

Causeway Bay, just past Wanchai, was once a middle-class Chinese community but is now primarily a business and tourist area filled with offices, hotels, restaurants, and Hong Kong's highest concentration of department stores.

North Point and Quarry Bay, farther east, once consisted solely of factories and tenements but are now full of gleaming new office complexes and small cafés.

Shaukiwan and Chai Wan, at the east end of Quarry Bay, were once very poor but are rapidly gentrifying as middle-class residents and businesses flee the high rents of Central.

Aberdeen, on the southwest side of the island, has a busy fishermen's harbor and a plethora of waterside attractions. Aberdeen also contains a factory area, Wong Chuk Hang, and the highway interchange for the Aberdeen Tunnel, which slices through the mountains and comes out at the Happy Valley Race Track.

Deep Water Bay is a scenic area reached by leaving Aberdeen and heading east on a winding ocean-front highway.

Repulse Bay, farther east, is another of Hong Kong's prestigious residential areas, with a very popular beach.

Stanley, reached by following the winding road, is a growing suburb known for bargain shopping.

Shek O, a pleasant seaside village on the southeast side of the island, is another old settlement that is a mix of village houses and baronial mansions.

Big Wave Bay, north of Shek O, has one of the territory's few surfing beaches.

Central and Western Districts

Central Hong Kong has an official name, Victoria City, but throughout the era of British reign, everyone has called it Central. Buildings in the district are both modern and ornate, gleaming in gold, silver, ivory, and ebony, with iridescent reflections of the harbor shimmering on their surfaces—this is just one of the faces with which the city enchants new visitors.

The Western District lies, as you might imagine, to the west of Central District, which is, of course, in the center of the north side of the island. Western begins with small Chinese shops that give way to large residential high-rises stretching out to Pok Fu Lam, a neighborhood popular among expat families.

Numbers in the text correspond to numbers in the margin and on the Central and Western Districts map.

A Good Walk

Walking is often the transportation of choice in Hong Kong's compact commercial areas, where taxis and buses can get stalled in rush-hour traffic. Take a day to explore Central District from the Star Ferry terminal up the Midlevels escalator to Hollywood Road and the Western District. Start at the **Star Ferry** ① terminal. One of the Totes (offtrack betting offices) is in front of the terminal, and to the right as you face inland are the main post office and the towering **Jardine House** ②, which is easy to spot because of its many round windows. Walk up the staircase behind Jardine House to **Exchange Square** ③, following the signs along the elevated walkway. It will take about five minutes to find your way through the pedestrian traffic jam.

Go back to the elevated walkway, past the Star Ferry pier, and beyond the Discovery Bay Ferry pier, to the **city hall complex** ④ (between Edinburgh Place and Connaught Road, which faces Queen's Pier and the harbor). From the city hall complex, continue on to the Connaught Road Central side of city hall and the underground walkway to **Statue Square** ⑤. The Victorian building on the square is the **Legislative Council Building** ⑥.

The modern glass-and-steel-structure at the end of the square is the headquarters of the **Hongkong & Shanghai Bank** ⑦. Just to the east is the old **Bank of China** ⑧ building, which houses the **Tsui Museum of Art.**

Catercorner from the Bank of China is a small park, **Chater Garden** ⑨. Head west, following the tracks of the double-decker trams that pass in front of the Hongkong & Shanghai Bank. This will take you along Des Voeux Road, lined with elegant shops and tall office buildings.

At the corner of Des Voeux Road and Pedder Street, turn left at the **Landmark** ⑩ shopping complex. Follow Pedder Street, which parallels the Landmark, and turn west on Queen's Road Central, one of the main shopping arteries. Central Market, on Queen's Road at the Queen Victoria Street crossing, used to be the city's largest public food market and now has a walkway on the top floor that connects to the **Midlevels Escalator** ⑪. Board the escalator and exit at **Hollywood Road** ⑫. This is not the end of the line, but it's a hot spot on every tourist itinerary and far more interesting than the residential sections you'll see if you keep climbing. Stop at **Man Mo Temple** ⑬, on Hollywood Road in the midst of antiques and curio shops. In the days before wheeled traffic, most of the steep, narrow lanes on the hillside were filled with steps. To reach **Upper Lascar Row** ⑭, also known as **Cat Street**, walk down the steps of Ladder Street, just across from Man Mo Temple.

From Cat Street head toward the Western District. Walk down Ladder Street back to Queen's Road Central. Walking west, you'll begin to find some of the best local color within the urban jungle. Turn right on Cleverly Street, then left. Both **Bonham Strand East and West** ⑮ have many little shops to explore, as does the adjacent **Wing Lok Street** ⑯. Follow Bonham Strand West to **Des Voeux Road West** ⑰. On the left side of the street as you continue west, you will find all kinds of shops selling preserved foods such as dried and salted fish, black mushrooms, and vegetables.

When you're ready to turn back, turn right on any side street and walk one block to Connaught Road West and then head east. Stop at **Western Market** ⑱, then turn onto **Queen's Road Central** ⑲ to get an interesting look at an herbal medicine shop.

TIMING

Set aside a whole day for this walk, especially if you want to browse or shop. A leisurely walk from Star Ferry terminal to Cat Street will take two to three hours. Plan about 30 minutes to look at the exhibition at the Tsui Museum in the Bank of China building and 20 minutes to see Man Mo Temple. From Cat Street to Western Market will take 1½ to 3 hours, depending on how much time you spend browsing.

The best strolling weather is in the dry season from late September to mid-December; the rest of the year you should carry a folding umbrella. If the rain gets heavy, duck into one of the thousands of stores and shopping arcades and engage in the favorite local sport: shopping and browsing.

Sights to See

❽ **Bank of China.** This structure, the former Bank of China building, is easy to recognize with its two Chinese stone lions guarding the front doorway. Built by Chinese Nationalists after World War II, this building was 20 ft higher than the adjacent Hongkong & Shanghai Bank edifice until the latter built its imposing new structure in the 1980s. Not to be outdone, the Bank of China commissioned I. M. Pei to design an even more impressive tower, which was completed in 1989. Across the street and a few doors east of the venerable institution, on Queen's Road Central, the new **Bank of China Tower** challenges its rival's influence on the landscape. A visiting architect recently said that the towers of finance in Hong Kong, which dominate the view as no

22

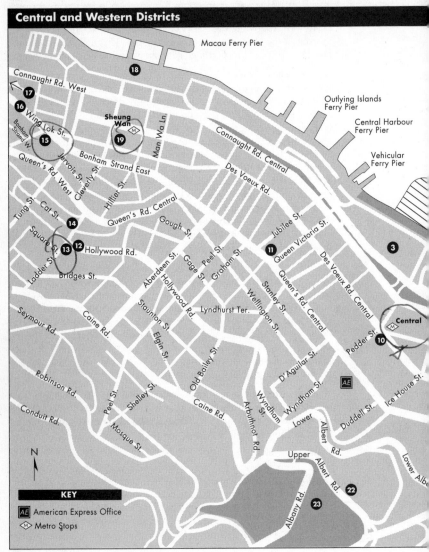

Macau Ferry Pier

Connaught Rd. West

Outlying Islands
Ferry Pier

Central Harbour
Ferry Pier

Vehicular
Ferry Pier

Sheung
Wan

Connaught Rd. Central

Wing Lok St.

Bonham Strand W.

Des Voeux Rd.

Bonham Strand East

Man Wa Ln.

Queen's Rd. West

Jervois St.

Cleverly St.

Hillier St.

Queen's Rd. Central

Gough St.

Jubilee St.

Queen Victoria St.

Des Voeux Rd. Central

Tung St.

Cat St.

Square St.

Ladder St.

Hollywood Rd.

Bridges St.

Aberdeen St.

Gage St.

Peel St.

Graham St.

Hollywood Rd.

Staunton St.

Wellington St.

Queen's Rd. Central

Stanley St.

Caine Rd.

Lyndhurst Ter.

Elgin St.

Pedder St.

Central

Seymour Rd.

D'Aguilar St.

Wyndham St.

Duddell St.

Ice House St.

Robinson Rd.

Peel St.

Shelley St.

Old Bailey St.

Caine Rd.

Arbuthnot Rd.

Wyndham St.

Lower Albert Rd.

Lower Albe

Conduit Rd.

Mosque St.

Upper

Albert Rd.

Albany Rd.

N

KEY

AE American Express Office

Ⓜ Metro Stops

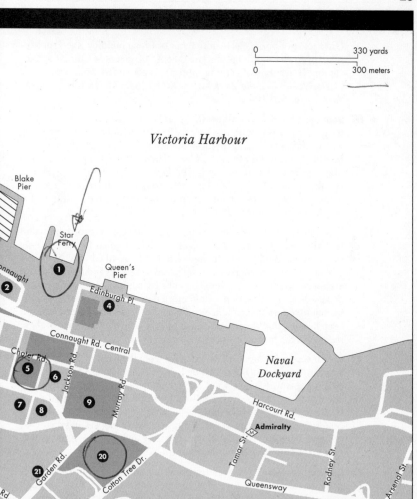

Victoria Harbour

church spires ever have, are an indication of the city's worship of an economy built around banking.

On the 11th floor of the former Bank of China building, the **Tsui Museum of Art** has holdings of more than 3,000 pieces of Chinese art, including collections of ceramics, bronze, and carved wood and ivory. ⊠ *Des Voeux Rd. and Bank St.,* ☎ *2868–2688.* ▦ *HK$30.* ☉ *Weekdays 10–6, Sat. 10–2.*

★ ⑮ **Bonham Strand East and West.** An area left relatively untouched by the modern world, the streets here are lined with traditional shops, many with open fronts. Among the most interesting are those selling live snakes, both for food and for medicinal uses. The snakes, from pythons to cobras, are imported from China and kept in cages outside the shops. Go ahead and sample a bowl of snake soup or an invigorating snake-gallbladder wine. The main season for the snake trade is from October through February.

Bonham Strand West is known for traditional Chinese medicines and herbal remedies. Many old shops have their original facades. Inside, walls are lined with drawers and shelves of jars filled with hundreds of strange-smelling ingredients, such as wood barks and insects, which are consumed dried and ground up, infused in hot water or tea, or taken as powders or pills. Some of the more innocuous remedies are made from ginseng, said to enhance virility and prolong life. Skeptics should keep in mind that the Chinese have been relying on the effects of these medicines for thousands of years.

⑨ **Chater Garden.** This small park, across from the Bank of China Tower, was the former home of the Hong Kong Cricket Club. A favorite local pastime was watching cricket players enjoying the game at a leisurely pace, oblivious to the traffic noise and bustle. The club, chased away by the high price of real estate, has moved to grounds outside the city center. Conservationists won the battle against developers and preserved the park, to the delight of all who come to sit and relax in this small, green oasis. ⊠ *Chater and Jackson Rds.*

❹ **City hall complex.** The architecture is unremarkable, but the promenade outside offers a good view of ships in the harbor. Stroll through the garden on almost any afternoon, and you'll see at least one or two wedding parties, usually with young Chinese newlyweds in elaborate Western regalia posing for a photographer. The registry at city hall is a popular spot for weddings, with more than 6,500 couples exchanging vows here each year. In addition to municipal offices, the complex contains a theater, a concert hall, and several libraries. (You can take out books if you bring your passport, proof of address, and a refundable deposit of HK$130 per book.) Many events in the annual **International Arts and Film Festival** are held here. ⊠ *Between Edinburgh Pl. and Connaught Rd.,* ☎ *2921–2840 or 2921–2555.* ☉ *Library: Mon.–Thurs. 10–7, Fri. 10–9, Sat. 10–5, Sun. 10–1.*

⑰ **Des Voeux Road West.** You'll recognize the tram tracks when you get to the west end of ☞ **Bonham Strand West.** On the left side of the street as you walk west, notice the many shops selling preserved foods—everything from dried and salted fish to black mushrooms. This is a good area for lunchtime dim sum.

❸ **Exchange Square.** Exchange Square consists of three gold- and silver-striped glass towers and contains some of the most expensive rental space on the island—indeed, in the world. In good weather local office workers like to buy take-out food from the various epicurean establishments in the square, including Häagen-Dazs, and picnic around the life-size bronze water buffalo between the towers. A few years ago you could see the harbor from this area, but now all you can behold is a new office development, the Central Station stop of the new Airport Railway, and the outlying islands' ferry pier, all built on reclaimed land, created by soil dredged from the harbor. Go up the escalator to the lobby of Exchange Square 1 to see the rotunda, which has exhibitions of a fairly trendy collection of contemporary art. ⊠ *Opposite Outlying Islands ferry pier,* ☎ *2522–1122.* ☼ *Weekdays 10–12:30 and 2:30–3:30.*

⑫ Hollywood Road. Here funerary shops sell traditional Chinese coffins and other elaborate ceremonial funerary items. Farther along, other shops sell different grades of rice, displayed in brass-banded wooden tubs. Rice is sold by the catty (about 1¼ pounds). Look to the left for a sign saying POSSESSION STREET, where Captain Charles Elliott of the British Royal Navy stepped ashore in 1841 and claimed Hong Kong for the British empire. It is interesting to note how far today's harbor is from this earlier shoreline—the result of a century of aggressive land reclamation.

Farther east along Hollywood Road are many antiques, curio, and junk shops, as well as shops selling every type of Asian art and handicraft. Some items are genuinely old, but most are not. Porcelain, embroidered robes, paintings, screens, snuff bottles, and wood and ivory carvings are among the many items found here in profusion. Bargain hard if you want a good price.

OFF THE BEATEN PATH

HONG KONG MUSEUM OF MEDICAL SCIENCES – This new museum, tucked away in an Edwardian-style building behind a small park in Midlevels, is worth the climb through tiny backstreets for anyone interested in the history of Chinese medicine in Hong Kong. Exhibitions show comparisons of how Chinese and Western medicines are used, examples of Chinese medicines of both animal and herbal origin, and a traditional Chinese medical practitioner's equipment, as well as several rooms devoted to Western medical subjects. To get here from Hollywood Road, follow Ladder Street behind Man Mo Temple, south and uphill to Square Street, which veers right, then left to Caine Lane. Follow a circular path going up about 300 ft around Caine Lane Garden, a park with colorful stucco structures, until you reach Number 2. ⊠ *2 Caine La., Midlevels, Hong Kong,* ☎ *2549–5123,* FAX *2559–9458.* ☜ *HK$10.* ☼ *Tues.–Sat. 10–5, Sun. 1–5.*

❼ Hongkong & Shanghai Bank. This modern glass-and-steel headquarters at the end of ☞ Statue Square, known simply as the Bank, houses the largest and most powerful financial institution in Hong Kong. ⊠ *Queen's Road Central, across from Statue Square.*

❷ Jardine House. To the left of the Star Ferry and easy to spot with its many round windows, this building, formerly Connaught Centre, was completed in 1973 and was one of Central's first skyscrapers. ⊠ *Connaught Place, across from Central Post Office.*

❿ The Landmark. At Pedder Street stands this rather overwhelming shopping complex with an atrium and European-style cafés. Here the same Gucci, Tiffany, and top designer boutiques that line 5th Avenue in New York and the Champs-Elysées in Paris have even higher prices because of stratospheric Hong Kong retail rents. Concerts and other events are presented free of charge. You'll find the latest addition to the complex—a moving carillon, with 3-ft-high figurines representing the 12 animals of the Chinese zodiac, rotating to a Chinese melody played by the bells that ring on the hour—on the corner of Queen's Road Central and Ice

House Street. ⊠ *Des Voeux Rd., between Ice House St. and Pedder St., no phone.* ⊙ *Building, 9 AM–midnight; most shops, 10–6.*

⑥ Legislative Council Building. Once the home of the Supreme Court and now headed for an uncertain future, the LegCo Building is one of the few remaining grand Victorian-style buildings left in this area. For most of Hong Kong's history as a British colony, the council had no real power, but starting in 1991 it had a majority of elected members who challenged the administration at sessions held every Wednesday. Since the handover in July 1997, all the seats have been occupied by a Beijing-appointed Provisional Legislature, made up of former LegCo members and new appointees likely to sympathize with the Chinese government's position on all issues. In front of the council building is the **Cenotaph,** a monument to all who lost their lives in the two world wars. ⊠ *Statue Square at Jackson Rd.*

★ ⑬ Man Mo Temple. Built in 1847 and dedicated to the gods of literature and of war—Man and Mo, respectively—this is Hong Kong Island's oldest temple. The statue of Man is dressed in green and holds a writing brush, while Mo is dressed in red and holds a sword. To their left is a shrine to Pao Kung, god of justice, whose face is painted black. To the right is Shing Wong, god of the city. Coils of incense hang from roof beams, filling the air with a heavy fragrance. The temple bell, cast in Canton in 1847, and the drum next to it are sounded to attract the gods' attention when a prayer is being offered. To check your fortune, stand in front of the altar, take one of the small bamboo cylinders available there, and shake it until one of the sticks falls out. The number on the stick corresponds to a written fortune. Here's the catch—the English translation of your fortune is in a book on sale in the temple. ⊠ *Hollywood Rd., at Ladder St., no phone.* ⊙ *Daily 9–6.*

⑪ Midlevels Escalator. Completed in 1993, this is actually a ½-mi-long combination of escalators and walkways that go through the steep incline between Central and Midlevels. The painless uphill climb provides an interesting view of small Chinese shops and gleaming residential high-rises, as well as the all-green **Jamia Mosque** (built in 1915), at Shelley Street. **Staunton Street,** one level above Hollywood Road, is now known as Hong Kong's SoHo (South of Hollywood), with a string of cafés and bars, including a most intriguing eatery, the Sherpa Himalayan Coffee Shop (you won't find one of these in New York or London!) at 11 Staunton Street.

Ride the escalators up between 10:20 AM and 11:30 PM. After 11:30 the escalators shut down, and in the mornings from 6 to 10, they reverse course and move downhill so that commuters living in Midlevels can get to work in Central. You can get off at any point and explore the side streets, which sell porcelain, clothes, and antiques (not necessarily authenticated). Notice that almost every building has a tiny makeshift altar to the ancestors, usually made of red paper with gold Chinese characters, with offerings of fruit and incense. ⊠ *Enter across from Central Market, at Queen's Road Central and Jubilee St.* ⊙ *Daily 6 AM–11:30 PM.*

⑲ Queen's Road Central. One of the main shopping arteries, this road has narrow lanes on either side; they are lined with tiny shops and stalls filled with inexpensive clothes and leather goods. Queen's Road Central was also once the seafront and site of the old military parade grounds.

Of the thousands of tiny shops and market stalls selling dried herbs, live snakes, and everything else imaginable to treat the body's vital energies, the **Eu Yan Sang Medical Hall** (⊠ 152 Queen's Central) is the one to visit for an education on how the Chinese use their traditional medicines. There are glass cases that show reindeer antlers, dried fungi, ginseng, and other standard medicinal items, cards printed in English explaining some of the uses, and men behind the counters who will happily sell you purported cures for anything from the common cold to impotence (the latter cure is usually slices of reindeer antler boiled into tea). One note of caution: Look all you want, but remember that Chinese medicines are not regulated by the Hong Kong government, and anything that sounds dubious or dangerous might be just that.

★ ❶ **Star Ferry.** Since 1898 the ferry terminal has been the gateway to the island for visitors and commuters crossing the harbor from Kowloon. Crossing the harbor on the Star Ferry and riding around Hong Kong Island on a double-deck tram are almost essential for first-time visitors. In front of the terminal you will usually see a few red rickshas. Once numbering in the thousands, these two-wheel man-powered taxis are all but gone. ⊠ *Enter terminal through tunnel next to Mandarin Hotel, Connaught Rd., and Connaught Place.* ☎ *1st class HK$2, 2nd class HK$1.70.* ☉ *6 AM–midnight.*

OFF THE BEATEN PATH

HONG KONG DOLPHIN WATCH – The Chinese white dolphin (actually pink to dark gray and found in waters from South Africa to Australia) is on its way to extinction in the South China Sea, largely because of dredging for the new airport. Hong Kong Dolphin Watch sponsors a Dolphin Discovery Cruise, departing three or four times a week. There is no guarantee you'll see a dolphin, but on most trips passengers see at least two or three jumping out of the water, rolling around, and showing their fins. The trip, which departs from Queen's Pier, next to City Hall, makes for an enjoyable day at sea, and tickets help raise money to build a sanctuary that would ensure the dolphins' survival. The cost includes a buffet lunch. Reservations should be made at least two weeks in advance. ⊠ *Box 4102, Central, Hong Kong,* ☎ *2984-1414,* FAX *2984-7799.* ☎ *HK$350.*

❺ **Statue Square.** A small oasis of green between Connaught Road Central and Chater Road that's filled with shaded walks and fountains, this square attracts office workers during lunchtime and hundreds of housemaids from the Philippines on the weekends. The statue in question is of a British colonialist, Sir Thomas Jackson, who was chief manager of the Bank of China from 1870 to 1902—so perhaps his statue will not stay here for much longer. The square is surrounded by some of the most important buildings in Hong Kong, including those housing the **Hong Kong Club**, the ☞ **Legislative Council**, and the ☞ **Bank of China**, and it is near the Central MTR station.

NEED A BREAK?

On the west side of Statue Square is the **Mandarin Oriental Hotel** (⊠ 5 Connaught Rd., ☎ 2522-0111), one of the finest hotels in the world. The mezzanine coffee lounge is a pleasant place to have a drink, or you can people-watch at the **Captain's Bar**, where billion-dollar deals are consummated over cognac.

⓮ **Upper Lascar Row.** Cat Street, as Upper Lascar Row is often called, is a vast flea market. You won't find Ming vases here—or anything else of significant monetary value—but you may come across an old Mao badge or an antique pot or teakettle.

More worthwhile for the art or antiques collector is the section of shops and stalls known as **Cat Street Galleries** (⊠ 38 Lok Ku Rd.), adjacent to the flea market and open 10–6 every day but Sunday. This is a growing new complex, with galleries selling every kind of craft, old but more often new. You can rest your feet and have coffee in the convenient little European café, Somethin' Brewin'.

18 **Western Market.** Built in 1906, the market is a fine example of mid-Victorian architecture. Once a produce market, it now consists of arcades, wide galleries, and a variety of souvenir shops: in short, a small version of London's Covent Garden. ⊠ *323 Connaught Rd. W.* ☉ *10 AM–11:45 PM.*

NEED A
BREAK?

Unwind at **Six Bugs Antiques & Café** (☎ 2581–4754), on the ground floor of the Western Market. This tiny, trendy establishment serves gourmet coffees and light fare 11 AM –11:45 PM daily amid a funky atmosphere of vintage curios and a jukebox that spins 45s.

16 **Wing Lok Street.** You can still find fascinating traditional items for sale on this street (off Queen's Road Central) lined with Chinese shops selling rattan goods, medicines, and the engraved seals called chops. You can have your initials engraved in Roman letters or Chinese characters on a chop made of plastic, bone, or jade. (Ivory is also available all over Hong Kong, but it is illegal to bring it into the United States.) It takes about an hour to engrave a chop, which you can pick up later or on the following day.

From Central to the Peak

The Midlevels area, south of Central's business district, climbs out of the hills, with luxury skyscrapers seeming to spring right from the tropical bush. The series of escalators carrying you up through the center of the development is a striking example of the use of technology to relieve the city's congestion, in the process saving valuable space and eliminating the traffic of a large road. Escalators run downhill in the morning, taking Midlevels residents to their jobs, and then uphill for the rest of the day. The Midlevels is also worth a visit to see Hong Kong University, the Botanical Gardens, and some of Hong Kong's few remaining examples of Victorian apartment architecture—although the latter are disappearing rapidly.

Victoria Peak, high above Midlevels, is known simply as the Peak and juts 1,805 ft above sea level. Residents here take special pride in the positions to which they have, quite literally, risen: It is the most exclusive residential area on the island.

Numbers in the text correspond to numbers in the margin and on the Central and Western Districts map.

A Good Tour

Most of the important colonial buildings of the Victorian era are in this area. Walking around can be tricky because of a series of elevated highways. However, there are pedestrian tunnels and overpasses. With a little patience and a good map, you should not have too much trouble finding your way about on foot. (Maps are available at the South China Morning Post Family Book Store, at the Star Ferry pier in Central.) The tour will culminate in a tram ride to Victoria Peak.

Start your walk at 2 Queen's Road Central, which is diagonally across the street from Chater Garden. From here you'll be heading uphill along Garden Road. Cross the street at the pedestrian overpass. Now you will be facing **Hong Kong Park** ⑳, where you'll find the **Museum of Tea Ware** and a large aviary.

Leave the garden and start climbing into the steep part of Central that merges into Midlevels. On the right is **St. John's Cathedral** ㉑. Continue up Garden Road and turn right on Upper Albert Road, passing **Government House** ㉒. Farther up Garden Road, up several staircases, is the **Zoological and Botanical Gardens** ㉓.

Stroll through the gardens, the zoo, and aviary. Swing back down Garden Road, cross the street, and go to the **Peak Tram** ㉔, just behind St. John's Building (not the cathedral, but a modern office building). Take the tram to **Victoria Peak** ㉕.

As an alternative to returning by the Peak Tram, you can catch Bus 15 or a cab to Central. This will take you on a trip as beautiful as the one on the tram, through the steep roads of the residential areas of Midlevels. You can also get to the Peak on the Number 15 minibus from the Star Ferry pier.

TIMING

The climb from Queen's Road Central to the Peak tram station will take about three hours if you stop to enjoy the park space. Spend about 40 minutes in the Museum of Tea Ware and at least 45 minutes strolling through Hong Kong Park's greenhouses and aviary, both of which can get crowded. Add on another 30 minutes for the zoo at the Zoological and Botanical Gardens, longer if you're in the mood for a green respite. The tram ride up the mountain will take about 20 minutes. Spend about an hour on the Peak.

Sights to See

American Library. This is the place to go for current and back issues of American magazines and books. Microfilm editions of the *New York Times* are also available. Materials cannot be checked out, but you can make photocopies for a small charge. It is next to impossible to get information about the library by telephone, so it's best to simply go there. ⊠ *American Consulate, 26 Garden Rd., Central,* ☎ *2523–9011.* ☉ *Weekdays 10–6.*

㉒ **Government House.** Constructed in 1891, this handsome white Victorian building was the official residence of the British governor. At press time Tung Chee Hwa, now Hong Kong's chief executive, had said he did not wish to reside there, so the building will become another relic from colonial days. Its fate is to be announced; whether it becomes a museum dedicated to a bygone era or is torn down for development is anyone's guess. ⊠ *Upper Albert Rd., just west of Garden Rd.*

★ ✋ ⓴ **Hong Kong Park.** A 25-acre marvel in the heart of Central, this park is composed of lakes, gardens, sports areas, a rain-forest aviary with 500 species of birds, and a greenhouse filled with 200 species of tropical and arid-region plants.

The park also contains Flagstaff House, the former official residence of the commander of the British forces and the city's oldest colonial building (built in 1846). The house is now the **Museum of Tea Ware**, and it holds displays on everything connected with the art of serving tea from the 7th century onward. The core collection, which includes Yi Xing tea ware (famous tea sets from Jiangsu Province, China), was donated by Dr. K. S. Lo, who wanted the public to share his appreciation for tea. There is also an exhibition of ceramics and silk from Dr. Lo's collection. ⊠ *Cotton Tree Dr., at park entrance,* ☎ *2869–0690.* ⌷ *Free.* ☉ *Thurs.–Tues. 10–5.*

㉔ **Peak Tram.** Housed in the Lower Peak Tram Terminus is the world's steepest funicular railway. It passes five intermediate stations en route to the upper terminal, 1,805 ft above sea level. The railway was opened in 1880 to transport people to the top of ☞ **Victoria Peak,** the highest hill overlooking Hong Kong Harbour. Before the tram, the only way to get to the top was to walk or take a bumpy ride up the steep steps in a sedan chair. The tram has two 72-seat cars, which are hauled up the hill by cables attached to electric motors. A free shuttle bus to and from the Peak Tram leaves from Edinburgh Place, next to city hall. ⌧ *Between Garden Rd. and Cotton Tree Dr.* 🚋 *HK$15 one-way, HK$27 round-trip.* 🕙 *Daily 7 AM–midnight; trams run every 10–15 min.*

㉑ **St. John's Cathedral.** An Anglican (Episcopal) church completed in 1849, the cathedral was built with Canton bricks in the shape of a cross. It serves as a good example of both Victorian-Gothic and Norman architecture. ⌧ *Garden Rd., up from Queen's Road Central, on west side of street just past large parking lot.* 🕙 *Daily 9–5. Sun. services open to the public.*

★ **㉕** **Victoria Peak.** The Chinese name for Victoria Peak is Tai Ping Shan (Mountain of Great Peace). It might become known by this name post-handover, but name change or not, this is one site built to last. The top of the peak is 1,805 ft above sea level, and on a clear day the panorama is breathtaking, offering a view of Hong Kong's islands stretching all the way up to the mainland shores. Besides being the most prestigious address to have in Hong Kong, the Peak offers highly hospitable parkland to visitors. It is a popular picnic spot, filled with beautiful walking paths that circle the peak. A lookout pavilion just below the summit was once part of a former governor's residence. The original gardens and country walks remain and are open to the public.

The **Peak Galleria** shopping mall and the **Peak Tower** next door have a wide selection of restaurants and boutiques selling souvenirs, clothes, and gifts. The Peak Tower has several attractions for children: The Peak Explorer is a virtual-reality ride through outer space, while the Rise of the Dragon takes you on a railcar through a series of animated scenes from Hong Kong's history, including a frighteningly accurate rendition of the 1907 typhoon that devastated the territory. There is also a Ripley's Believe It or Not Museum.

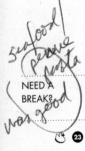

NEED A BREAK? On the Peak the nicest place to have a drink or a meal and enjoy the view is the **Peak Café** (⌧ 121 Peak Road, ☎ 2819–7868). If the weather is good, ask for a table in the garden.

㉓ **Zoological and Botanical Gardens.** A visit here is a delightful way to escape the city's traffic and crowds. In the early morning the spectacle of people practicing tai chi chuan (the ancient art of shadowboxing) is an interesting sight. The quiet pathways are lined with semitropical trees, shrubs, and flowers. The zoo has jaguars and gorillas, which for years were a source of friction between the government and animal rights groups, but the cages have been expanded to give the animals a better simulation of their natural habitat. As a result the jaguars sometimes hide in their rock caves, but they're certainly better off than they were a few years ago—in a tiny cage with nothing but raw steaks to occupy their attention. There is also an aviary with more than 300 species of birds, including a spectacular flock of pink flamingos. ⌧ *Upper Albert Rd., opposite Government House; enter on Garden Rd.* ☎ 2530-0155. 🚋 *Free.* 🕙 *Daily 6:30 AM–7 PM.*

OFF THE BEATEN PATH   **YAN YUEN SHEK** – Also known as Lovers' Rock, this is a shrine that many Chinese women visit every day, burning joss sticks and making offerings in search of a husband. The 6th, 16th, and 26th days of each lunar month are the most popular times. During the Maidens' Festival, held in August, fortune-tellers set up shop for the lovelorn. A visit here is best combined with a visit to the ☞ Zoological and Botanical Gardens.

Leave the gardens by the upper exit, east of the aviaries. Cross Garden Road and take the left fork (Magazine Gap Road) at the traffic circle. Take a sharp left onto Bowen Road, a pleasant street that is closed to traffic and has an almost rural feeling. From there Lovers' Rock is a 20- to 30-minute walk. To get back to town, walk to the Wong Nai Chung Gap Road traffic circle at the end of Bowen Road, where you can catch Bus 15 or 15B to the Peak or Bus 6 or 61 back to Exchange Square, or you can take a taxi.

Wanchai

Wanchai was once one of the five *wan,* areas the British set aside for Chinese residences, but it developed a reputation for vice and became a magnet for sailors on shore leave, as it was during the Vietnam War. Time changes everything, however: Sailors from all nations and military patrols still roam the streets when ships are in port, but if you come looking for the raunchy world of old Wanchai, you may be disappointed. Wanchai still has its nocturnal charms (☞ Chapter 7), but the "Wanch" of Richard Mason's novel, *The World of Suzie Wong,* seems a bit faded now.

Today, in addition to the old section, with its topless bars and massage parlors, Wanchai is a mixture of office buildings, restaurants, apartment buildings, and shops. The old Luk Kwok Hotel, better known as the Suzie Wong Hotel, has been replaced with a large modern hotel, but the novel's famous Lockhart Road, with its restaurants and seedy bars, British pubs, and tailors' shops, is still worth a stroll.

Numbers in the text correspond to numbers in the margin and on the Wanchai, Causeway Bay, Happy Valley, and North Point map.

A Good Walk

Walking is the best way to get around Wanchai, but the sights are not as spectacular as those of Central and Western. Take a circular walking tour starting from the junction of Queensway and **Queen's Road East** ①. This is a 10-minute ride from Central by tram or on Bus 5, or a few blocks from the Admiralty MRT stop.

Continue on Queen's Road East to Spring Garden Lane. Here you'll see the 66-story **Hopewell Centre** ②. After a few more blocks, turn left onto Wanchai Road, a busy market area selling a variety of foods, clothing, and household goods. It's a good place for browsing, especially along the narrow side alleyways. To the left are several small lanes leading to Johnston Road and more tram lines. There are a number of traditional shops here, including some selling household pets. Turn left on Johnston Road and follow the edge of Southorn Playground, a popular meeting place, especially for those looking for a game of cards or Chinese checkers.

Luard Road—along with cross streets Hennessy, Lockhart, and Jaffe roads—is in the heart of Old Wanchai. At night the area is alive with multicolor neon signs and a lively trade at bars, pubs, massage parlors, and restaurants. Hennessy Road, which roughly follows the line of the original harbor frontage, is one of the better shopping streets and another good place for browsing. Walk east on Hennessy Road to Fleming Road and turn north. Continue to Harbour Road, then head west to the **Academy for Performing Arts and Hong Kong Arts Centre** ③, in two adjacent buildings that serve as the heart of Hong Kong's cultural activities.

Continue on Harbour Road to Seafront Road and the **Hong Kong Convention and Exhibition Centre** ④. Circle back to Harbour Road and head east to take a look at the **Central Plaza** ⑤, one of the world's tallest buildings. The nearby Causeway Centre building houses the **Museum of Chinese Historical Relics** ⑥. To the east of Causeway Centre at Tonnochy Road is the **Wanchai Sports Grounds** ⑦.

From here you can taxi back to your hotel, catch the MTR at the Wanchai station, or continue walking along the harbor front to Wanchai Ferry pier for a ferry to Kowloon.

TIMING

If you stop to see the view from Hopewell Centre and the Hyatt and the exhibitions, as well as to browse, the tour around Wanchai will take about three hours.

Sights to See

❸ **Academy for Performing Arts and Hong Kong Arts Centre.** These two adjacent buildings are the center of Hong Kong's cultural life. They have excellent facilities for both exhibitions and performing arts. You can get information on the busy schedule of activities—ranging from dance performances and classical music recitals by local and visiting artists to productions staged by visiting dance troupes and theater companies—from local newspapers or the ticket reservations office. The Academy for Performing Arts was financed with horse-racing profits donated by the Royal Hong Kong Jockey Club. While you're at the Arts Centre, visit the **Pao Gallery** (4th and 5th floors), which hosts international and local exhibitions. ✉ *2 Harbour Rd., Wanchai,* ☎ *2582–0256.* ✆ *Free.* ☺ *Daily 10–8.*

NEED A BREAK?

For a bargain lunch, the restaurant at the Hong Kong Arts Centre has a soup and salad buffet daily for HK$65. ✉ *2 Harbour Rd., Wanchai.* ☺ *Daily 10–9.*

❺ **Central Plaza.** This office complex, completed in 1992, is worth noting simply because its 78 stories make it one of the tallest buildings in Asia. ✉ *Harbour Rd. and Fleming Rd.*

❹ **Hong Kong Convention and Exhibition Centre.** The center opened in 1988 as one of the largest and best-equipped meeting facilities in the world. It is the venue for annual international trade fairs, regional conferences, and hundreds of local events. It is adjoined by an office tower, a block of service apartments, and two hotels: the Grand Hyatt and the New World Harbour View. ✉ *Enter on Harbour Rd., between Fenwick Rd. and Fleming Rd.*

NEED A BREAK?

Adjoining the Convention and Exhibition Centre is the **Grand Hyatt Hotel.** Inside, the hotel lives up to the name *grand,* with a huge display of fresh flowers in the lobby and a swirling marble staircase on either side. Go up the staircase on the left to the lounge area, where you can relax over drinks or coffee while taking in a wonderful view of the harbor.

❷ **Hopewell Centre.** At 66 stories this is Hong Kong's third-tallest building. Circular in plan and with a slapdash aesthetic, it's known to detractors as the Stone Cigar. That criticism aside, the view atop the building from the **Revolving 66** (☎ 2862–6166) restaurant is splendid. Even if you don't plan to eat here, you may want to ride the exterior "glass-bullet" elevator. ✉ *183 Queen's Rd. E.*

❻ **Museum of Chinese Historical Relics.** Housed in the **Causeway Centre** building, the collection here covers 1,000 years of Chinese history and culture, with all types of arts and crafts on display. ⊠ *26 Harbour Rd.,* ☎ *2827–4692.* 🏛 *HK$5.* ⏰ *Weekdays 10–6, Sat. 1–6.*

❶ Queen's Road East. If you head east along this busy shopping street, you'll pass rice and food shops and stores selling rattan and traditional furniture, paper lanterns, and Chinese calligraphic materials. Shortly before reaching the Hopewell Centre, you may notice the altar of the **Tai Wong Temple** and smell the scent of smoldering joss sticks.

❼ Wanchai Sports Grounds. This sports complex opened in 1979 to provide world-class facilities for competitive athletic events. The grounds include a soccer field, a running track, a swimming pool, and an indoor games hall. ⊠ *East of Causeway Centre at Tonnochy Rd.*

Causeway Bay, Happy Valley, and North Point

Causeway Bay, one of Hong Kong's best shopping areas, also has a wide range of restaurants and a few sightseeing attractions. Much of the district can be easily reached from Central by the tram that runs along Hennessy Road or by the MTR to the Causeway Bay station.

The area east of Victoria Park offers very little for first-time visitors. North Point and Quarry Bay are both undeniably part of the "real" Hong Kong, which means tenements and factories. From Causeway Bay you can take the tram for a couple of miles through this area— perhaps the best way to get a feel for the environment.

Numbers in the text correspond to numbers in the margin and on the Wanchai, Causeway Bay, Happy Valley, and North Point map.

A Good Tour

If you come by taxi, a good starting point is the **Royal Hong Kong Yacht Club** ⑧, which overlooks the **Cargo Handling Basin** ⑨. Stroll around the harbor and have a look at the boats in the **Causeway Bay Typhoon Shelter** ⑩ and the **Noonday Gun** ⑪.

From Gloucester Road you can either walk or take a taxi to **Victoria Park** ⑫. Stroll around the park, where on a sunny day you can have lunch or beverages in the outdoor restaurant. From here exit onto Causeway Road and take a taxi to **Tin Hau Temple** ⑬. Take another taxi to **Kwun Yum Temple** ⑭. After seeing the temple, continue uphill on Tai Hang Road (a 15-minute walk or a brief ride by taxi or Bus 11) to **Aw Boon Haw (Tiger Balm) Gardens** ⑮, then take a taxi to the **Happy Valley Race Track** ⑯.

From here go to Chai Wan, site of the **Law Uk Folk Museum.** You can take a taxi from the racetrack all the way to Chai Wan, or ask to be dropped off at the Tin Hau MTR station. From here take the Island Line (the only line that stops here, designated in blue on the maps) in the direction of Chai Wan. Get off at Chai Wan, the end of the line, eight stops from Tin Hau. Follow signs pointing to the museum, on a small side street, a five-minute walk from the MTR station.

TIMING

Allow four to five hours to give yourself plenty of time to stroll around the park, catch taxis, and find the museum. Late morning, after the rush-hour traffic has cleared, is the best time to start off. It is difficult to find a taxi in Hong Kong during the early morning and late-afternoon rush hours or when it is raining heavily. Taxi drivers are not usually willing to wait for passengers while they sightsee, but in the middle of the day in reasonably good weather, there are usually plenty of taxis cruising the streets. They are not allowed to stop where there is a yel-

Wanchai, Causeway Bay, Happy Valley, and North Point

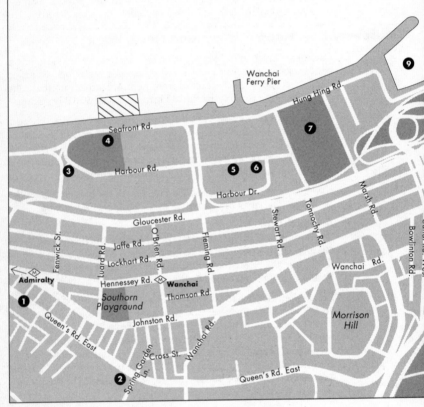

0 — 330 yards
0 — 300 meters

KEY
◇ Metro Stops

Victoria Harbour

Wanchai Ferry Pier

Hung Hing Rd.

Seafront Rd.

Harbour Rd.

Harbour Dr.

Gloucester Rd.

Jaffe Rd.

Lockhart Rd.

O'Brien Rd.

Fleming Rd.

Stewart Rd.

Tonnochy Rd.

Marsh Rd.

Bowrington Rd.

Wanchai Rd.

Admiralty

Fenwick St.

Hennessey Rd.

Wanchai

Southorn Playground

Thomson Rd.

Johnston Rd.

Queen's Rd. East

Spring Garden Ln.

Cross St.

Wanchai Rd.

Queen's Rd. East

Morrison Hill

④ ③ ⑤ ⑥ ⑦ ⑨ ① ②

Academy for Performing Arts and Hong Kong Arts Centre, **3**

Aw Boon Haw (Tiger Balm) Gardens, **15**

Cargo Handling Basin, **9**

Causeway Bay Typhoon Shelter, **10**

Central Plaza, **5**

Happy Valley Race Track, **16**

Hong Kong Convention and Exhibition Centre, **4**

Hopewell Centre, **2**

Kwun Yum Temple, **14**

Museum of Chinese Historical Relics, **6**

Noonday Gun, **11**

Queen's Road East, **1**

Royal Hong Kong Yacht Club, **8**

Tin Hau Temple, **13**

Victoria Park, **12**

Wanchai Sports Grounds, **7**

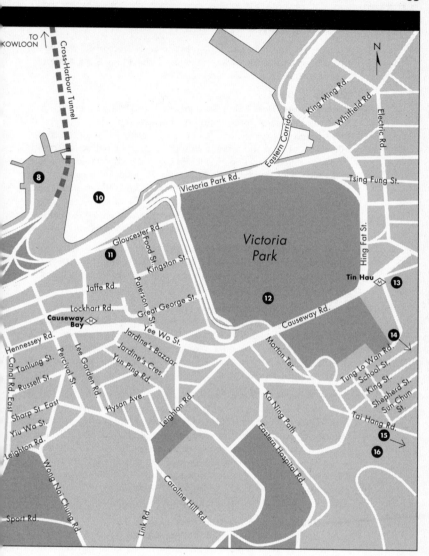

low line painted on the street near the curb, so look for designated taxi lanes, which appear every two or three blocks.

The dry season (from late September to early December) will be the nicest time to take this walk; if you are visiting Hong Kong at another time of year, take a folding umbrella.

Sights to See

★ ⑮ **Aw Boon Haw (Tiger Balm) Gardens.** Built in 1935 with profits from sales of a popular menthol balm, the gardens were the pet project of two Chinese brothers, who also built a mansion here. Eight acres of hillside are pocked and covered with grottoes and pavilions filled with garishly painted statues and models of Chinese gods, mythical animals, and scenes depicting fables and parables. It's great fun to explore, especially for children. Be forewarned: Some scenes of Taoist and Buddhist mythology are decidedly gruesome. There is also an ornate seven-story pagoda containing Buddhist relics and the ashes of monks and nuns. ⊠ *Tai Hang Rd., Happy Valley.* 🎟 *Free.* ☉ *Daily 9:30–4.*

⑨ **Cargo Handling Basin.** West of the Yacht Club and east of the Wan-chai Ferry pier, where you catch a ferry to Kowloon, you can watch the unloading of boats bringing cargo ashore from ships anchored in the harbor. ⊠ *Hung Hing Rd.*

⑩ **Causeway Bay Typhoon Shelter.** This boat basin was originally constructed as a safe haven in bad weather for sampan dwellers. As the number of fishing families who live in those small open-air boats has dwindled, the basin has filled with pleasure craft. At the west end of the shelter, however, you can still see a few sampans amid the sleek sailboats and restored junks.

⑯ **Happy Valley Race Track.** Every Wednesday night and one afternoon each weekend from September to mid-June, you can bet on horses here. Although it was completed in 1841, modern additions include a huge outdoor video screen for close-ups, slow motion, and instant replays. It is for members only, but you can obtain a special visitor's admission if you have been in Hong Kong for less than three weeks and are over 18. Your passport with a tourist visa stamp is required as proof. ⊠ *Hong Kong Jockey Club, 2 Sports Rd., Happy Valley,* ☎ *2966–8111 or 2966–8364.* 🎟 *HK$50 for entrance badge.*

⑭ **Kwun Yum Temple.** A house of worship dedicated to the goddess of mercy has stood on this site for 200 years, but the current structure is in a heavily renovated building and is mostly new, dating from 1986. Constructed on top of a huge boulder, it has a high ceiling and gallery. The temple is very popular with local believers. ⊠ *Lin Fa Kung St. W.* ☉ *Daily 9–nightfall.*

⑪ **Noonday Gun.** "In Hong Kong they strike a gong and fire off a noon-day gun," wrote Noel Coward in his song, "Mad Dogs and English-men." They still fire that gun at noon each day in a small enclosure overlooking the Yacht Club Basin and Typhoon Shelter, opposite the Excelsior Hotel and World Trade Centre. The tradition was started by Jardine Matheson and Co., the great *hong* (trading company) that inspired James Clavell's novels *Taipan* and *Noble House.* Jardine would fire a salute each time one of its ships arrived safely in the harbor. It is said this angered the local governor, who ordered the company to use a gun instead of a cannon and to fire it only as a noontime signal. The gun itself, with brass work polished bright, is a 3-pound Hotchkiss dating from 1901. Signs in English point to an unlikely looking door-way beside the Excelsior, which opens to the long underground tun-nel you must take to get to the viewing area. Last year the passageway was improved, with better signage all the way. ⊠ *Across from Excelsior Hotel, 281 Gloucester St.*

NEED A
BREAK?
Have coffee or lunch in the first-floor coffee shop of the **Excelsior Hotel** (⊠ 281 Gloucester Rd., ☎ 2894–8888), which overlooks the Yacht Club, and gaze at yachts docked in the harbor.

❽ Royal Hong Kong Yacht Club. The club is a place worth a visit, but it's not open to the public, so try to find a local resident who is a member, or who knows one, to give you guest privileges. If you belong to a yacht club at home, you may have reciprocal guest privileges. Once inside you are surrounded by glass-fronted cabinets containing silver prize trophies and a delightfully old-fashioned bar with magnificent views of the harbor. The menu in the members' restaurant is excellent. On weekends the place hums with activity, especially when there are races, a common event from spring through fall. The South China Sea Race to Manila is held every two years at Easter time. The next race takes place in spring 1998. Call the **Race Office** (☎ 2891–0013) for details. The club may drop the *Royal* from its name in the very near future. ⊠ *Off Hung Hing Rd.,* ☎ *2832–2817.*

⓭ Tin Hau Temple. On a street of the same name off Causeway Road, behind Park Cinema on the southeast side of ☞ **Victoria Park,** this temple is one of several in Hong Kong similarly named and dedicated to the goddess of the sea. Its decorative roof and old stone walls are noteworthy. The date of construction is unknown, but the temple bell was made in 1747. ⊠ *Tin Hau St., off Causeway Rd.*

⓬ Victoria Park. Beautifully landscaped with trees, shrubs, flowers, and lawns, this park has an aviary and recreational facilities for swimming, lawn bowling, tennis, roller-skating, and even go-cart racing. The Lantern Carnival is held here in mid-autumn, with the trees a mass of colored lights. Just before the Chinese New Year (late-January–early February), the park hosts a huge flower market. Here, too, you will find early morning practitioners of tai chi chuan. ⊠ *Gloucester Rd.*

OFF THE
BEATEN PATH
LAW UK FOLK MUSEUM – It's worth a trip to the end of the MTR line to see this museum, a 200-year-old house that belonged to a family of Hakkas, the farming people who originally inhabited Hong Kong Island and the peninsula all the way into what is now southern Guangdong province. Decorated as a period house, the museum displays rural furniture and farm implements. A photo exhibition shows you what bustling industrial Chai Wan looked like in the 1930s, when it was a peaceful bay inhabited only by fishermen and squatters. ⊠ *14 Kut Shing St.,* ☎ *2896–7006. 1 block from Chai Wan MTR station; outside the station turn left, then follow Kut Shing St. as it turns to the right.* ▣ *Free.* ☉ *Tues.–Sat. 10–1 and 2–6, Sun. 1–6.*

South Side

The south side of Hong Kong Island is largely residential, with points of interest nestled within the rolling hills. It is not a walkable area, but you can take a city bus or taxi from Central to both Stanley and Shek O and walk around.

Numbers in the text correspond to numbers in the margin and on the South Side of Hong Kong Island map.

A Good Tour

Start the tour at **Hong Kong University** ①, which you can easily reach by taxi from Central; visit the **Fung Ping Shan Museum,** on campus. Continuing around the west end of the island, you come to two huge housing developments: privately owned Pok Fu Lam, and government-sponsored Wah Fu Estate. Both overlook Lamma Island and are full of shops, recreational facilities, and banks. They are typical of Hong Kong's approach to mass housing. From here take a taxi downhill to **Aberdeen** ②. Continue to **Apleichau (Duck's Tongue) Island** ③, which can be reached by a bus across the bridge or by sampan.

You can take a taxi and go east of Aberdeen to **Ocean Park, Water World,** and **Middle Kingdom** ④, which are mostly of interest to children. You can spend the day here, or skip the theme parks and continue on by taxi from Aberdeen along the scenic waterside road to **Deep Water Bay** ⑤ and **Repulse Bay** ⑥. Taxi from there to **Stanley Bay** ⑦, where the main attraction is shopping at **Stanley Market.** Your final stop will be **Shek O** ⑧, the easternmost village on the south side of the island.

From Shek O the round-island route continues back to the north, to the housing and industrial estate of Chai Wan, where you have a choice of a fast journey back to Central on the MTR or a slow ride to Central on the two-decker tram that crosses the entire north side of the island via Quarry Bay, North Point, and Causeway Bay.

TIMING

If your time in Hong Kong is short, you can see all of these sights in a day. Start out early in the morning and plan to make Shek O your dinner stop. However, you can easily spend an entire day shopping in Stanley and another day on the beach at Shek O or hiking through Shek O Country Park.

Sightseeing around south Hong Kong Island is a year-round activity, except in very heavy rain. Shek O is worth visiting only in good weather. You can hike there at any time of year, while the beach is best from June to November.

Sights to See

❷ **Aberdeen.** Named after an English lord, not the Scottish city, Aberdeen got its start as a refuge for pirates some 200 years ago. The name *Hong Kong* (again, fragrant harbor in Cantonese) was first used to designate this area because it produced incense. The British later applied it to the entire island. After World War II Aberdeen became fairly commercial as the *tanka* (boat people) attracted tourists to their floating restaurants. The tanka continue to live on houseboats; although they may appear picturesque to occasional visitors, their economic conditions are depressing. Some visitors regret that many of these boat people are becoming factory workers, but drab and hard as that work may be, it's a definite improvement over their old way of life.

You can still see much of traditional Aberdeen, such as the **Aberdeen Cemetery** (⊠ Aberdeen Main Rd.), with its enormous gravestones, and side streets where you can find outdoor barbers at work and many dim sum restaurants. In the harbor, along with floating restaurants, there are some 3,000 junks and sampans, and you will undoubtedly be asked on board for a ride through the harbor. Use one of the licensed operators, which depart on 20-minute tours daily from 8 to 6 from the main Aberdeen seawall opposite Aberdeen Centre. Groups can bargain—a trip for four to six people should cost from HK$100 to HK$150. Individual tickets are HK$40.

South Side of Hong Kong

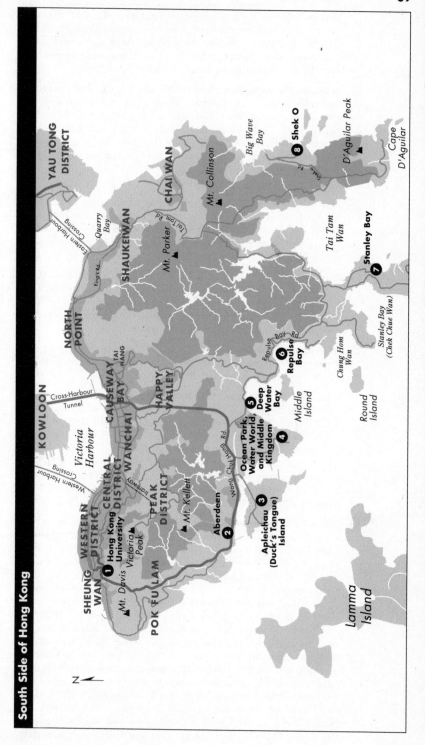

Also in Aberdeen is a famous **Tin Hau Temple,** whose ancient original bell and drum are still used at its opening and closing each day. Currently in a state of decline, this is one of several shrines to the goddess of the sea celebrated in the Tin Hau Festival in April and May, when hundreds of boats converge along the shore.

❸ Apleichau (Duck's Tongue) Island. To get here, you can take a bus across the bridge or arrive by sampan. The island has a boat-building yard where junks, yachts, and sampans are constructed, almost all without formal plans. Look to your right when crossing the bridge for a superb view of the harbor and its countless junks. Vehicles are not allowed to stop on the bridge, so you'll have to walk back if you'd like to take a picture.

On your left is a view of boats belonging to members of the Marina Club and the slightly less exclusive Aberdeen Boat Club, as well as the famous floating Jumbo Restaurant. A quiet, unspoiled area just a decade ago, Apleichau is now bursting at the seams with development—both public housing and a number of gleaming new private residential buildings and shopping malls.

❺ Deep Water Bay. On Island Road, just to the east of Ocean Park, Water World, and Middle Kingdom, this bay was the setting for the film *Love Is a Many-Splendored Thing,* and its deep coves are still beautiful. It has become a millionaire's paradise, home to Hong Kong's richest man, Li Ka-shing, a very private real-estate tycoon.

❶ Hong Kong University. Established in 1911, the university has a total of almost 10,000 undergraduate and graduate students. Most of its buildings are spread along Bonham Road.

On the campus is the **Fung Ping Shan Museum,** which contains an excellent collection of Chinese antiquities (ceramics and bronzes, some dating from 3,000 BC, fine paintings, lacquerware, and carvings in jade, stone, and wood). The museum also has the world's largest collection of Nestorian crosses of the Yuan Dynasty (1280–1368). In addition, it has superb pieces from pre-Christian periods: ritual vessels, decorative mirrors, and painted pottery. The museum is a bit out of the way, but it is a must for the curious and the true Chinese art lover. ⊠ *94 Bonham Rd.,* ☎ *2859–2114.* ▣ *Free.* ☉ *Mon.–Sat. 9:30–6.*

☝ **❹ Ocean Park, Water World,** and **Middle Kingdom.** These three attractions, east of Aberdeen, were built by the Royal Hong Kong Jockey Club. Ocean Park is on 170 acres of land overlooking the sea and is one of the world's largest oceanariums. It attracts daily crowds. On the lowland side are gardens, parks, and a children's zoo. A cable car, providing spectacular views of the entire south coast, can take you to the headland side and to Ocean Theatre, the world's largest marine mammal theater, where dolphins and a killer whale perform. There are seats for 4,000 people. There are also various rides, including a mammoth roller coaster. The adjacent 65-acre Water World is an aquatic fun park with slides, rapids, pools, and a wave cove. Middle Kingdom is a theme park depicting architecture, arts, crafts, and industry through 3,000 years of Chinese history. The complex has cultural shows, souvenir shops, and restaurants. ⊠ *Wong Chuk Hang Rd.,* ☎ *2873–8888 for Ocean Park, 2870–0268 for Middle Kingdom, or 2555–6055 for Water World.* ▣ *HK$140 for Ocean Park and Middle Kingdom, HK$65 for Water World.* ☉ *Ocean Park and Middle Kingdom: daily 10–6; Water World: June–Sept., daily 10–6.*

❻ Repulse Bay. Named after the British warship HMS *Repulse* (not, as some local wags say, after the pollution of its waters), the bay was the site of the famed Repulse Bay Hotel, which gained notoriety in December 1941 when invading Japanese clambered over the hills behind it and entered its gardens, which were being used as headquarters by the British. After a brief battle, the British surrendered. The hotel was demolished in 1982 and has been replaced with a luxury residential building, but replicas of its Repulse Bay Verandah Restaurant and Bamboo Bar were opened in 1986 and are run by the same people who operated the original hotel.

NEED A BREAK?	To indulge in an experience of colonial pampering, treat yourself to British high tea at the **Repulse Bay Verandah Restaurant and Bamboo Bar.** Tea is served daily from 3 to 5:30. ✉ 109 Repulse Bay Rd. ☎ 2812-9988. AE, DC, MC, V.

8 **Shek O.** The easternmost village on the south side of the island is filled with old houses, great mansions, a superb golf course and club, a few simple restaurants, a pretty beach, and fine views. Leave the little town square, full of small shops selling inflatable toys and other beach essentials, and take the curving path across a footbridge to the "island" of **Tai Tau Chau,** really a large rock with a lookout for scanning the South China Sea. Little more than a century ago this open water was ruled by pirates.

You can hike through **Shek O Country Park** in less than two hours. Look here for birds that are hard to find in Hong Kong, such as Kentish plovers, reef egrets, and black-headed gulls, as well as the colorful rufus-backed shrike and the bulbul.

NEED A BREAK?	A favorite place for lunch, drinks, or just outdoor café sitting is the **Black Sheep Restaurant,** in Shek O, a small establishment with an eclectic menu and the kind of relaxed ambience that makes you wonder if you're still in Hong Kong. ✉ From Shek O Village turn left at Thai restaurant by small traffic circle. Black Sheep is down road and around corner on right. ☎ 2809-2021. AE, MC, V.

7 **Stanley Bay.** It became notorious as the home of the largest prisoner-of-war camps in Hong Kong run by the Japanese during World War II. Today, Stanley is known for its picturesque beaches and its market, where casual clothing is sold at wholesale prices. Hong Kong has dozens of shops offering similar bargains, but it's more fun to shop for them in the countrified atmosphere around Stanley. You can also find ceramics, paintings, and books. Past the market, on Stanley Main Street, a strip of restaurants and pubs faces the bay. On the other side of the bay is a Tin Hau Temple, just beyond land that is being cleared for development. Part of this development is to be a public housing estate, which will give low-income residents a chance to live on prime waterfront property.

KOWLOON

Kowloon peninsula juts down from mainland China, directly across Victoria Harbour from Central. Legend has it Kowloon was named by a Chinese emperor who fled here during the Sung dynasty (960–1279). He counted eight hills on the peninsula and called them the Eight Dragons—so the account goes—but a servant reminded him that an emperor is also considered a dragon, and so the emperor called the region Gau-lung (nine dragons), which is Kowloon in the pinyin transliteration.

Kowloon is the site of most of Hong Kong's hotels. In the Old Tsim Sha Tsui district is the Victorian-era clock tower of the old Kowloon-Canton Railway station, the new Hong Kong Cultural Centre, the Peninsula Hotel, and the bustling Nathan Road area. The Tsim Sha Tsui East district lies on land reclaimed from the harbor and contains many luxury hotels and shopping centers, the Space Museum, and a waterfront esplanade. It is here you will find the new railroad station.

In the 1930s people took the Star Ferry from Hong Kong Island to Kowloon to stay overnight at the Peninsula Hotel, still elegant today, which was next door to the railroad station. The next morning they could board the Kowloon-Canton Railway trains for Peking, Moscow, London, and other Western cities. Today visitors can take a taxi through the Cross-Harbour Tunnel from Causeway Bay or Central to Kowloon or ride the MTR from Central to Kowloon in minutes. The Star Ferry, however, is still unquestionably the most exciting way to cross the harbor.

Numbers in the text correspond to numbers in the margin and on the Kowloon Peninsula map.

A Good Tour

From the Kowloon tip wend your way into the dense urban jungle of Tsim Sha Tsui from the **Star Ferry pier** ①, which is a 10-minute ferry ride from the pier on the Hong Kong side—and incidentally the most romantic way to see the harbor, day or night.

Stroll east along the water to the **Victoria Clock Tower**, then visit the **Hong Kong Cultural Centre** ②. Note the luxurious **Peninsula Hotel** ③, across from which you'll find the **Hong Kong Space Museum** ④. The **Hong Kong Museum of Art** ⑤ is behind the Space Museum.

Continue east on Salisbury Road in the direction of the **Tsim Sha Tsui East** ⑥ neighborhood, an area of reclaimed land. Turn left on Chatham Road South and continue north to the corner of Cheong Wan Road and the **Hong Kong Science Museum** ⑦. Backtrack a bit on Chatham Road to Granville Road or Cameron Road and turn right. The next main boulevard you come to will be **Nathan Road** ⑧. Head south a short way on Nathan Road, then turn right onto Haiphong Road to get to **Kowloon Park,** site of the **Hong Kong Museum of History** ⑨.

Return to Nathan Road and continue north three blocks to Jordan Road, make a left and then a right onto **Temple Street** ⑩. Follow Temple Street north to the **Kansu Street Jade Market** ⑪, to the west. Continue one block north of Kansu Street to the **Tin Hau Temple** ⑫.

From here you can either walk back down Nathan Road to the Jordan MTR stop and take it (the line shown in red on the maps) one stop to Mong Kok or take a taxi to the **Bird Market** ⑬. To get to the next stop, **Sung Dynasty Village** ⑭, take a taxi or take the MTR line from Mong Kok five stops to the Mei Foo station. From here it is a short walk along Lai Wan and Mei Lai roads.

The final stop, **Wong Tai Sin Temple** ⑮, is best reached by taxi if you're going there from Sung Dynasty Village. You can also take the green MTR line to Wong Tai Sin; the temple is directly opposite the station. To reach the green line from Mei Foo, you will have to backtrack. Take the red line back to Mong Kok, where you can catch a Quarry Bay–bound green line train. Go five stops to Wong Tai Sin.

TIMING

Plan half a day to stroll from the Star Ferry terminal to the Tin Hau Temple, stopping to see sights and shop along the way. Take at least an hour to see the Space Museum and the Museum of Art, another 45 minutes to see the Science Museum, and an hour for the Museum of History. Be spontaneous with your shopping time and compare prices before you make a decision. If you have two days to see Kowloon, take the walk from Star Ferry to Kowloon Park the first day, then on the second day start at Temple Street and continue to Wong Tai Sin Temple.

Start out around 10 AM to avoid the very heavy rush-hour traffic. The entire tour can be made in one day, but it will be a very tiring day, as Kowloon is crowded, noisy, and often frustrating to walk or drive through. This tour is appropriate at any time of year, but heavy rain and the excessive heat of summer might dampen your enthusiasm.

Sights to See

🖐 ⓭ **Bird Market.** On Hong Lok Street, two blocks from Nathan Road at the Mong Kok MTR stop, you'll find the famous market where old-timers sell antique cages and porcelain, along with, of course, little brown songbirds and colorful talking parrots. Stroll around and listen to the cacophony of birdcalls mingled with the chirp of grasshoppers that will become the birds' dinner. The street is under siege by developers who would like to build skyscrapers in its place, but a sort of stay of execution has been granted for another year. See it now, because it's hard to say exactly how much longer it will be there. ⊠ *Hong Lok St.* ⊙ *Daily 10–6.*

❷ **Hong Kong Cultural Centre.** This stark, architecturally controversial building has tiled walls inside and out, sloped roofs, and no windows—an irony since the view is superb. (However, a long, two-level promenade is just outside its doors, with plenty of seating to enjoy the view.) It houses a concert hall and two theaters. ⊠ *10 Salisbury Rd.,* ☎ *2734–2010.*

★ ❺ **Hong Kong Museum of Art.** The exterior is unexciting, but inside are five floors of well-designed galleries. One is devoted to historic photographs, prints, and artifacts of Hong Kong, Macau, and other parts of the Pearl River Delta. Other galleries feature Chinese antiquities and fine art and visiting exhibitions. ⊠ *10 Salisbury Rd.,* ☎ *2734–2167.* 🎟 *HK$10.* ⊙ *Tues.–Sat. 10–6; Sun. 1–6.*

★ ❾ **Hong Kong Museum of History.** The museum covers a broad expanse of the past with life-size dioramas depicting prehistoric scenes, the original fishing village, a 19th-century street, the Japanese occupation, and modern Hong Kong—all complete with sounds and smells. There is also a multiscreen slide show. ⊠ *Haiphong Rd.,* ☎ *2367–1124.* 🎟 *HK$10.* ⊙ *Mon.–Thurs. and Sat. 10–6, Sun. 1–6.*

🖐 ❼ **Hong Kong Science Museum.** More than 500 scientific and technological exhibits—including an energy machine, a miniature submarine, and the DC-3 that launched Cathay Pacific Airlines—emphasize interactive participation. The buildings look like giant Lego blocks. ⊠ *2 Science Museum Rd., corner of Cheong Wan Rd. and Chatham Rd.* ☎ *2732–3232.* 🎟 *HK$25.* ⊙ *Tues.–Fri. 1–9, weekends 10–9.*

★ 🖐 ❹ **Hong Kong Space Museum.** Across from the Peninsula Hotel, the dome-shape museum houses one of the most advanced planetariums in Asia. It also contains the **Hall of Solar Science,** whose solar telescope permits visitors a close look at the sun; **Exhibition Hall,** which houses several exhibits at a time on topics such as outer space and astronomy; and the **Space Theatre,** with Omnimax movies on space travel, sports, and natural wonders. Children under 6 are not admitted. ⊠ *10 Salis-*

44

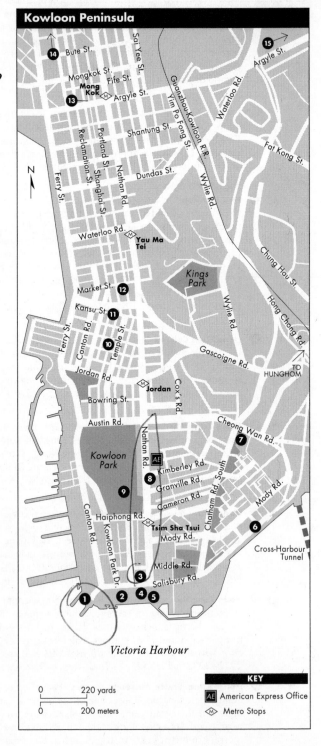

Kowloon Peninsula

Victoria Harbour

0 — 220 yards
0 — 200 meters

KEY

AE American Express Office

Ⓜ Metro Stops

bury Rd., ☎ 2734–9009. 🎟 HK$10. ⊙ Mon. and Wed.–Fri. 1–9, weekends 10–9; Space Theater, 7 shows daily from 2:30–8:30.

⓫ **Kansu Street Jade Market.** The daily jade market carries everything from fake jade pendants to precious carvings. If you don't know much about jade, take along someone who does, or you may pay a lot more than you should. The best time to visit is 10–noon. ⊠ Kansu St., off Nathan Rd. ⊙ Daily 9–6

ⓒ **Kowloon Park.** The former site of the Whitfield Military Barracks is today a restful, green oasis. Signs point the way to gardens with different landscaping themes. Try the Chinese Garden, which has a lotus pond, streams, a lake, and a nearby aviary with a colorful collection of rare birds. The **Jamia Masjid and Islamic Centre** is in the south end of the park, near the Haiphong Road entrance. This is Hong Kong's principal mosque. Built in 1984, it has four minarets, decorative arches, and a marble dome. ⊠ Just off Nathan Rd.

❽ **Nathan Road.** The most densely packed shopping mecca in the territory, the so-called Golden Mile runs for several miles both north and south and is filled with hotels and shops of every description. To the left and right are mazes of narrow streets lined with even more shops crammed with every possible type of merchandise—jewelry, electronics, clothes, souvenirs, and more (☞ Chapter 7). Expect to be besieged with street hawkers trying to sell you cheap "Rolexes."

❸ **Peninsula Hotel.** The exterior of this sumptuous hotel draws attention with a fleet of Rolls Royce taxis and doormen in white uniforms, while the huge colonnaded lobby has charm, grandeur, string quartets, and a plethora of celebrities (though with the opening of the Regent Hotel, no longer a monopoly on them). ⊠ Salisbury Rd., ☎ 2366–6251.

NEED A BREAK? Tsim Sha Tsui is short on quiet cafés, but the **Peninsula Hotel** offers high tea—frankly, the perfect way to rest your shopping feet in style. You even have options: Dine on a majestic array of scones and pastries in the lobby (daily 2–7 for HK$145 per person) or settle down for tea in the Verandah Restaurant (daily 3–5 at HK$155 per person).

❶ **Star Ferry Pier.** This is a convenient starting place for any tour of Kowloon. Here you will also find the bus terminal, with traffic going to all parts of Kowloon and to the New Territories. As you face the bus station, Ocean Terminal—where luxury cruise ships berth—is on your left. Inside this terminal, and in adjacent Harbour City, miles of air-conditioned shopping arcades are filled with hundreds of shops. To the right of Star Ferry is **Victoria Clock Tower,** all that is left of the Kowloon-Canton Railway Station, which once stood on this site. The new station, for travel within China, is a mile to the east.

OFF THE BEATEN PATH **HAN DYNASTY BURIAL VAULT** – It's worth a visit to the 1,600-year-old vault at Lei Cheng Uk Museum, in Sham Shui Po, Kowloon. The four barrel-vaulted brick chambers form a cross around a domed vault. The funerary objects are typical of the tombs of the Han dynasty (AD 25–AD 220). It was discovered in 1955 during excavations for the huge housing estate that now surrounds it. The easiest way to get here is to take Bus 2 from Kowloon Star Ferry terminal to Tonkin Street or catch the MTR to the Cheung Sha Wan station. ⊠ 41 Tonkin St., Lei Cheng Uk Resettlement Estate. 🎟 Free. ⊙ Mon.–Wed. and Fri.–Sat. 10–1 and 2–6; Sun. 1–6.

★ ♻ **⑭** **Sung Dynasty Village.** You'll go back in history hundreds of years when you visit this village northwest of Kowloon city. The complex re-creates the life of a village during the Sung dynasty, more than 1,000 years ago. There are faithful replicas of houses, shops, restaurants, and temples of the period. Observe craftspeople at work and other dressed in period costume. Visit on your own or take an organized tour, which can be arranged through your hotel tour desk. ⊠ *Sung Dynasty Village,* ☎ 2744–1022. ☒ *HK$120.* ☺ *Mon.–Sun. 10–8.*

★ **⑩** **Temple Street.** The heart of a busy shopping area, Temple Street is ideal for wandering and people-watching. By day you'll find market stalls with plenty of kitsch and a few worthwhile clothing bargains, but the best time to visit is after 8 PM, when the streets become an open-air market filled with street doctors offering cures for almost any complaint, fortune-tellers, and on most nights, Chinese opera.

Such nearby lanes as **Shanghai Street** and **Canton Road** are also worth a visit for their colorful shops and stalls selling everything from herbal remedies to jade and ivory. **Ning Po Street** is known for its shops selling paper kites and the colorful paper and bamboo models of worldly possessions that are burned at Chinese funerals.

⑫ **Tin Hau Temple.** One of Kowloon's oldest temples, this colorful sight is filled with incense and crowds of worshipers. You'll probably be encouraged to have a try with the fortune sticks, known as *chim* sticks. Each stick is numbered, and you shake them in a cardboard tube until one falls out. A fortune-teller asks you your date of birth and makes predictions from the stick based on numerology. ⊠ *Market St., 1 block north of Kansu St.* ☺ *Daily 7–5:30.*

⑥ **Tsim Sha Tsui East.** East on Salisbury Road, this area is part of the land reclamation that has transformed the entire district into a galaxy of luxury hotels, restaurants, and entertainment and shopping complexes.

★ **⑮** **Wong Tai Sin Temple.** Have your fortune told here at this large, colorful compound with a Buddhist shrine dedicated to a shepherd boy who was said to have magic healing powers. In addition to the main altar, the pavilions, and the arcade—where you'll find soothsayers and palm readers happy to interpret Wong Tai Sin's predictions for a small fee—there are two lovely Chinese gardens and a Confucian Hall. ☎ 2807–6177. ☒ *Small donation expected.* ☺ *Daily 7–5:30.*

THE NEW TERRITORIES

The visitor who has explored Hong Kong and Kowloon should go one step farther and spend at least a day in the New Territories. Here you can enjoy panoramas of forested mountainsides and visit some of the ancient temples and clan houses of the area.

Only about 15 mi (25 km) of land lie between Kowloon's waterfront and the pre-hand-over border with China—hence the New Territories' appellation as the Land Between. It is called the New Territories because it was the last area of land claimed by the British in extending their Hong Kong colony. Although most of the original farmland has given way to urban development, you will be surprised at the village flavor that remains in many areas, with small wet markets (the ground beneath them is always wet) selling fresh produce and live chickens and fish in small fishing towns along the water. The New Territories also has vast areas of country parks, including Tai Po Kou, a forest that has wild monkeys, near the Tai Po Kowloon-Canton Railway stop.

The sections below briefly highlight points of interest in the New Territories, circling clockwise out of Kowloon. The stops outlined below are far apart, so to explore the area on your own, you should probably rent a car or hire or chauffeur-driven auto for a day. The easiest way to see the region is to take a tour organized by the **Hong Kong Tourist Association** (☎ 2807–6543 Mon.–Sat. or ☎ 2807–6177 Sun. and holidays). The six-hour Land Between tour takes you to the Chuk Lam Shim Yuen (Bamboo Forest Monastery); Hong Kong's tallest mountain, Fanling; the Luen Wo Market; the Chinese border town of Luk Keng; the Plover Cove Country Park; Tai Po; and Chinese University. The Heritage tour goes to Sam Tung Uk, a restored 18th-century walled village; buildings along the Ping Shan Heritage Trail, some of which date to the 12th century; and other restored homes and ancestral halls from the era when the New Territories was the sleepy tip of southern China. Book through your hotel tour desk or an HKTA information center.

There are also nine Kowloon-Canton Railway stations between Kowloon and the Lo Wu station on the old Chinese border; you can get off at any of them. (At press time, a visa was required to enter China at Lo Wu.) A leaflet from the **Kowloon-Canton Railway Corporation** (☎ 2356–4488) outlines main attractions in the areas near railroad stations. Pick one up at the railroad station or any HKTA office. First-class fare to Sheung Shui, the stop before the old border is HK$17.

Numbers in the text correspond to numbers in the margin and on the New Territories and the Outer Islands map.

Western New Territories

A Good Tour

Start at **Chuk Lam Sim Yuen** ①, the Bamboo Forest Monastery. From here drive to **Ching Chung Koon Taoist Temple** ②, near the town of **Tuen Mun** ③. Then go on to **Miu Fat Buddhist Monastery** ④, on Castle Peak Road, a popular place for a vegetarian lunch.

Drive from here to **Lau Fau Shan** ⑤, a fishing town with a renowned market. Then visit **Kam Tin Walled Village** ⑥, a 17th-century enclave that's a regular stop on most tours; it's also accessible by Bus 51. Wander around the old village, then go up to the scenic town of **Lok Ma Chau** ⑦.

TIMING

This tour will take approximately one day. Plan to start in the morning and have lunch either at the Miu Fat monastery or in Lau Fau Shan. You can take this tour at any time of year, but naturally you'll miss the scenic views if it is raining heavily.

Sights to See

❷ **Ching Chung Koon Taoist Temple.** This huge temple, near the town of Tuen Mun, has room after room of altars, all filled with the heady scent of incense burning in bronze holders. On one side of the main entrance is a cast-iron bell with a circumference of about 5 ft. All large monasteries in ancient China had such bells, which were rung at daybreak to wake the monks and nuns for a day of work in the rice fields. On the other side of the entrance is a huge drum that was used to call the workers back in the evenings. Inside are rooms with walls of small pictures of the departed. Their relatives pay the temple to have these photos displayed so they can see their dearly departed as they pray. The temple also includes a retirement home, built from donations, which provides a quiet and serene atmosphere for the elderly. The grounds are beautiful, with plants and flowers, hundreds of dwarf shrubs, or-

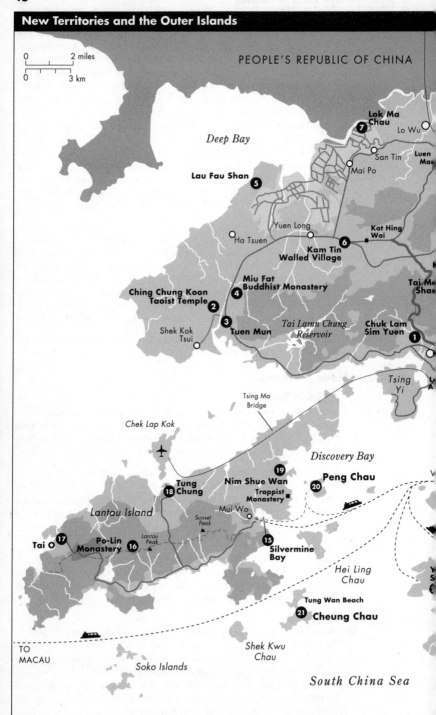

New Territories and the Outer Islands

PEOPLE'S REPUBLIC OF CHINA

0 — 2 miles
0 — 3 km

Deep Bay

Lok Ma Chau ❼

Lo Wu

Luen Ma

San Tin

○ Mai Po

Lau Fau Shan ❺

Yuen Long ○

Kat Hing Wai

Ha Tsuen ○

Kam Tin Walled Village ❻

Tai Me Sha

Miu Fat Buddhist Monastery ❹

Ching Chung Koon Taoist Temple ❷

❸ **Tuen Mun**

Tai Lamn Chung Reservoir

Chuk Lam Sim Yuen ❶

Shek Kok Tsui ○

Tsing Yi

L A

Tsing Ma Bridge

Chek Lap Kok

✈

Discovery Bay

Tung Chung ❽

Nim Shue Wan ❾

Peng Chau ❿

❷⓿

Trappist Monastery ■

Mui Wo ○

Lantau Island

Sunset Peak

Lantau Peak

Tai O ❼

Po-Lin Monastery ❻

❿ **Silvermine Bay**

Hei Ling Chau

Y S

Tung Wan Beach

❷❶ **Cheung Chau**

Shek Kwu Chau

TO MACAU

Soko Islands

South China Sea

N

Crooked Island

Sheung
Shai

8 **Fanling**

Wu Kau
Lang

*Plover Cove
Reservoir*

Tolo Channel

*Grass
Island*

**Tai Po
Market** **9**

Kam Shan

Pan
Chung

**Tolo Harbour and
Tap Mun Island**

**Tai Po Kau
ture Reserve**

**Chinese University
of Hong Kong**

10

Chek
Keng

4

THE NEW TERRITORIES

Amah Rock **13**

**Temple of Ten
housand Buddhas**

12 **11** **Shatin**

Sai Kung

uen Wan

**Sai Kung
Peninsula**

*Kau Sai
Chau*

High Island

**Chi Kok
usement
Park**

Sung Dynasty Village

Ho Chung

Port Shelter

*Basalt
Island*

KOWLOON

*Kowloon
Bay*

Yau Tong

Junk Bay

Tai Wan
Tau

toria
*Victoria
Harbour*

Tei Tong
Tsui

HONG KONG

*Tung Lung
Chau*

ng
ue Wan

23 **Sok Kwu Wan**

Stanley

*Lamma
Island*

*Stanley
Peninsula*

*Po Toi
Islands*

KEY	
▪▪▪	Hong Kong Metro
—	Rail Lines
⚓	**Ferry Lines**

namental fish ponds, and pagodas. ⊠ *Adjacent to Ching Chung LRT Station*.

① Chuk Lam Sim Yuen. The Bamboo Forest Monastery is one of Hong Kong's most impressive. It has three large statues of Buddha. Festival days bring large crowds of worshipers, proving the monastery's continuing importance to the Chinese.

⑥ Kam Tin Walled Village. A regular stop on most tours, this village was built in the 1600s as a fortified town belonging to the Tang clan. There are actually six walled villages around Kam Tin, but **Kat Hing Wai** is the most popular. The original walls are intact, with guardhouses on the four corners and arrow slits for fighting off attackers. But the image of antiquity is somewhat spoiled by the modern homes and their TV antennas looming over the ancient fortifications. Directly inside the main gate is a narrow street lined with shops selling souvenirs and mass-produced oil paintings.

⑤ Lau Fau Shan. In this village famous for its fish market you will find people selling freshly caught fish, dried fish, salted fish, and shellfish. Make your selection, then take it to one of the village's many restaurants and have it cooked to order. This is the oyster capital of Hong Kong, but don't eat them raw: Hepatitis is a serious problem in the territory.

⑦ Lok Ma Chau. The attraction here is a hillside view of vast fields and the Sham Chun River winding through them. If you plan to photograph senior citizens here, be aware your "models" will demand HK$1 for the privilege.

④ Miu Fat Buddhist Monastery. On Castle Peak Road near Tuen Mun, this is a popular place for a vegetarian lunch. The monastery itself is ornate, with large carved-stone animals guarding the front. Farther on is the village of **Yuen Long,** now completely redeveloped as an industrial and residential complex. ⊙ *Daily 10–6*.

③ Tuen Mun. With a population of almost a half million, this is one of Hong Kong's "new towns"—independent, small cities created to take the population spillover from the crowded areas of Kowloon and Hong Kong Island. They provide both industrial work sites and living accommodations near them for workers and their families. Other new towns are Tsuen Wan, Yuen Long, ☞ **Shatin,** Tai Po, Fanling, and Junk Bay. These seven towns now house more than 40% of Hong Kong's population.

Central New Territories

A Good Tour

The Central New Territories is accessible by KCR train. Start from the north end and take the train to the town of **Fanling** ⑧. You can take a taxi from the KCR stop to the Royal Hong Kong Golf Club and the **Luen Wo Market**.

Continuing on from the Fanling KCR stop, take the train south two stops to **Tai Po Market** ⑨, which runs along the streets near the train stop. Wander around the market, then take the KCR south one more stop, to the University station. This is the beginning of the campus of the **Chinese University of Hong Kong** ⑩. Take a campus bus or taxi to the **Art Gallery**, in the university's Institute of Chinese Studies Building.

Go back to the University station and take the train another stop south, to the **Shatin Racecourse,** which adjoins the Racecourse station.

Take a look around, then take the train one more stop south, to **Shatin** ⑪. From here you can take a taxi to the **Jubilee Sports Centre** and to the **Temple of Ten Thousand Buddhas** ⑫. The temple provides a view of **Amah Rock** ⑬ and **Tai Mo Shan** ⑭, Hong Kong's highest peak.

If you would like to spend some time enjoying the outdoors, the Central New Territories also has several attractive undeveloped areas: You can hike the **Tai Po Kau Nature Reserve,** explore the beaches and fishing villages of **Tap Mun Island,** or wander the forest and seaside trails of the **Sai Kung Peninsula.**

TIMING

Start this tour in the morning and plan to spend an entire day seeing the sights. You can tour this area at any time of year, as rain will not interfere with seeing most sights. However, if you plan to visit the Tai Po Kau Nature Reserve, Tap Mun Island, or the Sai Kung Peninsula, set aside a full day for each and go when the weather's decent.

Sights to See

⑬ **Amah Rock.** From the perch of the ☞ **Temple of Ten Thousand Buddhas** you can see this famous rock. Amah means nurse in English, and the rock, which resembles a woman with a child on her back, is popular with female worshipers.

⑩ **Chinese University of Hong Kong.** The **Art Gallery,** in the university's Institute of Chinese Studies Building, is well worth a visit. It has large exhibits of paintings and calligraphy from the Ming period to modern times. There are also important collections of bronze seals, carved jade flowers, and ceramics from South China. Take the KCR to University station and then take a campus bus or taxi. ⊠ *Tai Po Rd., Shatin, New Territories,* ☎ *2609–7416.* 🎟 *Free.* ☉ *Mon.–Sat. 10–4:30, Sun. 12:30–4:30. Closed between exhibitions.*

NEED A BREAK?

Across from the Chinese University campus is the popular **Yucca de Lac Restaurant,** which has outdoor dining facilities nestled in green hills along Tolo Harbour, affording a pleasant view of the university. ⊠ *Tai Po Rd., Ma Liu Shiu village,* ☎ *2691–1630.* ☉ *Daily 11–11. MC, V.*

OFF THE BEATEN PATH

TOLO HARBOUR AND TAP MUN ISLAND – About a 15-minute walk from the Chinese University along Tai Po Road is the Ma Liu Shui Ferry pier, the starting point for a ferry tour of the harbor and Tap Mun Island. The ferry (☎ 2807–6177 for schedule information) makes many stops, and if you take the 8:30 trip, you'll have time to hike around Tap Mun Island and still leave by late afternoon. For a break, there is a small village with a few Chinese restaurants, but you can also bring a picnic lunch. You should go only in sunny weather. Visit the New **Fisherman's Village,** on the southern tip of the island, populated mostly with Hakka fisherwomen. About a half mile north, near the western shore, is the ancient village of **Tap Mun,** where you'll see old women playing mah-jongg. **Tin Hau Temple** is less than a quarter mile north of the village. This huge structure, dedicated to Tin Hau, the goddess of the sea, is one of the oldest temples in Hong Kong; it sits at the top of a flight of steps that lead down into the water of the harbor. Inside are old model junks and, of course, a veiled figure of the goddess herself. Go to the east side of the island to see the **Tap Mun Cave** and some of the best-kept beaches in the territory.

⑧ **Fanling.** This town combines the serene atmosphere of the Royal Hong Kong Golf Club with the chaos of rapid growth. The nearby **Luen Wo Market** is a traditional Chinese market, well worth visiting. You might find snakes for sale here in the winter months, and you're sure to see whole dried chickens hanging on prominent display.

⓫ **Shatin.** Whether you enter Shatin by road or rail, you will be amazed to find this metropolis smack dab in the middle of the New Territories. Considered one of the "new towns," Shatin underwent a population explosion that took it from a town of 30,000 to one of more than a half million in 10 years. It is home to the **Shatin Racecourse** (⊠ Racecourse stop on KCR), Hong Kong's largest. Nearby is the huge **Jubilee Sports Centre,** a vast complex of tracks and training fields designed to give Hong Kong's athletes space to train under professional full-time coaches for international competition. Shatin is also home of **New Town Plaza** (⊠ adjacent to the Shatin KCR stop), the most extensive shopping complex in the New Territories; most stores are open 10–6:30.

OFF THE BEATEN PATH **SAI KUNG PENINSULA –** To the west of Shatin, the **Sai Kung Peninsula** consists mostly of park land. Take the MTR to Choi Hung and then Bus 92, Bus 96R, or Minibus 1 to Sai Kung Town. You can also take a taxi along **Clearwater Bay Road,** which will take you into forested areas and land that is only partially developed, with Spanish-style villas overlooking the sea. Stroll along the waterfront, and you'll see some of the most unusual marine life ever—inside tanks that are sitting outside restaurants. (If you choose to eat in a seafood restaurant, note once again that physicians caution against eating raw shellfish here because of hepatitis outbreaks.) To cruise around the harbor, rent a *kaido* (pronounced guy-doe; one of the small boats run by private operators) for about HK$130 round-trip, stopping at tiny **Yim Tin Tsai Island,** which has a rustic Catholic mission church built in 1890. **Sai Kung Country Park** has one of Hong Kong's most spectacular hiking trails (☞ Chapter 6), going through majestic hills overlooking the water. This excursion will take one day, and you should go only in sunny weather.

⓮ **Tai Mo Shan.** To the west of the ☞ Temple of Ten Thousand Buddhas is this mountain, Hong Kong's highest peak, rising 3,230 ft above sea level.

⓽ **Tai Po Market.** *Tai po* means "shopping place," and every visitor here discovers the town more than lives up to its name. In the heart of the region's breadbasket, Tai Po has long been a trading and meeting place for local farmers and fishermen. It is now being developed as an industrial center, with new housing and highways everywhere you look. It has a fine traditional market stretching along several blocks, with most action taking place outdoors. Adjacent to the market is the 100-year-old **Man Mo Temple.** ⊠ *Take KCR to Tai Po Market stop; market runs on street alongside the station.* ⊙ *Daily 9–6.*

OFF THE BEATEN PATH **TAI PO KAU NATURE RESERVE –** Take a detour east from Tai Po to the Tai Po Kau Nature Reserve. You can get there by bus from the Tai Po KCR stop, or take Bus 70 from Nathan Road at Jordan. You should go only in sunny weather. You can follow well-marked trails through the reserve's rain-forest vegetation and along its small meandering river. Look for exotic species of trees, many of which are labeled, including the joss stick tree, believed by some to be the tree that gave Hong Kong its name, which means "fragrant harbor." A "talking" post at the entrance to the forest plays recordings of the various birdsongs you are likely to hear as you wander along, such as that of the rufus turtledove and the greater necklaced laughing thrush. Be aware, however, that there are also less-friendly species here—snakes, porcupines, civet cats, scorpions, and some rather fierce-looking monkeys. The reserve is as safe as any wooded area, but you are advised to wear sturdy hiking boots and to refrain from getting too close to the monkeys. Exploring the reserve will take a full day; for breaks, bring snacks, a picnic lunch, and plenty of bottled water.

⑫ Temple of Ten Thousand Buddhas. You have to climb some 500 steps to reach this temple, nestled among the foothills of Shatin, but a visit is worth every step. Inside the main temple are nearly 13,000 gilded ceramic statues of Buddha, all virtually identical. They were made by Shanghai craftsmen and donated by worshipers. ⊠ *Shatin, no phone.* ▨ *Free.* ☾ *Daily dawn–dusk.*

THE OUTER ISLANDS

Looking out the airplane window on the approach to Kai Tak Airport on a fine day, you will see clusters of small islands dotting the South China Sea. Fishing fleets trawl slowly through the blue waters. Tiny round-bottom sampans scamper from one outcrop to another, ignoring the junks, ocean liners, and cargo ships steaming in and out of Hong Kong Harbour. Look closer, and you will see sandy coves, long strands of fine yellow sand washed by gentle surf, and countless tiny village settlements clinging to rocky bay shores and small sandbars.

These outer islands form the other Hong Kong, the unspoiled natural beauty that is as much a part of Hong Kong as Kowloon's crowded tenements or Hong Kong Island's concrete canyons. Unfortunately most visitors are caught up in the frantic urban experience and miss the opportunity to escape to this side of the territory. Try to go on a weekday; on weekends Hong Kongers pack the ferries as they flock to the islands.

In addition to Hong Kong Island and the mainland sections of Kowloon and the New Territories, 235 islands were under the control of the British until July 1997. The largest, Lantau, is bigger than Hong Kong Island; the smallest is just a few square feet of rock. Most are uninhabited. Others are gradually being developed but at nowhere near the pace of the main urban areas. A number of the outlying islands have been turned over to Vietnamese refugee camps and are off-limits unless you have special permission. But the four most accessible by ferry—Lantau, Lamma, Cheung Chau, and Peng Chau—have become popular residential areas and welcome visitors.

You can reach the islands by scheduled ferry services operated by the **Hong Kong and Yaumati Ferry Company** (☎ 2542–3081 or 2525–1108 for inquiries hot line). The ferries are easy to recognize by the large letters HKF painted on their funnels. You'll leave from the Outlying Districts Services Pier, in Central, on the land reclamation area behind ☞ **Exchange Square.** Ferry schedules are available at the information office on the pier. Round-trip fares vary from HK$15 to HK$50.

Numbers in the text correspond to numbers in the margin and on the New Territories and the Outer Islands map.

Lantau

The island of Lantau lies due west of Hong Kong. At 55 square mi (143 square km), it is almost twice the size of Hong Kong Island. For now—that is until development increases with the opening of the new airport on nearby Chek Lap Kok Island—Lantau's population is only 20,000, compared with Hong Kong Island's 1.5 million.

Visitors with historical interests will find many surprises on Lantau. The imperial hold on the islands of the South China Sea was tenuous, although at one time Lantau was the temporary home for an emperor of the Sung Dynasty. That was in 1277, when 10-year-old Emperor Ti Cheng and his small retinue set up camp just behind modern Silvermine Bay's beaches. They were fleeing the Mongol forces of Kublai Khan. The young emperor died on Lantau, and the Sung dynasty was crushed the following year, leaving no traces of the island's brief moment of imperial glory. There are traces, however, of Sung dynasty communities of the 13th century, including their kilns and burial sites. Many excavations on the island show evidence of even earlier settlements, some dating from Neolithic times.

A Good Tour

The ferry will take you to the town of Mui Wo on **Silvermine Bay** ⑮, an area being developed as a commuter suburb of Hong Kong Island. The island is very mountainous, so for a tour of the outlying villages, plan to hike (☞ Chapter 4) or take a bus. From the main ferry town, Mui Wo, the island's private bus services head out to the **Po-Lin Monastery** ⑯, home of a giant Buddha; **Tai O** ⑰, an ancient fishing village; and **Tung Chung** ⑱, which has a Sung dynasty fort.

Although the **Trappist monastery** near **Nim Shue Wan** ⑲ can be reached by bus from Silvermine Bay, you can also take a small passenger ferry, or kaido, between Peng Chau Island and Nim Shue Wan. You can also get to Nim Shue Wan from Discovery Bay: Take the ferry to this pristine suburban development from the ☞ **Star Ferry pier,** and from the Discovery Bay Ferry pier, turn left and walk to Nim Shue Wan, then head to the monastery.

TIMING

The ferry from Central to Silvermine Bay takes about one hour each way. After that it's up to you how long you spend on Lantau. The island is worth at least a full day's visit, even two. Visiting each of the attractions listed below will probably require a whole day, so choose the ones that seem most interesting to you. The best overnight accommodations are at the **Silvermine Beach Hotel** (☞ Chapter 4). Visitors may also stay overnight at the Po-Lin and Trappist monasteries. The HKTA has an information sheet on these and other accommodations available on Lantau.

Sights to See

⑲ **Nim Shue Wan.** For quiet and solitude, make the 90-minute hike through this old fishing village—where you might see the fishermen's grandchildren talking on their cellular phones—and the unspoiled woods and hills beyond to the **Trappist monastery** (✉ Grand Master, Trappist Haven, Lantau Island, Box 5, Peng Chau, Hong Kong, ☎ 2987–6286), on eastern Lantau. On the way you will see beaches that would be beautiful except for the astounding amount of trash thrown there or washed ashore. You can spend the night in the monastery's simple accommodations, but you must make reservations well in advance.

⑮ **Silvermine Bay.** The ferry will take you to this area, which is being developed as a commuter's suburb of Hong Kong Island. You can rent bicycles in front of the **Silvermine Beach Hotel** (☞ Chapter 4) for riding around the village of Mui Wo, still surrounded by picturesque terraced fields.

⑰ **Tai O.** Divided into two parts connected by a modern draw bridge, the village still has many stilt houses along the water as well as many fishing shanties. Visit the local temple, dedicated to Kuanti, the god of war, and taste local catches at the seafood restaurants. ⊠ *Take bus marked* TAI O *from Mui Wo village.*

⑯ Po-Lin Monastery. In the Precious Lotus Monastery, in the mountainous interior of the island, you will find the world's tallest outdoor bronze statue of Buddha, the **Tin Tan Buddha**—more than 100 ft high and weighing 275½ tons. The adjacent monastery, gaudy and exuberantly commercial, is also famous for the vegetarian meals served in the temple refectory. ⊠ *Take bus marked* PO-LIN MONASTERY *from Mui Wo, and ask driver to let you off at the monastery stop, from where you can follow signs.* 🖼 *Free.* ☉ *Daily dawn–dusk.*

⑱ Tung Chung. Here you can also visit an ancient **Sung dynasty fort,** which was evacuated by the Qing dynasty army in 1898, when the New Territories was leased to Britain. The fort is now an elementary school. Tung Chung's other attraction is its view of **Chek Lap Kok Island,** site of the new airport. By the time the airport opens, in April 1998, there will be bridges connecting Lantau with the New Territories and a tunnel connecting it to Hong Kong Island. There will also be a subway route in this vicinity, and high-rise buildings are sure to follow.

Peng Chau

The tiniest of Hong Kong's four major islands, Peng Chau was once home for just a few farmers and fishermen as well as a fireworks factory. Although the factory is now closed and the villagers have built three-story weekend retreats for Hong Kong's city folks, the community feeling remains.

Stand on the Peng Chau ferry quay and watch the kaido for Lantau's Trappist monastery sputter toward dark green hills. Choose your fresh shellfish from baskets held aloft by local fishermen bobbing in boats below the quay and then take what you've purchased to a café to be cooked. Then breathe in that stirring ambience of Hong Kong's islands— a mix of salt air, shrimp paste, and dried fish combined with a strong dose of local pride and a sense of independence, both of which have been lost in urban Hong Kong.

TIMING

The ferry from Central takes one hour each way. Go to Peng Chau in the afternoon, preferably on a sunny day. Plan on spending about two hours.

Sights to See

⑳ Peng Chau village. The village shopping district is known for its unpretentious little stores selling locally made porcelain at remarkably low prices. **Ming Lei Fong** (⊠ 10 Wing On St., ☎ 2987–7423) has Chinese elm-wood furniture, jewelry, and antique porcelain; it's open Sunday and by appointment during the week. **Elaine Gallery** (⊠ 26 Wing Hing St., ☎ 2983–0235) sells watercolors of Hong Kong.

Peng Chau doesn't have the lively café scene found on Lamma, but the **Forest** (⊠ 38C Wing Hing St., ☎ 2983–8837) is a popular watering hole among locals, with American home-style cooking and live music several nights a week.

Cheung Chau

Cheung Chau, southwest of Lantau and about one hour from Central by ferry, is Hong Kong's most crowded outlying island, with about 22,000 people, most of them living on the sandbar that connects the dumbbell-shape island's two hilly tips. It has a Mediterranean flavor that has attracted artists and writers from around the world, some of whom have created an expatriate artists' colony here.

There are no vehicles, so be prepared to walk around the island. Or as an alternative you can take one of the small sampans that provide ferry service throughout the year from Hong Kong Island to beaches on Cheung Chau—beaches that are virtually deserted and have clear water.

TIMING

The ferry from Central takes one hour each way. You can make Cheung Chau a day trip in good weather, or you can stay in reasonable comfort at the **Cheung Chau Warwick Hotel** (☞ Chapter 4), on East Bay at Tung Wan Beach, just north of Cheung Chau town.

Sights to See

㉑ **Cheung Chau village.** The entry into Cheung Chau's harbor, through lines of gaily bannered fishing boats, is an exhilarating experience. There is much history on Cheung Chau. There are pirate caves and ancient rock carvings along the waterfront just below the Warwick Hotel. Dining out is also a joy on Cheung Chau, where there are dozens of good open-air cafés on either side of the crowded sandbar township—both on the **Praya Promenade** along the waterfront and overlooking the main public beach at **Tung Wan.**

The 200-year-old **Pak Tai Temple,** dedicated to the protector of fishermen, is the site of the colorful Bun Festival, an annual springtime event and one of Hong Kong's most popular community galas. The festival originated in the 18th century as appeasement for the spirits of those killed by pirates, spirits who were thought to wreak plagues upon the village. Beside the main altar are four whalebones that came from the nearby sea. ⊠ ¼ *mi from ferry pier: Turn left from pier and go along waterfront until you see the temple, a slight uphill walk.* 🖾 *Free.* ☉ *Daily dawn–dusk.*

Lamma Island

For a glimpse of what rural China must have been like in past centuries, wander across Lamma Island, which faces the fishing port of Aberdeen on Hong Kong Island's south side. (The ferry from Central to Yung Shue Wan or Sok Kwu Wan takes about 40 minutes.) Here you'll see farmers, shielded from the sun by black-fringed straw hats, tending their vegetables, while fishermen gather shellfish, much as their ancestors did before them.

Lamma is also home to a bohemian contingent of expats, some of whom look as though they're in a time warp of their own, around 1968 or so. But there are just as many lawyers, journalists, and bankers who have come to escape the high rents of Hong Kong Island and spend their weekends relaxing on an island that has the feel of a casual beach community. Ignore the power station and cement factory and seek out the small bays along narrow paths that offer changing views of the ocean and Hong Kong Island.

TIMING

It takes about 55 minutes each way to reach Sok Kwu Wan by ferry from Central. Spend an afternoon hiking here or visit the village in the evening just for dinner. The ferry from Central to Yung Shue Wan takes about 50 minutes each way. Go to Yung Shue Wan in the afternoon (but only in good weather) and plan on staying until dinner.

Sights to See

Hung Shing Ye Beach. About midway between Sok Kwu Wan and Yung Shue Wan is Hung Shing Ye Beach, which is sometimes swimmable (don't go in if you see plastic bags and other refuse floating on the water). You can stay the night on Hung Shing Ye Beach at the **Concerto Inn** (☎ 2982–1668, FAX 2982–0022). Some of its 12 rooms have a good view, and the inn has a garden café as well.

㉓ **Sok Kwu Wan.** The smaller of Lamma's two villages, this is a good place to visit for a lunch or dinner at one of the long row of open-air harborside restaurants. You can also hike in the hills around the village.

㉒ **Yung Shue Wan.** By comparison with Sok Kwu Wan, Yung Shue Wan is buzzing with activity. Formerly a farming and fishing village, in the past decade it has become an enclave for expats, especially artists and journalists. Main Street is lined with boutiques and trendy restaurants. The ever-present smell of fish markets hovers around you as you wander into places that sell interesting pottery and baskets. **Silk Road Bazaar** (✉ 76 Main St., ☎ 2982–1200), a tiny stall, sells a striking selection of amber jewelry. It's only open on weekends, but appointments are available if you decide to visit on a weekday.

Other Islands

The adventurous visitor can try the more out-of-the-way islands, not quite as easy to reach but all the more rewarding for their remoteness. Besides Tap Mun and Yim Tin Tsai in the New Territories, here are two other favorites:

Ping Chau

This minuscule island, not to be confused with Peng Chau, is 1 sq mi of land lying in the far northeast of the New Territories, close to the mainland coast of China. It is almost deserted now and has a checkered history. Guns and opium were smuggled out of China through Ping Chau, and during the Cultural Revolution many mainlanders swam through shark-infested waters in hopes of reaching Ping Chau and the freedom of Hong Kong. The island's largest village, **Sha Tau,** is something of a ghost town, with many cottages boarded up, but here and there you'll find old farming families eager to take you in, maybe even for the night.

A large part of the island is country park, with footpaths overgrown with orchids, wild mint, and morning glory. Look for the strange rock formations at either end of the island. At the south end are two huge rocks known as the **Drum Rocks,** or Watchman's Tower Rocks. At the north end is a chunk of land that has broken away from the island. The Chinese say this represents the head of a dragon.

You must be prepared to stay for the night when you go, as the ferry runs only on weekends, departing Saturday and returning Sunday. Bring camping gear or accept the invitation of villagers to spend the night. Take the ferry from Ma Liu Shui near the University KCR stop. It departs on Saturday at 11:15 AM and returns Sunday at 1:10 PM. Call the HKTA hot line (☎ 2807–6177) for an update on the ferry schedule before you go.

Po Toi Islands

A chain of three barren little fishing islands, virtually unchanged since medieval times, is situated at the extreme southeast of Hong Kong's waters. Only Po Toi Island itself is virtually inhabited, with a population of less than 100. Go there for spectacular strolling and fine seafood restaurants.

Walk uphill past primitive dwellings, many deserted, to the Tin Hau Temple, or walk east through the hamlet of Wan Tsai, past banana and papaya groves, to Po Toi's famous **rock carvings.** The geometric patterns in these rocks are believed to have been carved during the local Bronze Age, about 2,500 years ago.

Getting to the islands is an all-day trip that will take some planning. The most convenient way to go to the Po Toi Islands is by junk. For a rental call **Simpson Marina** (☎ 2555–7349; ☞ Junking *in* Chapter 4). Ferries depart from Aberdeen on Tuesday, Thursday, and Saturday at 9 AM, returning from Po Toi at 10:30 AM, so you have to stay overnight if you want to explore the island. On Sunday and holidays you can get a morning ferry (10 or 11:30 from St. Stephen's Beach in Stanley) and return the same day, at 3 or 4. You can make the necessary reservations by calling 2554–4059, but you'll need the help of a Cantonese speaker, because no one answering the phone will speak English.

3 Dining

No matter how Chinese the surroundings are, Hong Kong's restaurants will not only lay feasts of carefully prepared Cantonese fare, but will transport you to lands beyond with superb international cuisine.

ANYWHERE YOU GO IN HONG KONG, in any direction you'd care to look, you're bound to see a restaurant sign. Establishments that sell prepared food are as old as Chinese culture itself, and because most people live in small apartments and have little space for home entertaining, restaurants are usually the chosen venues for special occasions and family get-togethers. Nowhere in the world is cooking more varied than in this city, where Cantonese cuisine (long regarded by Chinese gourmands as the most intricate and sophisticated in Asia) is joined by delights from not only other parts of China, but also nearly every other culinary region on earth. Whether it's French, Italian, Portuguese, Japanese, Indian, Thai, or specialty American food, the deeply rooted Chinese love of good food flourishes.

Be advised, however, that Hong Kong's extraordinary culinary vitality is offset by some of Asia's worst restaurants. Don't expect just any old neighborhood restaurant to turn out dreamy dishes.

Gastronomically speaking, the words *Chinese cuisine* don't mean much more than do *European cuisine*. The most populated country in the world has dozens of different cooking styles, though only five are prominent in Hong Kong. They are:

Cantonese. As 94% of the population comes from Guangdong (Canton) Province, this is the most popular style by far. This is fortunate because this semitropical province has the largest selection of fruits, vegetables, and meats. The Cantonese ideal is to bring out the natural taste of ingredients by cooking them quickly at very high temperatures. This creates *wok chi,* a fleeting energy that requires food to be served and eaten immediately. If it is properly prepared, you will never taste fresher food. Says international gourmet William Mark: "Only Cantonese chefs understand simplicity, purity, and variety." Menus are enormous.

Shanghai. Shanghai is a city of immigrants, not unlike New York and Hong Kong, and its cosmopolitan population has several culinary styles. Lying at the confluence of several rivers on the South China Sea, the city has especially good seafood. Shanghai crabs (actually from Suzhou) are winter favorites. Many dishes are fried in sesame oil or soy sauce and can be a bit greasy—no one can forget the famous "squirrel fish," so named because the oil-based sauce poured over the fish sizzles, or chatters, like a squirrel. This dish also originated in Suzhou but is featured in Shanghai restaurants.

Peking. Of course, Peking duck is a favorite, and nowhere is it better than in Hong Kong. It was originally an imperial Mongolian dish and is usually served in two (or three) courses. This is a northern noodle rather than a rice culture. Peking noodles, along with Mongolian barbecue and onion cakes, are inevitably ordered.

Szechuan. The spiciest Chinese food (also written in English as Sichuan) is now a favorite around the world. Rice, bamboo, wheat, river fish, shellfish, chicken, and pork dishes all have plenty of salt, anise, fennel seed, chili, and coriander. Ingredients are simmered, smoked, stirred, and steamed. The effect is an integrated flavor—the opposite of Cantonese food, where each ingredient has its own taste.

Chiu Chow. From near Canton, the Chiu Chow people have a gusty, hearty cuisine, which has never caught on in the West. It begins with

Iron Buddha tea and moves on to thick shark's fin soup, soya goose, whelk (tiny snails), bird's nest, and irresistible steamed lobsters served with tangerine jam.

A few more hints:

Dim sum restaurants serve tasty Chinese hors d'oeuvres and must be tried at lunch (or a bit earlier to avoid crowds). The staff pushes trolleys around while calling out the names of dishes; you point to what you want. Some, such as congealed blood and giblets, are esoteric; but others, such as steamed pork buns or spring rolls, are readily acceptable to most diners. Always checks the cost of items labeled "market price." Anything from a typhoon to heavy traffic can determine the cost. Ask for the exact price for your party's meal rather than for a *catty*, a unit in the Chinese weight system equal to about 1.1 pounds.

Tips are expected at most restaurants, even if a service charge is already added to the bill. In more traditional Chinese restaurants, tips are not expected. However, it is customary to leave small change.

Reservations are always a good idea; we note only when they're essential or when they are not accepted. Unless otherwise noted, the restaurants listed are open daily for lunch and dinner. We mention dress only when men are required to wear a jacket or a jacket and tie.

CATEGORY	COST*
$$$$	over HK$500 (US$64)
$$$	HK$300–HK$500 (US$38–US$64)
$$	HK$100–HK$300 (US$13–US$38)
$	under HK$100 (US$13)

per person, not including 10% service charge

HONG KONG ISLAND

Central

One of the busiest sections of the city, Central is a madhouse at lunchtime, when hungry office workers crowd the streets and eateries. Most restaurants have set lunches with speedy service, which makes it possible for most diners to get in and out within an hour; these are generally a good value. Evening dining is either supersmart or a quick bite followed by many drinks, specifically in an area called Lan Kwai Fong. The variety and the quality of dining have improved over the years, and there's now much to choose from in Central.

Asian

CANTONESE

$$$$ ✕ **Man Wah.** Although Cantonese restaurants, even upscale ones, are known for their lively, noisy atmosphere, this one is a Zen-like haven in the midst of busy Central. Silk paintings of Mandarins hang on the walls, gold-and-ebony hand-carved chopsticks adorn each table setting, and there's rosewood everywhere you look. The food is exquisite. A highlight is the sautéed fillet of sole with chilies in black bean sauce, which is delicately cooked to bring out the fish's fresh flavor, just as Cantonese cuisine should be. No detail, however small, is overlooked in taste or presentation; some dishes arrive with intricately carved garnishes. A smattering of dishes from other regions, like Peking duck and Szechuan tea-smoked pigeon, is also served. For dessert try poached pear in tangerine tea, an unusual specialty, to be savored slowly while watching the ships in Victoria Harbour go by. ✉ *Mandarin Oriental Hotel, 5 Connaught Rd.,* ☎ *2522–0111, ext. 4025. AE, DC, MC, V.*

Dining

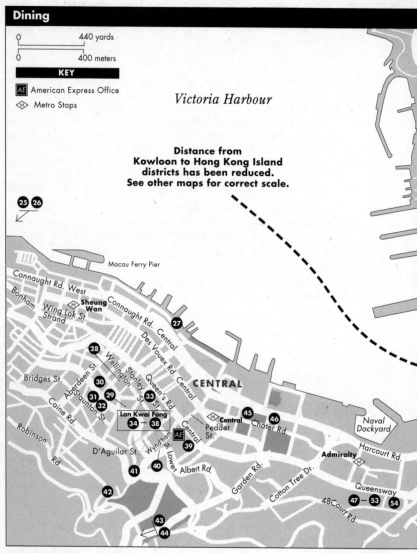

Distance from
Kowloon to Hong Kong Island
districts has been reduced.
See other maps for correct scale.

KEY

AE American Express Office

◇ Metro Stops

Victoria Harbour

Macau Ferry Pier

Connaught Rd. West

Bonham Strand

Wing Lok St.

Sheung Wan

Connaught Rd. Central

Des Voeux Rd. Central

Bridges St.

Aberdeen St.

Wellington St.

Stanley St.

Queen's Rd.

CENTRAL

Caine Rd.

Staunton St.

Lan Kwai Fong

Central

Pedder St.

Chater Rd.

Naval Dockyard

Robinson Rd.

D'Aguilar St.

Wyndham St.

Lower Albert Rd.

Garden Rd.

Admiralty

Harcourt Rd.

Cotton Tree Dr.

Queensway

48 Court Rd.

American Peking
Restaurant, **56**
Bali Restaurant, **1**
Black Sheep, **76**
Bodhi
Vegetarian, **6**
Cafe Deco Bar
and Grill, **44**
Casa Lisboa, **32**
Chinese
Restaurant, **15**
Chiu Chow
Garden, **64**

Chung Thai Food
Restaurant and Sea
Food, **21**
Dan Ryan's, **49**
Delaney's, **58**
Deli Lamma, **25**
Dim Sum, **69**
Dynasty, **62**
Farm House, **66**
Felix, **16**
Gaddi's, **17**
Golden Orchid Thai
Restaurant, **22**

Grappa's, **50**
Great Shanghai
Restaurant, **7**
Grissini, **63**
Hei Fung Terrace, **70**
Hunan Garden, **27**
Indochine 1929, **35**
Isshin, **67**
Jimmy's
Kitchen, **14, 39**
JW's California
Grill, **54**

Kung Tak Lam, **10**
Lancombe, **26**
Law Fu Kee Noodle
Shop, **28**
Le Tire Bouchon, **30**
Lucy's, **74**
Luk Yu Tea House, **33**
M at the Fringe, **40**
Man Wah, **45**
Moon Chuk, **68**
Mughal Room, **41**
Nadaman, **9**
Nepal, **31**
Nicholini's, **52**

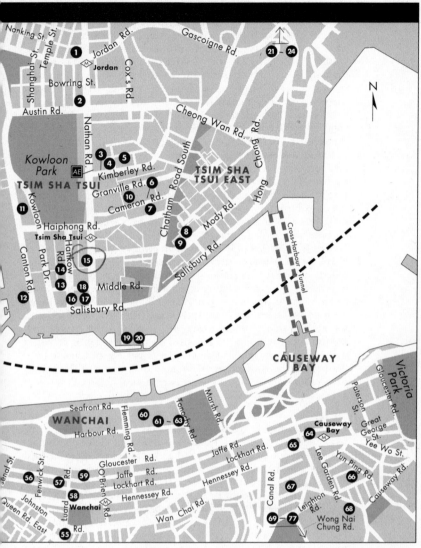

One Harbour
Road, **61**
Papillon, **29**
Peak Cafe, **43**
Peking Restaurant, **2**
Peking Shui Jiao, **59**
Petrus, **48**
Planet Hollywood, **12**
Plume, **19**
Post 97, **36**
Ricos, **42**
Sabatini, **8**

Saigon Beach, **57**
San Francisco Steak
House, **13**
San Shui
Restaurant, **23**
Shanghai
Shanghai, **46**
Shek O Chinese and
Thailand Seafood
Restaurant, **77**
Stanley's French
Restaurant, **73**
Stanley's Oriental, **72**
Steam and Stew
Inn, **55**

Summer Palace, **47**
Sun Hung Cheung
Hing, **4**
Szechuan Lau, **65**
Tables 88, **75**
Taiwan Beef
Noodle, **11**
Tiger's, **51**
Tokio Joe, **37**
Tso Choi Koon, **24**
Tutto Bene, **5**
Va Bene, **34**

The Verandah, **71**
The Viceroy, **60**
Wu Kong Shanghai
Restaurant, **18**
Yu, **20**
Yung Kee, **38**
Yunyan Szechuan
Restaurant, **3**
Zen, **53**

$$ ✕ **Yung Kee.** For more than a half century, this massive (five floors hold
★ some 5,000 guests) multistory eatery (you're taken upstairs in an ele-
vator by a woman wielding a mobile phone, which she uses to orga-
nize seating) has served Cantonese food amid riotous,
writhing-golden-dragon decor. Convenient to hotels and business in
Central, the restaurant attracts a varied clientele—from office work-
ers to visiting celebrities—all of whom receive the same cheerful, high-
energy service. Roast goose is a specialty, the skin beautifully crisp.
Seafood fanciers should try sautéed fillet of pomfret (a type of fish) with
chili and black bean sauce or one of the many expensive shark's fin
soups. ⊠ *32–40 Wellington St.,* ☎ *2522–1624. AE, DC, MC, V.*

$ ✕ **Law Fu Kee Noodle Shop.** To experience a down-to-earth and sim-
ple Cantonese meal, join the local folks who line up here for a quick
but filling lunch. Forget about nice decor and attentive service; you come
here for basic food—noodles and *congees* (rice porridges). Try won-
ton or ox brisket noodles and the beef or pig's kidney congee. The fa-
mous house specialty is the deep-fried fish balls with clam sauce. ⊠
50 Lyndhurst Terr., Central, ☎ *2850–6756;* ⊠ *140 Des Voeux Rd.,
Sheung Wan,* ☎ *2541–3080. No credit cards.*

$ ✕ **Luk Yu Tea House.** Food takes a backseat to atmosphere in this un-
official historical monument—Luk Yu is a living museum with ex-
traordinary character. It has been in business for more than 60 years
and as such lets you catch a rare glimpse of old colonial Hong Kong,
but from the Chinese (not British) perspective. The decor, including hand-
some carved wooden doors, hardwood paneling, marble facings, and,
unfortunately, spittoons (noisily used by the clientele), is definitely
worth seeing. The morning dim sum is popular with Chinese busi-
nesspeople, though the fare is no more than standard Cantonese.
Reservations can be difficult to get at peak meal hours unless you're
a regular. ⊠ *24–26 Stanley St.,* ☎ *2523–5464. No credit cards.*

PEKING

$$$–$$$$ ✕ **Hunan Garden.** Escape the hustle and bustle of Central in this serene
restaurant offering northern Chinese cuisine. Live Chinese music ac-
companies your gourmet journey. Highly recommended are the fried
fish butterflies appetizer: Carp pieces, thinly sliced and deep-fried with
a sweet coating, are crispy and sweet. The spicy fried chicken with chili
might set your lips and throat on fire. Stick with the codfish fillet with
fried minced beans (the chewy and nutty bean paste goes perfectly with
the fillet's soft texture). Also try the Shaoxing wine, served in tiny cups.
But first the waiter pours it into a silver container and rests it in a bucket
of hot water. Ask for lemon slices to go with the wine if you want a
more zesty aroma. ⊠ *The Forum, Exchange Sq., 3rd floor,* ☎ *2868–
2880. AE, DC, MC, V.*

SHANGHAI

$$$ ✕ **Shanghai Shanghai.** Following the trend of retro-Chinese restau-
rants that try to capture the essence of Shanghai in the 1930s, this new-
comer is the best of the bunch. Art deco touches, stained glass, discreet
private rooms, and wooden booths achieve the nostalgic effect. The
menu ranges from simple Shanghainese midnight snacks and cold appetizers to expensive shark's fin soup. After 9 PM the lights dim, and

a chanteuse comes onstage to croon Mandarin tunes—a song-request book is placed at every table. Reservations at least one week in advance are imperative because this intimately sized restaurant has become the hot spot for affluent Chinese reminiscing about the good old days— or imagining that they are there. ⊠ *Ritz Carlton Hotel, 3 Connaught Rd., Basement,* ☎ *2869–0328. Reservations essential. AE, DC, MC, V.*

INDIAN

$$ ✕ **Mughal Room.** You can get anything from a bargain set lunch to a
★ full banquet at one of the best Indian restaurants in town, and it's still good in the value-to-money category, too. The Mughlai cuisine, specializing in clay-oven cookery, is explained in a written introduction at the start of the menu. Each page bears an illustration and short history on one of the *mughals,* the ancient rulers of India, and offers mainly Indian, but also some other Asian, dishes. Select from the *bismillah* (appetizers): the chicken, lamb, and vegetarian *samosas* are fabulous, and serving dishes are huge. The tandoori *sabzi* are tomatoes and capsicum stuffed with mildly spiced cottage cheese and vegetable mash and then baked. The staff wears Bathan (a tribe from Pakistan) dress complete with curled-toe slippers of a past era and caps sporting a flag symbolizing bravery. The tasteful, muted decor is stylish, making it one of the posher curry houses in Hong Kong. ⊠ *Carfield Commercial Bldg., 75– 77 Wyndham St., 1st floor,* ☎ *2524–0107. AE, DC, MC, V.*

JAPANESE

$ ✕ **Tokio Joe.** This funky, casual Japanese joint serves up basic fare with finesse. Attention paid to design elements makes the atmosphere fun— beautiful ceramic pots line faux-fur walls, and food is thoughtfully presented. The *unaju don,* or fried eel with rice, comes in a lacquer box complete with assorted pickles in little bowls. The hot, tender flesh is tasty and fresh, and you can watch the chefs at work on their orders in a central bar area. They put a delightfully contemporary twist on certain dishes. For example, the house-special sushi roll contains a scrumptious mix of elements: deep-fried soft-shell crab, avocado, and crab roe. Also excellent is the *dobin mushi,* chicken vegetable soup served charmingly in a teapot, and for dessert try homemade sesame ice cream. ⊠ *16 Lan Kwai Fong,* ☎ *2525–1889. Reservations essential. AE, DC, MC, V.*

VIETNAMESE

$$$ ✕ **Indochine 1929.** The name directly evokes the period when the
★ French were in possession of what is modern-day Vietnam. The mood of the 1930s is gloriously, but subtly summoned by the decor—potted palms, old pictures, soothing lighting—and the dedicated service of the sarong-dressed staff. The chef travels regularly to Vietnam for inspirations and always comes up with exciting additions to the menu. Must-tries are the soft-shell crab and the Hanoi fried fish. Also sample an appetizer or two—vegetarian spring rolls and any salad will make a nice prelude to a satisfying dinner. Rice lovers shouldn't miss the Hue fried rice. The busy, chatty atmosphere, filled by a smart, casual crowd, is comfortable and relaxed. ⊠ *California Tower, 2nd floor, Lan Kwai Fong,* ☎ *2869–7399. AE, DC, MC, V.*

European
CONTINENTAL

$$$$
★ ✕ **M at the Fringe.** This spot above the Fringe Club sets itself apart with quirky yet classy decor and a seasonal menu that mixes Continental with Middle Eastern cuisine. It's hard to choose from so many dishes with intriguing descriptions. Whether it's pumpkin and almond tortelli pasta, crispy risotto, or grilled scallops wrapped in bacon, the combinations are truly as delicious as they are creative. The set lunches are a good value, and sweet tooths should visit on a Friday or Saturday night after dinner for the special dessert menu. Gingered crème brûlée and *Pavlova* (an Australian meringue and fruit delight) are perennial favorites; you can always succumb to the sampler platter for two. ✉ *South Block, 2 Lower Albert Rd., 1st floor,* ☎ *2877–4000. Reservations essential. AE, MC, V.*

$$ ✕ **Jimmy's Kitchen.** Probably the most famous —and still one of the best—of the territory's restaurants, this institution first opened for business in 1928. It has been catering to a deeply devoted Hong Kong clientele in one location or another ever since. Nicely decorated, it has comfortable booths, dark woodwork, lattice partitions, and brass work on the walls. The food is as charmingly old-fashioned as the place itself: Where else in Hong Kong can you find corned beef and cabbage? Other European specialties, including borscht, Stroganoff, goulash, and bangers and mash, are accompanied by the restaurant's traditional pickled onions. Their rhubarb tart is a must for dessert. ✉ *South China Bldg., 1 Wyndham St.,* ☎ *2526–5293. Lunch reservations essential. AE, DC, MC, V.*

$–$$ ✕ **Post 97.** With its image as a hip coffeehouse/nightspot and gathering point for the local intelligentsia, people sometimes forget just how good the food is here—and it won't break the bank. The menu features delicious pastas, salads, and sandwiches; there's a chalkboard of daily specials; and soups and desserts are almost always worthwhile. Post 97 has a 24-hour menu on weekends and is great for breakfast. People-watching potential and funky decor make this one of the most successful restaurants in Lan Kwai Fong. ✉ *9 Lan Kwai Fong,* ☎ *2810–9333. DC, MC, V.*

FRENCH

$$$–$$$$
★ ✕ **Papillon.** One block from the glittering Lan Kwai Fong area in a dead-end alley, this intimate restaurant is reminiscent of a small bistro in the south of France. Subdued lighting and black-and-white prints of Paris contribute to an atmosphere pleasant for both couples and groups. If you're hosting a private party or desire privacy, request a table at the back of the room, where curtains can be drawn. The mushroom soup and salmon tartare are satisfying starters, and the duck breast or sole fillet are good entrée choices. Don't miss out on the light-as-a-feather soufflé (try the ginger or Grand Marnier) to round out a hearty meal. The international wine list includes even Chinese and Chilean wines. Ask the manager to recommend food for you, and he'll match wines by the glass, too. ✉ *8 Wo On La.,* ☎ *2526–5965. Reservations essential. AE, DC, MC, V.*

$$$ ✕ **Le Tire Bouchon.** No longer tucked away on Old Bailey Street, this bistro's spacious new home includes a bar area and private rooms. The menu remains small and includes treasures such as sautéed chicken livers with red wine and duck-liver terrine. Also consider the Brittany-style monkfish, veal kidneys with cognac, and lamb noisettes with thyme flowers. There are more than 90 reasonably priced French wines from which to choose. ✉ *45 Graham St.,* ☎ *2523–5459. Reservations essential. AE, MC, V. Closed Sun.*

\$\$\$ ✕ **Va Bene.** This small, trendy northern Italian restaurant is a classy
★ combination of sleek Los Angeles decor and friendly, capable service.
An inventive menu includes melt-in-your-mouth risotto with shrimp
and orange, a wide selection of pasta dishes, and daily specials. Homemade breads are served with pesto and other freshly made dips, and
there is great tiramisu. ✉ *58–62 D'Aguilar St., Lan Kwai Fong,* ☎
2845–5577. AE, DC, MC, V.

Admiralty

Since this is essentially an office area and a series of large shopping
malls, much of the food offered meets the lunch demands of office workers and shoppers. However, with a major cinema and several good restaurants in the Pacific Place mall, it is a convenient place for dinner as
well.

Asian

CANTONESE

\$\$\$–\$\$\$\$ ✕ **Summer Palace.** Designed and named after Beijing's Summer Palace,
★ this luxurious Chinese kitchen lives up to its royal name—the food is
great and the setting is imperial. It has grand pillars, huge chandeliers,
and Chinese paintings on the walls. Try their dim sum during lunch
hour. The baked stuffed crab shell and deep-fried duckling in mashed
taro are also highly recommended. For a more exotic treat, try their
braised abalone and shark's fin soup. ✉ *Island Shangri-La, Pacific Place,
Supreme Court Rd., 5th floor,* ☎ *2820–8552. Reservations essential.
AE, DC, MC, V.*

\$\$\$ ✕ **Zen.** This upscale nouveau Cantonese restaurant is under the same
ownership as the ultrachic London eateries of the same name. Thin-
sliced pig's ears is one of the unusual specialties here, and Peking duck
is delicious (give advance notice if you want to try it). The more standard Cantonese dishes are quite delicately prepared and presented. Service is flawless, and the decor contemporary, with dramatic hanging
lights and a central waterfall. ✉ *The Mall, Pacific Place One, 88
Queensway,* ☎ *2845–4555. AE, DC, MC, V.*

PAN-ASIAN

\$\$\$ ✕ **Tiger's.** If you happen to be shopping in the Pacific Place mall and
need some sustenance, this is a good bet. Sit inside facing away from
the shopping atrium, and you can escape reality viewing the outrageous
decor here. Selections include seafood, vegetarian dishes, curries, tandoori offerings, and rice and noodles, with each dish identified by its
country of origin. The *banh cuon* (traditional homemade Vietnamese
steamed ravioli) is filled with crispy, mouthwatering pork and mushrooms that contrast with the delicate, translucent wrapper. *Pao phak
gap hed hom* (stir-fried fresh broccoli and Chinese mushrooms with
homemade oyster sauce) is equally tasty. ✉ *Basement, Pacific Place,
88 Queensway,* ☎ *2537–4682. AE, DC, MC, V.*

North American

\$\$–\$\$\$ ✕ **JW's California Grill.** This is the rare uptown hotel restaurant that
achieves a relaxed feeling. Sleek-looking yet supercomfortable seating
islands around the perimeter of the dining room are widely spaced for
privacy. A very attentive staff of waiters (they guarantee getting you
fed, watered, and back out the door quickly, if you ask) serves an eclectic menu of fresh California cuisine. Of particular note are honey-glazed
lamb chops and stir-fried lobster and prawns. Pasta here is also excellent,
as is the extensive list of American wines. ✉ *J. W. Marriott Hotel, Pacific Place, 88 Queensway,* ☎ *2841–3899. AE, DC, MC, V.*

$$ **✗ Dan Ryan's.** A popular bar, there is often only standing space here,
★ so book ahead for a table. Aside from beer, the menu offers a smat-
tering of international dishes—pasta and the like—but Dan Ryan's rep-
utation in town is for great burgers and soups served in bread bowls.
It's simple, rib-sticking stuff, but sometimes that's all you want, and
Dan Ryan's provides it without fuss or formality. ⊠ *114 Pacific Place,
88 Queensway,* ☎ *2845–4600. Reservations essential. AE, DC, MC,
V.*

European

ITALIAN

$$$–$$$$ **✗ Nicholini's.** This elegant, upscale Italian restaurant has a delightful
ambience, with bundles of beautiful flowers that light up the dining
room. Check out the bread trolley: It offers the most varieties of freshly
baked bread in town—bell pepper, mushroom, onion, nut, olive,
tomato, you name it. A complimentary appetizer is a prelude to a lovely
dinner, and a soothing sorbet cleanses the palate between courses. The
menu changes regularly—but minestrone soup or lobster salad is al-
ways a good way to kick off a hearty meal. ⊠ *Conrad International,
Pacific Place, 88 Queensway, 8th floor,* ☎ *2521–3838. Reservations
essential. AE, DC, MC, V.*

$$–$$$ **✗ Grappa's.** Don't let the mall location mislead you—Grappa's serves
★ superb Italian food. Once inside you can turn your back on the mall
and let the kindly staff look after you. The endless selection of pasta
dishes can prolong your decision, but nothing will be disappointing.
Excellent coffee and a range of bottled beers also make Grappa's a good
spot for a quick pick-me-up or an after-shopping rendezvous. ⊠ *132
Pacific Place, 88 Queensway,* ☎ *2868–0086. AE, DC, MC, V.*

FRENCH

$$$$ **✗ Petrus.** If fine dining is judged by the quality of food, service, and
★ ambience, Petrus simply aces. Chef Alain Verzeroli, who worked as the
executive sous chef at the world-renowned Joel Robuchon restaurant,
certainly cooks up to any high expectation. Every dish is delicately pre-
pared, and presentations rival the panoramic view. The salmon tartare
and tuna tartare are delightful starters, as are the ravioli and the black
truffle soup. Seafood lovers will rave about the monkfish, and the lamb
is another clear winner. The menu is ever-changing, and Petrus even
has a list of goose liver specialties to complement the house vintages.
There is a wide selection of French wines and even an extensive list of
half bottles. ⊠ *Island Shangri-La, Pacific Place, Supreme Court Rd.,
56th floor,* ☎ *2820–8590. Reservations essential. AE, D, MC, V.*

Midlevels

The world's largest outdoor escalator snakes through this part of Cen-
tral, transporting residents to and from work. To cater to this young
professional crowd, a slew of small eateries has sprung up along the
escalator's path in the last two years. Hop on the escalator after shop-
ping Hollywood Road, and you can spot everything from a Cajun restau-
rant to Finnish takeout. Just hop off when you see what you're
hungering for.

Asian

NEPALI

$$ **✗ Nepal.** If you're feeling adventurous but not quite up to an assault
★ on Everest, you can stimulate your imagination with a Yaktail or Yeti
Foot cocktail in this tiny Nepali restaurant. Don't be deceived by its
size—it has more to offer than you expect. Take a look at the Nepalese
wood carving, the *manne* (praying tools), and the musical instruments

as you enjoy the background Indian/Nepalese music. The menu has simple explanations of the cuisine. The *hanta tareko* (grilled eggplant) and *kaju sadeko* (fried cashew nuts) are good starters, and there's even a special Nepali soup, *golveda-ko-rash,* which is perfect for vegetarians. For a main course, the royal chicken, a light Nepali curry, is highly recommended; the sauce is creamy and mild and goes well with the Nepali rice. End the meal with the Nepalese ice cream, slightly firmer than ordinary ice cream, but not too rich. ⊠ *14 Staunton St.,* ☎ *2521–9108. Reservations essential. AE, DC, MC, V.*

European
PORTUGUESE

$$–$$$ ✕ **Casa Lisboa.** Fado music playing in the background, Portuguese oil
★   paintings lining the yellow walls, and bottles with eruptions of melted candle wax all add to the atmosphere. Replete with checkered tablecloths and painted pottery plates, the dimly lighted space is serviced by a professional but low-key staff. Choosing a starter from the ones offered is a challenge, with anything from Portuguese cheese and ham to snails with chili, garlic, and mushrooms available. Opt for the grilled sardines, and you won't be disappointed. Typically the menu features lots of codfish and chorizo options. The scallops with chorizo are served on a small wooden box with a plate that stays hot just long enough for you to cook the seafood, turning the scallops over yourself. The codfish soup is a divine broth of chunks of the flaked fish and slivers of garlic and coriander. There's an amusing set of special effects for the flambéed dish of king prawns, and remember to ask for the mashed potatoes *ze do pipa,* a fabulous mash with cheese, fish, and olives. All wines on the list are Portuguese (except for the champagne). ⊠ *21 Elgin St.,* ☎ *2869–9361. Reservations essential. AE, DC, MC, V.*

SPANISH

$$$ ✕ **Ricos.** This Spanish tapas bar serves a traditional and generally satisfying selection of food, but it's the wooden fittings and supercasual atmosphere that keep its fans loyal. People here always seem to be having a good time, and couples find the dark surroundings romantic. If you use the Midlevels escalator, go as far as Conduit Road and turn left; Ricos is just six doors down. ⊠ *44 Robinson Rd.,* ☎ *2840–0937. Reservations essential. AE, DC, MC, V.*

The Peak

Whether you take the tram or a taxi, on a clear day even the views en route will justify the trip to the highest spot to dine in Hong Kong. The view is spectacular, but if there are low clouds, you won't see a thing—although you can hear the city below you. There's a small selection of restaurants, but two compete for the number one position. For the view, stick with Cafe Deco, but old-timers stay loyal to the Peak Cafe.

Asian
PAN-ASIAN

$$$ ✕ **Cafe Deco Bar and Grill.** If you're in Hong Kong on a clear day, take the Peak tram up to the top to dine at this spiffy double-decker restaurant overlooking the city. Views *are* stunning. The decor is art deco to the hilt—you can spend an age looking at authentic period fittings. The menu includes an international range of choices: Chinese, Indian (there's a tandoor in the kitchen), Italian, Mexican, and Thai dishes, with dishes using *ancho* chilies or combining striped sea bass with fennel and pancetta. There is also an extremely reasonable wine list. Eat in the dining room, at the oyster bar, or in the ice cream parlor. The location is a favorite with visitors and residents alike. ✉ *Peak Galleria, 118 Peak Rd., 1st level,* ☎ *2849–5111. AE, DC, MC, V.*

$$–$$$ ✕ **Peak Cafe.** This café-restaurant opposite the top terminus of the Peak
★   tram is one of the most popular restaurants in the city because of its
casual and cozy ambience. When the weather is warm, the tables outside with views of the Lamma Channel are the best, but even in winter, wood stoves keep customers warm and content. The menu includes
plenty of tasty appetizers (try smoked salmon in pesto), as well as sandwiches, soups, and such Asian favorites as Hainan chicken and Thai
smoked duck. Their Indian tandoori dishes are reliably good—try ten-
der chicken marinated in yogurt and herbs or roasted Kashmiri potatoes, stuffed with nuts, bell peppers, and mushrooms. ✉ *121 Peak Rd.,*
☎ *2819–7868. Reservations essential. AE, DC, MC, V.*

Wanchai

At lunchtime Wanchai is just another jumble of people and not a particularly invigorating shopping area. But at night Wanchai comes into
its own. It's the primary nightlife destination, with fluorescent lights
stretching endlessly along the roads jam-packed with taxis and people
out for what will inevitably be a long night. Dining options are extreme—
from fail-safe five-star hotel luxury to street-level eateries that are authentic and welcoming, with fine food.

Asian

CANTONESE

$$$–$$$$ ✕ **Dynasty.** One of the two entrances to this hotel restaurant takes you
past a beautiful two-floor chandelier to typically subdued Cantonese
decor—beige tones, mirrors, unobtrusive fixtures. The beautiful crock-
ery design—especially commissioned for the New World hotel, in
Kowloon, and the New World Harbour View, in Wanchai, both with
a well-respected Dynasty restaurant—combines an art deco feel with
a Buddhist aesthetic. Palm trees and live traditional Chinese music pro-
vide a total contrast to the modernity on display outside the windows:
neon signs pushing Epson or Hitachi and the Wanchai Ferry travers-
ing the harbor. Sections on the menu are devoted to soup, chicken, pi-
geon, duck, and beef. If you really want to go all out, try the braised
imperial bird's nest with bamboo mushrooms and pigeon at HK$1,300.
Definitely try the roast suckling pig—thin skins on top of tiny buns,
although the melon balls accompanying this dish may present you with
a real chopstick challenge. ✉ *New World Harbour View, 1 Harbour
Rd.,* ☎ *2802–8888. Reservations essential. AE, DC, MC, V.*

$$$ ✕ **One Harbour Road.** One of five dining options set in the opulent
Grand Hyatt, this top-end Cantonese restaurant has typically muted
cream decor but with added extras—a glass roof for a view of the stars
at night and a two-tier layout that adds to the open feel. In the 1930s,
after Shanghai's economic boom faded, many of its citizens came to
Hong Kong to set up homes. One Harbour Road's design emulates the
elegant, art deco style of that period—you are even deposited in the
restaurant by a circular brass elevator. The food is classic hotel Cantonese—it's very fresh and beautifully presented, but the delicate flavors of this authentic regional food can often seem bland. Dim sum
offers a wide range of delicate and delicious little packages. Ask for a
single serving of lotus-leaf rice (in a large serving the fragrance of the
leaves can be lost on the rice inside). A selection of sauces, from XO
sauce (made from preserved scallops and chili) to mustard and soy sauces,
means you can perk up your dish if you wish. For dessert, the mango
pudding is a treat. ✉ *Grand Hyatt, 1 Harbour Rd., 7th and 8th floors,*
☎ *2588–1234, ext. 7338. Reservations essential. AE, DC, MC, V.*

$–$$ ✕ **Steam and Stew Inn.** You can't miss the red lanterns hanging at the restaurant's entrance in this short alley. This hole-in-the-wall with simple decorations boasts home-style and healthy Cantonese cooking (it serves red rice and doesn't use MSG—both considered rare in Hong Kong). Go for the steamed fish and eggplant casserole (one of the most popular items) instead of deep-fried dishes, of which they have a wide variety, including an irresistible deep-fried eel. For those concerned about cholesterol, you can request tailor-made dishes that use egg whites rather than whole eggs. Don't miss the double-boiled chicken and ginseng, which helps lower the body heat. They offer a seasonal menu as well as dim sum during lunch. This gem was opened seven years ago by a group of young professionals who craved inexpensive healthy Chinese dishes and draws a young clientele. ⊠ *21–23 Tai Wong Street East, Wanchai,* ☎ *2529–3913. MC, V.*

PAN-ASIAN

$$–$$$ ✕ **The Viceroy.** Mottled golden walls with murals, low-key music, and
★ a harbor view give the Viceroy a tranquil atmosphere for an evening meal. In summer be sure to book ahead for a table on the veranda, where you will feel the thrill of the Hong Kong skyline—huge neon lights and all. The menu is pan-Asian, primarily Indian with Thai and Indonesian dishes. *Kai hor bai teoy* (white-meat chicken in succulent parcels of pandanus leaves) is a favorite. The *kung kra borg* (juicy prawns wrapped in rice sheets with sweet and sour sauce) are superb. Even the humble samosas are royally presented, almost Japanese in manner with just two on a plate with tamarind sauce. For a sticky dessert combine *gulab jamun* (balls of deep-fried milk pastry soaked in sugar syrup and served warm) with a glass of Cointreau, a perfect accompaniment for this dish. ⊠ *Sun Hung Kai Centre, 30 Harbour Rd., 2nd floor,* ☎ *2827–7777. Lunch reservations essential. AE, DC, MC, V.*

PEKING

$ ✕ **American Peking Restaurant.** Pekinese cuisine is made up of hearty dishes suitable for the chilly climate of northern China (the site of modern-day Beijing). An overdecorated restaurant full of red-and-gold fixtures, the American Peking has been a gastronomic amenity in Hong Kong for more than 40 years. Favorites here include hot and sour soup, fried and steamed dumplings, and in the winter, delicious hot pots. Also try the excellent beggar's chicken (so called because it's cooked in clay and lotus leaves), minced pigeon, and, of course, Peking duck. Each meal begins with complimentary peanuts and sliced cucumber in vinegar—for practicing your chopstick skills. The name American Peking is fitting: The authenticity of the food is questionable, but it caters well to those unfamiliar with Chinese food. ⊠ *20 Lockhart Rd.,* ☎ *2527–7277 or 2527–7770. Weekend reservations essential. No credit cards.*

$ ✕ **Peking Shui Jiao.** This little noodle and dumpling shop serves up to eight different varieties including beef and leek, and vegetarian. *Shui jiao* dumplings, made in Beijing (Peking) and northern China, are crescent shaped, unlike Cantonese wontons, which are round. Choose either boiled or panfried dumplings. The decor is not exactly inviting at first glance—florescent lighting and hard, basic seating. But the prices are hard to beat, and the place is clean. Other than dumplings, Shanghai-style fried noodles and eggplant with garlic sauce are tasty. Come here for a quick bite before or after a performance at the nearby Arts Centre. ⊠ *118 Jaffe Rd.,* ☎ *2527–0289. No credit cards.*

VIETNAMESE

$ ✕ **Saigon Beach.** An absolute hole-in-the-wall, this tiny place can seat only about 20, so avoid the rush hours unless you don't mind standing. The decor, an amalgam of fishing gear—cheap plastic hung from nets, and the like—folding chairs, and Formica tables won't impress anyone. Instead, the extremely authentic Vietnamese fare and conviviality of elbow rubbing with people who know this is a find more than make up for the not-quite-prepossessing environs. ⊠ *66 Lockhart Rd.,* ☎ *2529–7823. No credit cards.*

European

IRISH

$–$$ ✕ **Delaney's.** There's much more to recommend this Irish pub than Guinness on draft. The decor was imported lock, stock, and beer barrel from the Emerald Isle, there's live music by Irish lads, and the very tasty food is well prepared. The leek and oatmeal soup is thick and satisfying enough to stave off a cold winter. The menu has good vegetarian choices, although there are also two hearty—and meaty—Irish stews from which to choose. Very crowded immediately after offices empty for the night, Delaney's is a better option for lunch, when things are less frantic: Dinner can be noisy and overrun by drinkers. ⊠ *1 Capital Pl., 18 Luard Rd., 2nd floor,* ☎ *2804–2880. Reservations essential. AE.*

ITALIAN

$$$$ ✕ **Grissini.** As you enter this sophisticated restaurant, you'll overlook the magnificent, some say over-the-top, Grand Hyatt lobby. The trompe l'oeil floor boggles the eyes and emphasizes the art-deco-meets-Tuscan-villa feel. Your fresh, delicate northern Italian meal begins with the long sticks of bread served at each table. The antipasto *misto* (mixed antipasto), pan-fried scallops and eggplant rolls are all great starters, and Grissini's risotto choices and flavorful fish entreés are not to be missed. This is also a great place to drink grappas, served with ceremony from a selection of curvaceous bottles with fitting nicknames like the UFO. ⊠ *Grand Hyatt, 1 Harbour Rd., 2nd floor,* ☎ *2588–1234. Reservations essential. AE, DC, MC, V.*

Causeway Bay

An absolute phenomenon on a Saturday afternoon, Causeway Bay, host to a series of large Japanese department stores, is one of the city's busiest shopping destinations. Consequently, the density of the population can be overwhelming. There are several pubs in the vicinity, but they are not concentrated in one strip. Likewise, there are several good restaurants, but to the uninitiated they can be hard to find. Times Square, a huge, modern shopping mall, has four floors of restaurants in one of its towers, and nearly all offer reliably good food, from Korean and Thai to American and French steak houses and regional Chinese offerings.

Asian

CANTONESE

\$\$ ✕ **Dim Sum.** Although most restaurants in Hong Kong serve dim sum
★ only at lunchtime, this elegant gem has broken the norm and offers
the delicate tidbits from dusk till dawn. The menu not only has Cantonese dim sum like the must-try *har gau* (steamed shrimp dumpling),
but also northern choices like chili prawn dumplings, Peking onion cakes,
and steamed buns. The chef's creative lobster bisque and abalone
dumplings are popular picks. This restaurant doesn't take lunch reservations on weekends and always attracts a long line. Arrive early or
admire the old Chinese advertisement posters and the antique telephone
while you wait. Happy Valley is close to Causeway Bay, but take a tram
or a cab to get here. ⊠ *63 Sing Woo Rd., Happy Valley,* ☎ *2834–
8893. AE, DC, MC, V.*

\$\$ ✕ **Farm House.** Don't confuse this restaurant with the fast-food chain
that's sprouted up all over the city. This excellent Cantonese restaurant serves MSG-free food with pride. It's a popular place for families
and small groups, whose conversations bring a lively buzz to the air.
Braised pigeon with garlic, stir-fried beef with red wine, and seafood
hot pots are popular items. The staff, attired in green uniforms, is efficient and friendly. ⊠ *A1A Plaza, 18 Hysan Ave.,* ☎ *2811–1881. AE,
MC, V.*

\$–\$\$ ✕ **Moon Chuk.** At the periphery of bustling Causeway Bay, Moon
Chuk offers a laid-back atmosphere and simple Cantonese food. Take
a look at the black-and-white pictures of the Prince's Building in Central back in 1924 and of old Hong Kong street scenes on the wall above
the booths. The rosewood furniture, with Chinese carvings on the
table legs, and the soothing lighting make for a warm hangout after a
day's shopping or sightseeing. Luxurious choices like abalone congee,
seafood congee, and shark's fin and prawn dumpling are served in addition to the typical congees and noodles. There's a separate dim sum
menu as well as a special menu with pictures for tourists. ⊠ *46
Leighton Rd., Causeway Bay,* ☎ *2808–0321. AE, MC, V.*

CHIU CHOW

\$\$ ✕ **Chiu Chow Garden.** Seafood-based Chiu Chow cuisine originated
in the area around Swatow on the China coast and is popular among
Chinese gourmets, although it's little known outside East Asia. Service
in this spacious, well-lighted restaurant tends to be slow, and getting
a waiter who speaks English is not always easy, but the food is delicious. Try Iron Buddha tea (served in thimble-size cups and packed with
caffeine), cold roast goose on a bed of fried blood (far better than it
sounds), Fukien abalone in a light ginger sauce, and delicious sautéed
shrimp and crabmeat balls served over crispy prawn crackers. There
are branches of Chiu Chow Garden in Jardine House and at Vicwood
Plaza, on Hong Kong Island. ⊠ *Hennessy Centre, 500 Hennessy Rd.,*
☎ *2577–3391. AE, DC, MC, V.*

JAPANESE

✕ **Isshin.** Of the many restaurants in the Times Square dining tower,
this is the only one serving Japanese cuisine, and it's interesting as much
for the decor as for the food. A basic sushi combination of 10 pieces
plus a tuna roll may not be cheap, but each is prepared to perfection.
Isshin's strongest suit is the variety of smaller items it offers, which could
qualify as a sort of rarefied dim sum menu. Soybean soup with mushrooms has a sharp, full-bodied flavor, and the three pieces of deep-fried
bean curd in soup are a rare experience: The crisp batter is garnished
with translucent shavings of fish, and the tofu interior melts in your
mouth. ⊠ *Times Sq., 13th floor,* ☎ *2506–2220. AE, DC, MC, V.*

SZECHUAN

$$ ✕ **Szechuan Lau.** Lovers of spicy, garlicky Szechuan food have come
★   to this no-frills-but-comfortable restaurant for many years. The place
     is always packed with both locals and visitors, and the noisy chatter
     of diners is part of the fun. Popular picks are hot garlic eggplant,
     smoked duck, and prawns in hot peppers on a sizzling platter. Small
     portions are available and advisable so you can taste more dishes. The
     staff is accustomed to Western guests. ⊠ *466 Lockhart Rd.*, ☎ *2891–
     9027. AE, MC, V.*

Repulse Bay

An exhilarating 20-minute bus ride from Central, Repulse Bay's beach
is one of the longest and cleanest in the territory. The Repulse Bay Hotel,
rebuilt as a luxury residential building, has several quality eateries and
shops.

CHINESE

$$–$$$ ✕ **Hei Fung Terrace.** Following the decorative setting of traditional
Suzhou gardens, the restaurant radiates the ancient and elegant am-
bience of a Chinese villa: traditional-style partitions, bamboo cur-
tains, imitation waterfalls, rocky walls and villa arches. The stewed
chicken with *huatiao* wine in casserole, though a bit oily, is a highlight.
Allow 30 minutes for its preparation since it takes time for the chicken
to be cooked and soaked in half a bottle of huatiao and sugar, thus ab-
sorbing the subtle aroma of the Chinese wine. The dim sum served at
lunch is also a treat. ⊠ *The Arcade, Repulse Bay Hotel, 109 Repulse
Bay Rd., 1st floor,* ☎ *2812–2622. AE, DC, MC, V.*

EUROPEAN

$$$ ✕ **The Verandah.** A great way to pass half a day is to wander into this
colonial replica and take afternoon tea (on Sundays and public holi-
days only). Finger sandwiches, scones, and pastries are accompanied
by a choice of Fortnum and Mason blends (orange pekoe, Darjeeling,
Earl Grey, Lapsang Souchong), Verveine tea from La Tisanerie, or coffee, all in a heavy classic silver service. Or you can partake of the Sunday brunch (11–2:30) for a full buffet of fruit, pancakes, and other
morning fare. The high ceilings, balustrades, wooden fixtures, and huge
windows hark back to Raffles, in Singapore, and the relaxed feel is a
welcome relief from the rigors of Hong Kong's city life. At dinner the
atmosphere becomes more formal, and you learn why this is considered one of the city's most romantic restaurants. The menu is mainly
European fare, with a small but excellent smattering of Asian-inspired
dishes like seared ahi tuna with wasabi. ⊠ *109 Repulse Bay Rd.,* ☎
2812–2722. AE, DC, MC, V.

Stanley Village

After an afternoon of intense haggling in Stanley Market, relax and
refuel at one of the many bordering restaurants. There are cheap pit
stops within the market itself as well as quite a few romantic upper-
end restaurants overlooking the sea. Even if you aren't a shopper, dinner in Stanley is a fine measure of how Hong Kong residents enjoy
themselves on weekends and in good weather.

Asian

PAN-ASIAN

$$–$$$ ✕ **Stanley's Oriental.** Designed like an eastern version of an a French
Quarter house in New Orleans, complete with ornate balconies and
ceiling fans, Stanley's Oriental has a menu that marries Eastern and
Western cuisines, matching Cajun and creole with Thai, Indian, and

Japanese. Try Thai curry or Cajun blackfish. Views of Stanley Bay are an additional pleasure. For a little romance, reserve a table on an upper level overlooking the water. ⊠ *90B Stanley Main St.,* ☏ *2813–9988. AE, DC, MC, V.*

European
CONTINENTAL

$$ ✕ **Lucy's.** Run by local catering whiz Lucy Humbert, Lucy's is done in brushed yellow paint with rattan chairs and bright fabrics covering cushions and sofas. The menu may not be extensive, but quality is high, and prices are low. Soups are always a good start, and try fish cakes or tagliatelle with salmon in vodka sauce. Each is well prepared, delicious, and presented with little touches that make you feel like someone cares. ⊠ *64 Stanley Main St. (just behind Park 'n' Shop),* ☏ *2813–9055. AE, DC, MC, V.*

$$–$$$ ✕ **Tables 88.** Housed in the two-story old Stanley police station, Tables 88 is certainly a spot worth visiting. Call it a museum or a gallery— the colonial-style building (a protected structure by the government) was originally constructed in 1859 and took two years to refurbish before the restaurant opened in 1991. The wooden fittings at the atrium bar were imported from a 120-year-old factory in Chicago to add a twist to the flint-stone ambience. There are nine rooms with various themes (cherry room, straw room, African room, to name a few) with hand-painted, sponge-finished walls and tailor-made artsy furniture. Don't miss the Strong Room (weapons storage room) on the ground floor. This architectural landmark serves eclectic international cuisine—from Hainan chicken rice to French seafood, as well as an extensive list of desserts. Try the soufflé and the warm apple crumble. Tables 88 has a selection of wine from California, Australia, Italy and France. ⊠ *88 Stanley Village Rd.,* ☏ *2813–6262. AE, DC, MC, V.*

FRENCH

$$–$$$ ✕ **Stanley's French Restaurant.** Have a drink at the bar downstairs as
★ you watch the world go by. Then head upstairs and pamper yourself: The rooftop dining experience takes your breath away. The regular menu is small in size but great in quality. The goose liver terrine with truffles and the warm marine lobster salad are both outstanding appetizers. Served on butter lettuce and topped with crispy taro chips, the salad's lobster and artichoke chunks mix perfectly with the subtle dressing. Seafood lovers will enjoy the delicately Cajun-spiced John Dory and the crisp baked salmon steak. Skate wing with capers and lemon sauce is another winner—it's only available during weekends and goes quickly. Check out the daily chalkboard menu and another separate menu for vegetarians. ⊠ *86–88 Stanley Main St.,* ☏ *2813–8873. Reservations essential. AE, DC, MC, V.*

Shek O

Shek O is a long trek, but it is a good bet for tourists who don't mind traveling for an adventurous meal. Once you've undertaken the journey—the longest one possible from Central, on Hong Kong Island— you'll be in need of some sustenance. Shek O is tiny, but the little seaside village boasts a few decent open-air restaurants.

Asian
CHINESE-THAI

$ ✕ **Shek O Chinese and Thailand Seafood Restaurant.** There's nothing particularly outstanding in decor or food here, but this is a legend in its own dinner time—it's just such *fun*. People arrive en masse on the weekend and sit for hours despite the relentless summer heat. The curious hybrid cuisine ensures plenty of rice, noodles, and fish dishes. The *tom yung kung* (spicy prawn and coconut soup) is always guaranteed to bring color to your cheeks, the green curry is a safe chicken choice, and the honey-fried squid is a must. The friendly holiday ambience is a real winner, and you can eat royally without breaking the bank. ⊠ *Main corner of Shek O, next to bus stop,* ☎ *2809–4426. Reservations required on weekends. No credit cards.*

International

$$ ✕ **Black Sheep.** This unpretentious, slightly offbeat place was opened by an artist, and it shows. There's a lot of *stuff* on the walls; look for the mounted chair, lamp, and clock. The changing menu—and music—is a mix of African (such as spicy pumpkin and squash soup), vegetarian (savory stuffed eggplant), crowd-pleasing (tasty lamb chops and salmon), and novelty items (the vegetarian Mooncake). The place attracts a lot of locals who hang around until there's a free table, so call ahead if you're making a special trip from a distant district. ⊠ *From Shek O village, turn left at Thai restaurant by small traffic circle; Black Sheep is down road and around corner on right,* ☎ *2809–2021. AE, MC, V.*

KOWLOON

Parts of Kowloon are among the most densely populated areas on the planet, and there's a corresponding abundance of dining opportunities. Many hotels located here for the view of Hong Kong Island (spectacular at night) have excellent restaurants, although they're uniformly expensive. On the street you may have just as much luck being adventurous and walking into places on a whim, though you take your chances. Some of the best finds are, however, in the back streets, where immigrants from all over Asia have brought with them their cooking skills from Vietnam, Thailand, and other countries.

Tsim Sha Tsui

Tsim Sha Tsui is on the tip of Kowloon and crammed with shops. From five-star deluxe hotels to holes-in-the- wall, this area also doesn't lack in dining options.

Asian

CANTONESE

$$$$ ✕ **Chinese Restaurant.** It takes some nerve to claim to be *the* Chinese restaurant in Hong Kong, but this one gets away with it. A postmodern interior is a new take on the traditional 1920s teahouse, and subdued lighting creates a mellow atmosphere. The talented kitchen staff's innovative Cantonese cooking is what makes the place stand out. The menu changes seasonally, though some oft-ordered items—papaya soup, crispy chicken skin, and stewed goose in brown ginger gravy—are always available and worth tasting. The Peking duck is out of this world, as is braised abalone on a bed of artichoke hearts. ⊠ *Hyatt Regency Hotel, 67 Nathan Rd.,* ☎ *2311–1234. Reservations essential. Jacket and tie. AE, DC, MC, V.*

PEKINESE

$$ ✕ **Peking Restaurant.** This place has been around for decades and its old-fashioned decor, admittedly not entirely well maintained, shows it. Waiters who are equally old will serve you, and that's part of the charm. The specialty here is Peking duck, and you don't have to order in advance as you do in many other places. Unfortunately, they don't bring out the whole bird and carve it at your table in grand style, but they will tailor the order to the size of your party. Other traditional dishes done well are lightly fried egg white mixed with vinegar and

Yangzhou fried rice with ham and peas. ✉ *227 Nathan Rd., 1st floor,* ☎ *2730–1315. No credit cards.*

$$ ✕ **Sun Hung Cheung Hing.** This old restaurant doesn't have fancy decor or exotic ingredients, but an authentic Northern China style of cooking. Adventurous eaters enjoy the sumptuous Mongolian barbecue—feel free to roll up your sleeves, mix the meat or vegetables in the special sauce (a mixture of 12 seasonings), and fry it on the table's built-in flat pan (the waiters are ready to cook it if you prefer not to, but it's extremely fun to cook, at least for the first two rounds). Sesame oil is used for the frying, which adds an irresistible aroma to the fresh ingredients and keeps the health-conscious happy. Peking hot pots and typical Northern dishes are also served. The prawns in chili is zingy and appetizing, and the dumplings are outstanding. ✉ *Kimberley Plaza, 45–47 Kimberley Rd., 1st floor,* ☎ *2369–3435. AE, DC, V.*

TAIWANESE

$ ✕ **Taiwan Beef Noodle.** The rosewood decor belies that this is just a down-to-earth noodle shop. Tasty Taiwanese snacks, dumplings, and noodles are a good way to refuel when shopping in this area. Try the Shanghai-style fried noodles as well as Taiwanese "chop suey." The shop is usually filled with a mix of locals and tourists, but table turnover is quick. ✉ *79–80 Canton Rd.,* ☎ *2892–2168. DC, MC, V.*

SHANGHAI

$–$$ ✕ **Wu Kong Shanghai Restaurant.** This unpretentious hole-in-the-wall
★ serves reasonably priced authentic Shanghainese cuisine. The cold pigeon with wine sauce, arranged in slices forming the shape of a bird, is excellent. Also try the vegetarian goose (bean-curd skin stuffed with vegetables) and imitation crabmeat (fried egg white). ✉ *Alpha House Basement, 27–33 Nathan Rd.,* ☎ *2366–7244. AE, DC, MC, V.*

SZECHUAN

$$ ✕ **Yunyan Szechuan Restaurant.** Szechuan cuisine is known for its burning spiciness, and a visit here can be a taste-bud tolerance test. The first challenge is the complimentary appetizer of spicy bean-curd shreds and peas. If you don't need a sip of tea to relieve your stinging throat, go for the dishes with three or even four chili signs on the menu, like poached sliced beef served in a pungent sauce and bean curd with minced meat and chili. For milder palates, deep-fried fish with sweet and sour sauce is stimulating. Szechuan hot dishes can be very oily, but the cold appetizers are refreshing. Don't forget to try the famous spicy, crispy beef. The beef, frozen and sliced paper-thin, is deep-fried into a crispy snack (imagine Chinese-style potato chips with a beefy flavor). The eggplant with garlic and chili sauce and the sliced chicken with mixed sauce are also highly recommended. For noodle lovers, tell the waiters how spicy you want your noodles to be: mild, hot, or very hot. ✉ *Miramar Shopping Centre, 1 Kimberley Rd., 4th floor,* ☎ *2375–0800. AE, DC, MC, V.*

ASIAN AND WESTERN

$$$$ ✕ **Yu.** This contemporary eatery is not only one of the best seafood restaurants, but one of the best in town in general. Walk in past a huge, curving aquarium inset in the wall, where gorgeous fish swim. The menu allows diners the maximum variety of seafood choices. There are at least six types of oysters, served on ice, glazed with champagne sauce, or prepared in a variety of other ways. There are a dozen or so fresh catches of the day, cooked to suit Asian or Western tastes, as well as East-meets-West specialties like sautéed Boston lobster with black beans and fine noodles. Service is outstanding, and so is the unobstructed view of the harbor and Central Plaza. ⊠ *Regent Hotel, 18 Salisbury Rd.,* ☏ *2721–1211. Reservations essential. AE, DC, MC, V.*

$$$$ ✗ **Felix.** The flagship of the Peninsula Hotel's new extension and designed by Philippe Starck, Felix perches on the 28th floor just beneath a helipad. At night the views of Hong Kong Island through the floor-to-ceiling glass wall are breathtaking. Every nook and cranny in this ultramodern space was touched by the French designer, from chairs bearing the faces of Starck's friends to sexy bathrooms with the best views in Hong Kong. The high-tech atmosphere can be unsettling for some—but its fans hail it as a "brasserie for the 21st century." The menu is also for culinary adventurists. The new Hawaiian chef boldly mixes some odd ingredients; popular items include lobster nachos, seared Sonoma foie gras with ginger-marinated figs, and barbecued lamb chops with gorgonzola risotto. After 9 PM the Felix gets buzzing, as the bar has become a popular place for a young crowd with money to burn. ⊠ *Peninsula Hotel, Salisbury Rd., 28th floor,* ☏ *2366–6251. DC, MC, V.*

CHINESE VEGETARIAN

$$ ✗ **Bodhi Vegetarian.** This small chain of restaurants offers some of the best Chinese vegetarian food in Hong Kong. The diverse selection will probably be a pleasant surprise to Westerners—even vegetarians. A wide array of vegetables, dozens of varieties of mushrooms, bird's nests, and noodles are often combined with tofu, prepared to suggest meat or fish. Try deep-fried taro (a potatolike vegetable) or stir-fried Chinese vegetables. Buddhist scrolls decorating the walls emphasize the philosophical roots of the menu. No alcohol is served. ⊠ *56 Cameron Rd., Tsim Sha Tsui,* ☏ *2739–2222. AE, DC, MC, V.*

$–$$ ✗ **Kung Tak Lam.** Health-conscious palates appreciate the simple Shanghainese vegetarian food here. Don't turn your back when you see the no-frills decor. It's the food that makes this joint so popular. Try the cold noodle plates, which come with an array of sauces to mix and make as sweet or as sour as you want. The bean-curd ravioli also deserves a big thumbs up. Nice prix fixes have unbelievably cheap prices. ⊠ *45–47 Carnarvon Rd., 1st floor,* ☏ *2367–7881. AE, DC, V.*

INDONESIAN

$ ✗ **Bali Restaurant.** This strange little place provides an inexpensive foray into the delights of Indonesian cuisine. There are traditional dishes—*nasi goreng* (fried rice with egg) and *gado gado* (salad with peanut dressing)—but also a whole section of noodles and curries. The curries tend to be tempered with coconut milk, so they're mild and creamy. Service is pretty much a family affair; wave your arms about for attention if they are all busy chatting. It's rarely completely packed, but cozy and well-worn booths ensure a bit of privacy (although the lurid red color may not compel you to stay too long). Off the beaten path and hardly what you'd call posh dining, Bali is nevertheless an interesting option. ⊠ *10 Nanking Rd., Jordan, Tsim Sha Tsui,* ☏ *2780–2902. No credit cards.*

JAPANESE

$$$$ ✗ **Nadaman.** Nadaman is one of the most authentic Japanese restaurants in town, where you can find fresh and succulent sushi and sashimi, sizzling Kobe beef *shabu-shabu* and tempting *teppanyaki.* Take a table seat or head straight to the sushi bar or the teppanyaki room. The exotic green tea or sesame ice cream are tasty finishing touches. ⊠ *Kowloon Shangri-La, 64 Mody Rd., Tsim Sha Tsui,* ☏ *2721–2111, ext. 8371. Reservations essential. AE, DC, MC, V.*

$–$$ ✕ **Great Shanghai Restaurant.** This restaurant isn't esteemed for its decor (which is old and dingy), but it's excellent for culinary adventurers and those who prefer the bold flavors of Shanghai food to the more delicate flavors of local Cantonese fare. You may not be ready for the sea blubber or braised turtle with sugar candy, but do try one of the boneless eel dishes, Shanghai-style yellow fish soup, beggar's chicken, or the excellent spiced soy duck. ⊠ *26 Prat Ave.,* ☎ *2366–8158 or 2366–2683. AE, DC, MC, V.*

European

FRENCH

$$$$ ✕ **Gaddi's.** Named after the Peninsula's first general manager, Leo Gaddi, who restored the hotel to its former glory after the Second World War, this gracious French restaurant has offered one of the top dining experiences in town for the last 40 years. The restaurant was completely refurbished in 1994. With huge chandeliers made in Paris, silver candelabras, and ankle-deep Tai Ping carpets, the decor is opulent and sumptuous. So is the food. Panfried goose liver, with a crispy skin, melts in your mouth. The warm lobster salad, the lobster with cider sauce, and the roast pigeon are also highlights. Don't decline the house soufflé, served in a portion big enough for two. The wine list, both extensive and expensive, has vintages from most parts of the world. ⊠ *Peninsula Hotel, Salisbury Rd.,* ☎ *2366–6251, ext. 3989. Reservations essential. Jacket and tie. AE, DC, MC, V.*

$$$$ ✕ **Plume.** Though serving fine European cuisine, this restaurant also has a tandoor and serves freshly made nan bread with pâté and butter. Highly recommended is the cream of artichoke soup with beluga. Served in a delicate espresso cup, it has been one of their signature dishes since the restaurant opened in 1980. And their wine cellar has a fine collection. The restaurant also features an elegant private dining space, the Baccarat Room, where luxurious tableware from Baccarat, Bernardaud, and Christofle are used. Enjoy a real Dionysian treat with their gorgeous enological glasses, and leave room for the cheese board and desserts like the ginger soufflé. ⊠ *The Regent, Salisbury Rd., Tim Sha Tsui,* ☎ *2721–1211. Reservations essential. Jacket and tie. AE, DC, MC, V.*

ITALIAN

$$$ ✕ **Sabatini.** Run by the Sabatini family, whose eateries in Rome, Japan, and Singapore go by the same name, this location has an unbeatable ambience for a romantic rendezvous. The warm rag-finished walls, wooden furnishings, and impeccable service make it a delightful dining experience. Pick your favorite light starters from the antipasti buffet table and move on to the excellent pasta dishes. The linguine Sabatini, cooked in a marvelous marinara sauce, is a great choice. For a main course, lobster prepared in a special Sabatini way—with lobster juice and tomato sauce—is also good. ⊠ *Royal Garden, 69 Mody Rd., 3rd floor,* ☎ *2733–2000. Reservations essential. AE, DC, V, MC.*

$$–$$$
★ ✕ **Tutto Bene.** The food here is trattoria in style—geared to light meals but with generous portions. The pizzas are great, and pastas come in a variety of shapes and colors (with squid-ink *pappardelle* and linguine). Vegetable fritters are fried in unbelievably light batter. After the food, the best things about this spot are the two areas in which to dine alfresco: in front on the terrace or in back, behind the kitchen, in a quaint garden setting. It's hard to find, so here's some help: Walk up Nathan Road away from the Star Ferry and turn right on Granville Road; turn left on Carnarvon Road and walk to the end, where you'll see a brick path leading up a hill—it looks like it's heading into a park-

ing lot. At the top turn right onto Knutsford Terrace. ⊠ *7 Knutsford Terr.,* ☎ *316–2116. AE, DC, MC, V.*

North American

$$–$$$ ╳ **San Francisco Steak House.** For more than 20 years this mock Barbary Coast eatery has been pleasing both locals and travelers with a combination of casual Bay Area atmosphere—dark paneled walls, red flocked wallpaper, and replicas of Powell Street cable cars—and American fare. The clam chowder is an original Boston recipe, and the cioppino is what you'd expect at Fisherman's Wharf. American Angus steaks are treated with the respect good meat deserves. Also excellent is the Canadian coho baby salmon, served whole. You can always ask for a burger; they're the best in town. All portions are very generous. ⊠ *7 Ashley Rd.,* ☎ *2735–7576. AE, DC, MC, V.*

$$ ╳ **Planet Hollywood.** Come see Jackie Chan's and Sylvester Stallone's handprints, grab a souvenir T-shirt, and enjoy a hilarious movie museum tour. The food, with a range of choices to satisfy both Eastern and Western palates, is satisfying, but it's the outrageous decor (movie pictures, props, and costumes) that packs a bigger bang. ⊠ *3 Canton Rd., Harbour City,* ☎ *2377–7888. AE, DC, MC, V.*

Kowloon City

With its close proximity to the airport, Kowloon City makes a good spot for convenient and authentic culinary treats—Hong Kong style. This neighborhood is very down-to-earth, and locals flock here for cheap, casual, and good meals.

Asian

CANTONESE

$–$$ ╳ **Tso Choi Koon.** If you're a delicate diner and prefer fine food, pass on this Cantonese home-cooking eatery. *Tso Choi* (Rough Dishes) is not everyone's cup of tea. Tripe lovers and haggis fans, however, might like to try the Chinese versions of some of their favorite dishes: Fried pig tripe, fried pig brain (which comes as an omelet), double boiled pig brain.. . . You get the idea. (The old generation in Hong Kong still likes these kinds of dishes while younger generations may demur.) The less adventurous can stick to creamy congee, fried chicken, or a fish fillet. The huge mirror on the wall features local celebrities' autographs, including TV cooking show host Martin Yan. ⊠ *17–19A Nga Tsin Wai Road, Kowloon City,* ☎ *2383–7170. No credit cards.*

THAI

$ ╳ **Golden Orchid Thai Restaurant.** Only a five-minute walk from the Kai Tak Airport is some of the best and most innovative Thai cuisine in the territory. The curry crab and the seafood curry in pumpkin are excellent. Adventurous eaters must not miss *mein come* (a kind of Thai leaf served with little bowls of spices and ingredients such as fried coconut, peanuts, garlic, chili, lime, and dried shrimp). Wrap whatever you want in the leaf and delve in. The steamed seafood cakes, served in Thai-imported stone pots, are also delicious. Try the roasted pork neck slices, prawn cakes, and rice with olives. Unlike most establishments in Hong Kong, the Golden Orchid doesn't insist on a service charge or accept tips, which makes this already cheap place an even bigger bargain. ⊠ *12 Lung Kong Rd., Kowloon City,* ☎ *2383–3076. V.*

Saikung

Saikung, renowned for its seafood restaurants and the neighborhood hill-walking tracks, is a town worth checking out. Many restaurants run adjoining seafood shops, so diners can pick fresh catch from tanks and have it cooked to order—steamed, fried, sautéed, or deep-fried with salt and pepper.

Seafood

$$–$$$ ✕ **San Shui Restaurant.** Just around the corner from the minibus terminal and cab stand, this restaurant clearly stands out, with its bamboo-and-mat decor and its white-and-green-checkered tablecloths. Get an outdoor table and watch the folks prepare their signature dish—bamboo char-grilled fish. The fish is skewered by split bamboo and grilled over a charcoal fire. ⊠ *11–15 Siu Yat Bldg., Saikung,* ☎ *2792–1828. AE, MC, V.*

$$–$$$ ✕ **Chung Thai Food Restaurant and Sea Food.** As its name shows, this seafood corner is best known for both Chinese and Thai cooking, prepared separately by chefs of both nationalities. Those with more spicy palates can try the Thai special fried crabs with curry and fried prawns with chili. Otherwise, pick any seafood you like from the store next door, and the chef can prepare it however you like—steaming is highly recommended for fresh fish as it retains its fresh taste and tender texture. ⊠ *93 Man Nin St., Saikung,* ☎ *2792–1481. Seafood shop,* ⊠ *5 Siu Yat Bldg., Hoi Pong Sq.,* ☎ *2792–8172. MC, V.*

OUTLYING AREAS

Lamma Island

Relatively easy to get to, Lamma Island is served by ferries from Central's pier approximately once an hour. Yung Shue Wan, where you disembark, has a collection of local seafood restaurants, one or two Western ones, and an odd assortment of shops.

Asian

CANTONESE

$ ✕ **Lancombe.** This Cantonese seafood restaurant is Lamma's best source for no-nonsense food at no-nonsense prices. The huge English/Cantonese menu features seafood, seafood, and more seafood. Try deep-fried squid, *garoupa* (a local fish) in sweet corn sauce, broccoli in garlic, and beef with black beans. Dishes come in three sizes; the small is sufficient for most. Go through the front of the restaurant via the kitchen (don't loiter, they're busy in there!) to the terrace out back, where you'll have a view of the sea and distant Peng Chau Island. ⊠ *47 Main St., Yung Shue Wan,* ☎ *2982–0881. No credit cards.*

International

$ ✕ **Deli Lamma.** This trendy but laid-back joint has more style than any other place on Lamma—with a designer bar made from old doors suspended from the ceiling on heavy chains and backgammon and chess boards painted on long tables along one wall, encouraging lazy afternoons with endless cups of coffee. Choose your fancy from two blackboards that will bear up to seven choices of pasta and "world" food—from Thai fish curry to British roasts and Indian curries. Yummy slabs of fresh garlic bread or salad come with your order. Service can be too laid-back, but it's always friendly. ⊠ *36 Main St., ground floor, Yung Shue Wan,* ☎ *2982–1583. No credit cards.*

4 Lodging

Hotel costs in Hong Kong are as steep as the hills, but after a day out amongst the crowds, you'll appreciate the professional service and cordial attention that accompany the expense.

ALTHOUGH MANY TOURISTS RUSHED to visit the territory during the last days of British rule in 1997, Hong Kong's status as a financial and business center and a gateway to the rest of China remains a strong attraction, especially to business travelers. In 1998 the new airport in Chek Lap Kok is due to open, as are the surrounding hotels. By the year 2000 at least seven new hotels are expected to provide thousands of new rooms.

Accommodations are very expensive in Hong Kong. Most hotels provide five-star amenities like magnificent views and high-tech facilities—and strive to please businesspeople with expense accounts at their disposal. To find a guest room for less than US$120 is difficult; expect to pay at least US$150 a night for a room of normal international standards. For that price you won't have a prime location, but you will have basic and reliable facilities—color TV, radio, telephone, same-day valet laundry service, room service, secretarial service, safe deposit box, refrigerator and minibar, and air-conditioning. Most hotels also have at least one restaurant and bar, a travel and tour-booking desk, and limousine or car rental.

Of course, Hong Kong *is* a business executive's paradise. Most major hotels have business centers that provide secretarial, translation, courier, telex, fax, and printing services—even personal computers (charges vary from hotel to hotel so check prices before renting). Executive floors or clubs have become a standard perk in well-established hotels. Typically these floors have extra concierge services, complimentary breakfasts and cocktails, express check-in, personalized stationery, a well-equipped business center, and an area for guests to meet with their business contacts. Many hotels have ballrooms, and most have smaller meeting and conference rooms. For an overview of Hong Kong meeting, convention, and incentive facilities, contact the **Convention and Incentive Department** (⊠ Hong Kong Tourist Association, 10/F, Citicorp Centre, 18 Whitfield Rd., North Point, Hong Kong Island, ☎ 2807–6543).

Book your rooms well in advance for a trip to Hong Kong, especially in March and from September through early December, the high seasons of conventions and conferences. Some hotels offer attractive seasonal packages, and it is usually less expensive to book through a travel agent.

The **Hong Kong Tourist Association** (HKTA) publishes a *Hotel Guide,* listing members' rates, services, and facilities. The brochure is published once a year, making it at least one price hike behind. The HKTA does not arrange hotel reservations. The Hong Kong Hotel Association (HKHA) does, at no extra charge but only through its reservations office at Kai Tak International Airport, which is immediately beyond the customs area; there will also be an office at the new airport.

Choosing where to stay in Hong Kong depends on the purpose of your visit. Thanks to the three tunnels that run underneath the harbor, the Star Ferry, and the Mass Transit Railway (MTR) subway, it no longer matters whether you stay "Hong Kong side" or "Kowloon side": The other side is only minutes away by MTR.

If you want to avoid the main tourist accommodation areas, there are a few alternatives, all in the New Territories and outlying islands, which are also generally less expensive than lodgings on Hong Kong Island or in Kowloon.

Our categories for hotel rates are based on the average price for a standard double room for two people; a single person in a double room will get a slightly lower rate. Prices will be higher for a larger room or for a room with a view. All rates are subject to a 10% service charge and a 5% government tax, which is used to fund the activities of the HKTA. Accommodations are listed by three geographical areas—Hong Kong Island, Kowloon, and New Territories and the Outer Islands— and are alphabetical within each price category.

The 800 numbers listed below are for use in the United States.

CATEGORY	COST*
$$$$	over HK$2,500 (US$310)
$$$	HK$1,800–HK$2,500 (US$225–US$310)
$$	HK$1,200–HK$1,800 (US$150–US$225)
$	under HK$1,200 (US$150)

All prices are for a double room, not including 10% service charge and 5% tax.

HONG KONG ISLAND

If you need to be near the city's financial hub, you'll prefer the Central District, on Hong Kong Island, but will pay for the convenience and views. Central is as busy as New York City on weekdays, but except for the Lan Kwai Fong area, it is quiet at night and on weekends. Wanchai, east of Central, was once a sailor's dream of Suzie Wong types and booze. It still has plenty of nightlife, but new office high-rises and the Convention and Exhibition Centre now draw businesspeople. Causeway Bay, farther east, is an ideal area for shopping or sampling lots of different restaurants. Happy Valley is near the racetrack and Hong Kong Stadium, the territory's largest sports stadium. Hotels have also sprung up farther east along the MTR line in residential North Point and Taikoo Shing.

Central

$$$$ 🏨 **Conrad International.** This luxurious business hotel resides in a gleaming white oval-shape tower rising from Pacific Place, an upscale complex with a multistory mall on the edge of Central. The rooms, in the top 21 floors of the 61-story building, have dramatic views of the harbor and city. In each room or suite, guests are welcomed by a Conrad teddy bear upon turn-down, and a rubber ducky in the bathroom adds another homey touch. On-staff masseurs can massage you in the comfort of your own room on request. The four floors of executive rooms have in-room Internet access (which also provides E-mail access), fax machines, and even personal step machines. Brasserie on the Eighth restaurant is popular for its French fare and views of the park; Nicholini's is one of the city's top spots for Italian cuisine (☞ Chapter 3). ⊠ *Pacific Place, 88 Queensway,* ☎ *2521–3838, 800/445–8667 in the U.S.,* ℻ *2521–3888. 513 rooms, 58 suites. 4 restaurants, bar and lounge, pool, health club, business services. AE, DC, MC, V.*

$$$$ 🏨 **Furama.** In the heart of Central and popular with business travelers, this hotel has been one of the best known in the territory for 25 years. For the past three years Furama has been the official lodging for international teams competing in the spring Rugby Sevens. Last year players, managers, and coaches took up more than 350 rooms. For beautiful views of either Chater Garden and Victoria Peak or city hall and Victoria Harbor, ask for a room above the 17th floor. The revolving rooftop restaurant and bar offer the ultimate panorama, as well as a spectacular daily lunch and dinner buffet of Chinese, Japanese, and Western dishes. Its wine room is stocked with hundreds of wines to be sam-

pled by bottle or glass. On the ground floor a bakery sells delicious snacks to famished shoppers. ⊠ *1 Connaught Rd.,* ☎ *2525–5111, 800/ 426–3135 in the U.S.,* FAX *2845–9339. 473 rooms, 43 suites. 5 restaurants, bar and lounge, 3 no-smoking floors, health club, shops, business services. AE, DC, MC, V.*

$$$$ ⊞ **Island Shangri-La.** Within the Pacific Place complex, this hotel
★ sparkles with more than 780 dazzling Austrian crystal chandeliers; no matter where you go, these opulent decorations hang overhead—in the lobby, in the restaurants, and in every single room. This deluxe hotel has a fantastic view of both the harbor and the Peak and also has the world's largest Chinese landscape painting, *The Great Motherland of China* (16 stories high), which took six months for the 40 artists from Beijing to create. Rooms are on the 39th to 55th floor, are classy and sophisticated, and surround the atrium where the painting hangs. Extralarge desks in each room are handy for business travelers, who can also plug in notebook computers readily. You can eat very well at the renowned French eatery Petrus and the imperial Chinese outlet Summer Palace (☞ Chapter 3). The pool and health club overlook Hong Kong Park. ⊠ *Supreme Court Rd., 2 Pacific Place, 88 Queensway,* ☎ *2877–3838, 800/942–5050 in the U.S.,* FAX *2521–8742. 565 rooms. 4 restaurants, bar and lounge, 4 no-smoking floors, pool, barbershop, beauty salon, health club, shops, business services. AE, DC, MC, V.*

$$$$ ⊞ **J. W. Marriott.** This elegant American-style hotel was the first to open at Pacific Place. A box-shape 27-story building, it has an extravagant glass-walled atrium lobby filled with plants and a cascading waterfall. Rooms have harbor and mountain views and endless amenities, including data ports for modem or fax machines and 50 pay movies on demand. J. W.'s serves popular California cuisine (☞ Chapter 3), and function rooms suitable for a variety of events are convenient for business travelers. There is a well-equipped 24-hour gym. ⊠ *Pacific Place, 88 Queensway,* ☎ *2810–3000, 800/228–9290 in the U.S.,* FAX *2845–0737. 604 rooms, 27 suites. 3 restaurants, 2 bars and lounge, pool, health club, business services. AE, DC, MC, V.*

$$$$ ⊞ **Mandarin Oriental.** Celebrated by travel writers as one of the world's
★ great hotels, the Mandarin Oriental represents Hong Kong's high end, serving the well-heeled and the business elite since 1963. It has balconies off most rooms—although many have lost their harbor view as reclamation has moved the hotel back from the waterfront. Take the opportunity to greet Robert Chan, who has been guarding the prestigious entranceway for more than two decades. The vast lobby is decorated with Asian antiques, and a live band performs in the mezzanine Clipper Lounge early in the evening. Comfortable guest rooms have antique maps and prints, traditional wooden furnishings, Eastern knickknacks, and accents of black-and-gold glamour. The well-mannered staff provides extremely efficient service. Man Wah, on the 25th floor, serves Cantonese cuisine in a genteel atmosphere (☞ Chapter 3). Centrally located beside the Star Ferry concourse, the Mandarin is rightfully the choice of many celebrities and VIPs. Read the thoughtful good-night note left on your pillow by the turn-down service; it may give you a sweet dream. ⊠ *5 Connaught Rd.,* ☎ *2522—0111, 800/ 526–6566 in the U.S.,* FAX *2810–6190. 489 rooms, 58 suites. 4 restaurants, 3 bars, indoor pool, barbershop, beauty salon, health club, business services. AE, DC, MC, V.*

$$$$ ⊞ **Ritz-Carlton.** Next to the Furama on the prime block between Chater
★ and Connaught roads, the Ritz makes its relatively small self stand out with a sophisticated exterior recalling art deco New York. The interior has an elegant, refined atmosphere created by European antiques and reproductions mixed with Asian accents. Everything from Chippendale-style furniture to gilt-frame mirrors is spotless and shining. The

Lodging

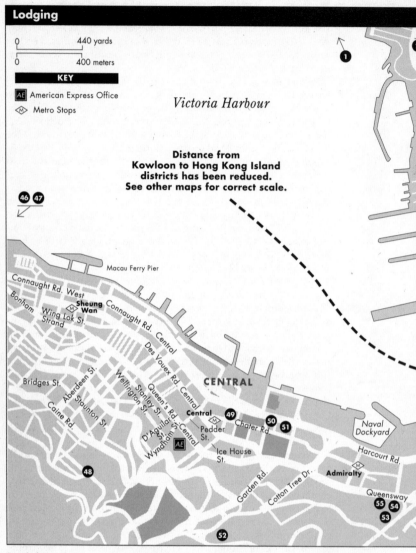

| 0 | 440 yards |
| 0 | 400 meters |

KEY

AE American Express Office

M Metro Stops

Victoria Harbour

Distance from Kowloon to Hong Kong Island districts has been reduced. See other maps for correct scale.

Macau Ferry Pier

Connaught Rd. West

Bonham Strand

Wing Lok St.

Sheung Wan

Connaught Rd. Central

Des Voeux Rd. Central

Bridges St.

Aberdeen St.

Staunton St.

Caine Rd.

Wellington St.

Stanley St.

Queen's Rd. Central

D'Aguilar St.

Wyndham St.

CENTRAL

Central

Pedder St.

Ice House St.

Chater Rd.

Garden Rd.

Cotton Tree Dr.

Admiralty

Naval Dockyard

Harcourt Rd.

Queensway

Bangkok Royal, **15**

Beach Resort Hotel, **19**

Bishop Lei International House, **48**

Booth Lodge, **5**

BP International House, **13**

Caritas Bianchi Lodge, **6**

Century, **60**

Cheung Chau Warwick, **46**

City Garden, **69**

Concourse, **8**

Conrad International, **53**

Eaton, **10**

Emperor Byron Hotel, **62**

The Excelsior, **66**

Furama, **51**

Garden View International House, **52**

Gold Coast, **1**

Grand Hyatt, **59**

Grand Plaza, **63**

Grand Stanford Harbour View, **36**

Grand Tower, **7**

Guangdong, **24**

Harbour Plaza, **20**

Harbour View International House, **57**

Holiday Inn Golden Mile, **30**

Holy Carpenter Church Guest House, **17**

Hong Kong Renaissance, **28**

Hongkong, **39**

Hotel Nikko, **37**

Hyatt Regency, **29**

Imperial, **31**

International, **23**

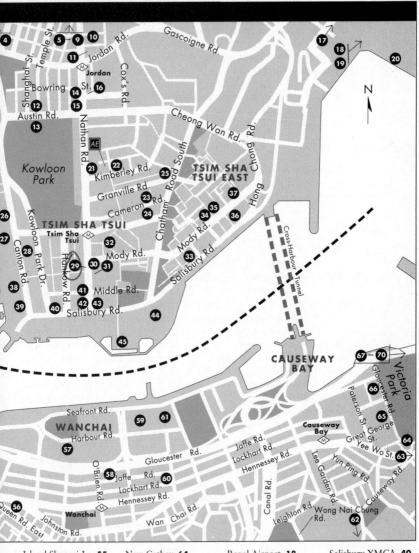

Island Shangri-La, **55**
J.W. Marriot, **54**
Kowloon, **41**
Kowloon Panda, **2**
Kowloon
Shangri-La, **33**
Luk Kwok, **58**
Majestic, **11**
Mandarin Oriental, **49**
Marco Polo, **27**
Metropole, **9**
Miramar, **21**
New Astor, **32**

New Cathay, **64**
Newton, **68**
New World, **45**
New World Harbour
View, **61**
Park Lane, **65**
Pearl Seaview, **12**
Peninsula, **42**
Prince, **26**
Prudential, **16**
Ramada Hotel
Kowloon, **25**

Regal Airport, **18**
Regal Hongkong
Hotel, **67**
Regal Kowloon, **35**
Regal Riverside, **3**
The Regent, **44**
Ritz-Carlton, **50**
Royal Garden, **34**
Royal Pacific, **38**
Royal Park, **4**

Salisbury YMCA, **40**
Shamrock, **14**
Sheraton Hong Kong
Hotel and Towers, **43**
Silvermine Beach
Hotel, **47**
South China, **70**
The Wesley, **56**
Windsor, **22**

large guest rooms, all with marble bath, honor bar, and colonial-style rosewood furniture, overlook either Victoria Harbor or Chater Garden. The main restaurant, Toscana, serves northern Italian cuisine, and a special macrobiotic dining program is available in the coffee shop and on the room service menu. The Executive Business Center has Internet and E-mail access as well as computer workstations and color printers. ⊠ *Connaught Rd.,* ☎ *2877–6666, 800/241–3333 in the U.S.,* FAX *2877–6778. 216 rooms and suites. 5 restaurants, bar, lounge, no-smoking floors, pool, health club, shops, business services. AE, DC, MC. V.*

Midlevels

$$ 🏨 **Bishop Lei International House.** Owned and operated by the Catholic diocese, this guest house is in a residential area of the Midlevels. Rooms are clean and functional, and half have a harbor view. The clientele tends to be church groups, academics, and students. It has a fully-equipped business center, a workout room, a pool, and a restaurant serving Chinese and Western meals. ⊠ *4 Robinson Rd.,* ☎ *2868–0828,* FAX *2868–1551. 123 rooms, 80 suites. Restaurant, pool, exercise room, business services. AE, DC, MC, V.*

$ 🏨 **Garden View International House.** This attractive, cylindrical guest
★ house on a hill overlooking the botanical gardens and harbor is run by the YWCA. It has well-designed rooms that make excellent use of small, irregular shapes and emphasize the picture windows. If you want to do your own cooking, ask for a suite with a kitchenette (with microwave oven). Otherwise, there is a coffee shop serving European and Asian dishes. Guests can also use the swimming pool and gymnasium in the adjoining YWCA. Garden View is a five-minute drive (Bus 12A or Minibus 1A) from Central and just a few minutes from the Peak Tram station. ⊠ *1 MacDonnell Rd.,* ☎ *2877–3737,* FAX *2845–6263. 130 rooms and suites. Coffee shop, pool, business services. AE, DC, MC, V.*

Wanchai

$$$$ 🏨 **Grand Hyatt.** No expense was spared in building this opulent black-
★ marble-faced hotel, which adjoins the Hong Kong Convention Centre. The art deco lobby is graced by a hand-painted ceiling by Italian artist Paola Dindo. The Italian Grissini and Cantonese One Harbour Road restaurants are notable (☞ Chapter 3), and the ground-floor breakfast buffet is a decadent feast. The restaurants are popular with locals, who also line up to get into JJ's, the nightclub and disco. Seventy percent of the guest rooms have harbor views, while the remaining ones overlook the 11th-floor pool, garden, and vast recreation deck shared by the New World Harbour View. The business center features an IBM room with IBM's latest technology and software, and access to Reuters Business Briefing is available. The Grand Hyatt is close to the Wanchai Star Ferry, yet its location assures less foot traffic than other high-profile hotels. Perhaps that's why Sir Andrew Lloyd Webber stayed here when his musical *Cats* came to town and why celebrities like Luciano Pavarotti, Cindy Crawford, Sylvester Stallone, and Bruce Willis sign the guest list. ⊠ *1 Harbour Rd.,* ☎ *2588–1234, 800/233–1234 in the U.S.,* FAX *2802–0677. 536 rooms, 36 suites. 4 restaurants, bar and lounge, pool, beauty salon, driving range, 2 tennis courts, exercise room, nightclub. AE, DC, MC, V.*

$$$ 🏨 **Century.** This 23-story hotel is ideal for conventioneers—it's a five-minute walk by covered overpass (a lifesaver in steamy summer months) from the convention center and the MTR. The hotel caters to business travelers, offering a well-equipped business center and executive floors.

Rooms are modern, with wooden furniture painted in pastels. The 24-hour coffee shop is in keeping with Wanchai's nightlife reputation. It also features a health club with an open-air pool, a gymnasium, and a golf driving bay. There is also a popular independently run Shanghainese restaurant and a karaoke lounge within the complex. ⊠ *238 Jaffe Rd.*, ☎ *2598–8888*, ℻ *2598–8866. 492 rooms, 24 suites. 4 restaurants, bar, 4 no-smoking floors, pool, health club, shops, business services. AE, DC, MC, V.*

$$–$$$ 🏨 **Luk Kwok.** This contemporary hotel and office tower designed by Hong Kong's leading architect Remo Riva has replaced the Wanchai landmark of the same name immortalized in Richard Mason's novel, *The World of Suzie Wong.* Luk Kwok's appeal is its proximity to the Convention Centre, the Academy for Performing Arts, and the Arts Centre. Room decor is clean and simple, with contemporary furniture; higher floors afford mountain or city views. It has a good Chinese restaurant but no bar. ⊠ *72 Gloucester Rd.*, ☎ *2866–2166*, ℻ *2866–2622. 194 rooms, 2 suites. 2 restaurants, 1 no-smoking floor, business services. AE, DC, MC, V.*

$$$ 🏨 **New World Harbour View.** Sharing the Convention Centre complex with the Grand Hyatt is this more modest but equally attractive hotel. Guest rooms are moderate size and have modern decor with plenty of beveled-glass mirrors. Right above the Convention Centre, 65% of the rooms offer a panoramic harbor and airport view. There are fax machines in every guest room. Amenities include excellent Chinese and Western restaurants, a cozy bar, pools, gardens, jogging trails, tennis courts, and health club facilities on the recreation deck between the two hotels. The free-form pool is Hong Kong's largest, complete with lagoons and an alfresco dining area near it. The lobby lounge is a popular rendezvous for local and visiting businesspeople. ⊠ *1 Harbour Rd.*, ☎ *2802–8888 or 2731–3488*, ℻ *2802–8833 or 2721–0741. 809 rooms, 53 suites. 3 restaurants, 2 bars, 9 no-smoking floors, pool, barbershop, beauty salon, health club, shops, business services. AE, DC, MC, V.*

$$ 🏨 **The Wesley.** Opened in 1992 on the site of the old Soldiers and Sailors Home, this 21-story moderately (for Hong Kong) priced hotel is a short walk from the Convention Centre, the Academy for Performing Arts, and the MTR. The rooms are small but pleasantly furnished, and the corner "suites" have alcove work areas—very convenient for businesspeople. A tram stop is outside the door, and Pacific Place is close by, as are the bars of Wanchai. ⊠ *22 Hennessy Rd.*, ☎ *2866–6688*, ℻ *2866–6613. 251 rooms. Restaurant, coffee shop. AE, DC, MC, V.*

$–$$ 🏨 **Harbour View International House.** This waterfront YMCA property offers small but clean and relatively inexpensive accommodations close to the Wanchai Star Ferry Pier. The best rooms face the harbor. It's a good bargain for travelers who plan to attend cultural events in the evenings; the Arts Centre and Academy for Performing Arts is next door. Opposite Harbour View is the Convention and Exhibition Centre, the most popular venue for large-scale exhibitions and conferences in the territory. The hostel provides free shuttle service to Causeway Bay and the Central Star Ferry. ⊠ *4 Harbour Rd.*, ☎ *2802–0111*, ℻ *2802–9063. 320 rooms. Restaurant. AE, DC, MC, V.*

Causeway Bay

$$$$ 🏨 **Park Lane.** This elegant hotel, with an imposing facade reminiscent of London's Knightsbridge area, overlooks Victoria Park and backs onto one of Hong Kong Island's busiest shopping, entertainment, and business areas. The lobby is extraordinarily spacious, and all rooms have luxurious marble bathrooms, elegant handcrafted furniture, and marvelous views of the harbor or Victoria Park, or both. The rooftop restaurant has a panoramic view and serves international cuisine with a touch of Asian flavor. Those who can't resist the shopping temptation may never find time to use the well-equipped fitness center, but they will probably have enough exercise walking the two-floor shopping arcade. There are 17 retail outlets including designer boutiques such as agnes b, Enrico Coveri, and Perry Ellis. ⊠ *310 Gloucester Rd.,* ☎ *2890–3355,* ℻ *2576–7853. 775 rooms, 29 suites. 2 restaurants, bar, 5 no-smoking floors, beauty salon, health club, shops, business services. AE, DC, MC, V.*

$$$$ 🖼 **Regal Hongkong Hotel.** The slightly over-the-top decor in this 33-story hotel leans toward European, with masses of marble and a dramatic lobby with high windows, Louis XIV furniture, and a huge mural depicting a Mediterranean scene. The front desk area is small but doesn't affect the efficient service. Gilded elevators lead to guest rooms with maple-inlay furniture crafted by local artisans, walls and carpets in muted earth tones, and brightly colored bedspreads. Bathrooms are spacious, with triangular tubs. There are four executive floors. The dining rooms are sumptuous, especially the top-floor Mediterranean restaurant, with great views of Victoria Park. The rooftop pool and terrace is an escape from the hustle and bustle of the area. Close to the Hong Kong Stadium and the Happy Valley race course, as well as the city's most popular shopping area, this deluxe hotel is one of the most convenient spots to stay. ⊠ *88 Yee Wo St.,* ☎ *2890–6633, 800/222–8888 in the U.S.,* ℻ *2881–0777. 393 rooms, 32 suites. 4 restaurants, bar and lounge, 3 no-smoking floors, pool, health club, shops, business services. AE, DC, MC, V.*

$$$ 🖼 **The Excelsior.** The Excelsior opened in 1974 and remains one of the
★   city's most popular hotels. It is a veteran that readily adapts to the changing demands of the group and business markets. Eighty percent of the rooms enjoy a splendid sea view, including the Hong Kong Yacht Club's neatly aligned yachts and boats. The location is ideal for shopping and dining. At Talk Of The Town, the top-floor restaurant-cum-bar-cum-nightclub you can sample a creative East-meets-West cuisine while listening to live music. The fitness-minded will appreciate the rooftop tennis courts, the well-equipped gym, and the jogging track in adjacent Victoria Park. Of course, business travelers are well provided for. On a historical note, the hotel sits on the first plot of land auctioned by the British government when Hong Kong became a colony in 1841. ⊠ *281 Gloucester Rd.,* ☎ *2894–8888,* ℻ *2895–6459. 875 rooms, 22 suites. 4 restaurants, 2 bars, 5 no-smoking floors, indoor tennis court, beauty salon, health club, shops, business services. AE, DC, MC, V.*

$ 🖼 **New Cathay.** A Chinese-managed hotel close to Victoria Park, this hotel is fairly basic and is favored by Asian tour groups and Westerners on a budget. Rooms are very small but have the necessities of air-conditioning, TV, and tea- and coffeemakers. ⊠ *17 Tung Lo Wan Rd.,* ☎ *2577–8211,* ℻ *2576–9365. 225 rooms and 3 suites. 2 restaurants. AE, DC, MC, V.*

Happy Valley

$$ 🖼 **Emperor Byron Hotel.** Opened in July 1996, this new kid on the block is the most convenient spot for horse-racing fanatics. It is just a few minutes' walk to the Happy Valley racetrack and 5–10 minutes by taxi to the Causeway Bay shopping area. The hotel mainly caters to business and corporate travelers. Corridors are narrow, and rooms are clean and functional. ⊠ *1A Wang Tak St.,* ☎ *2893–9406,* ℻ *2834–6700.*

157 rooms, 1 suite. 2 restaurants, bar, business services. AE, DC, MC, V.

Quarry Bay

$$–$$$ ⊞ **Grand Plaza.** This hotel, part of a large residential-commercial-entertainment complex, is a little out of the way, but it's connected to the Taikoo MTR station and has enough space for a vast recreational club with a huge pool, squash courts, a billiard room, a gymnasium, an aerobics hall, a miniature golf course, a playground, and a jogging track. There are evening barbecues on the garden terrace, an upmarket coffee shop, and extensive shopping in the adjoining Jusco department store. ⊠ *2 Kornhill Rd.,* ☎ *2886–0011,* FAX *2886–1738. 208 rooms and 40 suites. 3 restaurants, indoor pool, tennis court, miniature golf, health club, squash courts, badminton, billiards, business services. AE, DC, MC, V.*

North Point

$$ ⊞ **City Garden.** Although not as close to the MTR as its brochure suggests, this hotel has the advantage of being easily accessible to the Eastern Corridor Expressway, which links Causeway Bay to Taikoo Shing and the Eastern Harbour crossing. Rooms are basic and rather small. The hotel caters to Asian tour groups and has a good Cantonese restaurant. ⊠ *9 City Garden Rd.,* ☎ *2887–2888,* FAX *2887–1111. 611 rooms, 2 suites. 2 restaurants, pool, sauna, health club, business services. AE, DC, MC, V.*

$$ ⊞ **Newton.** In a boxy high-rise that is functional yet relatively featureless, this hotel's advantages are its nearness to the Fortress Hill MTR station and its pleasant bar-restaurant, which has live entertainment. Rooms are small but adequate. ⊠ *218 Electric Rd.,* ☎ *2807–2333,* FAX *2807–1221. 354 rooms, 8 suites. Restaurant, bar and lounge, coffee shop, pool, sauna, business services. AE, DC, MC, V.*

$$ ⊞ **South China.** Managed by a mainland Chinese company and so naturally attracting groups from mainland China, this is a small, functional hotel, with a large Chinese restaurant and bar. It is some distance from the Wanchai MTR. ⊠ *67 Java Rd.,* ☎ *2503–1168,* FAX *2512–8698. 204 rooms. 2 restaurants, business services. AE, DC, MC, V.*

KOWLOON

Most hotels in Hong Kong are on the Kowloon Peninsula, which includes Tsim Sha Tsui, Tsim Sha Tsui East, Harbour City, and the Yau Ma Tei and Mong Kok districts, just north of Tsim Sha Tsui. The fabled Golden Mile of shopping on Nathan Road runs through Tsim Sha Tsui. Back streets are filled with restaurants, stores, and hotels.

Tsim Sha Tsui East is a grid of modern office blocks (many with restaurants or nightclubs) and luxury hotels. This area has been created on land reclaimed from the harbor in the last decade, so none of the hotels is very old. Hung Hom includes a noisy old residential area and a recently developed private housing complex with cinemas and shops.

North of Tsim Sha Tsui are Yau Ma Tei and Mong Kok, which have more of the older, smaller, moderately priced hotels. Most are on or very near Nathan Road and are probably the best bets for economy-minded visitors. Excellent bus service and the MTR make it possible to reach the center of Tsim Sha Tsui quickly.

Hung Hom

$$$ 🏨 **Harbour Plaza.** Opened in summer 1995, this 20-story glass-clad hotel can well claim unique harbor views—it is the first hotel in the recently developed Hung Hom waterfront area, between the railroad terminus and the airport. There's a terrific view of Victoria Harbour, the South China Sea, the airport, the Eastern Corridor, and even the fishing folk at the waterfront. Hotel buses shuttle all day to and from the airport and Tsim Sha Tsui; the railway station where trains leave for China is five minutes away. The atrium lobby is spacious and well designed, with good harbor views from lounges on two levels. Rooms are large and contemporary. For dining there are a Japanese *robatayaki* barbecue, a Cantonese restaurant, a Western grill, and a fun pub called the Pit Stop, which features actual racing cars. The opulent hotel also has a large, scenic rooftop pool as well as a fitness center and health spa. ⊠ *20 Tak Fung St., Hung Hom, Kowloon,* ☎ *2621–3188,* 📠 *2621–3311. 385 rooms, 30 suites. 4 restaurants, lounge and pub, pool, beauty salon, health club, shops, business services. AE, DC, MC, V.*

$ 🏨 **Holy Carpenter Church Guest House.** In the center of the discount shopping and industrial district of Hung Hom, this small, 18-year-old hostel is close to the Kai Tak airport and train station. It is mostly used by budget travelers who are able to book at least a month in advance and just want a place to sleep. ⊠ *1 Dyer Ave., Hunghom,* ☎ *2362–0301,* 📠 *2362–2193. 14 rooms. MC, V.*

Kowloon City

$$$$ 🏨 **Regal Airport.** A three-minute stroll through an air-conditioned walkway leads you from Regal to Kai Tak Airport's customs area. It's the perfect place to stay if you're moving on quickly or have airport-related business (there is a half-price day-use discount for transit passengers). But remember, Kai Tak will close once the new aiport at Chek Lap Kok opens in April 1998. The best rooms face the airport as does the Five Continents restaurant, where you get excellent international meals and marvelous picture-window views. Wash down a cocktail at the top-floor Flying Machine Bar, which also provides a superb harbor and airport view and live music. All rooms are fully soundproofed. A regular shuttle bus transports guests from the hotel to Nathan Road or the Tsim Sha Tsui East business and shopping areas. ⊠ *30 Sa Po Rd.,* ☎ *2718–0333,* 📠 *2718–4111. 368 rooms, 21 suites. 4 restaurants, lounge, pub, no-smoking floors, barbershop, beauty salon, shops, business services. AE, DC, MC, V.*

Tsim Sha Tsui

$$$$ 🏨 **Hyatt Regency.** Its white facade, ground-floor shopping arcade, and dramatic marble-and-teak lobby exude glamour. The Buddhist Gods of Hospitality guarding the spacious lobby's reception area are meant to give visitors warm blessings and ensure them a nice stay. The hotel has a gallery of Asian antiques and the award-winning Chinese Restaurant (☞ Chapter 3). The hotel is five minutes from the Star Ferry and next door to the Tsim Sha Tsui MTR station. ⊠ *67 Nathan Rd., Tsim Sha Tsui,* ☎ *2311–1234, 800/233–1234 in the U.S.,* 📠 *2739–8701. 706 rooms, 17 suites. 4 restaurants, coffee shop, no-smoking rooms, shops, business services. AE, DC, MC, V.*

$$$$ 🏨 **Peninsula.** The Pen is a legend—not merely for its opulent and
★   deluxe facilities but for its 70-year history; this grand old lady was established on December 11, 1928. She has won over the world's classiest guests—celebrities like Warren Beatty, Charlie Chaplin, Muhammed Ali, Ronald Reagan and the Princess of Wales. Just like a grandmother,

the Pen has witnessed the changes of the territory—it had the most glorious time before it became a shelter for refugees during World War II and was later taken over by the Japanese to become an elegant military headquarters. The Pen is one of the most famous hotels in the world—and regarded as one of the best. Its taste and old-world style are evident everywhere: colonial architecture, a columned and gilt-corniced lobby where high tea is served (a prestigious rendezvous in town), a fleet of Rolls-Royces, attentive room valets, and luxurious bath accessories. In 1994 the Pen added a 30-story tower with twin helipads. The 132 spacious new guest rooms and suites are decorated with the same classically European deep blue, gold, and ivory fabrics; Chinese prints and furniture provide a subtle Eastern accent. All rooms feature silent fax machines and the Pen's famous shoe box (staff will retrieve the shoes through the opening from the corridor and have them cleaned). A superb spa houses a Roman-style pool, a sundeck, a Jacuzzi, a sauna, and a steam bath to treat you like royalty. The hotel houses Gaddi's, one of the finest restaurants in town, and the poshest of the posh rooftop restaurants, Felix (☞ Chapter 3). What more can we say. ✉ *Salisbury Rd., Tsim Sha Tsui,* ☎ *2366–6251,* ℻ *2722–4170. 246 rooms, 54 suites. 7 restaurants, bar, pool, beauty salon, health club, shops, business services, helipad. AE, DC, MC, V.*

$$$$ 🏨 **The Regent.** This first-class hotel is for those who want nothing but
★ the best. The elegantly modern Regent, on the southernmost tip of Tsim Sha Tsui, offers luxurious guest rooms and spectacular harbor views from the very edge of the waterfront. Glittering trees and shrubs at the hotel's entrance light up light up, creating a Christmas-like ambience each night, and bellboys clad in spotless white mark the prelude of a classy stay. Rooms are spacious and bright, delicately decorated in a sophisticated and contemporary style. Thick carpet, glass-top working desks and comfy beds, together with dignified and helpful service, assure travelers the comforts of home. Take advantage of the hotel's Jacuzzi and renowned spa and massage treatments. The East-meets-West seafood restaurant Yu and the fine dining room Plume are standouts in Hong Kong (☞ Chapter 3). Club Shanghai recaptures the atmosphere of a Shanghai nightclub in the 1920s and '30s. The hotel's Rolls Royce and Mercedes limo fleet and the largest privately owned collection of Daimler limos outside the United Kingdom will you chauffeur you on request. ✉ *18 Salisbury Rd., Tsim Sha Tsui,* ☎ *2721–1211, 800/545–4000 in the U.S.,* ℻ *2739–4546. 508 rooms, 94 suites. 5 restaurants, pool, health club, shops, business services. AE, DC, MC, V.*

$$$$ 🏨 **Sheraton Hong Kong Hotel and Towers.** This Sheraton, with a trademark four-floor atrium lobby, is across the street from the Space Museum, at the south end of the fabled Golden Mile. Guest rooms are done in soft pastels and contemporary furniture and offer a choice of harbor, city, or courtyard views. Make sure you visit the rooftop pool and terrace via the exterior glass elevator, and Someplace Else, an art deco café popular as a happy-hour hangout. Fitness facilities are state of the art. ✉ *20 Nathan Rd., Tsim Sha Tsui,* ☎ *2369–1111, 800/334–8484 in the U.S.,* ℻ *2739–8707. 806 rooms, 26 suites. 6 restaurants, 2 no-smoking floors, pool, health club, shops, business services. AE, DC, MC, V.*

$$$–$$$$ 🏨 **Holiday Inn Golden Mile.** On the Golden Mile of Nathan Road, the hub of Kowloon's business and shopping area, this business-style hotel has been popular for more than 20 years. It was recently refurbished, and the exterior has a contemporary architectural style that allows sweeping views of Nathan Road. Cafe Vienna, with floor-to-ceiling windows, is decorated with potted plants and trees, and has an oasislike ambience. The café can feed you day and night with its lunch and dinner buffets, à la carte menu, afternoon tea, and late-night buffet. ⊠ *50 Nathan Rd., Tsim Sha Tsui,* ☎ *2369–3111, 800/465–4329 in the U.S.,* FAX *2369–8016. 591 rooms, 9 suites. 3 restaurants, bar and lounge, 100 no-smoking rooms, pool, health club, shops, business services. AE, DC, MC, V.*

$$$–$$$$ ⊞ **Hongkong.** German tourists might raise a glass to this hotel's promi-
   ★   nent and outrageous Oktoberfest celebration. It holds the record for hosting the largest of such gatherings—up to 1,000 each night during the festive month. A member of Marco Polo hotels (formerly known as Omni hotels), it is also renowned for its evening entertainment at Gripps, an American-style bar and restaurant, which features impersonation bands such as the Australian Beatles, Babba, and an Elvis Presley impersonator. The hotel is in the wharf-side Harbour City complex, next to the Star Ferry, along with its sister hotels the Marco Polo and the Prince. The complex houses offices, shopping malls, movie theaters and restaurants and is close to pop-culture landmarks Hard Rock Cafe and Planet Hollywood. All fun aside, the Hongkong has an excellent reputation with business travelers for efficiency. ⊠ *Harbour City, Tsim Sha Tsui,* ☎ *2113–0088, 800/843–6664 in the U.S.,* FAX *2113–0011. 621 rooms, 44 suites. 6 restaurants, lounge, no-smoking floor, pool, barbershop, beauty salon, shops, business services. AE, DC, MC, V.*

$$$–$$$$ ⊞ **Hong Kong Renaissance.** The lobby of this 19-story building is newly redecorated with black-and-white marble and onyx columns, an intricate gilt railing on the grand staircase, a new barrel-vault ceiling, and custom-made rock-crystal chandeliers—radiating an opulent but intimate ambience. Guest rooms are spacious and tasteful, and the best (and more expensive) have harbor views. The Bostonian restaurant has a great selection of American seafood dishes, and you'll have fun with the crayons and huge drawing paper on the tables. The best drawings each month are framed on the wall. Asian palates will love the innovative and delicately presented Chinese dishes at T'ang Court. All suites and rooms on Renaissance Club executive floors have fax machines and computer modem outlets. ⊠ *8 Peking Rd., Tsim Sha Tsui,* ☎ *2375–1133, 800/854–7854 in the U.S.,* FAX *2375–6611. 473 rooms, 27 suites. 3 restaurants, lounge, 4 no-smoking floors, pool, health club, shops, business services. AE, DC, MC, V.*

$$$ ⊞ **Marco Polo.** This 16-story hotel in the shopping and commercial area along Canton Road is close to the Ferry Pier and is environment friendly. Papers are recycled, and bags and toiletries are biodegradable, but the most unique touch at this modern hotel are the little green plants in each room. Each plant is adopted by a hotel associate, and a tag placed next to the plant reminds guests to care for the environment. Rooms and suites are homey and a there is a well-established business center. Guests can use the Hongkong's pool. ⊠ *Harbour City, Canton Rd., Tsim Sha Tsui,* ☎ *2113–0088, 800/843–6664 in the U.S.,* FAX *2113–0022. 384 rooms, 56 suites. 3 restaurants, 3 no-smoking floors, barbershop, shops, business services. AE, DC, MC, V.*

$$$ ⊞ **Miramar.** Opened in 1948, Miramar was Hong Kong's first post–World War II hotel. It was originally owned by the Spanish Catholic Mission and was intended to provide shelter for missionaries expelled from China. As tourism blossomed in the territory, the priests changed their plan and turned the premises into a hotel. At the top of the Golden Mile and across from Kowloon Park, the Miramar has a vast lobby with a dramatic stained-glass ceiling that radiates a traditional Asian touch. It was recently refurbished and now features a grand ballroom and an expanded foyer coffee shop. The adjacent Miramar Shopping Centre has two Chinese restaurants and a brewery coffee shop.

The hotel is close to both the Jordan and Tsim Sha Tsui MTR stations. ✉ *130 Nathan Rd., Tsim Sha Tsui,* ☎ *2368–1111,* FAX *2369–1788. 550 rooms. Restaurants, bar, no-smoking floor, shops, business services. AE, DC, MC, V.*

$$$ 🏨 **New World.** This hotel, with beautifully landscaped gardens and terraces, is part of a huge shopping complex on the southeast tip of Tsim Sha Tsui. The decor is pleasantly postmodern, with contemporary furniture throughout. Rooms are spacious and comfy. It has a good selection of restaurants and evening entertainment, including the Panorama restaurant, which true to its name offers one of the best panoramic harbor views in town, and Catwalk, a popular disco. ✉ *22 Salisbury Rd., Tsim Sha Tsui,* ☎ *2369–4111,* FAX *2369–9387. 501 rooms, 42 suites. 3 restaurants, 2 lounges, no-smoking floor, pool, beauty salon, health club, dance club, business services. AE, DC, MC, V.*

$$$ 🏨 **Prince.** Like its neighbors in the Harbour City complex (the Hongkong and Marco Polo), the Prince is very convenient to upscale shops and cinemas and to the restaurants and shops of Tsim Sha Tsui. It is also nearby the China Hong Kong Terminal, where ferries, boats and buses depart for destinations in China. Most rooms overlook expansive Kowloon Park, and some suites have views of Victoria Harbour. The Spice Market restaurant serves Southeast Asian buffets and an international menu. Guests can use the pool at the Hongkong Hotel, which is just a six-minute walk. ✉ *Harbour City, Tsim Sha Tsui,* ☎ *2113– 1888, 800/843–6664 in the U.S.,* FAX *2113–0066. 345 rooms, 51 suites. Restaurant, deli, bar, no-smoking floor, shops, business services. AE, DC, MC, V.*

$$ 🏨 **Guangdong.** This mainland Chinese–managed hotel is popular among Southeast Asian and Chinese visitors. Comfortable rooms, with beige walls and nondescript French furniture, look out on the street below, which is usually bustling with shoppers and patrons of the many local restaurants and bars. There are no bars or live entertainment in-house, but you don't have to travel far to find evening activities. The best views are on or above the ninth floor. The Canton Court restaurant serves only mediocre Cantonese cuisine. ✉ *18 Prat Ave., Tsim Sha Tsui,* ☎ *2739–3311,* FAX *2721–1137. 234 rooms, 11 suites. 2 restaurants, shops, business services. AE, DC, MC, V.*

$$ 🏨 **Imperial.** This small hotel lacks its own bars, lounges, restaurants, and live entertainment; however, its location on the Golden Mile of Nathan Road means you don't have to walk far for any product or service. Rooms are cramped and basic, without any decoration to speak of. Nearby is the popular Mad Dogs pub, frequented by many local expats, the Space Museum, the Cultural Centre, the MTR, and the Star Ferry. ✉ *30 Nathan Rd., Tsim Sha Tsui,* ☎ *2366–2201,* FAX *2311–2360. 209 rooms, 6 suites. AE, DC, MC, V.*

$$ 🏨 **Kowloon.** A shimmering mirrored exterior and a chrome, glass, and
★ marble lobby reflect the Kowloon's high efficiency and high-tech amenities. Kowloon, which means "nine dragons" in Chinese, is the hotel's design theme. The triangular windows and the pointed lobby ceiling, made from hundreds of hand-blown Venetian glass pyramids, symbolize dragons' sharp teeth. Kowloon is the first hotel in Hong Kong to establish an E-mail address for each room for guests to use during their stay and has plans to include Internet access in the future. Each room is equipped with a Telecentre, a 14-inch interactive television that provides updated information including flight details and word processing. On the southern tip of Nathan Road's Golden Mile, you are just minutes from the Star Ferry and next door to the MTR. You have a choice of restaurants and are entitled to signing privileges in Peninsula hotel facilities. ✉ *19–21 Nathan Rd., Tsim Sha Tsui,* ☎ *2369–*

8698, FAX *2739–9811. 728 rooms, 8 suites. 3 restaurants, no-smoking floors, beauty salon, shops, business services. AE, DC, MC, V.*

$$ ⊞ **New Astor.** This small and inviting, triangle-shape hotel is on a busy corner of Old Tsim Sha Tsui across the road from the MTR. Rooms have standard dark-wood furniture and basic facilities such as mini-bar, hair dryer, and refrigerator. Ask for a room with a coffeemaker if you're a java lover. Guests tend to be groups from China and the more affluent backpackers. Just a short walk away is Granville Road, where fashion outlets cluster. ⊠ *11 Carnarvon Rd., Tsim Sha Tsui,* ☏ *2366–7261,* FAX *2722–7122. 147 rooms, 1 suite. Restaurant, shops,* business services. AE, DC, MC, V.

$$ ⊞ **Ramada Hotel Kowloon.** This modern hotel is relatively small and tries for a home-away-from-home ambience. A fireplace in the lobby and comfortably furnished rooms with natural wood throughout create a cozy atmosphere. The bar and karaoke attract many young locals. ⊠ *73–75 Chatham Rd., South Tsim Sha Tsui,* ☏ *2311–1100, 800/854–7854 in the U.S.,* FAX *2311–6000. 203 rooms, 2 suites. 2 restaurants, bar, shops, business services. AE, DC, MC, V.*

$$ ⊞ **Royal Pacific.** Right on the Tsim Sha Tsui waterfront, this hotel is part of the China Hong Kong City complex, which includes the terminal for ferries to China. Rooms are small but attractive and equipped with tea- and coffeemakers. The hotel is connected to Kowloon Park by a footbridge and is close to cinemas and shopping areas. Among its restaurants is one that serves excellent Swiss food. ⊠ *33 Canton Rd., Kowloon,* ☏ *2736–1188,* FAX *2736–1212. 641 rooms, 42 suites. 3 restaurants, bar, health club, squash, business services. AE, DC, MC, V.*

$$ ⊞ **Windsor.** This humble but smart little hotel offers clean, functional accommodations just east of the Nathan Road Golden Mile of shopping and entertainment. It has a coffee-shop-cum-bar and business services. When taking a cab here, specify your destination as the hotel (both the Windsor Cinema, and in Causeway Bay, the Windsor House are more widely known). ⊠ *39–43A Kimberley Rd., Tsim Sha Tsui,* ☏ *2739–5665,* FAX *2722–6670. 165 rooms, 1 suite. 2 restaurants, bar, business services. AE, DC, MC, V.*

$ ⊞ **International.** Like other budget lodgings in the territory, this lower-end hotel provides the literal basics—don't expect to be pampered. A bright orange lobby helps prepare you for the pink-and-orange color scheme of the rooms, the best of which face Cameron Road and have balconies facing the bright lights and active nightlife of Tsim Sha Tsui. Rooms and facilities are considerably worn and shoddy. ⊠ *33 Cameron Rd., Tsim Sha Tsui,* ☏ *2366–3381,* FAX *2369–5381. 91 rooms, 2 suites. Restaurant. MC, V.*

$ ⊞ **Salisbury YMCA.** If you can't afford the Pen, cross the street and
★   settle at this five-star Y, where you can enjoy the same magnificent harbor view at a fraction of the price. You can't compare the YMCAs in Hong Kong with the Ys in other parts of the world—in terms of both price tag and services. The Salisbury YMCA, Hong Kong's most popular, sits on a huge, sterile-looking block opposite the Cultural Centre, Space Museum and Art Museum—an excellent location for theater and art performance crawls. Rooms are clean, and you'll have superb recreational facilities including a well-equipped fitness center, a sauna, a Jacuzzi, and a dance studio. It also has a chapel and a beautiful garden. The restaurants serve good, cheap food, and the shops are bargain-priced. ⊠ *41 Salisbury Rd., Tsim Sha Tsui,* ☏ *2369–2211,* FAX *2739–9315. 318 rooms, 62 suites. 3 restaurants, 2 indoor pools, health club, squash, shops. AE, DC, MC, V.*

Tsim Sha Tsui East

$$$$ ⚅ **Kowloon Shangri-La.** This classy hotel caters mainly to business trav-
★ elers and features a 24-hour business center and a fax and personal
computer outlet in each room; global vision teleconferencing is also
available on request. The elevator carpets highlight the day of the
week and are changed at midnight to remind guests of their schedule
from the moment the elevator door opens. The modern, pastel rooms
are large by Hong Kong standards. A variety of in-house restaurants
serves Japanese, Chinese, French, and American cuisines, and a bar and
lounge offer live entertainment, including string quartets and harp
and piano music. Views are of Victoria Harbour or the city. Pamper
yourself with the sauna and solarium services. The owners' attention
to detail, the expert, loyal staff, and the regular fine-tuning of facilities ensure repeat business. ✉ *64 Mody Rd., Tsim Sha Tsui East,* ☎
2721–2111, 800/942–5050 in the U.S., 🖷 *2723–8686. 692 rooms,
31 suites. 5 restaurants, bar and lounge, no-smoking floor, indoor
pool, barbershop, health club, shops, business services. AE, DC, MC,
V.*

$$$ ⚅ **Grand Stanford Harbour View.** At the east end of Tsim Sha Tsui East,
this luxury hotel (formerly a Holiday Inn Crowne Plaza) has an un-
obstructed harbor view from more than half its rooms. The elegant lobby
is spacious, and the large guest rooms are done in warm earth tones
with finely crafted wooden furniture. Its restaurants are locally well
known, including Mistral, which serves Italian cuisine, but particularly
Tiffany's New York Bar, which celebrates the Roaring '20s with an-
tique furniture, Tiffany glass ceilings, and American entertainment. The
hotel has extensive recreational facilities including a year-round swim-
ming pool and a health club. Grand Stanford is an Inter-Continental
Global Partner. ✉ *70 Mody Rd., Tsim Sha Tsui East,* ☎ *2721–5161,*
🖷 *2732–2233. 554 rooms, 25 suites. 4 restaurants, pool, health club,
shops, business services. AE, DC, MC, V.*

$$$ ⚅ **Hotel Nikko.** Part of the Japanese Nikko chain, this luxury harbor-
front hotel at the far end of Tsim Sha Tsui East attracts mostly Japa-
nese tourists. You can brush up on your Japanese and learn the gracious
national greeting—an enthusiastic smile and a bowing back. Guest rooms
have an attractive Asian style, and suites are more contemporary than
the regular rooms. Nearly 200 rooms enjoy a magnificent harbor view.
The Sagano restaurant serves freshly imported ingredients from Japan
and is one of the most popular in Hong Kong. ✉ *72 Mody Rd., Tsim
Sha Tsui East,* ☎ *2739–1111, 800/862–9354 in the U.S.,* 🖷 *2311–
3122. 444 rooms, 18 suites. 4 restaurants, lounges and bar, pool, barbershop, beauty salon, health club, shops, business services. AE, DC,
MC, V.*

$$$ ⚅ **Regal Kowloon.** If you favor a French environment, check in at the
Regal. The lobby has an impressive tapestry, and Louis XVI–style fur-
niture graces one of the lounges and the guest rooms. Rooms are dec-
orated in peach and green, with chintz bedspreads and curtains. Le
Restaurant de France has a gorgeous dining room with French Regency
decor and a menu based on that of Maxim de Paris. ✉ *71 Mody Rd.,
Tsim Sha Tsui East,* ☎ *2722–1818, 800/222–8888 in the U.S.,* 🖷
*2369–6950. 600 rooms, 34 suites. 4 restaurants, bar and lounge, 2
no-smoking floors, beauty salon, health club, shops, business services.
AE, DC, MC, V.*

$$$ ⚅ **Royal Garden.** An exquisite garden atrium with lush greenery and
whispering running water rises from the ground floor to the hotel's
rooftop. Glass-sided elevators, live classical music, trailing greenery,
and trickling streams give the Royal Garden serenity. Guest rooms, all
of which surround the atrium, are Asian in style. Guests especially ap-

preciate Sabatini, sister to the famous Roman restaurant (☞ Chapter 3), and the rooftop state-of-the-art health club with indoor-outdoor pool and spa services. The pool, fashioned after an ancient Roman bath with fountains, a colorful sun mosaic, and underwater music, is heated and covered during winter by a huge bubble top. ✉ *69 Mody Rd., Tsim Sha Tsui East,* ☎ *2721–5215,* ℻ *2369–9976. 377 rooms, 45 suites. 6 restaurants, pub, no-smoking floor, indoor-outdoor pool, beauty salon, spa, health club, shops, dance club, business services. AE, DC, MC, V.*

Yau Ma Tei and Mong Kok

$$ 🏨 **BP International House.** Built by the Boy Scouts Association, this hotel next to Kowloon Park provides excellent value. A portrait of BP himself—Baron Robert Baden-Powell, founder of the Boy Scouts—hangs in the spacious lobby. The rooms are small and hostel-like despite the hotel-like cost but are equipped with multichannel TVs, telephones, and electronic key cards. Most rooms have a panoramic view of Victoria Harbour and a clear view of the busy area of Kowloon. There is a multipurpose hall on the upper ground level for exhibitions, conventions, and concerts, and the hotel has one of the biggest health clubs in town. It also has self-service coin laundry—a major attraction for budget travelers. You can park in the 530-space garage on the premises. Finding a parking space in Hong Kong is far more difficult than getting a room. ✉ *8 Austin Rd., Yau Ma Tei,* ☎ *2376–1111,* ℻ *2376–1333. 529 rooms, 6 suites. 2 restaurants, health club, coin laundry, business services, parking (fee). AE, DC, MC, V.*

$$ 🏨 **Concourse.** One of Hong Kong's nicer budget hotels, the Concourse is run by the China Travel Service. It's tucked away from the main street but is only a minute's walk from the Prince Edward MTR station, in Mong Kok. Rooms are basic and functional, and the hotel also provides business services. It is in a perfect location to enjoy a glimpse of the real, down-to-earth life of Hong Kong. Sip coffee (or a mixture of tea and coffee—it's quite strong) at a local coffee house or slurp a bowl of noodles at one of the holes-in-the-wall. There are loads of simple eateries around this area and an active nightlife scene nearby. The hotel has a Chinese and a Korean restaurant. ✉ *22 Lai Chi Kok Rd., Mong Kok,* ☎ *2397–6683,* ℻ *2381–3768. 425 rooms, 5 suites. 2 restaurants, coffee shop, bar, business services. AE, DC, MC, V.*

$$ 🏨 **Eaton.** In a brick-red shopping and cinema complex in the middle of Nathan Road, Eaton provides quick access to Hong Kong's down-to-earth street nightlife. It's within spitting distance of Temple Street, the busy night market with fortune tellers, opera singers and vendors. Rooms are clean and modern, with all the basic necessities. There is a swimming pool and a gym on the top floor. The hotel also provides business services. ✉ *380 Nathan Rd., Yau Ma Tei,* ☎ *2782–1818,* ℻ *2782–5563. 486 rooms. 2 restaurants, bar, 5 no-smoking floors, pool, health club, business services. AE, DC, MC, V.*

$$ 🏨 **Grand Tower.** Above a shopping mall in the busiest part of Kowloon, Grand Tower gives tourists access to the real Hong Kong. This mall isn't for designer goods, but for ordinary items from cushion covers and knickknacks to watches, clothes, and shoes. Bird Street (where many Chinese walk and talk, together with their caged birds) and the Ladies' Market are a short walk away, as is the Mong Kok MTR. Rooms are adequately clean and functional. ✉ *627–641 Nathan Rd., Mong Kok,* ☎ *2789–0011,* ℻ *2789–1000, 536 rooms, 13 suites. 3 restaurants, barbershop, beauty salon, shops, business services. AE, DC, MC, V.*

$$ 🏨 **Majestic.** This hotel is on the site of the old Majestic Cinema on upper Nathan Road. The lobby is clean and plain, and the sparsely furnished rooms have contemporary furniture, a minibar, a TV, and a refrigerator. All suites are equipped with fax machines. Facilities are barely basic—there is no pool or gym, and for dining and imbibing there is only a coffee shop and a bar. But in the same complex are a cinema and shops; and many restaurants—running the gamut from Chinese food to Malaysian cuisine—are in the area. The Jordan MTR is nearby. ✉ *348 Nathan Rd., Yau Ma Tei,* ☎ *2781–1333,* FAX *2781–1773. 387 rooms. Bar, coffee shop, no-smoking floor, shops, cinema, business services. AE, DC, MC, V.*

$$ 🏨 **Pearl Seaview.** Reclamation of the harbor front and construction have taken away most of this slender hotel's sea view, but it has compensatory features. Guest rooms are very small, but the restaurant has bargain-priced buffets, especially for lunches. The hotel attracts tour groups from Europe and Asia. It's convenient to the Yau Ma Tei MTR and is on Shanghai Street, where traditional Hong Kong still holds out, with shops selling handmade kitchenware, temple offerings, and wedding dresses. Temple Street, a must-see of Hong Kong street nightlife, is nearby, as is the territory's artistic movie house, Broadway Cinematheque (☞ Chapter 5). ✉ *268 Shanghai St., Yau Ma Tei,* ☎ *2782–0882,* FAX *2388–1919. 255 rooms. Restaurant, bar, lounge. AE, DC, MC, V.*

$$ 🏨 **Prudential.** Rising from a busy corner on upper Nathan Road, with the Jordan MTR station beneath it, this hotel is a great find if you have a modest budget. Rooms are spacious and offer interesting city views. It shares a building with a lively shopping mall and has its own pool, sauna, and gym. ✉ *222 Nathan Rd., Yau Ma Tei,* ☎ *2311–8222,* FAX *2367–1304. 415 rooms, 19 suites. Bar, coffee shop, pool, shops, business services. AE, DC, MC, V.*

$–$$ 🏨 **The Metropole.** Just north of the major shopping area along Nathan Road, the Metropole is a hidden delight in Yau Ma Tei. On its facade is a 150-ft steel mural titled *Magnificent China,* which features the scenic attractions of China. Rooms are clean and modern, with simple decor that reflects a harmonic melange of the East and West. The rooftop pool and health club offer a relaxing atmosphere. Executive travelers can take a minute to enjoy a sip of the welcome champagne on arrival before getting their hands on the computers at the business center. The hotel's Chinese restaurant, House of Tang, serves authentic Szechuan food. ✉ *75 Waterloo Rd., Yau Ma Tei,* ☎ *2761–1711 or 800/227–5663,* FAX *2761–0769. 487 rooms. 3 restaurants, bar, pool, health club, business services. AE, DC, MC, V.*

$ 🏨 **Bangkok Royal.** Just off Nathan Road and steps from the Jordan MTR, this hotel has rooms that are sparsely decorated, somewhat down at the heels, but clean. The 20 top-floor rooms were closed at press time, and only 56 rooms remain at your service. There are no bars or lounges, but there is a good Thai restaurant on the lobby floor (it is the *Bangkok* Royal, after all), and you are within walking distance of the restaurants and entertainment of Nathan Road. ✉ *2 Pilkem St., Yau Ma Tei,* ☎ *2735–9181,* FAX *2730–2209. 56 rooms. 2 restaurants. AE, DC, MC, V.*

$ 🏨 **Booth Lodge.** This pleasant contemporary retreat near the Jade Market is operated by the Salvation Army. But don't be turned off—the facilities are not of the donated kind. In fact, everything in this recently renovated lodge is clean, bright, and new, from crisply painted walls to starched sheets on the double beds. The lobby is a study in minimalism and has an officelike atmosphere, but the Booth is a good value. It is also close to the Yau Ma Tei MTR. ✉ *11 Wing Sing La., Yau Ma Tei,* ☎ *2771–9266,* FAX *2385–1140. 53 rooms. Restaurant. AE, MC, V.*

$ 🏨 **Caritas Bianchi Lodge.** This clean and friendly lodge done in simple modern decor has basic facilities including TV, minibar, air-conditioning and private bathroom. Just around the corner from busy Nathan Road, the lodge is also close to the Jade Market and the nightly Temple Street Market. ⊠ *4 Cliff Rd., Yau Ma Tei,* ☎ *2388–1111,* 🆊 *2770–6669. 90 rooms, 2 suites. Restaurant. AE, DC, MC, V.*

$ 🏨 **Shamrock.** With rooms that are more spacious than elegant and an atmosphere best described as old-fashioned (the hotel is more than 40 years old), the Shamrock is still a good bargain. It is just north of Kowloon Park and steps from the Jordan MTR. ⊠ *223 Nathan Rd., Yau Ma Tei,* ☎ *2735–2271,* 🆊 *2736–7354. 148 rooms. Restaurant. AE, DC, MC, V.*

THE NEW TERRITORIES AND THE OUTER ISLANDS

Tsuen Wan's Kowloon Panda has helped alleviate the shortage of first-class accommodations in the fast-developing New Territories and has been welcomed by business travelers involved in manufacturing here. Accommodations are still limited on the outlying islands, although some (such as Cheung Chau) have a booming business in rooms to rent, with agents displaying photographs of available rentals on placards that line the waterfront opposite the ferry pier.

The New Territories

$$$ 🏨 **Regal Riverside.** In one of the territory's new towns, this large, modern hotel overlooks the Shing Mun River in the foothills of Shatin. Rooms have river and garden views, are done in pastel colors, and have contemporary furniture. The Riverside has Hong Kong's largest hotel disco and a health club that's home to Hong Kong's only float capsule, purported to soothe away the day's pressures. You can also join the healthy horde of people jogging or cycling along the river path or just watch the rowers practice. The hotel is a few minutes from the territory's busiest shopping—the New Town Plaza. Shuttle service leaves every hour to the plaza and every half hour to Tsim Sha Tsui. ⊠ *Tai Chung Kiu Rd., Shatin,* ☎ *2649–7878, 800/222–8888 in the U.S.,* 🆊 *2637–4748. 786 rooms, 44 suites. 7 restaurants, bar, no-smoking floor, pool, barbershop, beauty salon, health club, shops, dance club, business services. AE, DC, MC, V.*

$$ 🏨 **Beach Resort Hotel.** If you're a water-sports freak, stay here. Although the beach isn't particularly impressive, the water-sports facilities are— sailing, windsurfing, canoeing; speed boats, water scooters, rowing dinghies, pedal boats, aqua bikes. . . You name it. Beginners can ask for coaching while experienced players can rent the equipment and head out to sea. Landlubbers can check out the archery and beach volleyball grounds. On the waterfront of Saikung, the hotel is only 10 minutes' walk from the town and sumptuous seafood restaurants. The hotel also has a weekend flea market, a barbecue area, and restaurants that serve Thai, Chinese, and Western cuisines. ⊠ *Tai Mong Tsui Rd. (off Hiram's Hwy., a mile past Saikung town), New Territories,* ☎ *2791–1068* 🆊 *2791–2274. 32 rooms and suites. Restaurants, bar, picnic area, pool, tennis court, archery, volleyball. AE, DC, MC, V.*

$$ 🏨 **Gold Coast.** Opened in 1994, this is Hong Kong's first conference resort. Its vast complex on the western harbor front of Kowloon is served by special ferries from Central, 30 minutes away, and there are shuttle buses to the MTR and the airport. The hotel has extravagant decor, with acres of marble, miles of wrought-iron balustrades, a grand ball-

room, and palm-court atriums. The resort has a large marina, a water-sports area, tennis courts, pitch-and-putt golf, an all-service spa, and even an archery range. It has gained a reputation among conference organizers for facilities that can accommodate 1,200 people. It faces the beautiful beach that held 300,000 people during New Year's fireworks last year. It is also the only hotel in Hong Kong with assault equipment for Outward Bound courses. ⊠ *1 Castle Peak Rd., Tuen Mun, New Territories,* ☎ *2452–8888,* 𝔽𝔸𝕏 *2440–7368. 443 rooms. 4 restaurants, 3 bars, pool, beauty salon, spa, 2 tennis courts, health club, squash, business services. AE, DC, MC, V.*

$$–$$$ ⊞ **Kowloon Panda.** You can't miss the huge panda facade on the side of the largest hotel in the western New Territories; its 30 stories dominate the skyline of bustling Tsuen Wan. The decor is reminiscent of hotels in Tokyo's Ginza district, with lots of open-plan lounges and ultramodern rooms in warm and natural tones. Some rooms offer harbor views. On the premises are a pool, a health club, business and meeting facilities, a variety of restaurants, and a department store. Executive guests of the Mega Club also enjoy Nintendo and access to the Internet in their rooms. Complimentary bus service is available to and from Tsim Sha Tsui and Mongkok, and the MTR is nearby. ⊠ *3 Tsuen Wan St., Tsuen Wan,* ☎ *2409–1111,* 𝔽𝔸𝕏 *2409–1818. 971 rooms, 55 suites. 4 restaurants, 2 bars, no-smoking floor, pool, health club, shops, business services. AE, DC, MC, V.*

$$–$$$ ⊞ **Royal Park.** Right next to New Town Plaza, the busiest shopping mall in the territory, this 16-story hotel is far out yet easily accessed by train and buses. It's also the closest hotel to the Shatin Racecourse. The lobby has a deep color scheme, and rooms have bay windows providing a panoramic view of Shatin. Four rooms are specially designed for the disabled. ⊠ *8 Pak Hok Ting St., Shatin,* ☎ *2601–2111,* 𝔽𝔸𝕏 *2601–3666. 436 rooms, 12 suites. 4 restaurants, lounge, pool, tennis court, exercise room, jogging, business services. AE, DC, MC, V.*

Cheung Chau Island

$ ⊞ **Cheung Chau Warwick.** Miles from the fast-paced city, this little gem on the beach aims to assure you a carefree and relaxed stay—no business services or executive floor, but a nice pool and a sandy beach. The six-story hotel is only an hour by ferry from Hong Kong Island and is a popular getaway for Hong Kong families. There are no cars on the leisurely island; the hotel is just a 10-minute walk from the pier. ⊠ *East Bay, Cheung Chau,* ☎ *2981–0081,* 𝔽𝔸𝕏 *2981–9174. 71 rooms. 2 restaurants, pool, beach. AE, DC, MC, V.*

Lantau Island

$–$$ ⊞ **Silvermine Beach Hotel.** Lying along the bay, this resort in Mui Wo escapes the hecticness of Hong Kong. A ferry from Hong Kong Island will get you here in an hour, and the hotel is a five-minute walk from the pier. The resort has a pool (open only in summer) and a tennis court and runs daily guided tours of the island. Hop on one of the hotel's air-conditioned coaches and embark on a grand tour to the bronze statue Tin Tan Buddha, the Po Lin Monastery, and Tai O fishing village. You'll be glad you hiked one of the many sections of the Lantau Island trail—the scenery is expansive. ⊠ *D.D. 2, Lot 648 Silvermine Bay, Mui Wo, Lantau Island,* ☎ *2984–8295,* 𝔽𝔸𝕏 *2984–1907. 135 rooms. Restaurants, pool, exercise room. AE, DC, MC, V.*

5 Nightlife and the Arts

Hong Kongers play as hard as they work, and have many distractions from which to choose. Whether you follow the pulsing neons signs to garish entertainment or book ahead for a classical performance, Hong Kong is a city for night-crawling.

NIGHTLIFE

The handover? What handover? Despite the change of sovereignty when Britain returned Hong Kong to China last year, the town continues to party hard with its night owl activities. Hong Kong is a 24-hour city. When the sun sets, the pace doesn't stop—it just proceeds in a more carefree style. There are night markets, a zillion restaurants (from five-star eateries to holes-in-the-wall), sophisticated piano bars, elegant lounges, superstrobed discos, cozy bars, smoky jazz dens, topless bars and hostess clubs, marble massage parlors, cabarets, and, of course, the karaoke (video sing-along) bars, oh so popular with locals.

All premises licensed to serve alcohol are subject to stringent fire, safety, and sanitary controls. True clubs, as distinct from public premises, are less strictly controlled, and wise visitors should think twice before succumbing to the city's raunchier hideaways. If you stumble into one, check out cover and hostess charges *before* you get too comfortable. Pay for each round of drinks as it's served (by cash rather than credit card), and never sign any blank checks. As in every tourist destination, the art of the tourist rip-off is well practiced. To be safest, visit spots that are sign-carrying members of the Hong Kong Tourist Association (HKTA). You can pick up its free membership listing (including approved restaurants and nightspots) at any HKTA information office.

Take note, too, of Hong Kong's laws. You must be over 18 to be served alcohol. Drugs, obscene publications, and unlicensed gambling are ostensibly illegal. There is some consumer protection, but the generally helpful police, many of whom speak English, expect every visitor to know the meaning of caveat emptor (let the buyer beware).

Following is a checklist of some suggested drinking and dancing spots (with telephone numbers where reservations are possible or wise). Many of Hong Kong's smarter nightspots are in hotels.

Fast-paced, competitive Hong Kong is a world of change where buildings seem to vanish overnight and new fads emerge weekly. Don't be surprised if our listing includes some spots that have changed their decor or name or have closed since these words were set in type.

Cabarets and Nightclubs

The biggest and best old-fashioned nightclub-restaurants are Chinese, where the cuisine is Cantonese, as are most of the singers. Big-name local balladeers and stars singing what's called Cantopop make guest appearances. Though modest by Las Vegas standards, the shows can be entertaining, as at the massive **Ocean City Restaurant & Night Club** (⊠ New World Centre, Tsim Sha Tsui, ☎ 2369–9688).

Ocean Centre's **Ocean Palace Restaurant & Night Club** (⊠ Harbour City, Canton Rd., Tsim Sha Tsui, ☎ 2730–7111) is a favorite for Hong Kong family and wedding parties.

At the nightclub-restaurant **Golden Crown** (⊠ 94 Nathan Rd., ☎ 2366–6291), locals and tourists dine and dance the night away.

Club 97 (⊠ 8–11 Lan Kwai Fong, Central, ☎ 2810–9333) is a small, glitzy, often crowded nightclub for gatherings of the "beautiful people." It is open from 9 PM to 4 AM or later, as long as there are customers. The nightly entrance fee is appropriately HK$97.

Propaganda (⊠ 1/F, 30–32 Wyndham St., Central, ☎ 2868–1316) is one of the most popular clubs and also the only gay club in the territory, but the crowds won't arrive until well after midnight. The cavernous entrance leads to a dark, intimate disco with a comfy lounge.

Cocktail and Piano Bars

Sophisticated and elegant cocktail bars are the norm at all luxury hotels. You'll find live music (usually Filipino trios with a female singer, occasionally international acts) in gleaming decor. Some venues have a small dance floor. Hong Kong's happy hours typically run from late afternoon to early evening, with two drinks for the price of one.

High-altitude harbor gazing is the main attraction at the Island Shangri-La's 56th-floor **Cyrano** music lounge (⊠ 2 Pacific Place, 88 Queensway, Hong Kong, ☎ 2820–8591). The Peninsula's **Felix Bar** (⊠ Salisbury Rd., Tsim Sha Tsui, ☎ 2366–6251) is a must for visitors. It not only has a brilliant view of the island, but the impressive bar and disco were designed by visionary Philippe Starck. Go up in the bubble elevator to the Sheraton's **Sky Lounge** (⊠ 20 Nathan Rd., Tsim Sha Tsui, 18th Floor, ☎ 2369–1111) in time for sunset, and you won't be disappointed. At the Excelsior's **Talk of the Town** (⊠ 281 Gloucester Rd., Causeway Bay, ☎ 2837–6786) you'll be greeted by a 270-degree vista of Hong Kong Harbour.

Marvelous harbor views are also part of the appeal of **Gripps** (⊠ Harbour City, Tsim Sha Tsui, ☎ 2113–0088), the nightspot in the Hongkong Hotel; it has ocean-liner–level views of the harbor and a central bar modeled on a high-class London pub. There is entertainment nightly by visiting pianists and touring cover bands. The New World Harbour View's **Oasis Bar** (⊠ 1 Harbour Rd., Wanchai, ☎ 2802–8888) has a unique glass roof and harbor scenery, albeit slightly obstructed because of the Convention and Exhibition Centre's new extension.

Feeling pampered is your pleasure at the Peninsula's **Bar** or its club-like **Verandah** (⊠ Salisbury Rd., Tsim Sha Tsui, ☎ 2366–6251). The socially aware go to the Peninsula's lobby; sit to the right of the Peninsula's entrance to be where the cream of society traditionally lounges. The Mandarin Oriental's mezzanine **Clipper Lounge** (⊠ 5 Connaught Rd., Central, ☎ 2825–1935) is perfect for a relaxing drink after a long day of shopping or touring. The **Regent's lobby lounge** (⊠ 18 Salisbury Rd., Tsim Sha Tsui, ☎ 2721–1211) is a place to see and be seen. Be ready to chat about the fashion industry with the parade of Armani-clad and Chanel-scented men and women.

Pubs

Pubs can be found in all areas of Hong Kong. Some places are dives but may serve cheap drinks, while others are more upper class and, of course, charge more. Live music is often provided by a local band, and most pubs offer snacks.

Off-duty Central business folk flock to the pirate-galleon **Pier One** at Jardine House (⊠ In front of Star Ferry Terminal, Central, ☎ 2526–3061) for an à la carte lunch or a reasonably priced dinner buffet.

Central's British-managed, oak-beamed **Bull & Bear** is in Hutchison House, on Lambeth Walk (⊠ 10 Harcourt Rd., ☎ 2526–1953). This place draws all types—a large share of whom are English expats—serves standard pub fare, and is known to get a little rowdy on weekends.

Both branches of the Irish pub **Delaney's** (⊠ G/F, Multifield Plaza, 3 Prat Ave., Kowloon, ☎ 2301–3980; ⊠ 2/F One Capital Place, 18 Luard Rd., Wanchai, ☎ 2804–2880) have interiors made in Ireland and shipped to Hong Kong. The pubs seem totally authentic in furnishings and atmosphere. There's Guinness and Delaney's ale (a specialty microbrew) on tap, corner snugs (small, private rooms), and a menu of Irish specialties. It's not cheap except for happy hour, when both pubs are usually packed.

In Wanchai, pub hopping is best practiced by the energetic and easy-to-please. The **Horse & Groom** (⊠ 161 Lockhart Rd., ☎ 2507–2517) is down at the heels but certainly a true pub. Its neighboring **Old China Hand Tavern** (⊠ 104 Lockhart Rd., ☎ 2527–9174) has been here since time immemorial, and the decor suffers accordingly, but it makes for authentic pub atmosphere. A popular drinking hole is **BB's Bar and Brasserie** (⊠ 114–120 Lockhart Rd., ☎ 2529–7702), which can be rather fashionable. **Dali's** (⊠ G/F, 76 Jaffe Rd., ☎ 2528–3113) attracts the district's suited business types. **Ridgeway's** (⊠ 1/F, Empire Land Commercial Bldg., 81–85 Lockhart Rd., ☎ 2866–6608) has pool tables. The **Flying Pig** (⊠ 2/F, Empire Land Commercial Bldg., 81–85 Lockhart Rd., ☎ 2865–3730) has amusing and original decor. For a reasonable hotel drinking hole, try the Excelsior Hotel's **Dickens Bar** (⊠ 281 Gloucester Rd., ☎ 2837–6782), which provides live music on most nights.

Or if it's not too hot, you can sit at an outdoor table at Causeway Bay's **King's Arms** (⊠ Sunning Plaza, 1 Sunning Rd., ☎ 2895–6557), one of Hong Kong's few city-center beer gardens. The convivial outdoor area is a great place to meet other visitors.

A favorite bar in this part of town is the **Jump** (⊠ Causeway Bay Plaza 2, 7th floor, 463 Lockhart Rd., Wanchai, ☎ 2832–9007). Formerly China Jump (the name change was political), this pub flies in professional bartenders from across the world who skillfully flare (toss bottles) to concoct some strange brews—consider the FBI, a combination of ice cream and vodka. Beware the dentist's chair, however, unless you like to sip your margaritas upside down.

Over in Tsim Sha Tsui a diverse, happy crowd frequents the Aussie-style **Kangaroo Pub** (⊠ 35 Haiphong Rd., ☎ 2376–0083), which has good pub food and interesting views of Kowloon Park.

Rick's Cafe (⊠ 4 Hart Ave., Tsim Sha Tsui, ☎ 2367–2939), a local hangout, is a restaurant-pub decorated à la *Casablanca,* with potted palms, ceiling fans, and posters of Bogie and Bergman (there's also a branch on Lockhart Road in Wanchai). **Grammy's Lounge** (⊠ 2A Hart Ave., ☎ 2368–3833) features Filipino-led sing-alongs and attracts a rowdy crowd. **Ned Kelly's Last Stand** (⊠ 11A Ashley Rd., Tsim Sha Tsui, ☎ 2376–0562) is an institution with Aussie-style beer and grub and loud, fun live jazz in the evening. For Central's Lan Kwai Fong area *see* For Singles *below.*

A trendy place in Tsim Sha Tsui is an out-of-the-way strip called Knutsford Terrace, where a new breed of bars and restaurants has recently made its home. Tropical rhythms can be found at the Caribbean-inspired **Bahama Mama's** (⊠ 4–5 Knutsford Terr., ☎ 2368–2121), where there's world music. You wouldn't think that **Chasers** (⊠ 2–3 Knutsford Terr., ☎ 2367–9487), fitted with genuine English antiques, including chairs, lamps, and prints, would be as groovy as it is. With live pop music most evenings, young locals love it.

Wine Bars

Western stockbrokers and financial types unwind in Central's **Brown's Wine Bar** (⊠ 2/F Tower 2, Exchange Sq., ☎ 2523–7003). It has excellent British food and a splendid bar.

For an intimate encounter, try **Le Tire Bouchon** (✉ 9 Old Bailey St., Central, ☎ 2523–5459), which dispenses tasty bistro meals and fine wines by the glass.

Tiny, classy **Juliette's** (✉ 6 Hoi Ping Rd., Causeway Bay, ☎ 2882–5460) provides a cozy ambience for chuppie (Hong Kong's Chinese yuppies) couples and just-left-work corporate types.

Pacific Wine Cellars (✉ Basement, Seibu, Pacific Place, 88 Queensway, Admiralty, ☎ 2971–3897) is tucked away behind tall shelves of vintage wines in Seibu's magnificent basement grocery store. Mainly suits and wandering shoppers discover this joint.

Pomeroy's (✉ The Mall, Pacific Place, Level 3, ☎ 2523–4772) is a congenial if rather noisy place where crowds gather—especially at happy hour.

Jazz and Folk Clubs

Since 1989 jazz lovers have enjoyed great performances at the **Jazz Club** (✉ 2/F, California Entertainment Bldg., 34–36 D'Aguilar St., Central, ☎ 2845–8477). The club boasts a wide selection of local jazz, R&B, and soul talent as well as top-notch international acts every month, including harmonica player extraordinaire Carey Bell and bluesmen Georgie Fame and Joe Louis Walker.

Ned Kelly's Last Stand (☞ Pubs, *above*) is an Aussie-managed home for pub grub and Dixieland, courtesy of Ken Bennett's Kowloon Honkers. Get here early, before 10 PM, to get a comfortable seat.

Wanchai's unpretentious alternative to the topless bar scene is the **Wanch** (✉ 54 Jaffe Rd., ☎ 2861–1621), known for its live local folk and rock performances. The interesting Hong Kong–theme decor (remember *Love Is a Many Splendored Thing*?) is also worth a visit.

There are many rousing evenings when Filipinos take on American country-and-western music in **Bar City** (✉ New World Centre, Tsim Sha Tsui, ☎ 2369–8571). It is particularly popular with young locals.

Hardy's Folk Club (✉ 35 D'Aguilar St., Central, ☎ 2522–4448) is another Hong Kong rarity—there's an open stage for anyone to get up and give it a go. Several steps away from karaoke, there's also usually a guitarist who takes requests. Singers vary from the talented amateur to the self-conscious Western transient to dismal one-drink-too-many wailers. It can be awful or awfully amusing.

Discos

At the discos in Hong Kong, young people with money to spend prance about in the latest fashions (both the fashions and the dancing can be worrisome). Whether it's thigh-high PVC boots, neon-color tops, or life-preserver-type jackets, if the clothes are in the windows of hip shops, the young guns are wearing them. Cover charges are high by American standards; entrance to the smarter spots can be HK$100 or more (much more on the eves of major public holidays), although this usually entitles you to two drinks. If discos aren't your taste and dance parties are, look out for posters in Lan Kwai Fong and Wanchai that scream about the latest international DJ (usually very well known) arriving in town to play for one night only. Some bars and restaurants also hold weekly or monthly club nights, and music ranges from funk and jazz to house and easy listening.

The perennial favorite nightspot is **JJs** (✉ Grand Hyatt, 1 Harbour Rd., Hong Kong, ☎ 2588–1234), the Grand Hyatt's entertainment center. It contains a disco and a pizza lounge with a dartboard and a bar screening major sporting events, but it is remembered most for its flashy disco lights, good house band in the music room, and the wall-to-wall suits and their escorts.

The **Catwalk,** in the New World Hotel (⊠ 22 Salisbury Rd., Tsim Sha Tsui, ☎ 2369–4111), has a disco, a live band, and karaoke lounges. Antler chandeliers hang from the ceiling, and cat prints cover the floors, walls, staircase and even windows.

Both branches of **Rick's Cafe** (⊠ 4 Hart Ave., Tsim Sha Tsui, ☎ 2376–2939; ⊠ 78–82 Jaffe Rd., Wanchai, ☎ 2528–1812) are practically disco institutions, and despite being among the oldest, they remain favorites. If you arrive after midnight on weekends, be prepared to join the lines to get in.

The **Lost City** (⊠ Chinachem Golden Plaza, 77 Mody Rd., Tsim Sha Tsui East, ☎ 2311–1111) is undoubtedly the most popular and thriving disco for young Chinese. Described as a "multifunctional entertainment complex," it's a cross among a cheesy B-grade film set, Las Vegas camp glamour, and an over-the-top Broadway production. It's contains a massive 100,000 sq ft of disco areas, karaoke rooms, a kitschy café, and plenty of zebra-striped sofas and chairs.

Japanese tourists gravitate to the Park Lane Hotel's **Starlight** (⊠ 310 Gloucester Rd., Causeway Bay, ☎ 2890–3355). Some tourists check out the Japanese high-tech **Zodiac** disco, known for its Cantopop, in the New World Centre's Bar City drinking complex (⊠ Salisbury Rd., Tsim Sha Tsui, ☎ 2369–8571). A ticket will also admit you to Bar City's other two bars.

Joe Bananas (⊠ 23 Luard Rd., Wanchai, ☎ 2529–1811) is a legend in its own drinking time. This disco-cum-bar strictly excludes the military and people dressed too casually—no shorts, sneakers, or T-shirts. This is a yuppie favorite, and there's frequently a line to get in. The evening starts with friends meeting up for drinks—the cocktails are lethal, by the way—but later in the night the tables are pushed aside, and the dancers have their way.

The dance floor at the **Big Apple Pub and Disco** (⊠ Basement, 20 Luard Rd., Wanchai, ☎ 2529–3461) gets going in the wee hours of the morning—and keeps going. There is a sleaze factor involved with this joint, but it's one of the best places to dance and is a favorite among the clubbers and dance-party crowd who wander out into the morning air to finally go home to their beds. **Neptune Disco II** (⊠ 98–108 Jaffe Rd., Wanchai, ☎ 2865–2238) is another late-night haunt for the dance-till-you-drop set.

Hostess Clubs

These are clubs in name only. Hong Kong's better ones are multimillion-dollar operations with hundreds of presentable hostess-companions of many races. Computerized time clocks on each table tabulate companionship charges in timed units—the costs are clearly detailed on table cards, as are standard drink tabs. The clubs' dance floors are often larger than those at discos, and they have one or more live bands and a scheduled lineup of singers. They also have dozens of fancily furnished private rooms—with partitioned lounges and the ubiquitous karaoke setup—that are often palatially comfortable. Local and visiting businessmen adore these rooms—and the multilingual hostesses. Business is so good the clubs are willing to allow visitors *not* to ask for companionship. The better clubs are on a par with music lounges in deluxe hotels, though they cost a little more. Their happy hours start in the afternoon, when many have a sort of tea-dance ambience, and continue through to mid-evening. Peak hours are 10 PM–4 AM. Be aware that many hostess-oriented clubs, whether seedy or posh, are also prostitution fronts.

Club BBoss is the grandest and most boisterous hostess club, in Tsim Sha Tsui East's Mandarin Plaza (☎ 2369–2883). Executives, mostly locals, entertain in this oddly named club, tended by a staff of more than 1,000. If your VIP room is too far from the entrance, you can hire an electrified vintage Rolls Royce and purr around an indoor roadway. Be warned that this is tycoon territory, where a bottle of brandy can cost HK$18,000. Along the harbor, in New World Centre, are **Club Cabaret** (☎ 2369–8431) and **Club Deluxe** (☎ 2721–0277), both luxurious dance lounges.

As its name implies, **Club Kokusai** (⊠ 81 Nathan Rd., Tsim Sha Tsui, ☎ 2367–6969) appeals to visitors from the Land of the Rising Yen. As in other clubs, karaoke dominates here.

Mandarin Palace (⊠ 24 Marsh Rd., ☎ 2575–6551) is a comfortable grand Wanchai nightclub where clients can indulge their singing aspirations in karaoke duets with the hostesses until the wee hours.

For Singles

Hong Kong is full of single people, possibly because of the transient nature of the town or because their hardworking lifestyle leaves them no time for relationships. Either way, there's a rampant singles scene, with people out looking for that special someone or even that special someone just for tonight. Taking yourself to any of the major bar and club areas will guarantee sheer numbers; the rest, as they say, is up to you.

Many Westerners and chuppies choose to meet in crowded comfort in the Lan Kwai Fong area, a hillside section around Central's D'Aguilar Street with many appetizing bistros, wine bars, and cafés.

Singles mix happily at **California** (⊠ 24–26 Lan Kwai Fong, Central, ☎ 2521–1345), a laid-back American-style restaurant for all ages. It has a late-night disco most nights. The tiny bar of **La Dolce Vita** (⊠ G/F, 9 Lan Kwai Fong, Central, ☎ 2810–9333), underneath its sister restaurant Post 97 and next to its other sibling, Club 97, often spills out onto the pavement. With sleek decor, this is a place to be seen, and the cliques tend to be a tad pretentious.

Cheery Western crowds gather at Scottish Victorian pub **Mad Dogs** (⊠ Century Sq., 1 D'Aguilar St., Central, ☎ 2810–1000), also in the Lan Kwai Fong area, as well as in Tsim Sha Tsui near the Sheraton Hotel (⊠ 32 Nathan Rd., ☎ 2301–2222). **Schnurrbart** (⊠ Winner Bldg., 29 D'Aguilar St., Central, ☎ 2523–4700) is a friendly German pub. For a low-key evening, try **Hardy's Folk Bar** (☞ Jazz and Folk Clubs, *above*).

Just on the outskirts of the Fong is the fashionable **Petticoat Lane** (⊠ 2 Tun Wo La., Central, ☎ 2973–0642)—a little difficult to find but definitely worth the wandering (it's near the Midlevels escalator between Lyndhurst Terrace and Hollywood Road). It opened as a gay bar, but individuals of all sexual preferences lounge in its opulent, plush pink setting and quaint outdoor area.

The arts-minded mingle at the **Fringe Club** (⊠ 2 Lower Albert Rd., Central, ☎ 2521–7251), in a historic redbrick building that also houses the members-only Foreign Correspondents Club. The Fringe Club is home to Hong Kong's alternative arts scene. Another drinking favorite for the casual is **Club 64** (✉ 12–14 Wing Wah La., Central, ☎ 2523–2801), where you can get a cheap drink in a setting that's cozy but a little run-down. Above Club 64 is the trendy **Le Jardin** (✉ 10 Wing Wah La., Central, ☎ 2526–2717). It has a lovely outdoor terrace that overlooks a not-so-lovely alley, but it still has a good cosmopolitan ambience.

The gay bar **Zip** (✉ 2 Glenealy, Central, ☎ 2523–3595) has a futuristic interior with loads of silver decor, TV screens, and multicolor lights high on the walls. It's very popular and worth a visit.

Solo businessmen can always find someone to talk to at hotel bars, frequented by both locals and expatriates. The Hyatt's **Chin Chin** or **Nathan's** (✉ 67 Nathan Rd., Tsim Sha Tsui, ☎ 2311–1234) and the **Chinnery,** in the Mandarin Oriental, all have their appeal.

THE ARTS

The most comprehensive calendar of cultural events is *HK Magazine,* a free weekly newspaper distributed each Friday to many restaurants, stores, and bars. You can also read daily reviews in the "Life" section of the *Hong Kong Standard* and its weekend *Hong Kong Life* magazine. The other English-language newspaper, the *South China Morning Post,* lists events and has an entertainment pullout every Friday called *WE.* Highlights of other weekly happenings are listed in the *TV Times,* which comes out every Thursday.

City hall (✉ By Star Ferry, Hong Kong Island, ☎ 2921–2840) has posters and huge bulletin boards listing events and ticket availability. Tickets for cultural events held in government centers can be purchased in booths on the ground floor by the main entrance. **URBTIX** outlets are the easiest place to purchase tickets for most general performances. There are branches at city hall and at the Hong Kong Arts Centre (☎ 2734–9009 for bookings and information). The free monthly *City News* newspaper also lists events and is available at city hall.

Dance

Hong Kong Dance Company. This ensemble has been promoting the art of Chinese dance and choreographing new works with historical themes since 1981. The 30-odd members are experts in folk and classical dance. Sponsored by the Urban Council, they perform about three times a month throughout the territory. ☎ *2853–2642.*

Hong Kong Ballet. This is Hong Kong's first professional ballet company and vocational ballet school. It is Western oriented, in both its classical and contemporary repertoire, and performs at schools, auditoriums, and festivals. ☎ *2573–7398.*

City Contemporary Dance Company. (☎ 2326–8597). Dedicated to contemporary dance, this group presents innovative programs inspired by Hong Kong themes. Performances are usually held at the Hong Kong Arts Centre (☞ *above*).

Drama

Chung Ying Theatre Company. A professional company of Chinese actors performs plays (most of them original) mainly in Cantonese. Regular guest performers include English mime artist Peta Lily. ☎ *2521–6628.*

Fringe Club. An enormous amount of alternative theater, ranging from one-person shows to full dramatic performances, is presented at this club, the only one of its kind to offer facilities to amateur drama, music, and dance groups. Short-run contemporary plays by American and English writers are also presented as well as shows by independent local groups. It is an ideal starting point for anyone interested in seeing how less established arts groups are getting along. ☎ 2521–7251.

Zuni Icosahedron. The best-known avant-garde group puts on new drama and dance (usually in Cantonese) at various locations. ☎ 2893–8419.

Festivals and Special Events

There's a veritable festival season in Hong Kong from January to April each year, when the Fringe, Arts, Food, and Film festivals are held back to back. Then there are a few smaller festivals throughout the year. The festivals showcase diverse local and international shows and performers. Often a group of artists gets together a few works, sponsorship is granted, and before you know it, it's proclaimed a festival. Following are the regular cultural festivals—but don't be surprised if a festival turns up that's not on the list.

Hong Kong Fringe Festival (January). Often scooping up top-notch performers from the Edinburgh Fringe in the United Kingdom as well as the Melbourne and Sydney festivals in Australia, the Hong Kong Fringe Festival hosts an assorted heap of international and local drama, dance, music, and light entertainment. The quality can be patchy, but that's part of the fun, and tickets for shows are usually relatively cheap.

Hong Kong Arts Festival (February–March). For many this festival is the cultural highlight of the year. It embraces four weeks of world-class music, dance and drama from around the globe. Most acts sell out far in advance. Information abroad can be obtained through the HKTA. In Hong Kong Island, city hall has all the schedules up on boards so you can see what's sold out.

Hong Kong Food Festival (March). This festival—with two weeks of food, glorious food—is designed to give tourists a sampling of the territory's diverse culinary options. The festival holds a smorgasbord of events, including cooking classes with world-renowned chefs, tours of famous restaurants and tea houses, and an amusing waiters' race and cheerleading competition. Brochures and more information are available at the HKTA.

Hong Kong International Film Festival (April). Two weeks of films and documentaries representing virtually every country in the world give Hong Kong film fans a good run for their money. There is neither commercial interest specifically involved nor a competition, and the festival frequently focuses on hot spots in global cinema, as well as special sections on restored Mandarin classics, commendable locally made films, and many other Asian productions. It's difficult to get tickets for evening performances, but seats at daytime shows, which begin around noon, are usually available from URBTIX (☎ 2734–9009 for information). Brochures are available at city hall and other Urban Council and Regional Council outlets.

Chinese Opera Fortnight (September). For two weeks, traditional Cantonese, Peking, Soochow, Chekiang, and Chiu Chow opera is presented in the City Hall Theatre, Concert Hall, and Ko Shan Theatre.

Festival of Asian Arts (October–November). Perhaps Asia's major cultural festival, this event showcases more than 150 artistic events (dance, music, and theater) from as far afield as Australia, Bhutan, Hawaii, and Mongolia. It is staged not only in concert halls but also at playgrounds throughout the territory. It is held biennially in even-numbered years.

Film

With only two main studios (the sweet-faced action hero Jackie Chan owns one of them), Hong Kong is the movie-making capital of Asia and is second to Hollywood when it comes to exporting films. Unlike Western shoot-em-ups, the camera work in martial art flicks emphasizes the ricochet choreography of physical combat.

If you're looking for more than just a visual feast (something in English, or with subtitles), visit **Broadway Cinematheque** (⊠ Prosperous Garden, 3 Public Square St., Yau Ma Tei, ☎ 2332–9000 or 2384–6281 for ticket reservations). The art house's train-station–like design is award-winning; foreign and independent films are announced on a departure board (local films are rare). You can read the latest reel-world magazines from around the globe in the minilibrary, view laser discs, or access the Internet. A shop sells new and vintage film posters, and there's a coffee bar as well. To get here, use the Temple Street exit at the Yau Ma Tei MTR.

Performance Halls

Hong Kong Island

City hall (☞ *above*). Classical music, theatrical performances, films, and art exhibitions are presented at this complex's large auditorium, recital hall, and theater.

Hong Kong Arts Centre. Several floors of auditoriums, rehearsal halls, and recital rooms welcome local and visiting groups to perform here. Some of the best independent, classic, and documentary films from around the world are shown here, often with themes focusing on a particular country, period, or well-known director. ⊠ *2 Harbour Rd., Wanchai,* ☎ *2582–0200.*

Hong Kong Fringe Club. This club hosts some of Hong Kong's most innovative visiting and local entertainment and art exhibitions. Shows range from the blatantly amateur to the dazzlingly professional. It also has good jazz, avant-garde drama, and many other events. ⊠ *2 Lower Albert Rd., Central,* ☎ *2521–7251.*

Queen Elizabeth Stadium. Although basically a sports stadium, this 3,500-seat venue frequently presents ballet and orchestral and pop concerts. ⊠ *18 Oi Kwan Rd., Wanchai,* ☎ *2591–1346.*

Hong Kong Academy for Performing Arts. This arts school has two major theaters each seating 1,600 people, plus a 200-seat studio theater and a 500-seat outdoor theater. Performances include local and international theater, modern and classical dance, and music concerts. ⊠ *1 Gloucester Rd., Wanchai,* ☎ *2584–8500.*

Kowloon

Hong Kong Coliseum. This 12,000-plus seat stadium presents everything from basketball to ballet, skating polar bears to local and international pop stars. ⊠ *9 Cheong Wan Rd., Hung Hom Railway Station, Hung Hom,* ☎ *2355–7234.*

Hong Kong Cultural Centre. This venue for shows and conferences contains the Grand Theatre, which seats 1,750, and a concert hall, which accommodates 2,100. The center is used by visiting and local artists, whose performances range from opera to ballet to orchestral music. ⊠ *10 Salisbury Rd.,* ☎ *2734–2009.*

University Hall. This modern auditorium belongs to Baptist University and usually hosts pop concerts. It also offers dance and symphony concerts. Few big names book here, but there's plenty of local talent to check out. ⊠ *224 Waterloo Rd.,* ☎ *2339–5182.*

The New Territories

Tsuen Wan Town Hall. Although it's off the beaten track, this auditorium has a constant stream of local and international performers. Groups include everything from the Warsaw Philharmonic to troupes of Chinese acrobats. It has a seating capacity of 1,424 and probably the best acoustics of any performance hall in Hong Kong. ⊠ *72 Tai Ho Rd., Tsuen Wan,* ☎ *2414–0144; Tsuen Wan MTR Station.*

Shatin Town Hall. This impressive building, attached to New Town Plaza, an enormous shopping arcade, is a five-minute walk from the KCR station at Shatin. It hosts cultural events including dance, drama, and concert performances. ⊠ *1 Yuen Wo Rd., Shatin,* ☎ *2694–2511.*

Performing Arts Ensembles

Regular performances are held by several permanent arts ensembles in the territory. Some survive with government support, others are subsidized by private organizations.

Hong Kong Philharmonic Orchestra. More than 100 musicians from Hong Kong, the United States, and Europe perform everything from classical to avant-garde to contemporary music by Chinese composers. Former soloists include Vladimir Ashkenazy, Rudolf Firkusny, and Maureen Forrester. Performances are usually held Friday and Saturday at 8 PM in city hall or in recital halls in the New Territories (☎ 2721–2030 for ticket information).

Hong Kong Chinese Orchestra. Created in 1977 by the Urban Council, this group performs only Chinese works. The orchestra consists of strings, plucked instruments, wind, and percussion. Each work is specially arranged and orchestrated for each concert (☎ 2853–2622 for further information).

Chinese Opera

Cantonese Opera. There are 10 Cantonese opera troupes in Hong Kong, as well as many amateur singing groups. These groups perform "street opera," for example, in the Shanghai Street Night Market on Sunday, while others perform at temple fairs, in city hall, or in playgrounds under the auspices of the Urban Council (☎ 2867–5125). Visitors unfamiliar with the form are sometimes alienated by the strange sounds of this highly complex and extremely sophisticated art form. Every gesture has its own meaning; in fact, there are 50 different gestures for the hand alone. Props attached to the costumes are similarly intricate and are used in exceptional ways. For example, the principal female will often wear 5-ft-long pheasant tails attached to her headdress. Anger is shown by dropping the head and shaking it in a circular fashion so the feathers move in a perfect circle. Surprise is shown by what's called nodding the feathers. One can also "dance with the feathers" to show a mixture of anger and determination. The orchestral instruments punctuate the singing. It is best to have a local friend translate the gestures, since the stories are so complex they make Wagner or Verdi librettos seem almost simplistic.

Peking Opera. A highly stylized musical performance, this type of opera employs higher-pitched voices than Cantonese opera. This is an older opera form and more respected for its classical traditions. Several troupes visit Hong Kong from the People's Republic of China each year, and their meticulous training is well regarded. They perform in city hall or at special temple ceremonies. Call the Urban Council (☎ 2867–5125) for further information.

6 Outdoor Activities and Sports

Hong Kong's international reputation for fast-paced urbanism doesn't prepare most visitors for the wide range of sports and outdoor activities available. You can test your luck at a horse-racing track, hike a well-developed network of trails, learn a martial art, or simply loaf about on one of the region's lovely beaches.

Updated by
Jan Alexander

AS YOU MIGHT EXPECT IN THE hometown of Jackie Chan, Hong Kong is a place where high-octane activity never seems to stop, whether it's on the stock exchange floor, in the gym, or in the racing stands. You won't find much baseball or American-style football, but the local cricket, soccer, and rugby teams are the British imports least likely to become casualties of the handover. And if you happen to be in town for horse-racing season, don't miss the spectacle. Hong Kong has the world's highest per-capita horse-race betting turnover. Total money spent at the racetrack for the 1995–96 season, the latest for which figures are available, was US$10.5 billion, or $1,690 for every member of the population. Check weekly activity schedules at a Hong Kong Tourist Association information booth for listings on spectator-sport events.

If you want to be a participant in local activities, you can join the men and women doing tai chi in the public parks (if you care to get up at 6 AM). And, of course, if you've ever dreamed of studying martial arts, this is the place to start. Hong Kong residents are partial to hiking in the mountains and sailing into the more remote stretches of the South China Sea, beyond Victoria Harbour. Golf and tennis are also widely available.

PARTICIPANT SPORTS

Hong Kong has long been known as a club-oriented city, and whether you're into golf, sailing, squash, or tennis, you'll find that the best facilities are available at members-only clubs. However, the following clubs have reciprocal privileges with clubs outside Hong Kong:

The Hong Kong Jockey Club offers free entry to its members enclosure during racing season but not use of club recreational facilities. Visitors with reciprocal privileges at the Hong Kong Golf Club are allowed 14 free rounds of golf each year. Other clubs with reciprocal policies are the Royal Hong Kong Yacht Club, (the "Royal" may be dropped soon), Hong Kong Cricket Club, Kowloon Cricket Club, Hong Kong Football Club, Hong Kong Country Club, Kowloon Club, Hong Kong Club, and Ladies' Recreation Club.

Before you leave for Hong Kong, check with your club to see if it has an arrangement with one there. If so, you'll need to take along your membership card, a letter of introduction, and, often, your passport when you visit the affiliated establishment in Hong Kong. Call when you arrive to book facilities or ask your hotel concierge to make arrangements.

Golf

Three Hong Kong golf clubs allow visitors with reciprocal privileges from a club at home to play their courses.

The **Clearwater Bay Golf and Country Club,** in the New Territories, has five outdoor and two indoor tennis courts, three indoor squash courts, and two indoor badminton courts, as well as an outdoor pool, a health spa, and an 18-hole golf course. Together with the Hong Kong Tourist Association (HKTA), the club sponsors a Sports and Recreation Tour, allowing visitors to tour the facilities and play golf. ✉ *Clearwater Bay Rd., Saikung Peninsula,* ☎ *2719–1595 or 2335–3885 for booking office (*☎ *2801–7177 for HKTA tour).* ✉ *Greens fees HK$1,200 for 18 holes, tour cost HK$380 plus greens fees. Cart, club, and shoe rentals available; no lessons.*

The **Discovery Bay Golf Club,** on Lantau Island, has an 18-hole course open to visitors on weekdays. ⊠ *Take Discovery Bay ferry from Star Ferry pier in Central, then catch bus to course (call club for current bus-line info),* ☎ *2987–7271 or 2987–7273.* ⊞ *Greens fees HK$1,400, club rental HK$150, golf-cart rental HK$300, and shoe rental HK$150. Lessons: HK$500–HK$600 per hr.*

The **Hong Kong Golf Club** (formerly the Royal Hong Kong Golf Club) allows visitors to play on its three 18-hole courses at Fanling in the New Territories. ⊠ *Just off Fanling Hwy.,* ☎ *2670–1211 for bookings, 2670–0647 for club rentals (HK$250).* ⊞ *Greens fees HK$1,400 for 18 holes. Lessons: HK$250–HK$400 per half hour, HK$290–HK$1,270 for 18-hole coaching, depending on pro.*

The **Tuen Mun Golf Centre** is a public center with 100 golf driving bays and a practice green. ⊠ *Lung Mun Rd., Tuen Mun,* ☎ *2466–2600.* ⊞ *HK$11 per bay, HK$11 per club, and HK$11 per hour per 30 balls.* ⊙ *Tues., Wed., and Fri.–Sun. 8 AM–10 PM, Mon. and Thurs. 1–10.*

Health Clubs

Most health clubs require membership, and the person behind the desk will look at you blankly if you try to explain your health club at home might have a reciprocal arrangement. The majority of first-class hotels have health clubs on their premises. And the following two health clubs will let you enter for a reasonable day rate.

California Fitness Center (⊠ 1 Wellington St., Central, ☎ 2522–5229) costs HK$150 per day.

Tom Turk Fitness Club (⊠ Citibank Tower, Citibank Plaza, 3 Garden Rd., 3rd floor, Central, ☎ 2521–4541; ⊠ International House, 8 Austin Rd., Tsim Sha Tsui, ☎ 2736–7188) charges HK$115 for a day visit, HK$200 after 5.

Hiking

Hong Kong's well-kept and reasonably well-marked hiking trails, never more than a few hours from civilization, are one of its best-kept secrets. While visitors are busy shopping, the colony's residents are hitting the trails to escape the bustle and noise. A day's hike (or two days if you're prepared to camp out) takes a bit of planning, but it's well worth the effort. You'll see the best of Hong Kong, looking out over the expanse of islands from the low, rugged mountains, and discover exotic birds and shrubbery in the wild bush land, as you meander through rolling hillsides and highland plateaus. You'll feel farther than you really are from the buildings below, which seem almost insignificant from this perspective.

However, don't expect to find the wilderness wholly unspoiled. Few upland areas escape Hong Kong's relentless plague of hill fires for more than few years at a time. Some are caused by dried-out vegetation, others erupt from small graveside fires set by locals to clear the land around ancestors' eternal resting spots. You may run into a knee-high charcoal forest of scorched grass and saplings. In more frequented areas, a layer of metal cans, heat-twisted plastic water bottles, and other rubbish lie exposed, staring through the blackened stems. Partly because of these fires, most of Hong Kong's forests, except for a few spots in the New Territories, support no obvious wildlife other than birds— and mosquitoes. Bring along repellent.

Gear

In addition to insect repellent, you'll need sturdy shoes or boots, a small knapsack, sunblock, a hat or sunglasses, and a supply of water and food. If you hike the Hong Kong Trail, there is one stretch of urban development where you can stop and replenish your groceries. Wear layered clothing—the weather in the hills tends to be very warm during the day and colder toward nightfall. If you're planning to camp, carry a sleeping bag and tent.

Great Outdoor Clothing Company (⊠ Silvercord Bldg., 30 Canton Rd., Tsim Sha Tsui, ☎ 2730–9009) doesn't offer the same range of camping equipment, backpacks, sleeping bags, and clothes you'd find in the United States or in the United Kingdom, but it'll do in a pinch.

Timberland (⊠ 2nd floor, Pacific Place, Admiralty, ☎ 2868–0845) sells hiking boots, although you may also want to look in any of the dozens of small shops on Fa Yuen Street in Mong Kok, Kowloon.

Maps

Before you go, pick up trail maps at the **Government Publications Centre** (⊠ Pacific Place, Government Office, ground floor, 66 Queensway, Admiralty, ☎ 2537–1910). Ask for the blueprints of the trails and the Countryside Series maps. The HM20C series comprises handsome four-color maps, but it's not very reliable.

Trails

You can hike through any of the territory's country parks and around any of the accessible outlying islands, but the following are four of the most popular hiking trails.

Hong Kong Trail. The most practical for first-time trailblazers, the Hong Kong Trail wends for approximately 30 mi (48 km) over Hong Kong Island, from **Victoria Peak** to the beach community of **Shek O.** The full hike takes two days. The trail offers a panoramic view of the island with all of its history and splendor and passes through some dense forest untouched by development or fires. Follow the map to the starting point on the Peak (you can get there by tram or taxi) and take the trail down through **Pok Fu Lam.** Toward the end of the first day you'll reach **Wang Nai Cheung Gap,** where a road connects Happy Valley to the south side of the island. You can buy food at the grocery market at Parkview Apartments here and continue your hike, or take a bus or taxi back to your hotel. On the second day hike through **Tai Tam Country Park,** then climb **Dragons Back Ridge** toward the northeastern part of the island. From here the trail takes you down to the unspoiled rural village at **Big Wave Bay.** Between here and Shek O you'll see lavish estates. From **Shek O** you can take a bus or taxi home.

Lantau Trail. This trail is the toughest—three days if you follow the entire route—but you can break off at a number of points. You can even retreat to a monastery to rest your feet. A long, arduous day's walk will take you from **Silvermine Bay** (☞ Outer Islands *in* Chapter 2), which you reach by ferry from Central, to the **Po-Lin Monastery.** You'll walk over Sunset Peak, then down and up again to the top of **Lantau Peak,** Hong Kong's second-highest mountain. From here you drop straight down to the monastery. You can stay here for the night, either in the monastery dorms or the Lantau Tea Gardens cottages, or take a bus back to Silvermine Bay. Begin your second day from the monastery (take the bus there if you returned to Silvermine Bay). On this branch of the trail, you hike to the picturesque fishing village of **Tai O.** The scenery along this walk, past the Shek Pik Reservoir, is quite spectacular. From the monastery make your way through the highland meadows of **South**

Lantau Park, then turn north. You'll pass a number of small monasteries before dropping down to Tai O. From the village you might want to turn back. If you're going to camp and continue on the trail, be sure to bring a three-day supply of water, and be prepared to spend the night in complete wilderness. The trail from Tai O follows the remote west coast of Lantau to **Fan Lau,** site of an old fort and one of Hong Kong's mysterious prehistoric circles of stones. Return to Silvermine Bay on the path alongside the catchment channels, where water from the mountains flows down.

McLehose Trail. A splendidly isolated 60-mi (97-km) path through the New Territories (a four- or five-day hike) starts at **Tsak Yue Wu,** beyond Sai Kung, and circles the **High Island Reservoir** before breaking north. Climb through **Sai Kung Country Park** to a steep section of the trail, up the mountain called **Ma On Shan.** Then turn south for a high-ridge walk through **Ma On Shan Country Park.** From here you walk west along the ridges of eight mountains, also known as the Eight Dragons, which gave Kowloon its name. (The last emperor of the Sung dynasty is thought to have named the peninsula Nine Dragons after these eight peaks, plus himself as the ninth.) You may see wild monkeys on the trail near Eagles Nest. After you cross Tai Po Road, the path follows along ridge tops toward **Tai Mo Mountain,** 3,161 ft above sea level. This is the tallest mountain in Hong Kong and sometimes gets snow at the top. Continuing west, the trail drops gradually to **Tai Lam Reservoir** and then to **Tuen Mun,** where you can catch public transportation.

Wilson Trail. Hong Kong's newest major trail opened in 1996 and runs 48 mi (78 km) from Stanley Gap on Hong Kong Island to Nam Chung in the northeastern New Territories. You have to cross the harbor by MTR at Quarry Bay to complete the entire walk. The trail has been laid out with steps paved with stone and footbridges at steep sections and across streams. Clearly marked with signs and information boards, this popular walk is divided into 10 sections. You can take just one or two of these, since the whole trail takes about 31 hours to traverse. It begins at Stanley Gap Road, on the south end of Hong Kong Island, and it takes you through rugged peaks that offer a panoramic view of Repulse Bay and the nearby Round and Middle islands. This first part, Section 1, is only for the very fit. Much of the trail requires walking up steep mountain grades. For an easier walk, try Section 7, which takes you along a greenery-filled fairly level path that winds past the eastern shore of the Sing Mun Reservoir in the New Territories and then descends to Tai Po, where there is a sweeping view of Tolo Harbour. Other sections will take you through the monkey forest at the Kowloon Hill Fitness Trail (Section 5), over mountains, and past charming Chinese villages.

Jogging

The best stretch of land for jogging is Bowen Road. It's a 5-mi (8-km) run back and forth on a wooded street that is closed to vehicular traffic. Victoria Park at Causeway Bay also has an official jogging track.

The **Hong Kong Running Club** is open to all levels of ability, including those training for marathons, and meets every Sunday morning at 7 from April to December. There is no charge to visitors, though there is a small joining fee (HK$150) to cover printed handouts of articles on running safety, nutrition, and other concerns. Dr. Bill Andress, who runs the club, recommends shorter runs in the oppressively hot summer months and cautions against starting a running program at that time if you aren't accustomed to the steam-bath weather. ✉ *Meet at* *the parking lot in front of Adventist Hospital, 40 Stubbs Rd., Happy Valley, ☏ 2574–6211, ext. 888 (ask for director of health).*

Junking

As boating styles go, junking—dining on the water aboard large pleasure craft that also serve as platforms for swimmers and water-skiers—is unique to Hong Kong. This leisure activity has become so popular there is now a fairly large junk-building industry producing highly varnished, plushly appointed, air-conditioned junks up to 80 ft long.

These floating rumpus rooms serve a purpose, especially for citizens living on Hong Kong Island who suffer from "rock fever" and need to escape through a day on the water. Because so much drinking takes place, the junks are also known as "gin junks," commanded by "weekend admirals." If anyone so much as breathes an invitation for junking, grab it.

You can also rent a junk. The pilot will take you to your choice of the following outer islands: Cheung Chau, Lamma, Lantau, Po Toi, or the islands in Sai Kung Harbour. **Simpson Marine Ltd.** (✉ Aberdeen Marina Tower, 8 Shun Wan Rd., Aberdeen, ☏ 2555–7349) is an established charter operator whose crewed junks can hold 35–45 people. Costs start at HK$2,200 for an eight-hour day trip or a four-hour night trip during the week, HK$4,500 on summer weekends. The price goes up on holidays.

Other established charter outfits recommended by the HKTA include the following:

Boatique (✉ Aberdeen Marina Club, Shop 10–11, ground floor, Aberdeen Marina Bldg., 8 Shum Wan Rd., Aberdeen, ☏ 2555–9355).

Jubilee International Tour Centre (✉ Man Yee Bldg., 60 Des Voeux Rd., Room 302–303, Central, ☏ 2530–0530).

Martial Arts

C. S. Tang at the **Hong Kong Chinese Martial Arts Association** (☏ 2798–2763) can provide information on where to find short-term martial-arts instruction, with courses that last from 10 days to a few months.

The **Martial Arts School** (✉ 446 Hennessy Rd., Causeway Bay, ☏ 2891–1044) of master Luk Chi Fu uses the white-crane system of internal-strength training. This method is one of the schools of *chi kung* or *noi kung,* the names for internal-strength kung fu, as opposed to the more violent type seen in the movies. This gentler version is said to be the forerunner of yoga. The technique relies on quick thinking, controlled breathing, and an instant grasp of the situation at hand. At the advanced level, a student can absorb blows and use spears and knives as if they were an extension of his or her body. Now run by the master's son, Luk Chung Mau, the school is open to visitors who are in Hong Kong for a few weeks.

The **South China Athletic Association** (✉ Caroline Hill Rd., Causeway Bay, ☏ 2665–0834) has classes in the lion dance, in kickboxing, and in the uses of weaponry.

Parachuting

The **Hong Kong Parachuting Club** holds weekend courses at Sai Kung, where you can jump from a fixed-wing aircraft to the airfield. Caution: Before you leave home, make sure your health insurance policy covers you for injuries incurred abroad. ☎ 2834–4391 or 2488–5447. ◻ HK$3,400 for course and parachute rental.

Skating

Cityplaza II, on Hong Kong Island, has a first-class ice-skating rink. ◻ 1111 Kings Rd., Taikoo Shing, ☎ 2885–4697. ◻ HK$50 per person weekdays, HK$60 per person weekends. All sessions are 2 hrs.

Festival Walk in Yau Yat Tsuen, is an entertainment complex adjacent to the Kowloon Tong train station. At press time, the complex was still under construction, but when complete, it will house the largest ice-skating rink in Hong Kong. Call for further information. ☎ 2844–3888.

Sailing

To go sailing, you must belong to a yacht club that has reciprocal privileges with one in Hong Kong. Contact the **Hong Kong Yacht Club** (☎ 2832–2817) to make arrangements. Sometimes members need crews for weekend races, so experienced sailors can go to the club and check the "crew wanted" board in the club's Course Room.

Scuba Diving

Bunn's Divers Institute (◻ 188 Wanchai Rd., Wanchai, ☎ 2893–7899) offers outings for qualified divers to such areas as Sai Kung. The cost of a day trip runs HK$480 if you bring your own equipment and HK$800 if you need to rent gear. You must bring or rent a tank ($70 each; you'll need one each for morning and afternoon).

Mandarin Divers (◻ Aberdeen Marina Tower, 8 Shun Wan Rd., Aberdeen, ☎ 2554–7110) offers two-week open-water training for a cost of HK$4,500, including boat rental, equipment, and certification (medical certificate required).

Squash

The **Hong Kong Urban Council** (☎ 2868–0000) runs many public squash courts in the territory and provides a **central booking service** (☎ 2521–5072); bookings can be made up to 10 days in advance, and you should book as early as possible. Bring a passport for identification. Most courts are open from 7 AM to 10 PM or 11 PM and cost HK$46–HK$50 for 45 minutes. The Urban Council can answer questions about locations of courts, or you can contact the following directly.

Harbour Road Indoor Games Hall (◻ 27 Harbour Rd., Wanchai, ☎ 2827–9684).
Hong Kong Squash Centre (◻ Cotton Tree Dr. across from Peak Tram Terminal, Central, ☎ 2521–5072).
Laichikok Park (◻ Lai Wan Rd., Kowloon, ☎ 2745–2796).
Victoria Park (◻ Hing Fat St., Causeway Bay, ☎ 2570–6186).

Swimming

Public swimming pools are filled to capacity in summer and closed in winter. Most visitors use the pools in their hotels. ☞ Beaches, *below.*

Tennis

Although there are a limited number of public tennis courts, they are usually completely booked far in advance. To book a public tennis court, you will need identification such as a passport. Most courts are open from 6 AM or 7 AM to 10 PM or 11 PM and cost HK$34 in the daytime and HK$46 in the evenings. Further information is available through the Hong Kong Urban Council (☞ Squash, *above*) and the **Hong Kong Tennis Association** (⊠ Sports House, Room 1021, 1 Stadium Path, So Kon Po, Causeway Bay, Hong Kong, ☎ 2504–8266). The following are courts open to the public:

Bowen Road Courts (⊠ Bowen Rd., Happy Valley, ☎ 2528–2983), four courts.

Hong Kong Tennis Centre (⊠ Wongneichong Gap, Happy Valley, ☎ 2574–9122), 17 courts.

Kowloon Tsai Park (⊠ Kowloon Tong, ☎ 2336–7878), eight courts.

Victoria Park (⊠ Causeway Bay, ☎ 2570–6186), 14 courts.

Waterskiing

Contact the **Waterski Club** (⊠ At the pier at Deep Water Bay Beach, ☎ 2812–0391) to rent a speedboat, equipment, and the services of a driver, or ask your hotel front desk for names and numbers of other outfitters. The cost is usually about HK$580 per hour.

Windsurfing

The popularity of this sport was on the decline until Hong Kong's native daughter Lee Lai-shan sailed off with the gold medal in the 1996 Summer Olympics. Now windsurfing centers at Stanley Beach, on Hong Kong Island, and Tun Wan Beach, on Cheung Chau Island, will gladly start you on the path to Olympic glory with lessons (approximately HK$250 for four hours spread over two days) and board rentals (HK$55 per hour). Other beaches that have stands where you can rent boards are the small beach opposite the main beach at Shek O, Hong Kong Island; Tolo Harbour, near Taipa in the New Territories; and Sha Ha Beach, in front of the Surf Hotel at Sai Kung, also in the New Territories. For further information call the **Windsurfing Association of Hong Kong** (⊠ Sports House, 1 Stadium Path, Room 1101, So Kon To, Causeway Bay, ☎ 2504–8255).

SPECTATOR SPORTS

Cricket Fighting

The ancient Chinese sport of cricket fighting (that's cricket as in insect, not as in the sport) is hidden from visitors, so ask for directions from a local friend. If you see someone wandering in a market, carrying a washtub, and softly calling, *"Tau, chi choot"* ("Come to see the crickets fight"), follow him.

Horse Racing and Gambling

Horse racing is the nearest thing in Hong Kong to a national sport. It is a multimillion-dollar-a-year business, employing thousands of people and drawing crowds that are almost crazed in their eagerness to rid themselves of their hard-earned money. Even if you're not a gambler, it's worth going to one of Hong Kong's two tracks just to see the crowds. In fact, in a place where gambling has developed into a mania, it may come as a surprise to learn that most forms of gambling are forbidden. Excluding the stock market, which is by far the territory's biggest single gambling event, the only legalized forms of gambling are horse racing and the lottery. Nearby Macau (☞ Chapter 8) is another story—there you can get your fill of casino gambling.

The Sport of Kings is run under a monopoly by the Royal Hong Kong Jockey Club, one of the most politically powerful entities in the territory. Profits go to charity and community organizations. The race season runs from September or October through May. Some 65 races are held at one or the other of the two courses, most often on Saturdays and Sundays, with an occasional Wednesday or Thursday night session. Check with the **Hong Kong Tourist Association hot line** (☎ 2807–6390) for a season schedule. You can view races from the Members' Stand at both tracks by showing your passport and paying HK$50 for a badge. Both courses have huge video screens at the finish line so that gamblers can see what is happening each foot of the way.

The **Happy Valley Racecourse** (✉ Hong Kong Jockey Club, 2 Sports Rd., Happy Valley, ☎ 2966-8111 or 2966–8364) on Hong Kong Island is one of Hong Kong's most beloved institutions and host to most of the night races, which are usually held on Saturday or Sunday.

The **Shatin Racecourse** (✉ Tai Po Rd., Shatin, next to Racecourse KCR station, ☎ 2966–6520) in the New Territories is newer than Happy Valley and is one of the most modern racecourses in the world. Most races held here are run in the day on Saturday or Sunday. The easiest way to get here is by KCR train. When a race is being held, the KCR detours to the Racecourse stop, between Sha Tin and University. There is a walkway from the station that takes you directly to the race track. By car, take the exit marked Racecourse from Tai Po Road, just past central Shatin.

Rugby

One weekend every spring Hong Kong hosts the international tournament of Sevens-a-Side teams at the Hong Kong Stadium, and the whole town goes rugby mad. In 1998 the tournament will be held March 28–29. To avoid camping outside the stadium all night to buy tickets, you can purchase them in advance from an overseas agent. For a list of agents contact Beth Coalter at the **Hong Kong Rugby Football Union** (✉ Sports House, 1 Stadium Path, Room 2003, So Kon Po, Causeway Bay, ☎ 2504–8300, FAX 2576–7237).

BEACHES

Few tourists think of Hong Kong as a place for swimming or sunbathing. Yet Hong Kong has hundreds of beaches, about 30 of which are "gazetted"—cleaned and maintained by the government, with services that include lifeguards, floats, and swimming-zone safety markers.

The scenery is breathtaking, but pollution is a problem in Hong Kong waters, so we wouldn't advise you to spend the whole day in the water. For this reason we've restricted our recommendations to the beaches that offer a variety of activities as alternatives to swimming. Check with the HKTA before taking the plunge, and don't swim if a red flag—indicating either pollution or an approaching storm—is hoisted. The red flag is often flying at Big Wave Bay (on Hong Kong Island, south side) because of the rough surf. Check with the HKTA or listen to announcements on radio or TV before heading out there.

Swimming is extremely popular with the locals, which means that most beaches are packed on summer weekends and public holidays. The more popular beaches, such as Repulse Bay, are busy day and night throughout the summer. Shortly after the Mid-Autumn Festival in

September, local people stop using the beaches. This is a good time for visitors to enjoy them, especially since the weather is warm year-round.

Almost all the beaches can be reached by public transportation, but knowing which bus to catch and where to get off can be difficult. Most bus drivers have neither the time nor the ability to give instructions in English. Pick up bus maps at the HKTA information booths before you start out. Or you can take a taxi all the way to any of the beaches on Hong Kong Island and still have change for lunch! Beaches on outlying islands are reached by Hong Kong Ferry from Central and are often a short walk from the pier.

Hong Kong Island

Big Wave Bay, Hong Kong's only surfing beach, often lives up to its name and is frequently closed for swimming because of high surf. When the red flag goes up, signaling dangerous waves, get out of the water. The beach has kiosks, barbecue pits, a playground, changing rooms, showers, and toilets. ⊠ *From Shau Ki Wan take Bus 9 to the parking lot at Big Wave Bay Rd.; you have to walk for about 20 min down several hills to get to the beach.*

At **Deep Water Bay** the action starts at dawn every morning, all year long, when members of the Polar Bear Club go for a dip. The beach is packed in summer, when there are lifeguards, swimming rafts, and safety-zone markers, plus a police reporting center. Barbecue pits, showers, and rest rooms are open year-round. A taxi from Central will take about 20 minutes. ⊠ *By public transport, take Bus 6A from Exchange Sq. Bus Terminus. For a scenic route, take Bus 70 from Exchange Sq. to Aberdeen and change to Bus 73, which passes the beach en route to Stanley.*

Repulse Bay is Hong Kong's answer to Coney Island, except it's a hundred times more beautiful. It has changing rooms, showers, toilets, swimming rafts, swimming safety-zone markers, and playgrounds. There are also several Chinese restaurants, as well as kiosks serving light refreshments. The beach has an interesting building at one end resembling a Chinese temple, with large statues of Tin Hau, goddess of the sea, and Kwun Yum, goddess of mercy. Small rowboats are available for rent at the beach. ⊠ *Take Bus 6, 6A, 64, 260, or 262 from Exchange Sq., or Bus 73 from Aberdeen. Most drivers on this route speak English and can tell you when to get off.*

Shek O is almost Mediterranean in aspect. A fine, wide beach with nearby shops and restaurants, it has refreshment kiosks, barbecue pits, lifeguards, swimming rafts, playgrounds, changing rooms, showers, and toilets. This is one of the few beaches directly accessible by bus. ⊠ *Take the MTR from Central to Shau Ki Wan (there is a bus from Central to Shau Ki Wan, but it takes hours), then Bus 9 to the end of the line.*

Stanley Main, a wide sweep of beach, is popular with the Hobie Cat crowd and has a refreshment kiosk, swimming rafts, changing rooms, showers, and toilets, plus a nearby market. ⊠ *Take a taxi from Central; or Bus 6, 6A, or 260 from Exchange Sq.; or Bus 73 from Aberdeen.*

Turtle Cove, isolated but picturesque, has lifeguards and rafts in summer, barbecue pits, a refreshment kiosk, changing rooms, showers, and toilets. ⊠ *From Central take the MTR to Sai Wan Ho and change to Bus 14; get off on Tai Tam Rd. after passing the dam of Tai Tuk Reservoir.*

The New Territories

Expansive Sai Kung Peninsula has some of the most beautiful beaches, and many are easily reached by public transportation. Here are the three most popular beaches in Sai Kung:

Pak Sha Chau is a gem of a beach, with brilliant golden sand. It's on a grassy island near Sai Kung Town and can only be reached by sampan. (Go to a pier and look for sampans. A driver will probably approach you. You must negotiate a fee but expect to pay about HK$100.) Amenities include barbecue pits and toilets. ⊠ *Take MTR to Choi Hung, then Bus 92 to Saikung.*

Sha Ha's waters are sometimes dirty, but because it is rather shallow far out from shore, it's ideal for beginning windsurfers. You can take lessons or rent a board at the Kent Windsurfing Centre. Facilities include refreshment kiosks, a coffee shop, and a Chinese restaurant in the adjacent Surf Hotel. ⊠ *Take MTR to Choi Hung, then Bus 92 to the end of the line at Saikung, and walk or take a taxi for about a mile.*

Silverstrand is always crowded on summer weekends. Although a little rocky in spots, it has good, soft sand and all the facilities, including changing rooms, showers, and toilets. ⊠ *MTR to Choi Hung, then Bus 92 or taxi.*

The Outer Islands

If you want to make a longer day of it, take a morning ferry to Lamma, Lantau, or Cheung Chau. One option is to combine the beach trip with a sightseeing tour of the island.

Cheung Sha is a very popular beach, only a short taxi or bus ride from the Silvermine Bay ferry pier. It has a sandy beach a mile long and is excellent for swimming. All the standard facilities are available. ⊠ *Take the ferry from Central to Silvermine Bay. Buses meet the ferry every half hr on weekdays; on Sun. and holidays buses leave when full, which will not take long on a sunny day.*

Hung Shing Ye, on Lamma Island, is very popular with local young people. There are no swimming rafts, but there are showers, toilets, changing rooms, barbecue pits, and a kiosk. ⊠ *Take the ferry from Central to Yung Shue Wan and then walk over a low hill.*

Lo So Shing, also on Lamma Island and popular with local families, is an easy hike on a paved path from the fishing village of Sok Kwu Wan. Facilities include a kiosk, barbecue pits, swimming rafts, changing rooms, showers, and toilets. ⊠ *Take a ferry from Central to Sok Kwu Wan and then walk for 20–30 min.*

Tung Wan is the main beach on Cheung Chau Island, and its wide sweep of golden sand is hardly visible on weekends because it's so crowded with sunbathers. At one end is the Warwick Hotel. There are plenty of restaurants along the beach for refreshments, seafood, and shade. The standard amenities are available. ⊠ *Take the ferry from Central to Cheung Chau ferry pier and walk 5 min through the village to the beach.*

7 Shopping

Although Hong Kong is no longer the mercantile paradise it once was, many shopping aficionados still swear by it, and they return year after year for such items as Chinese antiques, Chinese porcelain, pearls, watches, cameras, eyeglasses, silk sheets and kimonos, tailor-made suits, and designer clothes found in off-the-beaten-path outlets.

Updated By
Jan Alexander

SINCE THE 1980S RAPIDLY RISING RETAIL RENTS have put a damper on the megabargains for which Hong Kong was once known. Although retail prices here are still well below those of many Asian and European cities, you will probably find that clothes, computers, and many electronic items cost about the same as or slightly more than they do in the United States. This is not to say you won't find some good values and, of course, a wide range of unique items—with the added bonus of no sales tax.

Few of the outdoor market sellers will bargain with you now. In the electronic shops in Tsim Sha Tsui, however, salesmen will frequently drop the list price slightly, by about 5%. Nor is it uncommon for jewelers in the midprice range to offer you a discount of 10%–20% if you look at a few items and seem moderately interested. Be wary if a salesperson tries to drop the price much lower, however; you might go home to find you've purchased an inferior or defective item.

A rule of thumb: Tiffany's, Dior, Waterford, and the other designer boutiques with branches all over the world will probably not offer bargains. Stick to local shops (choose those with the HKTA membership sticker in the window, which signals consumer protection) and to items made in Hong Kong or other parts of Asia.

If you're really determined to shop till you drop, **Asian Cajun Ltd.** (⊠ 12 Scenic Villa Dr., 4th floor, Pokfulam, ☎ 2817–3687, ℻ 2855–9571) offers customized shopping tours for visitors looking for good buys in antiques, art, jewelry, designer clothes, and specialty items. Escorted tours, which visit hard-to-find shops and private dealers, are US$100 per hour, with a three-hour minimum, for up to four people. There is an extra hourly charge for a car and driver.

MAJOR SHOPPING AREAS

Hong Kong Island

Western District

From the edge of Central to Kennedy Town (take the MTR to Sheung Wan or the tram to Western Market) is Western District, one of the oldest and most typically Chinese areas of Hong Kong. Here you'll can find craftsmen making mah-jongg tiles, opera costumes, fans, and chops (seals carved in stone with engraved initials); Chinese medicine shops selling ginseng, snake musk, shark fins, and powdered lizards; rice shops and rattan-furniture dealers; and cobblers, tinkers, and tailors. Here, too, you will find alleyways in which merchants have set up small stalls filled with knickknacks and curios.

Also in Western, opposite Central Market, is the huge **Chinese Merchandise Emporium,** with a vast display of reasonably priced goods, from luggage to antiques, made in China. Next to the Emporium, on **Pottinger Street,** are stalls selling every kind of button, bow, zipper, and sewing gadget. Cloth Alley, or Wing On Street, is nearby, and so is Wellington Street, where you'll find a variety of picture framers, mah-jongg makers, and small boutiques. Going west, don't miss **Man Wa Lane,** where you can buy your personal Chinese chop. In this area you will also find Western's two largest department stores: Sincere and Wing On.

Nearby is the Victorian redbrick structure of **Western Market.** Built in 1906 as a produce market, it is now similar to London's Covent Gar-

Shopping Centers, Department Stores, & Markets

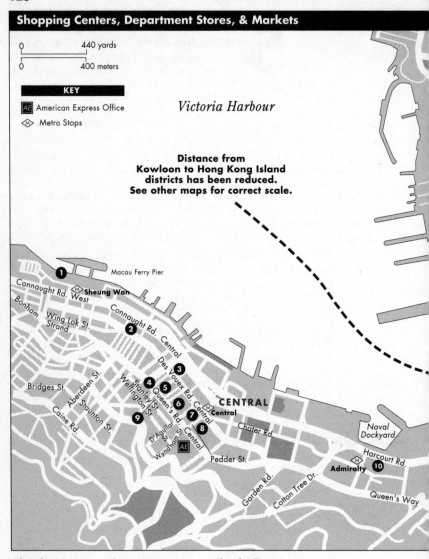

0		440 yards
0		400 meters

KEY

🅰🇪 American Express Office

◈ Metro Stops

Victoria Harbour

Distance from Kowloon to Hong Kong Island districts has been reduced. See other maps for correct scale.

Macau Ferry Pier

Connaught Rd. West

Sheung Wan

Bonham Strand

Wing Lok St.

Connaught Rd. Central

Bridges St.

Aberdeen St.

Wellington St.

Stanley St.

Des Voeux Rd. Central

Queen's Rd. Central

CENTRAL

Central

Caine Rd.

Staunton St.

D'Aguilar St.

Wyndham St.

Queen's Rd. Central

Chater Rd.

Naval Dockyard

Pedder St.

Garden Rd.

Cotton Tree Dr.

Harcourt Rd.

Admiralty

Queen's Way

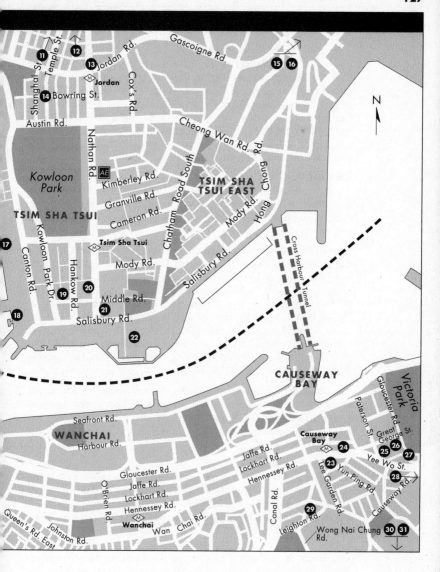

den. The first two floors are filled with shops selling crafts, toys, jewelry, collectibles, and fabrics.

The streets behind Western Market are some of the best places to soak up some of Hong Kong's traditional Chinese atmosphere. **Wing Lok Street** and **Bonham Strand West** are excellent browsing areas, with their herbal shops, snake gall-bladder wine shops—visit **She Wong Yuen** (✉ 89–93 Bonham Strand) for a taste—and shops selling rice, tea, and Chinese medicines. Heading uphill, don't miss the stalls selling bric-a-brac on **Ladder Street,** which angles down from Queen's Road in Central to Hollywood and Caine roads. **Hollywood Road** is the place to look for Chinese antiques and collectibles.

Central District

The financial and business center of Hong Kong, Central offers an extraordinary mixture of boutiques, department stores, hotel shopping arcades, and narrow lanes full of vendors selling inexpensive clothing and knockoffs of designer goods.

Lane Crawford, east of the Chinese Merchandise Emporium, is Hong Kong's most luxurious department store. Central is also home to a branch of Chinese Arts & Crafts, which carries small collections of upscale clothing, linen, silk, jewelry, and art objects. Other exclusive shops can be found in Central's major business and shopping complexes, including the **Landmark Central Building, Prince's Building, Nine Queen's Road, Swire House,** and **Pacific Place,** and in hotel shopping arcades, such as those of the **Mandarin Oriental** and **Furama Kempinski** hotels. **Shanghai Tang,** on Pedder Street, has fine silk Mandarin jackets for men and women, as well as an exciting array of campy chinoiserie.

You can hunt for bargains on clothing, shoes, woolens, handbags, and accessories in the stalls that fill **East and West Li Yuen Streets,** between Queen's Road and Des Voeux Road. **Wyndham** and **On Lan** streets have several good embroidery and linen shops, and **D'Aguilar Street** has flower stalls.

Wanchai District

More famous for its Suzie Wong–style nighttime meanderings than for daytime shopping, Wanchai still has some interesting spots for the curious or adventurous shopper. Tattoos, for instance, are available on **Lockhart Road,** and traditional Chinese bamboo birdcages on **Johnston Road.** Wandering through the lanes between Johnston Road and Queen's Road East, with their vegetable and fruit markets, you can find dozens of stalls selling buttons and bows and inexpensive clothes. In tiny **Spring Garden Lane,** you will also find several small factory outlets. **Queen's Road East** (near its junction with Queensway) is famous for shops that make blackwood and rosewood furniture and camphor-wood chests. There are more furniture shops on **Wanchai Road,** off Queen's Road East.

Happy Valley

Happy Valley is a good area to shop for shoes. Follow **Wong Nai Chung Road** around the eastern edge of the racecourse to **Leighton Road.** At the intersection of these two roads you will find several shops that make shoes, boots, and handbags to order at reasonable prices. The nearby **Leighton Centre** has several fashionable boutiques, toy shops, and accessory shops, but prices are higher here than they are in nearby Causeway Bay.

Causeway Bay

Four large Japanese department stores dominate Causeway Bay: **Mitsukoshi, Jumbo Sogo, Daimaru,** and **Matsuzakaya. Times Square** is a megamall with 12 floors of shopping, from the high-end Lane Crawford to run-of-the-mill moderate boutique chains. The main branch of the China Products Company chain is here, as is the Windsor House branch of Lane Crawford. **Hennessy Road** is filled with shops selling jewelry, watches, stereos, cameras, and electronic goods, and parallel **Lockhart Road** has several good shoe stores. The **Excelsior Hotel Shopping Centre** features a wide range of art, gift, and souvenir shops. **Vogue Alley** has boutiques where you can see the best work of Hong Kong's own fashion designers. The street called **Jardine's Bazaar,** a traditional favorite for inexpensive clothing, has strictly bottom-of-the-barrel merchandise now, but turn into the alley off the street to experience a bustling "wet market" (so called because the vendors are perpetually hosing down their produce), where Chinese housewives shop for fresh produce and for fresh chickens, which are slaughtered on the spot.

Eastern District

The Eastern District, which includes North Point, Quarry Bay, and Shaukiwan, is more of a residential and restaurant area than an exciting shopping area. The best shopping is found in Quarry Bay's huge **Cityplaza I & II** complex, which houses Hong Kong's largest department store, UNY, as well as hundreds of shops, ice-skating and roller-skating rinks, gardens, and restaurants.

Stanley Market

The most popular shopping area on the south side of the island is Stanley Market. It's not quite the bargain mecca it used to be, but if you comb through the stalls, you can still find some good buys in sportswear and casual clothing. It's also a good place to shop for linens. Steer clear of the antiques and handicrafts, however. Lately, the prices have risen way out of proportion to the quality of the items. The area around the **Main Street** section of the market has a trendy, artsy ambience. On the way to Stanley Market, stop at **Repulse Bay**'s shopping arcade, which has several stores selling fine reproductions of traditional Chinese furniture. Nearby, on Beach Road, is the **Lido Bazaar,** a series of stalls selling souvenirs, curios, jewelry, and clothing.

Kowloon

Tsim Sha Tsui District

Tsim Sha Tsui, known for its Golden Mile of shopping along **Nathan Road,** is justifiably popular with tourists for its hundreds of stereo, camera, jewelry, cosmetic, fashion, and souvenir shops. Branching off Nathan Road are narrow streets lined with shops crowded with every possible type of merchandise. Explore **Granville Road,** with its embroidery and porcelain shops and clothing factory outlets (not as plentiful as they were a few years ago, but worth a look for serious bargain hunters), and **Mody Road,** with its souvenir-shop alleys. Tsim Sha Tsui also has the **Yue Hwa Chinese Products Emporium,** the Japanese **Isetan** department store, the huge upscale **World of Joyce** mall, and three large and well-stocked branches of **Chinese Arts & Crafts.** Two of Hong Kong's largest shopping complexes—the multistory maze of the **New World Shopping Centre** and the vast, air-conditioned **Harbour City**—are found here. And the new **Tsim Sha Tsui East** area provides a host of other complexes.

Hung Hom District

Travel east of Tsim Sha Tsui to Hung Hom, the center of Hong Kong's jewelry and textile-manufacturing industries, for a tremendous selection of designer and factory-outlet bargains. Many are found on **Man Yue Street.**

SHOPPING CENTERS

Hong Kong Island

The Admiralty (✉ Queensway, Central, MTR: Admiralty) complex comprises a large selection of shops clustered in four shopping centers: Queensway Plaza, United Centre, Pacific Place, and Admiralty Centre. They are connected to one another by elevated covered walkways. **United Centre** is worth visiting just for Tequila Kola, which sells imported furniture, fabrics, and gifts. **Admiralty Centre** has reasonably priced optical shops and men's tailors, a chop maker, and an excellent carpet shop. **Pacific Place** has four floors of upscale shops and restaurants; its flagship department store, **Seibu** (☎ 2877–3627), has upmarket products and a vast, varied food department in the basement.

Cityplaza I & II (✉ 1111 Kings Rd., Taikoo Shing, MTR: Taikoo Shing), one of Hong Kong's busiest shopping centers, is popular with families because of its ice-skating rink, bowling alley, and weekly cultural shows. Many shops carry children's clothing, with labels such as Les Enfants, Crocodile, Peter Pan, and Crystal. Its selection of more than 400 shops includes plenty of clothing stores for men and women and a number of toy stores.

The Landmark (✉ Des Voeux Rd. and Pedder St., Central, MTR: Central) is one of Central's most prestigious shopping sites and is home to **Celine, Loewe, D'Urban, Gucci, Joyce, Hermès of Paris,** and other chichi designer boutiques. There are also art galleries and fine jewelry shops. A pedestrian bridge links the Landmark with shopping arcades at the Swire House, Jardine House, Prince's Building, Mandarin Oriental Hotel, and Nine Queen's Road.

Shun Tak Centre (✉ 200 Connaught Rd., MTR: Sheung Wan). Emerging from the MTR you'll find yourself at the Shun Tak Centre Shopping Arcade (at Macau Ferry Terminal), where a selection of boutiques features clothing, handbags, toys, and novelties. Most are chain stores found all over Hong Kong, so there is no particular reason to make a special trip to Shun Tak. But if you're waiting for the Macau Ferry and in the mood to shop, have a look around.

Times Square (✉ 1 Matheson St., Causeway Bay, MTR: Causeway Bay) is a gleaming new complex that packs in most of Hong Kong's best-known stores, including **Lane Crawford,** into 12 frenzied floors. An indoor atrium has floor shows with everything from heavy metal music to fashion shows to local movie star appearances. There are also a cinema complex and a dozen or so eateries.

Kowloon

Harbour City (✉ Canton Rd., Tsim Sha Tsui, next to the Star Ferry Terminal; MTR or Star Ferry to Tsim Sha Tsui) is Hong Kong's—and one of the world's—largest shopping complexes; if you can't find it here, it probably doesn't exist. Harbour City houses **Ocean Terminal, Ocean Centre, Ocean Galleries,** and the **Hong Kong Omni Hotel.** At last count there were some 50 restaurants and 600 shops, including 36 shoe stores and 31 jewelry and watch stores. The complex contains a vast **Toys 'R Us** (✉ Ocean Terminal, ☎ 2730–9462) and a large branch of Britain's **Marks & Spencer** (✉ Ocean Centre, ☎ 2926–3318).

New World Shopping Centre (✉ 18 Salisbury Rd., Tsim Sha Tsui; MTR: Tsim Sha Tsui, then walk to Salisbury Rd.) is a harbor-front shopping center (next to the New World Hotel) that has four floors of fashion and leather boutiques, jewelry shops, restaurants, optical shops, tailors, stereo stores, arts and crafts shops, and the Japanese **Tokyu de-**

partment store. The **Regent Hotel Shopping Arcade** (⊠ Salisbury Rd., Tsim Sha Tsui), featuring mostly designer boutiques, can be reached through the New World Shopping Centre.

Tsim Sha Tsui East, an area of hotels, shops, and offices east of Chatham Road, is accessible via a minibus from the Kowloon Star Ferry, or you can board the hovercraft ferry at Central Star Pier. There are 15 different shopping plazas clustered in this area, including Wing On Plaza, Tsim Sha Tsui Centre, Empire Centre, Houston Centre, South Seas Centre, and Energy Plaza. Prices are reasonable, and the atmosphere is lively.

DEPARTMENT STORES

Some of these department stores hold Sunday sales, and all hold seasonal sales. But stay clear of these unless you have great stamina.

Chinese

The many Chinese-product stores give shoppers some of the most unusual and spectacular buys in Hong Kong—sometimes at better prices than in the rest of China. Whether you are looking for pearls, gold, jade, silk jackets, fur hats, Chinese stationery, or just a pair of chopsticks, you cannot go wrong with these stores. Most are open seven days a week but are crowded on Saturday, Sunday sale days, and during weekdays at lunchtime. These shopkeepers are expert at packing, shipping, and mailing goods abroad, but are not so talented in the finer art of pleasant service.

China Products Company (⊠ 19–31 Yee Wo St., Causeway Bay, next to Victoria Park, ☎ 2890–8321; ⊠ 54 Nathan Rd., Tsim Sha Tsui, ☎ 2739–3839) offers a fairly wide and good-quality selection of goods, including household items.

Chinese Arts & Crafts (⊠ Prince's Bldg., Central; Pacific Place, Admiralty; 26 Harbour Rd., Wanchai; Star House, Silvercord Centre; and 233 Nathan Rd., Tsim Sha Tsui; ☎ 2827–6667 for information). This chain is particularly good for fabrics, white porcelain, silk-embroidered clothing, jewelry, and carpets. Our favorite specialty item here is the large globe with blue lapis oceans and land masses inlaid in semiprecious stones, all for a mere HK$70,000.

Chinese Merchandise Emporium (⊠ 92–104 Queen's Rd., Central, ☎ 2524–1051) serves a bustling local clientele. The fabric, toy, and stationery departments are particularly good here.

Chung Kiu Chinese Products Emporium (⊠ 528–532 Nathan Rd., Yau Ma Tei, ☎ 2780–2351) specializes in arts and crafts but also has a good selection of traditional Chinese clothing and fine silk lingerie.

Shanghai Tang Department Store (⊠ 12 Pedder St., Central, ☎ 2525–7333), on the ground floor of the Pedder Building, is the current retro rage in Hong Kong, selling old-fashioned Mandarin suits for men and women. Custom-made suits start around HK$5,000, including fabric from a large selection of Chinese silks. You can also have a cheongsam made for HK$2,500–HK$3,500, including fabric. The store also has a line of ready-to-wear Mandarin suits and kimonos in unisex styles, all in the HK$1,500 to HK$2,000 range, and Chinese memorabilia, including novelty watches depicting Mao Zedong and Deng Xiao Ping.

Yue Hwa Chinese Products Emporium (⊠ 143–161 Nathan Rd., Tsim Sha Tsui, ☎ 2739–3888; ⊠ 54–64 Nathan Rd., Tsim Sha Tsui, ☎ 2368–9165; ⊠ 301–309 Nathan Rd., Yau Ma Tei, ☎ 2384–0084) carries a broad selection of Chinese goods and has a popular medicine counter.

Japanese

Seibu (⊠ The Mall, Pacific Place, Admiralty, ☎ 2877–3627), one of many popular Japanese department stores in Hong Kong, holds the distinction of being the most upscale of the upscale. Check out Seibu for state-of-the-art fashions from Western and Japanese designers, inventive gifts, and an exotic food hall in the basement.

Yaohan (⊠ Whampoa Gardens, Hung Hom, New Territories, ☎ 2766–0338; ⊠ New Town Plaza, 18 Sha Tin Centre Rd., New Territories, ☎ 2697–9338) is out of the way but worth the trip for its food department. You can reach Whampoa Gardens by bus from the Star Ferry terminal, in Tsim Sha Tsui. To get to New Town Plaza, take the KCR to Shatin. The shopping center is right above the station.

Western

The Dragon Seed (⊠ 39 Queen's Rd., Central, ☎ 2524–2016; ⊠ New World Centre, 18–24 Salisbury Rd., Tsim Sha Tsui, ☎ 2721–3980) department store has two branches. The branch at Queen's Road has a wide range of classic European clothing and shoes. The New World Centre store has men's and women's clothing departments and a gift shop.

Joyce Boutique (⊠ The Galleria, 9 Queen's Road Central, tel. 2810–1120) is a local retailer with a concept approach—the hushed interior and beautifully displayed upscale merchandise are meant to reflect the tastes of the owner, local businesswoman and socialite Joyce Ma. In addition to the latest in Western designer fashions for women and men, Joyce sells unique household items. Be forewarned that the svelte and beautiful young sales' clerks sometimes treat Western browsers with disdain, unless they look ready to drop a wad of cash.

Lane Crawford is the most prestigious Western-style department store of all, with prices to match. Special sales here can be exhausting because everyone pushes and shoves to find bargains. The store at **One Pacific Place** (⊠ 88 Queensway, Admiralty, ☎ 2845–1838) is the best. There are branches in Windsor House, Causeway Bay; Times Square, and Pacific Place on the Hong Kong side; and in Ocean Terminal in Tsim Sha Tsui, Kowloon.

MARKETS, BAZAARS, AND ALLEYS

In Hong Kong each district has an Urban Council–run market that sells fresh fruit, vegetables, meat, seafood, and live chickens (you should know that some slaughtering of fowl takes place). Surrounding the markets are small stores that sell every imaginable kitchen and bathroom appliance, as well as clothes and even electronic goods.

Around heavy pedestrian areas you'll find illegal hawkers with a wide variety of cheap goods, but the buyer should beware—constantly on the lookout for the police, the vendors may literally run off with their goods. If so, get out of their way! In summer they can be often found in Tsim Sha Tsui in front of the Hyatt, around Granville and Mody roads, and at the Star Ferry terminal.

The street bazaars and markets give you some of the best of Hong Kong shopping—good bargains, exciting atmosphere, and a fascinating setting. Famous Cat Street, the curio haunt in Upper Lascar Row, running behind the Central and Western districts, is full of small high-quality Chinese antiques shops now, but in the street outside you'll still find plenty of hawkers selling inexpensive jewelry, opium pipes, Mao buttons, and assorted paraphernalia. In Kowloon, outside the Mong Kok

MTR station, is the Women's Market, with outdoor stalls full of women's clothes. If you rummage around enough, you might find a designer item at a rock-bottom price.

The Flower Market (⊠ Flower St. near Prince Edward MTR station) is a collection of street stalls offering cut flowers and potted plants, with a few outlets specializing in plastic plants and silk flowers.

The Jade Market (⊠ Kansu St. off Nathan Rd., Yau Ma Tei) displays jade in every form, color, shape, and size. The market is full of traders conducting intriguing deals and of keen-witted sellers trying to lure tourists. Some trinkets are reasonably priced, but unless you know a lot about jade, don't be tempted into buying expensive items.

The Kowloon City Market (⊠ Take Bus 5, 5C, or 1A from Star Ferry in Kowloon and get off opposite the airport), near the airport, is a favorite with local bargain hunters because of its huge array of clothes, porcelain, household goods, and electrical gadgets.

The Lido Bazaar (⊠ Beach Rd., Repulse Bay) is a series of small stalls selling souvenirs, costume jewelry, bags, belts, and some clothing.

Li Yuen Streets East and West (⊠ Between Queen's and Des Voeux Rds., Central) offer some of the best bargains in fashions, with or without famous brand names. Many shops here also sell trendy jewelry and accessories. You can also find traditional Chinese quilted jackets. Bags of every variety, many in designer styles, are particularly good buys. A note of warning: Watch out for pickpockets in these crowded lanes.

Stanley Village Market (Bus 6, 6A, or 260 from the Central Bus Terminus) is a popular haunt for Western residents and tourists looking for designer sportswear, washable silk, and cashmere sweaters at factory outlet prices and in Western sizes. **China Town** (⊠ 39 Stanley Main St.) has bargains on cashmere sweaters. **Sun and Moon Fashion Shop** (⊠ 18A–B Stanley Main St.) sells casual wear, with good bargains on such familiar names as L.L. Bean, Yves St. Laurent, and Talbot's. **Allan Janny Ltd.** (⊠ 17 Stanley New St.) has antique furniture and porcelain ware. Stanley Market is also a good place to buy linens. **Tong's Sheets and Linen Co.** (⊠ 55–57 Stanley St.) has sheets, tablecloths, and brocade pillow covers, as well as silk kimonos and pajamas. The market is at its most enjoyable on weekdays, when it's less crowded.

Temple Street (⊠ Kowloon, near Jordan MTR station) becomes an open-air market at night, filled with a colorful collection of clothes, handbags, electrical goods, gadgets, and all sorts of household items. By the light of lamps strung up between stalls, hawkers try to catch the eye of shoppers by flinging clothes up from their stalls; Cantonese opera competes with pop music, and there's the constant chatter of vendors' cries and shoppers' bargaining. The market stretches for almost a mile and is one of Hong Kong's liveliest nighttime shopping experiences.

SPECIALTY STORES

Antiques

The unofficial word from Hong Kong's antiques dealers is that most ancient porcelain, textiles, and specialty furniture will not be available after the Chinese takeover. China has laws against taking items more than 120 years old out of the country, and it is expected to apply the same ruling to Hong Kong. To be sure, a great deal of merchandise is smuggled out of China anyway, but shops dealing with very old pieces expect to lose much of their export business, so these shops will stop handling anything that might be affected by the law. Everyday furniture and pottery are not considered national treasures and will not be affected.

Auction Houses

If you know what you are after, keep an eye out for auction announcements in the classified section of the *South China Morning Post*.

Lammert Brothers (⊠ Union Commercial Bldg., 12–16 Lyndhurst Terr., mezzanine floor, Central, ☎ 2545–9859) holds regular carpet and antiques sales.

Victoria Auctioneers (⊠ Century Sq., 1–13 D'Aguilar St., 16th floor, Central, ☎ 2524–7611) has sales of ceramics, paintings, and jewelry.

Shops

HOLLYWOOD ROAD AREA

If you have more curiosity than cash, Hollywood Road is a fun place to visit. The street, running from Central to Western, is undeniably the best place for poking about in shops and stalls selling antiques from many Asian countries. Treasures are hidden away among a jumble of old family curio shops, sidewalk junk stalls, slick new display windows, and dilapidated warehouses.

C. L. Ma Antiques (⊠ 43–55 Wyndham St., Central, ☎ 2525–4369) has Ming dynasty–style reproductions, especially large carved chests and tables made of unlacquered wood.

Dynasty Furniture Co. (⊠ 68-A Hollywood Rd., Central, ☎ 2369–6940) has small netsukes skillfully carved out of tagua, a rain-forest nut that looks a lot like ivory.

Eastern Dreams (⊠ 47A Hollywood Rd., Central, ☎ 2544–2804; ⊠ 4 Shelley St., Central, ☎ 2524–4787) has antique and reproduction furniture, screens, and curios.

Honeychurch Antiques (⊠ 29 Hollywood Rd., Central, ☎ 2543–2433) is known especially for antique silver jewelry from Southeast Asia, China, and England.

Schoeni Fine Arts (⊠ 27 Hollywood Rd., Central, ☎ 2542–3143) sells Japanese, Chinese, and Thai antiques; Chinese silverware, such as opium boxes; and rare Chinese pottery.

True Arts & Curios (⊠ 91 Hollywood Rd., tel. 2559–1485) is a cluttered store with good buys in embroidered items (including slippers for bound feet), silver, porcelain, and snuff bottles.

Yue Po Chai Antique Co. (⊠ 132–136 Hollywood Rd., Central, ☎ 2540–4374) is one of Hollywood Road's oldest shops, and it has a vast and varied stock.

CAT STREET

Cat Street (or Upper Lascar Row), once famous for its thieves' market of secondhand stolen goods, now has almost as many small antiques shops as Hollywood Road itself; they are behind the outdoor stalls selling old—or at least old-looking—jewelry, curios, and assorted bits of junk.

Cat Street Galleries (⊠ 38 Lok Ku Rd., Sheung Wan, Western, ☎ 2541–8908) is a ground-floor mall of shops selling porcelain and furniture.

China Art (⊠ 15 Upper Lascar Row, Western, ☎ 2542–0982) has fine furnishings, mostly from the Suzhou area of China, and offers tours, usually once a month, to its warehouse in southern China.

OTHER AREAS

Alvin Lo & Co. (⊠ 2 Exchange Sq., Central, ☎ 2524–3395) has porcelain vases and figurines, mostly from the Qing and Ming dynasties, with some even older.

Altfield Gallery (⊠ Prince's Bldg., Central, ☎ 2537–6370) carries furniture, fabrics, and collectibles from all over Asia.

Charlotte Horstmann and Gerald Godfrey (✉ Ocean Terminal, Tsim Sha Tsui, ☎ 2735–7167) is good for wood carvings, bronze ware, and furniture.

Eileen Kershaw (✉ Peninsula Hotel, Tsim Sha Tsui, ☎ 2366–4083) has fine Chinese porcelain and jade carvings.

Nishiki Gallery (✉ 1 Exchange Sq., Central, ☎ 2845–2551) specializes in Japanese dolls, prints, and kimonos, 19th-century export silver, and Chinese blackwood furniture.

Teresa Coleman (✉ 79 Wyndham St., Central, ☎ 2526–2450) carries antique embroidered pieces.

Art

At a time when recession has caused most of the high-profile art buyers of Japan and the West to fade into the background, Hong Kong's economic boom has made the city a hot spot for art collecting. There is a lively contemporary gallery scene, much of it concentrating on the best work coming out of China and Southeast Asia today, and the **Art Asia Expo** (✉ Hong Kong Convention Centre, Wanchai), held every November, when galleries from all over the world arrive with work for sale.

Auction Houses

The two major auction houses from the West have branches in Hong Kong. Call for information about upcoming events.

Christie's Swire (✉ Gloucester Tower, Suite 1107–09, Landmark, Central, ☎ 2521–5396) has frequent auctions of Chinese art and antiques, as well as periodic auctions of European artists and contemporary works.

Sotheby's (✉ 2 Exchange Sq., 1st floor, ☎ 2524–8121) specializes in Chinese work, such as antiques and paintings from private collections, and estate jewelry and porcelains.

Galleries

Asian Art News, a bimonthly magazine, on sale at the bigger newsstands around town for HK$50, is a good guide to what is happening in galleries around the region. If you're interested in a firsthand view of the new trends in Asian art, plan to spend a day gallery hopping in Central and the Lan Kwai Fong area.

Alisan Fine Arts Ltd. (✉ Prince's Bldg., Central, ☎ 2526–1091) was one of the first galleries in Hong Kong to promote Chinese artists living abroad and has a wide range of contemporary art with an East-meets-West flavor.

Galerie La Vong (✉ 1 Lan Kwai Fong, 13th floor, Central, ☎ 2869–6863) is the place to see the works of today's leading Vietnamese artists, many of whose creations reveal an intriguing combination of French Impressionist and traditional Chinese influences. Many paintings from the 1960s and 1970s are on newsprint because canvas was unavailable during the Vietnam War.

Fringe Gallery (✉ 2 Lower Albert Rd., Central, ☎ 2521–7251) is part of the Fringe Club and is a showcase for young, not-yet-famous Hong Kong artists, both Chinese and expat.

Hanart TZ Gallery (✉ Old Bank of China Bldg., 2A Des Voeux Rd., 5th floor, Central, ☎ 2526–9019) shows contemporary Chinese artists from the mainland, Taiwan, Hong Kong, and abroad.

LKF Gallery (✉ Lan Kwai Fong House, 5–6 Lan Kwai Fong, 1st floor, Central, ☎ 2524–8976) exhibits a trendy blend of contemporary Eastern and Western abstract art.

Plum Blossoms Gallery (✉ Coda Plaza, 51 Garden Rd., 17th floor, Central [across from the Botanical Gardens], ☎ 2521–2189) shows Chinese and Western art, along with antique textiles and Tibetan carpets.

Sandra Walters (✉ 28 Arbuthnot Rd. [enter at 9 Glenealy Rd.], Central, ☎ 2522–1137), who for years owned the Mandarin Oriental Fine Arts Gallery, has moved to a public showroom showing a wide range of late-19th-century to contemporary Western and Chinese art. Call for an appointment.

Schoeni Art Gallery (✉ Coda Plaza, 51 Garden Rd., 18th floor, Central, ☎ 2869–8802) exhibits a dramatic mix of abstract, realist, and political paintings by contemporary mainland-Chinese artists. Once a year Schoeni hosts a show of European masters.

Wagner Art Gallery (✉ Lusitano Bldg., 4 Duddell St., 7th floor, Central, ☎ 2521–7882) is owned by an Australian couple who are making it their mission to introduce the best Australian artists to the territory. From time to time there are also shows of major contemporary names.

Wattis Fine Art (✉ 20 Hollywood Rd., 2nd floor, Central, ☎ 2524–5302) specializes in 18th- to 20th-century European paintings and the work of contemporary artists living in Hong Kong, both Chinese and expat.

Zee Stone Gallery (✉ 3 Exchange Sq., Central, ☎ 2845–4476; ✉ Yu Yuet Bldg., 43–55 Wyndham St., Central, ☎ 2810–5895) displays a combination of contemporary Chinese paintings and antique Tibetan silver and carpets. The Wyndam Street branch sells Chinese furniture as well.

Framers

It may be worth it to have your artwork framed in Hong Kong because prices are much lower than in Europe and the United States. The following framers are reputable and centrally located:

Man Fong (✉ 1 Lyndhurst Tower, Lyndhurst Terr., Central, ☎ 2522–6923).

Po Shu Frame & Glass Co. (✉ 255 Queen's Rd. E, ground floor, Wanchai, ☎ 2573–7334).

Wah Cheong (✉ 15 Hollywood Rd., Central, ☎ 2523–1900).

Cameras, Lenses, and Binoculars

Many of Hong Kong's thousands of camera shops are clustered in the Lock Road–lower Nathan Road area of Tsim Sha Tsui, in the back streets of Central, and on Hennessy Road in Causeway Bay. If in doubt about where to shop for such items, stick to HKTA-member shops. Pick up the HKTA shopping guide at any of its visitor centers. All reputable dealers should give you a one-year worldwide guarantee. If you are interested in buying a number of different items in the shop (most also stock binoculars, calculators, radios, and other electronic gadgets), you should be able to bargain for a good discount. Unauthorized dealers, who obtain their camera gear illegally from sources other than the official agent, may not provide a proper guarantee—although you may pick up better bargains in these outlets.

Photo Scientific Appliances (✉ 6 Stanley St., ☎ 2522–1903) is the place where local photographers shop for nearly all of their equipment. Expect good prices on both new and used cameras, lenses, video cameras, and accessories.

Williams Photo Supply (✉ Prince's Bldg., ☎ 2522–8437) stocks an array of photography needs.

Carpets and Rugs

Regular imports from elsewhere in China and from Iran, India, Pakistan, Afghanistan, and Kashmir make carpets and rugs a very good buy in Hong Kong. There are also plenty of carpets made locally. Though prices have increased in recent years, carpets are still cheaper in Hong Kong than they are in Europe and the United States.

Chinese Carpets

Branches of China Products and Chinese Arts & Crafts (☞ Department Stores, *above*) give the best selection and price range.

Carpet World (✉ 46 Morrison Hill Rd., Wanchai, ☎ 2893–0202; ✉ Ocean Terminal, Harbour City, Tsim Sha Tsui, ☎ 2730–4275) has a wide selection.

Tai Ping Carpets (✉ Hutchison House, 10 Harcourt Rd., ground floor, Central, ☎ 2522–7138; ✉ Wing On Plaza, 62 Mody Rd., Tsim Sha Tsui East, ☎ 2369–4061) is highly regarded for locally made carpets, especially for custom-made rugs and wall-to-wall carpets. The store takes 2½–3 months to make specially ordered carpets; customers can specify color, thickness, and even the direction of the weave. There is a showroom on the ground floor of Hutchison House. Tai Ping's occasional sales are well worth attending; check the classified section of the *South China Morning Post* for dates.

Other Asian Carpets

On Upper Wyndham Street, in Central, you will find several shops selling Central Asian, Persian, Turkish, Indian, Pakistani, Tibetan, and Afghan rugs—though don't expect miraculously low prices. Note: Because of customs regulations, American citizens are rarely allowed to import Persian rugs into the United States (☞ Customs and Duties *in* the Gold Guide).

Mir Oriental Carpets (✉ 52 Wyndham St., ☎ 2521–5641) is one of the most appealing of the Wyndham shops for its service and large stock. New selections arrive frequently.

Oriental Arts (✉ 44 Wyndham St., ☎ 2869–8123) has a large stock of carpets from India, Tibet, the Middle East, and Central Asia.

Tribal Rugs Ltd. (✉ Admiralty Centre, 18 Harcourt Rd., 2nd floor, ☎ 2529–0576), a bit out of the way in a run-of-the-mill shopping mall, is larger than the carpet shops on Wyndham Street and definitely worth a visit. Rugs from many locations are stacked almost from floor to ceiling.

Ceramics

For a full range of ceramic Chinese tableware, visit the various China Products Company stores (☞ Department Stores, *above*). They also offer fantastic bargains on attractively designed vases, bowls, and table lamps. Inexpensive buys can also be found in the streets of Tsim Sha Tsui, the shopping centers of Tsim Sha Tsui East and Harbour City, the Kowloon City Market, and the shops along Queen's Road East in Wanchai.

Antiques and Reproductions

Mei Ping (✉ 55 Wellington St., Central, ☎ 2521–3566) has unusual and very beautiful reproductions of Chinese vases and bowls.

Sheung Yu Ceramic Arts (✉ Vita Tower, 29 Wong Chuk Hang Rd., Aberdeen, ☎ 2555–6542) carries good reproductions.

Yue Po Chai Antique Co. (✉ 132–136 Hollywood Rd., Central, next to Man Mo Temple, ☎ 2540–4374) is the best spot for antique ceramic items.

English Porcelain

You can buy the finest names in European porcelain in Hong Kong, though you will pay as much as you would at home.

Craig's (✉ St. George's Bldg., 2 Ice House St., Central, ☎ 2522–8726; ✉ Ocean Terminal, Tsim Sha Tsui, ☎ 2730–8930) has some of the best finds in fine English porcelain dinner, tea, and coffee sets, including Royal Crown Derby, Royal Doulton, Royal Worcester, Spode, and Wedgwood china.

Factory Outlets

Ah Chow Factory (✉ Room 1–3, Hong Kong Industrial Centre, 489–491 Castle Peak Rd., Block B, 7th floor, Laichikok, ☎ 2745–1511) is a popular spot for deals. Take the MTR to the Laichikok station and follow exit signs to Leighton Textile Building/Tung Chau West.

Overjoy Porcelain (✉ 10–18 Chun Pin St., 1st floor, Kwai Chung, New Territories, ☎ 2487–0615) has good bargains. Take the MTR to the Kwai Hing station, then grab a taxi.

Chocolates

Chocolate Boutique (✉ Regent Hotel, 18 Salisbury Rd., Room 44, basement arcade, Tsim Sha Tsui, ☎ 2721–1211) makes its own chocolates on the premises.

The Mandarin Shop (✉ Mandarin Oriental Hotel, 5 Connaught Rd., Central, ☎ 2825–4084) has an irresistible selection of chocolate truffles.

See's Candies (✉ 11 Pedder St., the Landmark, Central, ☎ 2523–4977), flown in fresh from California daily, are available in their outlets, including the main branch in the Landmark, as well as in Ocean Terminal, Tsim Sha Tsui.

Clothing (Children's)

There are plenty of stores in Hong Kong that sell Western-style ready-to-wear children's clothing. You can also find fabulous traditional Chinese-style clothing for tots in two clothing alleys in Central—Li Yuen streets East and West.

Baba's (✉ Prince's Bldg., Central, ☎ 2523–7212) has traditional English-style smocks and rompers.

Crocodile Garments Ltd. (✉ The Mall, Pacific Place, Central, ☎ 2524–3172; ✉ Ocean Terminal, Tsim Sha Tsui, ☎ 2735–5136; and other locations all over town) sells Western-style kids' clothes.

G2000 (✉ Manning House, 38 Queen's Rd., Central, ☎ 2522–4449; ✉ New World Centre, Tsim Sha Tsui, ☎ 2369–0911) has a standard range of children's wear.

Mothercare (✉ Windsor House, 311 Gloucester Rd., Causeway Bay, ☎ 2882–3468; ✉ Prince's Bldg., Central, ☎ 2523–5704; ✉ Ocean Terminal, Tsim Sha Tsui, ☎ 2735–5738), a British firm, carries baby clothing and maternity wear.

Clothing (Tailor-Made)

Along with Hong Kong's multitude of ready-to-wear clothing shops, you can still find Chinese tailors to make suits, dresses, and evening gowns. Unfortunately, many of the next generation in tailors' families are leaving the business, so don't wait too long to visit their shops. All tailors keep records of clients' measurements, so satisfied customers can make repeat orders by mail or telephone. Keep a copy of the original measurements in case you need to change them. Here are some other do's and don'ts:

- For a suit, overcoat, or jacket, give the tailor plenty of time—at least three to five days—and allow for a minimum of two proper fittings plus a final one for finishing touches. Shirts can be done in a day, but you will get better quality if you allow more time.

- Tailors in hotels or other major shopping centers may be more expensive, but they are conveniently located and will be more accustomed to Western styles and fittings.

- Have a good idea of what you want before you go to the tailor. Often the best method is to take a suit you want copied. Go through the details carefully, and make sure they are listed on the order form, together with a swatch of the material ordered (the swatch is essential).

- When you pay a deposit (which should not be more than 50% of the final cost), make sure the receipt includes all relevant details: the date of delivery, the description of the material, and any special requirements.

For Men

Ascot Chang (⊠ Prince's Bldg., Central, ☎ 2523–3663; Peninsula Hotel, Tsim Sha Tsui, ☎ 2366–2398; Regent Hotel, Tsim Sha Tsui, ☎ 2367–8319) has specialized in making shirts for men since 1949. Clients have included George Bush and Andy Williams.

H. Baromon Ltd. (⊠ Swire House, Connaught Rd., Central, ☎ 2523–6845) has been making suits for the territory's business barons for more than 40 years.

A-Man Hing Cheong Co., Ltd. (⊠ Mandarin Oriental Hotel, Central, ☎ 2522–3336) is known for European-cut suits and custom shirts and has its own list of distinguished clients.

W. W. Chan & Sons (⊠ Burlington House, 92–94 Nathan Rd., Tsim Sha Tsui, ☎ 2366–9738) is known for top-quality classic cuts and has bolts and bolts of fine European fabrics from which to choose. Chan will make alterations for the lifetime of the suit, which should be about 20 years. Chan tailors also travel to the United States several times a year to fill orders for their customers. If you have a suit made here and leave your address, they will let you know when they plan to be in town.

Tom Li at Leading Company (⊠ Hyatt Regency Shopping Arcade, Nathan Rd., Tsim Sha Tsui, ☎ 2366–2737) is a more modestly priced tailor, recommended by locals, who makes stylish suits for men and women.

For Women

You will find that tailors do their best work on tailored suits, coats, and dresses and do not do as well with more fluid styles or knit fabrics. Tailors are the place to order a traditional Chinese cheongsam. You can bring in something you want copied or find a style in one of the tailor's catalogs. You can also bring in a photograph from a magazine or if you're skilled with pencil and paper and sure of what you want, bring in a sketch.

A good tailor has a wide selection of fabrics, but you can also bring in your own. Visit the Chinese Arts & Crafts (☞ Department Stores, *above*) branches for beautiful Chinese brocades. **Western Market** (⊠ Des Voeux Rd., Sheung Wan) has fabrics on the second floor. One detail frequently overlooked is buttons. Your tailor will probably offer you buttons made of the suit fabric at no extra charge, but if you prefer to select your own, you'll find a dazzling array of buttons in jade, mother-of-pearl, brass, and more ordinary materials at **Wu Sim Ming**

(☎ 2543–6328), the small tailor shop on the ground floor of Western Market.

Irene Fashions (✉ Burlington House, 92–94 Nathan Rd., Tsim Sha Tsui, ☎ 2367–5588) is the women's division of W. W. Chan.

Mode Elegante (✉ Peninsula Hotel, Tsim Sha Tsui, ☎ 2366–8153) has become known for high-fashion suits for the executive woman.

Bobby's Fashions (✉ Mirador Mansion, 5 Carnarvon Rd., Tsim Sha Tsui, ☎ 2724–2615) is a favorite of local expats.

Clothing (Women's)

You need just glance around the streets of Central to see that Hong Kong is one of the world's capitals of chic. Most of the best-known European retail names have stores in Hong Kong, and the territory is starting to produce some interesting and often very trendy designers of its own. For innovative, youthful creations, many by Hong Kong's own up-and-coming designers, check out the boutiques that line Vogue Alley, which starts at the intersection of Paterson and Kingston streets in Causeway Bay. For upscale women's wear and designer boutiques, Central and five-star hotels are the best places to look. Remember that most major hotels have a shopping arcade. Consult the HKTA's Shopping Guide, available at HKTA visitor centers, for complete listings of branches of these stores.

Computers

All the big names sell in Hong Kong. If you are going to buy, make sure the machine will work on the voltage in your country; an IBM or IBM clone personal computer sold in Hong Kong works on 220 volts, while the identical machine in the United States works on 110 volts. Servicing is a major concern, too. The real bargains in computers are the locally made versions of the most popular brands. The following computer stores are members of the HKTA and considered reputable:

Continental Computer Systems (✉ Hing Tai Commercial Bldg., 114 Wing Lok St., Room 202, Sheung Wan, ☎ 2854–2233) has reasonable prices on IBM clones and Macs, both desktop and notebook models.

Expert Computer Store (✉ Times Square, 1 Matheson St., Causeway Bay, ☎ 2506–3318; ✉ 113 Des Voeux Rd., Central, ☎ 2581–9113) has good deals on desktop Pentiums, modems, printers, and some software.

Mastertech Office Automation (✉ Star Computer City, Star House, 2nd floor, 3 Salisbury Rd., Tsim Sha Tsui, ☎ 2736–7263) carries a full line of office equipment and desktop computers.

One Take Computer Shop (✉ New Capital Computer Plaza, 85–95 Un Chau St., Sham Shui Po, ☎ 2728–0045) offers desktops, laptops, and accessories at low prices.

Electronic Gimmicks and Gadgets

Special Interest Electronic Co. (✉ Hutchison House, 10 Harcourt Rd., Central, ☎ 2526–3648) has hundreds of strange and not-so-strange electronic devices crammed into a tiny space.

Factory Outlets

Hong Kong used to be the factory-outlet center of the world, the place where European and American labels were manufactured and the overruns sold at close-to-wholesale prices. Those days are long gone, but because many garments manufactured elsewhere in China and in other developing countries still come through Hong Kong's duty-free port, you can find samples and overruns in the territory's many outlets. Discounts generally run a mere 20%–30% off retail, but comb through everything, and more often than not you'll be able to bag at least one fabulous bargain. One word of caution, however: check the garment carefully for damage and fading. Outlets do not accept returns.

The biggest surprise about outlets is how conveniently located some of the best ones are. If you came to Hong Kong to shop, don't miss the Pedder Building in the heart of Central and a number of small outlets tucked away in the Lan Kwai Fong area.

Pedder Building
The Pedder Building (⊠ 12 Pedder St., Central), just a few feet from a Central MTR exit, contains five floors of small shops. The number of shops offering discounts of around 30% off retail—and sometimes more—seems to be growing rather than shrinking now, after a couple of years of an upscale trend. (The **Anne Klein Shop** [☎ 2521–2547], however, is the building's first full-fledged retail store, so don't venture through that particular door if discounts are what you're after.)

Blanc deChine (☎ 2524–7875), not a discount store, has beautiful Chinese clothes, in similar styles to those at the more famous Shanghai Tang but in subtler colors, plus reproductions of antique snuffboxes as well as silver mirrors and picture frames. **Cascal** (☎ 2523–4999) has Celine, Dior, and Prada bags at about 20% off retail. **Ca Va** (☎ 2537–7174) has fabulous knitwear, along with suits and designer casual wear. **Labels Plus** (☎ 2521–8811) has some men's fashions as well as women's daytime separates. **La Place** (☎ 2868–3163) has youthful fashions, Prada bags, and a large selection of Chanel jackets at about 20% off retail. **Shopper's World–Safari** (☎ 2523–1950) has more variety than most outlets and a small upstairs department with men's fashions. The **Silkwear House** (☎ 2877–2373) has blouses with Nordstrom, Saks, and Tahari labels going for a song.

The Pedder Building also has a number of linen shops. **Hongkong & Shanghai Lace Co.** (☎ 2522–4408) has sheets, duvet covers, and table linens, as well as a line of children's clothes, at fairly low prices. **Swatow Linen Lace Co.** (☎ 2522–8547 has embroidered sheets, tablecloths, and doilies from the Swatow region of China.

Lan Kwai Fong Area
The small area of Central made up of Lan Kwai Fong and its intersecting streets is another good place to outlet-shop. Ask passersby for directions if you have trouble finding Lan Kwai Fong; it's small and tucked away but is well known to residents because of its nightlife.

Anna's Collection (⊠ 3rd floor, Grand Progress Bldg., 15–16 Lan Kwai Fong ☎ 2501–4955) has Emanuel and Country Road, plus a selection of designer fashions in sizes over 16.

Gat (⊠ Cosmos Bldg., 8–11 Lan Kwai Fong, 7th floor, ☎ 2524–9896; ⊠ Kowloon's Taurus Bldg., 21A–B Granville Rd., 12th floor, Tsim Sha Tsui, ☎ 2722–6287; and ⊠ 22 Yee Wo St., Causeway Bay, ☎ 2808–1053) carries Kenar, sometimes at as much as 40% to 50% off U.S. retail prices. There have been reports, however, of rayon sweaters from Gat coming unraveled and the store refusing to give refunds or exchanges, so shop carefully.

IN Fashion (⊠ 9A Grand Progress Bldg., 15–16 Lan Kwai Fong, ☎ 2877–9590) carries career wear and casual clothes by Ann Taylor, Laura Ashley, Next, Talbot's, and an occasional item designed for Nordstrom, as well as designer ball gowns.

Moda Mia (⊠ Grand Progress Bldg., 15–16 Lan Kwai Fong St., ☎ 2868–4798) has Italian suits, bags, and belts at a slight discount and a fine selection of men's Italian ties for HK$350.

Pot Pourri (⊠ Wong Chung Ming Commercial Bldg., 16 Wyndham St., 12th floor, ☎ 2525—1111) has Talbot's, Emanuel Ungaro, and Fenn Wright & Manson.

Ricki's (⊠ Cosmos Bldg., 8–11 Lan Kwai Fong, Room 8–11, ☎ 2877–1552) from time to time carries Emanuel Ungaro, Episode, Donna Karan, Tahari, Jaeger, Ellen Tracy, and Just Cotton.

Zeno Fashions (⊠ Man Cheung Bldg., 15–17 Wyndham St., Block B, ☎ 2868–4850) stocks mostly career wear, from labels such as Ellen Tracy, Emmanuel Ungaro, Episode, Krizia, Banana Republic, and Country Road.

Laichikok

There are a number of outlets worth visiting within a few blocks of Kowloon's Laichikok MTR station.

Le Baron (⊠ 4th floor, Flat B Yeung Chung [No. 6] Industrial Bldg., 19 Cheung Shun St., ☎ 2785–0863) has some of the best buys in cashmere in the territory, which makes the trouble of finding this building worth it: Almost at the end of Cheung Shun Street, enter through the garage and use the single elevator on the far right. It's in an office with a sign that says HEYRO DEVELOPMENT CO. LTD. Go into the office, then enter the showroom through the second door on the right.

Mia Fashion Designs (⊠ Ardour Centre, 680 Castle Peak Rd., ground floor, ☎ 2745–9771) is a small store, easy to find compared to other outlets in the area, that carries silk and cotton blouses and lingerie, often with Nordstrom labels, at bargain-basement prices.

Rotterdam (⊠ Kee Wah Industrial Bldg., 666 Castle Peak Rd., 12th floor, ☎ 2741–2586) has women's designer clothes, sometimes at almost-giveaway prices.

Other Outlets

Coast 2 Coast Design Warehouse (⊠ Hing Wai Centre, 7 Tin Wan Praya Rd., Room 1904, Aberdeen, ☎ 2870–0191) has clothes, crystal, linens, and ceramics at up to 50% off retail prices.

Diane Freis Factory Outlet (⊠ Kaiser Estate, Phase I, 41 Man Yue St., Hung Hom, ☎ 2362–1760) has discounts of around 30% on Hong Kong–based designer Diane Freis' day-wear concoctions and her elaborate cocktail dresses. Ask your hotel concierge about the bus to the outlets in Hung Hom. Many other outlets here have branches in Central, so you may decide it's not worth the trip.

Fair Factor (⊠ 44 Granville Rd., no phone) has plenty of uninteresting items, but you may be rewarded with some real finds—such as items by GAP, Adrienne Vittadini, Villager, and Victoria's Secret, going for a mere HK$50 to HK$100.

Fashions of 7th Avenue (⊠ Sing Pao Centre, 8 Queen's Rd., 12th floor, Central, ☎ 2868–4208; ⊠ Shopping Arcade, Convention Plaza, 1 Harbour Rd., Wanchai, ☎ 2824–0619; ⊠ Kaiser Estate, Phase III, Hok Yuen St., Hung Hom, Kowloon, ☎ 2764–4655) is known for its casual knit sportswear and classic suits.

The Joyce Warehouse (⊠ 34 Horizon Plaza, 2 Lee Wing St., Ap Lei Chau, ☎ 2814–8313) has taken shopaholic locals by storm. This is the outlet for women's and men's fashions sold in the ritzy Joyce Boutiques in Central and Pacific Place, with labels by such major designers as Jil Sander and Giorgio Armani. Prices for each garment are reduced by about 10% each month, so the longer the piece stays on the rack, the less it costs. The outlet is open from Tuesday to Saturday 10–6 and Sunday 12–6. Take Bus 90 from Exchange Square and get off at the Ap Lei Chau stop. From there it's easiest get a taxi to Horizon Plaza, a three- to four-minute ride.

Klaxon (⊠ 188-C Mody Rd., ☎ 2367–9881) is the best of a number of stores on Haiphong Road across from Kowloon Park.

Timothy Fashion Co. (⊠ Kaiser Estate, Phase I, 41 Man Yue St., Hung Hom, Kowloon, ☎ 2362–2389) has classic wool sweaters for men and women at good prices. Silk garments for men and women and lingerie are also good buys here, but you can find a similar selection in Tsim Sha Tsui, so don't go all the way to Hung Hom if these are all you're after.

TSL Jewellery Showroom (⊠ Summit Bldg., 30 Man Yue St., Hung Hom, ☎ 2764–4109; ⊠ Wah Ming Bldg., 34 Wong Chuk Hang Rd., Aberdeen, ☎ 2873–2618) has fairly good prices on diamonds and other precious stones in unique settings, and both locations have an on-premises workshop where you can watch the jewelry being made.

Furniture and Furnishings

Hong Kong has seen a tremendous boom in the home-decor market in recent years, and manufacturers of furniture and home furnishings have been quick to increase production. Rosewood furniture is a very popular buy in Hong Kong, as are several other specialty woods. A number of old-style shops specialize in the rich-looking blackwood furniture that originated in southern China at the turn of the century; chairs, chests, couches, and other pieces can be found at the west end of Hollywood Road, near Man Mo Temple. Queen's Road East and nearby Wanchai Road are good sources for camphor-wood chests, as is Canton Road in Kowloon.

Reproductions are common, so "antique" furniture should be inspected carefully. Traits of genuinely old pieces are: a mature sheen on the wood, slight gaps at joints as a result of natural drying and shrinking of the wood, signs of former restorations, and signs of gradual wear, especially at leg bottoms. Keep in mind, too, that blackwood, rosewood, and teak must be properly dried, seasoned, and aged to prevent pieces from cracking in climates that are less humid than Hong Kong's. Even in more humid areas, the dryness of winter heating systems can cause harm.

The Banyan Tree (⊠ Prince's Bldg., Central, ☎ 2523–5561; ⊠ Repulse Bay Shopping Arcade, Repulse Bay, ☎ 2592–8721; ⊠ Ocean Terminal, Harbour City, Tsim Sha Tsui, ☎ 2730–6631; ⊠ Times Square, 1 Matheson St., Causeway Bay, ☎ 2506–3850) has furniture and bric-a-brac, both old and new, from Europe, India, and Southeast Asia. An excellent buy spotted here recently was a Chinese bird cage for $700. Lesser quality birdcages go for more than $800 at Stanley Market. You can arrange to visit Banyan Tree's warehouse by calling its office (☎ 2877–8303). You will not receive a discount if you buy from the warehouse, but you will have the chance to see—and buy—pieces that have just arrived.

Cathay Arts (⊠ Ocean Centre, ☎ 2730–6193) is one of many rosewood furniture dealers that can be found in the Harbour City complex at Tsim Sha Tsui.

IDOS Gallery (⊠ Highgrade Bldg., 111 Chatham Rs., Tsim Sha Tsui, ☎ 2739–2882; ⊠ 88 Sun On Village, Hiram's Hwy., Sai Kung, Kowloon, ☎ 2791–4882) has wrought-iron furniture and colorful ceramics from Indonesia.

Luen Wo Hong (⊠ 88–90 Queen's Rd. E, Wanchai, ☎ 2527–8344) has reproductions of antique blackwood and elm-wood furniture.

Luk's Furniture (✉ 52–64 Aberdeen Main Rd., Aberdeen, ☎ 2553–4125) is a bit off the beaten path, but it has two floors of rosewood and lacquer furniture, as well as Korean chests, all at warehouse prices. You can place custom orders here.

Queen's Road East, in Wanchai, the great furniture retail and manufacturing area, offers everything from full rosewood dining sets in Ming style to furniture in French, English, or Chinese styles. Custom-made orders are accepted in most shops here. **Choy Lee Co. Ltd.** (✉ 1 Queen's Rd. E, ☎ 2527–3709) is the most famous.

Tequila Kola (✉ main showroom, United Centre, Admiralty, ☎ 2520–1611; ✉ Prince's Bldg., Central, ☎ 2877–3295) has reproductions of antique wrought-iron beds, one-of-a-kind furniture, home accessories, and jewelry from various corners of Asia.

Furs

It seems bizarre that Hong Kong, with its tropical climate, should have so many fur shops. But fur is a good buy here, with high-quality skins, meticulous tailoring, excellent hand finishing, and competitive prices.

Siberian Fur Store (✉ 29 Des Voeux Rd., Central, ☎ 2522–1380; ✉ 21 Chatham Rd., Tsim Sha Tsui, ☎ 2366–7039) has a particularly fashionable selection of mink, fox and other furs, all at reasonable prices.

Handicrafts and Curios

The traditional crafts of China include a fascinating range of items: lanterns, temple rubbings, screen paintings, paper cuttings, seal engravings, and wooden birds.

Banyan Tree (☞ Antiques, *above*) carries a pricey but attractive selection of items from different Asian countries.

Design Selection (✉ 75 Wyndham St., Central, ☎ 2525–8339) has a good selection of Indian fabrics.

Kinari (✉ Anson House, 61 Wyndham St., Central, ☎ 2869–6827) sells crafts and antiques from all over Southeast Asia.

Mountain Folkcraft (✉ 12 Wo On La., Central, ☎ 2525–3199) offers a varied collection of fascinating curios. From Queen's Road Central walk up D'Aguilar Street, past Wellington Street, then turn right onto Wo On Lane.

Vincent Sum Designs Ltd. (✉ 15 Lyndhurst Terr., Central, ☎ 2542–2610) carries Indonesian silver, crafts, and batiks.

The Welfare Handicrafts Shop (✉ Jardine House, Shop 7 basement, 1 Connaught Pl., Central, ☎ 2524–3356; ✉ Salisbury Rd., Tsim Sha Tsui, ☎ 2366–6979), next to the YMCA, stocks a good collection of inexpensive Chinese handicrafts for both adults and children. All profits go to charity.

Jewelry

Jewelry is the most popular item among visitors to Hong Kong. It is not subject to any local tax or duty, so prices are normally much lower than they are in most other places. Turnover is fast, competition fierce, and the selection fantastic.

Settings for diamonds and other gems will also cost less here than in most Western cities, but check your country's customs regulations, as some countries charge a great deal more for imported set jewelry than for unset gems. Hong Kong law requires all jewelers to indicate on every gold item displayed or offered for sale both the number of carats and the identity of the shop or manufacturer—make sure these marks are present. Also, check the current gold prices, which most stores will have displayed, against the price of the gold item you are thinking of buying.

Gems

DIAMONDS

As one of the world's largest diamond-trading centers, Hong Kong offers these gems at prices that are at least 10% lower than world-market levels. When buying diamonds, check the four Cs: color, clarity, carat (size), and cut. Shop only in reputable outlets—those recommended by someone who lives in Hong Kong or listed in the Hong Kong Tourist Association's shopping guide (available in HKTA visitor centers). For information or advice, call the **Diamond Importers Association** (☎ 2523–5497).

PEARLS

Pearls, another good buy, should be checked for color against a white background. Shades include white, silvery white, light pink, darker pink, and cream. Cultured pearls usually have a perfect round shape, semibaroque pearls have slight imperfections, and baroque pearls are distinctly misshapen. Check for luster, which is never found in synthetics. Freshwater pearls from China, which look like rough grains of rice, are inexpensive and look lovely in several twisted strands. Jewelry shops with a good selection of pearls include the following:

Po Kwong (⌧ 82 Queen's Rd., Centrall, ☎ 2521–4686) specializes in stringed pearls from Australia and the South Seas and will add clasps to your specifications.
K. S. Sze & Sons (⌧ Mandarin Oriental Hotel, ☎ 2524–2803) is known for its fair prices on pearl necklaces and other designs.
Trio Pearl (⌧ Peninsula Hotel, Tsim Sha Tsui, ☎ 2367–9171) has beautiful one-of-a-kind designs in pearl jewelry.

JADE

Hong Kong's most famous stone, jade comes not only in green but in shades of purple, orange, yellow, brown, white, and violet. Although you'll see trinkets and figurines purported to be made of jade everywhere in Hong Kong, high-quality jade is rare and expensive. Translucency and evenness of color and texture determine jade's value. Translucent, deep emerald green Emperor's jade is the most expensive. Be careful not to pay jade prices for green stones, such as aventurine, bowenite, soapstone, serpentine, and Australian jade. Many of the pieces for sale at the Kansu Street **Jade Market** (☞ Markets, Bazaars, and Alleys, *above*) are made of these impostors; but the endless sea of stalls brimming with trinkets of every size, shape, and color makes a visit worthwhile. If you are wary of spending any money on Kansu Street, visit the following:

Chow Sang Sang (⌧ 229 Nathan Rd., Tsim Sha Tsui, ☎ 2730–3241, and 17 smaller branches around town) has jade necklaces, bracelets, and brooches in traditional Chinese designs.
Chow Tai Fook (⌧ 29 Queens Rd., Central, ☎ 2523–7128, and 15 branches) is a good place to shop for fine jade.
Tsim Sha Tsui's Jade House (⌧ 162 Ocean Terminal, Tsim Sha Tsui, ☎ 2736–1232) has a wide selection of jade in a rainbow of hues, including deep green, in loose stones and settings, mostly of traditional Chinese design.

Jewelers

Chan Che Kee (⌧ 18 Pottinger St., Central, ☎ 2522–6402) has fist-size 14- to 18-carat gold Chinese zodiac animals, a unique gift; other small stores on Pottinger Street also carry the animals.

Chinese Arts & Crafts (☞ Department Stores, *above*) stores have a wide selection of jade, pearls, and gold as well as porcelain, jewelry, and enamelware.

China Handicrafts & Gem House (✉ 25A Mody Rd., Tsim Sha Tsui East, ☎ 2311–9703) sells loose gemstones.

Just Gold (✉ 47 Queen's Rd., Central, ☎ 2869–0799; ✉ 27 Nathan Rd., Tsim Sha Tsui, ☎ 2312–1120; and 14 other branches) specializes in delicate gold jewelry, a favorite among the Hong Kong Chinese; prices rarely go past HK$5,000.

Kai-Yin Lo (✉ The Mall, Pacific Place, Admiralty, ☎ 2840–0066; ✉ Mandarin Hotel, Central, ☎ 2524–8238; ✉ Peninsula Hotel, Tsim Sha Tsui, ☎ 2721–9623) has fabulous modern jewelry with an Asian influence.

Leather Bags and Belts

Italian bags, belts and briefcases are popular status symbols in Hong Kong, but you'll pay top dollar for them. Locally made leather bags are clearly of inferior quality—the leather isn't as soft, and the smell isn't nearly as luxurious as that of fine European leather. But if you're looking for some bargain-basement buys, check out the locally produced designer copies on Li Yuen streets East and West, in Central, and in other shopping lanes. The leather-garment industry is a growing one, and although most of the production is for export, some good buys can be found in the factory outlets in Hung Hom, Kowloon. Medium-quality bags and belts from the local manufacturer Goldlion can be found at Chinese Arts & Crafts (☞ Department Stores, *above*) stores.

For top-brand international products, visit department stores such as Lane Crawford, Wing On, and Sincere and the Japanese stores in Causeway Bay: Daimaru, Mitsukoshi, Matsuzakaya, and Sogo. All stock leather by designer brands, such as Nina Ricci, Cartier, Lancel, Il Bisonte, Comtesse, Guido Borelli, Caran d'Ache, Franco Pugi, and Christian Dior. You may find the prices higher than they are at home, however.

Linens, Silks, Embroideries

Pure silk shantung, silk and gold brocade, silk velvet, silk damask, and printed silk crepe de chine are just some of the exquisite materials available in Hong Kong at reasonable prices. The best selections are in the China Products, Chinese Arts & Crafts, and Yue Hwa stores (☞ Department stores, *above*). Ready-to-wear silk garments, from mandarin coats and cheongsams to negligees, dresses, blouses, and slacks are good buys at Chinese Arts & Crafts.

Irish linen, Swiss cotton, Thai silk, and Indian, Malay, and Indonesian fabric are among the imported cloths available in Hong Kong. Many can be found on Wing On Lane in Central. Vincent Sum Designs specializes in Indonesian batik; a small selection can also be found in Mountain Folkcraft (☞ Handicrafts and Curios, *above*). Thai silk is about the same price in Hong Kong as it is in Bangkok. Fabrics from India are available from Design Selection (☞ Handicrafts and Curios, *above*).

The best buys from China are hand-embroidered and appliquéd linen and cotton. You can find a magnificent range of tablecloths, place mats, napkins, and handkerchiefs in the China Products Company and Chinese Arts & Crafts (☞ Department Stores, *above*) stores and in linen shops in Stanley Market. You should also look in the various shops on Wyndham and On Lan streets in Central. When buying hand-embroidered items, be certain the edges are properly overcast and beware of machine-made versions being passed off as handmade.

Martial Arts Supplies

There are hundreds of martial arts schools and supply shops in Hong Kong, especially in the areas of Mong Kok, Yau Ma Tei, and Wanchai, but often they are hidden away in back streets and up narrow stairways. The most convenient place to buy your drum cymbal, leather boots, sword, whip, double dagger, studded wrist bracelet, Bruce Lee *kempo* gloves, and other kung-fu exotica is **Kung Fu Supplies Co.** (⊠ 188 Johnston Rd., Wanchai, ☎ 2891–1912).

Miscellaneous Chinese Gifts

If you are really stuck for a gift idea, think Chinese. Some of the most unusual gifts are often the simplest. How about an embroidered silk kimono or a pair of finely painted black-lacquer chopsticks? Or a Chinese chop, engraved with your friend's name in Chinese? These are available at shops throughout Hong Kong. For chop ideas, take a walk down Man Wa Lane in Central (⊠ Opposite Wing On department store, 26 Des Voeux Rd.). For those who live in cold climates, wonderful *mien laps* (padded silk jackets) are sold in the alleys of Central or in the various shops featuring Chinese products. Another unusual item for rainy weather—or even as a decorative display—is a hand-painted Chinese umbrella, available very inexpensively at Chinese Arts & Crafts and China Products Company (☞ Department Stores, *above*). Chinese tea, packed in colorful traditional tins, can be picked up in the teahouses in Bonham Strand and Wing Lok Street in Western. A bit more expensive, but a novel idea, are padded tea baskets with teapot and teacups or tiered bamboo food baskets, which also make good sewing baskets.

Optical Goods

There are a vast number of optical shops in Hong Kong, and some surprising good bargains, too. Soft contact lenses, hard lenses, and frames for glasses go for considerably less than in many other places. All the latest styles and best-quality frames are available at leading optical shops at prices generally much lower than in Europe and the United States.

The Optical Shop (⊠ Main branch: Prince's Bldg., Central, ☎ 2523–8385) is the fanciest and probably the most reliable optical store and has branches throughout Hong Kong. An eye test using the latest equipment is provided free.

Perfume and Cosmetics

Although aromatic ointments were believed to have been used by the Egyptians more than 5,000 years ago, it was Asia that made the major contributions to the art of perfumery. Today, however, Chinese perfumes are hardly a match for Western fragrances. Scented sandalwood soap is the one exception (the Maxam label in Chinese Product stores is prettily packaged). Western perfume and cosmetics are expensive in Hong Kong. Until a few years ago the territory imposed a substantial cosmetics tax. Even after that was dropped, retailers didn't want to risk lowering their profit margins. You can, however, buy most of your favorite brands at department stores such as Wing On and Sincere and at the following stores.

The Body Shop (✉ The Landmark, ☎ 2845–5238; ✉ Pacific Place, ☎ 2524–2853; ✉ Ocean Centre, Tsim Sha Tsui, ☎ 2736–7736) has branches all over Hong Kong.

Red Earth (✉ Seibu, Pacific Place, ☎ 2801–7937; ✉ The Landmark, ☎ 2877–6599), an Australian manufacturer of all-natural cosmetics, has several convenient branches. Try the glycerine soaps, which come in almost every imaginable color and scent.

Watson's (✉ Princes Bldg., Central, ☎ 2522–5153; ✉ Entertainment Bldg., 30 Queens Rd., Central, ☎ 2868–4388; ✉ Pacific Place, Admiralty, ☎ 2523–2885; ✉ Everest Bldg., 241 Nathan Rd., Tsim Sha Tsui, ☎ 2735–5033; other locations around town) is a full-service drug store with a good selection of major cosmetic and makeup brands, including some interesting Asian lines of bath oils, body lotions, and soaps in flower and fruit scents.

Shoes

The place to buy shoes in Hong Kong is on Wong Nai Chung Road, in Happy Valley next to the racecourse. Here you will find many shoe shops selling inexpensive locally made shoes and Japanese-made shoes, as well as copies of European designer shoes, boots, and bags. If you have small feet, these shops can offer excellent buys. If you wear size 8 or larger, you'll probably have trouble finding shoes that fit well. The merchants are also particularly good at making shoes and bags, covered with silk or satin, to match an outfit. If you leave your size chart, you can make future purchases through mail order.

Top-name Italian and other European shoes can be found in the department stores and shopping centers. But don't expect prices for designer shoes to be much less than they are back home.

Kow Hoo Shoe Company (✉ Prince's Bldg., 1st floor, Central, ☎ 2523–0489) has great cowboy boots in knee-high calfskin.

Lee Kee Boot & Shoe Makers (✉ 19–21B Hankow Rd., Tsim Sha Tsui, ☎ 2367–1180) custom-makes shoes for both men and women and is renowned for its skill in copying specific styles at reasonable prices.

Mayer Shoes (✉ Mandarin Oriental Hotel, Central, ☎ 2524–3317) has an excellent range of styles and leathers for men and women.

Maylia Shoe Co. (✉ The Peninsula Arcade, mezzanine floor, Salisbury Rd., Tsim Sha Tsui, ☎ 2367–1635) has more women's than men's shoes, with lizard-skin shoes starting at around HK$2,500, and a wide range of designer handbag copies.

Sporting Goods

Hong Kong is an excellent place to buy sports gear, thanks to high volume and reasonable prices.

Bunns Diving Equipment (✉ 188 Wanchai Rd., Wanchai, ☎ 2572–1629) is the place for water-sports enthusiasts, with sailing, waterskiing, surfing, and snorkeling gear (including wet suits).

Marathon Sports (✉ Tak Shing House, Theatre La., 20 Des Voeux Rd., Central, ☎ 2810–4521; ✉ Pacific Place, Admiralty, ☎ 2524–6992; ✉ Ocean Terminal, Harbour City, Tsim Sha Tsui, ☎ 2730–6160) carries a good range of equipment and clothing for tennis players and golfers.

Po Kee Fishing Tackle Company (✉ 6 Hillier St., Central, ☎ 2543–7541; ✉ Ocean Terminal, Harbour City, Tsim Sha Tsui, ☎ 2730–4562) has everything to outfit fishermen.

World Top Sports Goods Ltd. (✉ Swire House, Pedder St. entrance, Central, ☎ 2521–3703; ✉ 9 Carnarvon Rd., Tsim Sha Tsui, ☎ 2721–

3188; ⊠ 49 Hankow Rd., Tsim Sha Tsui, ☎ 2376–2937) carries a comprehensive range of sports equipment.

Stereo Equipment

Hennessy Road in Causeway Bay has long been the mecca for finding stereo gear, although many small shops on Central's Queen Victoria and Stanley streets and on Tsim Sha Tsui's Nathan Road offer a similar variety of goods. Be sure to compare prices before buying, as they can vary widely. Also make sure that guarantees are applicable in your own country. It helps to know exactly what you want, since most shopkeepers don't have the room or inclination to give you a chance to test and compare sound systems. However, some major manufacturers do have individual showrooms where you can test the equipment before buying. The shopkeeper will be able to direct you. Another tip: Though most of the export gear sold in Hong Kong has fuses or dual wiring that can be used in any country, it pays to double-check.

Tea

Cha (tea) falls into three types: green (unfermented), black (fermented), and oolong (semifermented). Various flavors include jasmine, chrysanthemum, rose, and narcissus. Loong Ching Green Tea and Jasmine Green Tea are among the most popular, and they're often available in attractive tins. These make inexpensive but unusual gifts.

If you wanted to buy a ton of tea, you could probably do so in Hong Kong's most famous tea area—Western District on Hong Kong Island. Walk down Queen's Road West and Des Voeux Road West, and you will find dozens of tea merchants and dealers. You can also buy packages or small tins of Chinese tea in the tea shops of the Western District or at the various Chinese product stores and leading supermarkets, such as Park 'n' Shop.

Cheng Leung Wing (⊠ 526 Queen's Rd. W, no phone) is a tea purveyor in the heart of the tea district.
Fook Ming Tong Tea Shop (⊠ Prince's Bldg., Central, ☎ 2521–0337; other branches at Mitsukoshi and Sogo stores in Causeway Bay and Ocean Terminal, Harbour Centre, Tsim Sha Tsui) is a mecca for the sophisticated tea shopper. You can get superb teas in beautifully designed tins or invest in some antique clay tea ware.
Luk Yu Teahouse (⊠ 24 Stanley St., ☎ 2523–5464), the oldest and most famous of Hong Kong's teahouses, is where to go if you want to enjoy a cup of cha in traditional style; you can also get dim sum.
Tea Zen (⊠ House for Tea Connoisseurs, 290 Queen's Rd., ground floor, Central, Sheung Wan, ☎ 2544–1375) offers a range of teas in a simple atmosphere.

TVs and VCRs

Color TV systems vary throughout the world, so it's important to be certain the TV set or videocassette recorder you purchase in Hong Kong has a system compatible to the one in your country. Hong Kong, Australia, Great Britain, and most European countries use the PAL system. The United States uses the NTSC system, and France and Russia use the SECAM system. Before you buy, tell the shopkeeper where you will be using your TV or video recorder. In most cases you will be able to get the right model without any problems. The HKTA has a useful brochure called Shopping Guide to "Video Equipment."

Watches

You will have no trouble finding watches in Hong Kong. Street stalls, department stores, and shops overflow with every variety, style, and brand name imaginable, many with irresistible gadgets. But remember Hong Kong's remarkable talent for imitation. A superbargain gold "Rolex" may have hidden flaws—cheap local mechanisms, for instance, or "gold" that rusts. Stick to officially appointed dealers carrying the manufacturers' signs if you want to be sure you're getting the real thing. When buying an expensive watch, check the serial number against the manufacturer's guarantee certificate and ask the salesperson to open the case to check the movement serial number. If an expensive band is attached, find out whether it is from the original manufacturer or is locally made, as this will dramatically affect the price (originals are much more expensive). You should obtain a detailed receipt, the manufacturer's guarantee, and a worldwide warranty for all items.

Artland Watch Co. Ltd. (✉ Corner of Ice House St. and Des Voeux Rd., Central, ☎ 2523–8872; ✉ 62A Nathan Rd., Tsim Sha Tsui, ☎ 2366–4508) has top-of-the-market buys.

City Chain (✉ 14 branches in Hong Kong, 29 in Kowloon) is good for less expensive brands.

8 Side Trip to Macau

Macau is priming itself as it becomes more than just a side trip destination. Arrivals at the international airport are on the rise as the city restores its decorative facades and builds museums and parks. Despite the bustle, the Portuguese territory retains the charm of its quiet, cobblestoned neighborhoods.

By Shann
Davies

IF HISTORY BALANCED ITS BOOKS, today no one would be skimming over the 40-mi (64-km) waterway from Hong Kong to Macau or flying into its international airport. After all, the Portuguese-administered enclave of 9 sq mi (23½ sq km) on the South China coast lost any commercial or political significance a century and a half ago.

How and why has it survived? One clue can be found on any of the fast ferries that bring in the majority of visitors. Most passengers will be Hong Kong Chinese heading for the casinos, which have provided the territory with much of its revenue since legal gambling was introduced in the 1840s as an attempt to compensate for the loss of entrepôt trade to newly founded Hong Kong.

Also on board might be Jesuit priests and Roman Catholic nuns, both Chinese and European, who run vital centuries-old charities and tend to one of Asia's oldest and most devout Christian communities. Just as likely on the ferry may be Buddhist priests, who help maintain Macau's firm faith in its Chinese traditions. There could also be foreign tourists—more than a million per year—textile and toy buyers, British engineers, Swiss chefs, French showgirls, and bar hostesses from Southeast Asia. In their different ways all prove there's plenty of life left in the grande dame of the China coast.

The voyage is a pleasant progress between hilly green islands—some a part of Hong Kong, most sparsely populated extensions of China's Zhuhai Special Economic Zone. As it appears on the skyline, Macau jolts the imagination. Hills crowned with a lighthouse and a church spire, a blur of pastel buildings, and tree-lined avenues all confirm this is a bit of transplanted Iberia, settled in 1557 by the Portuguese as Europe's first outpost in China.

Macau is 90 mi (144 km) south of Guangzhou (Canton to Westerners), the traditional port for China's trade with foreign "barbarians." In the 16th century, however, its traders were forbidden by the emperor to deal with Japan, whose shogun had imposed a ban on China trade. The Portuguese saw their chance and soon were making fabulous fortunes from their command of trade between the two Asian countries and Europe. Among the cargoes that passed through Macau were silk, tea, and porcelain from China, silver and lacquerware from Japan, spices and sandalwood from the East Indies, muslin from India, gems from Persia, wild animals and ivory from Africa, foodstuffs from Brazil, and European clocks, telescopes, and cannons.

Macau's golden age came to an abrupt end with the closure of Japan and the loss of Portugal's mercantile power to the Dutch and English. Northern Europeans and Americans sent their Indiamen and clipper ships to Macau to barter ginseng, furs, woolens, and opium for tea and silk. Their merchants treated the city as their own but, with their rents and customs duties, helped Macau survive. Then, in the mid-19th century, Hong Kong was founded, and the merchants moved out, leaving Macau a backwater.

In the early part of this century, Macau was cast by movie producers and novelists as a den of sin, sex, and spies. True, it had casinos, brothels, opium parlors, and secret agents; but, in fact, it was a small, pale shadow of Shanghai and Hong Kong. Today any traveler in search of wild and wicked Macau will be disappointed, and so will romantics looking for a colonial twilight. As you approach through the ocher waters of the silt-heavy Pearl River estuary, the reality of modern

Macau is unavoidable. High-rise apartments and office blocks mask the hillsides, multistory factories cover land reclaimed from the sea, and construction hammers insist this is no longer a sleepy old town.

The modern prosperity comes from taxes on gambling and the export of textiles, toys, electronics, furniture, luggage, and ceramics. Like Hong Kong, Macau is a duty-free port where anyone can set up a business with minimal taxation or government restrictions. As a result, there is little evidence of city planning, and many new skyscrapers are grotesque. However, some building projects have benefited Macau. These include the University of Macau and the racetrack on Taipa Island, a handful of handsome hotels, and a number of superbly restored or re-created historical buildings.

Relations with China have never been better, with ever-increasing two-way trade and joint ventures in Zhongshan, the neighboring Chinese county. Macau's close proximity to China also makes it a popular gateway for excursions across the border. Following the Sino-British agreement that handed Hong Kong back to China in 1997, the Portuguese negotiated the resumption of Chinese sovereignty over Macau, which will take place on December 20, 1999.

Macau has a population of about 450,000, and most live in the 3½ sq mi (9 sq km) of the mainland peninsula and on newly developing Taipa Island, with small communities on the mostly rural island of Coloane. About 95% of the inhabitants are Chinese, many of long-standing residence. About 7,000 people speak Portuguese as their first language, but only a few come from Portugal; the others are Macanese from old, established Eurasian families. The more transient residents tend to be expatriate Europeans, Americans, and Australians, plus several thousand nightclub hostesses from Thailand and the Philippines. Although Portuguese is the official language and Cantonese the most widely spoken, English is generally understood in places frequented by tourists.

Pleasures and Pastimes

Casinos

The glamorous images summoned by the word *casino* should be checked at the door with your cameras before you enter the Macau variety. Here you'll find no opulent floor shows, no free drinks, no jet-setters in evening dress, and no suave croupiers. What you will find is no-frills, no-holds-barred, no-questions-asked gambling. Open 24 hours a day, most rooms are noisy, smoky, shabby, and in constant use. The gamblers, mostly Hong Kong Chinese, are businesspeople, housewives, servants, factory workers, and students, united in their passion—and what a passion it is! There is almost certainly more money wagered, won, and lost in Macau's casinos than in any others in the world. Sociedade de Turismo e Diversoes de Macau (STDM), the syndicate that has the gambling franchise, admits the total amount is in excess of HK$100 billion annually. In return for the franchise, STDM is paying the government a premium of HK$1.3 billion (about US$162.5 million) over a 10-year period, plus 26% to 30% of gross income and money to build homes for 2,000 families, provide new passenger ferries, and keep the harbor dredged. The syndicate does not complain, so judge the profits for yourself.

Dining

Although East and West have clashed in many respects, when it came to cooking there was instant rapprochement, and it happened in Macau. By the time the Portuguese arrived, they had learned a lot about the eating habits of countries throughout their new empire. They adopted many ingredients grown and used in the Americas and Africa and brought them to China. The Portuguese were the first to introduce China to peanuts, green beans, pineapples, lettuce, sweet potatoes, and shrimp paste, as well as a variety of spices from Africa and India. In China the Portuguese discovered tea, rhubarb, tangerines, ginger, soy sauce, and the Cantonese art of fast frying to seal in flavor.

Over the centuries a unique Macanese cuisine developed, with dishes adapted from Portugal, Brazil, Mozambique, Goa, Malacca, and, of course, China. Today some ingredients are imported, but most are available, fresh each day, from the bountiful waters south of Macau and the rich farmland just across the China border. One good example of Macanese food is the misleadingly named Portuguese chicken, which would be an exotic alien in Europe. It consists of chunks of chicken baked with potatoes, coconut, tomato, olive oil, curry, olives, and saffron. Extremely popular family dishes include *minchi* (minced pork and diced potatoes panfried with soy), pork baked with tamarind, and duckling cooked in its own blood, all of which are served with rice.

Lodging
In the past decade Macau has caught up with neighboring Hong Kong in its international first-class accommodations. Some of the world's leading hotel groups are now represented here, in some cases with more resort services than in Hong Kong and always at lower rates. Plus Macau has two *pousadas,* marvelous examples of Portuguese inns with distinctive Macanese characteristics. By and large Macau's hotels depend on Hong Kong residents, who often make plans to visit at the last moment, so business fluctuates with weather conditions and holidays. The result is sizable discounts usually available for midweek stays. These are best obtained through Hong Kong travel agents or through the hotel itself. Macau's hotels are so much less expensive than Hong Kong's that when you consider other Macau plusses, like a laid-back environment and easy access to Hong Kong and China, you may want to make your visit more than just a day trip.

Serendipity
Like any territory with a long multicultural past, Macau is packed with interesting things to see and do that overlap one another. This tends to unravel any neatly organized itinerary or program, but makes your experience unique because you will inevitably succumb to the invitation of mysterious courtyards, baroque churches, colonial squares, imaginative museums, quiet cemeteries, and bustling street markets. Often you'll stumble on some celebration, a religious procession, the opening of a new shop, fireworks displays, or performances by artists in a music or arts festival. Forget your schedule and enjoy the moment.

EXPLORING

Macau divides quite conveniently into eight areas, including Taipa and Coloane Islands to the south, which can be seen separately or back to back. The city is compact but can be confusing because it has grown over the centuries according to happenstance rather than planning, so a modern urban sprawl is imposed on a colonial European trading settlement. This makes for street patterns that can be as frustrating as they are fascinating. To add to the puzzle, the government in recent years has replaced all the old street numbers with site numbers, which is why you find buildings on one block addressed 8, 16, 56, and 68 for example. The solution is to use reference points, as we have in the following itineraries.

Numbers in the text correspond to numbers in the margin and on the Macau and Taipa and Coloane Islands maps.

The Outer Harbour

The district between the Ferry Terminal and Lisboa Hotel is part of modern Macau, with hotels, restaurants, nightclubs, casinos, museums, and sports facilities that include the grandstands and start/finish straightaway of the Grand Prix circuit. There has been massive reclamation of the harbor for new office and apartment blocks.

A Good Walk

Like most visitors, you'll probably arrive at the **Ferry Terminal** ①, from which you can easily get a cab or bus to your destination of choice. From the departure level, cross the walkway over the waterfront Avenida da Amizade to the **Jai Alai Casino** ② and witness the frantic gambling action. Continue along Rua Luís Gonzaga Gomes to the **Macau Forum** ③ and Tourist Activities Centre (CAT), where you'll find the unique Grand Prix and Wine museums. Walk a block to Avenida da Amizade for a coffee break in the Mandarin Oriental Hotel's attractive lobby or join the local families relaxing in nearby Outer Harbour Park. At the end of the avenue is the Lisboa Hotel, an extraordinary landmark as well as a place to eat, drink, gamble, dance, watch a striptease show, shop, or play video games.

TIMING

This walk, with museum visits, will take about two hours. Nearby Guia Hill is the starting point for the tranquil Restoration Macau walk (see below); or if you want to get right into the thick of Macau, take a cab to Sanmalo (☞ Downtown, *below*).

Sights to See

❶ **Ferry Terminal.** The Dutch, who failed to take Macau in 1622, disembarked at this site. The three-story terminal is attractive and efficient, with restaurants, tourist information, hotel, car rental, and travel agencies, a bank and automatic teller machine, duty-free shops, and luggage lockers. Outside is the grandstand of the annual Grand Prix and a reservoir with a computer-controlled cyberfountain of 292 water jets that play regularly though the day and are lighted after dark. ✉ *Av. da Amizade at the reservoir.*

❷ **Jai Alai Casino and Nightclub Complex.** The Basque sport for which it was built failed to attract enough business, so the complex was converted into the busiest casino in town, with some of the best nightclubs, cinemas, and restaurants. ✉ *Terminal Marítimo do Porto Exterior, off Av. da Amizade.*

❸ **Macau Forum.** This multipurpose facility has a large stadium that seats 4,000 and is used for sports events or pop concerts and an auditorium with 350 seats for operas and plays. The adjoining Tourism Activities Centre, usually known by its Portuguese initials CAT, has two museums. Oldest is the **Grand Prix Museum,** which tells the story of the races that began in 1953. It features some of the cars and motorbikes that have raced here over the years, photos, videos, memorabilia, mockups of a pit stop and a rescue operation, plus two simulators— one of which is interactive—in which you can experience the sensation of driving in the Grand Prix.

The **Wine Museum** illustrates the history of wine making with photographs, maps and paintings, antique wine presses, Portuguese wine fraternity costumes, and 750 different Portuguese wines. ✉ *Rua Luís Gonzaga Gomes. Grand Prix Museum:* ☎ *798–4126.* ✆ *10 patacas,*

Macau

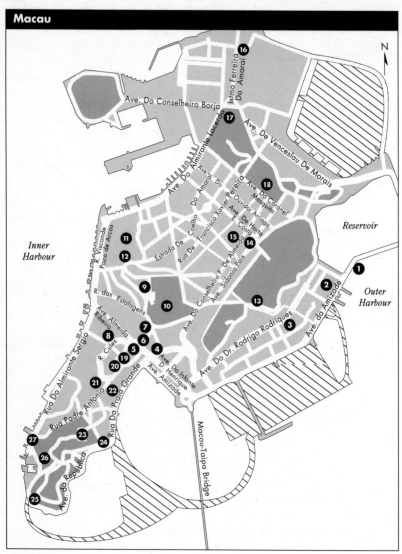

20 patacas for simulator rides. ☉ *Daily 10–6.* Wine Museum:☎ 798–
4108. ⊠ *15 patacas (includes first glass of wine).* ☉ *Daily 10–6.*

Downtown

For a relatively straightforward introduction to the many-layered and
often contradictory character of Macau, stroll the mile or so of the main
street, Avenida Almeida Ribeiro, generally known by its Chinese name,
Sanmalo.

A Good Walk

Avenida Almeida Ribeiro (Sanmalo) stretches from the Rua Da Praia
Grande to the Inner Harbour. Begin at the east end, where the Banco
Nacional Ultramarino faces the Bank of China, then proceed past the
row of 1920s shop houses, with balconied facades, and the Art Deco
General Post Office ④ to Leal Senado Square. Take a look in the white-
washed gallery of the **Leal Senado** ⑤ and have a stroll around the lively
square to visit the **Santa Casa da Misericordia** charity ⑥ and **São
Domingos** church ⑦. The main tourist office is also on the square, with
brochures, books, and souvenirs. Continue down Sanmalo and note
the variety of facades: China Coast shop houses, fortresslike pawnshops,
Portuguese baroque mansions, chrome-and-glass office blocks. At
street level you'll find restaurants, banks, hotels, the small Kam Pek
casino, and shops selling gold jewelry, bargain-priced clothing, antiques,
medicines (Western and Chinese), dried and salted fish, and liquor. Make
a left on Travessa do Mastro to reach **Rua da Felicidade** ⑧, a street of
attractively restored facades housing restaurants and shops. Follow the
street until it ends at the busy Inner Harbour and floating casino.

TIMING
This walk will take anywhere from 30 minutes to an hour and a half,
depending on whether there's an interesting exhibition in the Leal
Senado Gallery and if shopping is on your agenda.

Sights to See

④ General Post Office. This handsome arcaded building, dating from the
early 20th century, contains the telephone exchange and a thriving phi-
lately department. ⊠ *Largo do Senado, at Av. Almeida Ribeiro,* ☎ 396–
8516.

⑤ Leal Senado. The Loyal Senate is the focal point of downtown and looks
out on **Largo do Senado** (Senate Square), which is paved Portuguese
style with black-and-white tiles in a wave pattern and furnished with
benches, plants, and a fountain in the shape of an armillary sphere. Vehicles are banned, and the square is a pedestrian haven. The Leal Senado
is a superb example of colonial architecture, constructed in the late 18th
century to house the senate of leading citizens—at the time far more
powerful than the governors, who usually served their appointed time
and then returned to Portugal. Today the senate, with some elected and
some appointed members, acts as the municipal government, with its
president holding the same power as a mayor. Inside the building a beautiful stone staircase leads to wrought-iron gates that open onto a charming garden. The foyer and garden are open during working hours, and
there are frequent art and history exhibitions in the foyer and gallery.

The original **national library** is also housed within the Leal Senado. A
superb copy of the classic Portuguese library in Mafra, it holds possibly the best collection of books in English about China's history, society, economy, and culture. Much was inherited from the British- and
American-managed Chinese Customs House. The library also has rare

books from the early days of the Portuguese empire and bound copies of old Macau newspapers. Scholars and others are welcome to browse or study; there's also a nice view of the square. ⊠ *Largo do Senado, 2nd floor, at Rua Dr. Soares.* ⊘ *Mon.–Sat. 1–7.*

⑧ Rua da Felicidade. In the past the Street of Happiness was the heart of the red-light district. Few brothels have survived the competition from sauna and massage parlors; most have been replaced by budget hotels and restaurants. In 1996 the Cultural Institute of Macau decided to restore the appearance of the old China Coast and fitted traditional facades to all the buildings on the street. The result is stunning, with red wooden lattices over the windows, retractable red canopies and gray-stone gateways to shrine-filled courtyards. The new look has helped business in the area, especially in the evening when food stalls with stools and tiny tables are set out. Lights blaze from open-front restaurants, laundries, tailor shops, and family living rooms. The pungent smell of cooking pervades the streets, and it seems as if most of Macau's 450,000 people have fled their tiny apartments to eat out, relax, and socialize. ⊠ *Off Av. Almeida Ribeiro at Travessa do Mastro.*

⑥ Santa Casa da Misericordia. Portugal's Holy House of Mercy is the oldest Christian charity on the China coast. Founded in 1569, its headquarters occupies this handsome baroque building on Largo do Senado, and its offices administer homes for the elderly, kitchens for the poor, clinics, and a leprosarium. Its president is by tradition the senate president. On the second floor, closed to the public, a reception room contains paintings of benefactress Marta Merop and Macau's first bishop, Dom Belchior, along with the latter's cross and skull. ⊠ *Largo do Senado, next to GPO.*

⑦ São Domingos. Possibly the most beautiful church in Macau, with a magnificent cream-and-white baroque altar of graceful columns, fine statues, and a forest of candles and flower vases, São Domingos (St. Dominic's) was built in the 17th century by Dominicans. It has had a stormy history: In 1644 a Portuguese officer was murdered at the altar by a mob during mass; in 1707 the church was besieged by the governor's troops when the Dominicans sided with the Pope against the Jesuits on the question of whether ancestor worship should be permitted among Chinese Christian converts. After three days the soldiers broke down the doors and briefly imprisoned the priests. (At press time the church was closed for a total renovation, scheduled for completion in 1998.) ⊠ *Rua de São Domingos, at Largo do Senado.*

The Old Citadel

The most remarkable early buildings in Macau were on or around the centrally located **Monte Hill**, and those that have survived eloquently recall the golden era of Portugal's worldwide empire.

A Good Walk

The best way to approach the old citadel is from Senate Square. Take the Rua da São Domingos, to the right of São Domingos Church, turn left on Rua da Palha, which runs into Rua de São Paulo, which leads to the dramatic free-standing facade of **St. Paul's** ⑨. Go up the steps, visit the Museum of Sacred Art, then cross the road to view the remains of the **Monte Fort** ⑩, which holds the new **City Museum**. Return down the stone staircase and turn right onto Rua de São Paulo. Pass the antiques and souvenir shops and arrive at the Praça Luís Camões park. People-watch in the **Camões Grotto and Garden** ⑪ and relax in the shade of giant banyan trees. Finally go next door to Number 22 and remember former Western visitors in the **Old Protestant Cemetery** ⑫.

Pick up
the phone.

Pick up
the miles.

Calling Card

415 555 1234 2244
J.D. SMITH

WORLDPHONE

Use your MCI Card® to make an international call from virtually anywhere in the world and earn frequent flyer miles on one of seven major airlines.

Enroll in an MCI Airline Partner Program today. In the U.S., call **1-800-FLY-FREE.** Overseas, call MCI collect at **1-916-567-5151.**

1. To use your MCI Card, just dial the WorldPhone access number of the country you're calling from.
   (For a complete listing of codes, visit www.mci.com.)
2. Dial or give the operator your MCI Card number.
3. Dial or give the number you're calling.

# **Bahrain**	800-002	# **Kuwait**	800-MCI (800-624)
# **Brunei**	800-011	**Lebanon** ⁑	600-MCI (600-624)
# **China** ❖	108-12	# **Macao**	0800-131
For a Mandarin-speaking		# **Malaysia** (CC) ♦	800-0012
operator	108-17	# **Philippines** (CC) ♦	
# **Cyprus** ♦	080-90000	To call using PLDT ■	105-14
# **Egypt** ♦	355-5770	To call using PHILCOM ■	1026-14
(Outside of Cairo, dial 02 first)		Philippines IIIC via PLDT	
# **Federated States of Micronesia**	624	in Tagalog ■	105-15
# **Fiji**	004-890-1002	Philippines IIIC via PHILCOM	
# **Guam** (CC)	950-1022	in Tagalog ■	1026-12
# **Hong Kong** (CC)	800-1121	# **Qatar** ★	0800-012-77
# **India** (CC) ❖	000-127	# **Saipan** (CC) ⁑	950-1022
# **Indonesia** (CC) ♦	001-801-11	# **Saudi Arabia** (CC)	1-800-11
Iran ⁑	(Special Phones Only)	# **Singapore**	8000-112-112
# **Israel** (CC)	177-150-2727	# **Sri Lanka**	440-100
# **Japan** (CC) ♦		(Outside of Colombo, dial 01 first)	
To call using KDD ■	0039-121▶	# **Syria**	0800
To call using IDC ■	0066-55-121	# **Taiwan** (CC) ♦	0080-13-4567
To call using ITJ ■	0044-11-121	# **Thailand** ★	001-999-1-2001
# **Jordan**	18-800-001	# **United Arab Emirates** ♦	800-111
# **Korea** (CC)		**Vietnam** ●	1201-1022
To call using KT ■	009-14	**Yemen**	008-00-102
To call using DACOM ■	00309-12		
Phone Booths ⁑	Red Button 03,		
	then press ★		
Military Bases	550-2255		

Is this a great time, or what? :-)

Urban planning.

CITYPACKS

The ultimate guide to the city—a complete pocket guide plus a full-size color map.

TIMING

Although it depends on how much time you spend in the museums, the walk should take about two hours.

Sights to See

⑪ Camões Grotto and Garden. Macau's most popular public park is frequented from dawn to dusk by people practicing tai chi chuan (shadowboxing), young lovers, students, and men carrying their caged songbirds for a walk or huddled over games of Chinese chess. The garden houses the Orient Foundation and was originally the private grounds of the former Camões Museum and later headquarters for the British East India Company. In 1785 it was used by French cartographer La Perouse for a small observatory aimed at China. The garden was taken over by the city in 1886 and a heroic bronze bust of Camões, Portugal's greatest poet (who is believed to have lived here in 1557), was installed in a rocky alcove. Nearby, a wall of stone slabs is inscribed with poems by various contemporary writers praising Camões and Macau. At the entrance to the grotto a modern bronze sculpture honors the friendship between Portugal and China. Some rooms of the Casa Garden contain historic and artistic exhibits, and there is an art gallery in the basement. ⊠ *13 Praça Luis de Camões,* ☎ *554–699.* ⬛ *Free.* ⊙ *Gardens dawn–dusk, house weekdays 9:30–6.*

⑩ Monte Fort. Standing on the hill overlooking St. Paul's, this fort was built by the Jesuits and completed in 1623. In 1622 it was the scene of Macau's most famous battle. The Dutch, jealous of Portugal's power in Asia, invaded the territory, which was protected by a small force of soldiers, African slaves, and priests. As the Dutch closed in on Monte, a lucky cannon shot, fired by one of the priests, hit the enemy's powder supply, and in the ensuing confusion the Dutch were driven back to sea. In 1626 the first full-time governor of Macau evicted the Jesuits from the fort. For the next century and a half it was the residence and office of Macau's governors. The fort's buildings were destroyed by fire in 1835, but the great walls remain, along with the cannon. The fort has since become a popular park and was even used as an auditorium for an open-air performance of *The Barber of Seville* during an international music festival. Now the **City Museum** is being installed on top of and in the excavated foundations of the fort, with exhibits showing Macau's history as a gateway between East and West. It is scheduled to open in late 1997. ⊠ *Between Rua D. Belchior Carneiro and Calçda do Monte.* ⬛ *Free.* ⊙ *Daily 10–6.*

⑫ Old Protestant Cemetery. This "corner of some foreign field" is the last resting place of more than 150 Americans and British. It is a tranquil retreat where tombstones recall the troubles and triumphs of Westerners in 19th-century China. Some of the names are familiar: George Chinnery; Captain Henry Churchill, great granduncle of Sir Winston; Joseph Adams, grandson of John Adams, the second U.S. president; Robert Morrison, who translated the Bible into Chinese; opium traders Thomas Beale, Captain John Crockett, and James Innes; Swedish historian Anders Ljungstedt; and American engineer John P. Williams. In addition, there are graves of sailors who were victims of battle, accident, or disease. ⊠ *22 Praça Luis Camões.* ⊙ *Daily 9-6.*

⑨ St. Paul's. Today the symbol of Macau, this church was built between 1602 and 1627 by exiled Japanese Christians and local craftsmen under the direction of the Jesuits. It was attached to the first Western-style university in Asia, attended by such scholars as Matteo Ricci and Adam Van Schall, who studied here before going to the court in Peking. The college, along with most of the fort and the body of the church, was destroyed in a disastrous fire in 1835. The story of the church is told on its carved stone facade and in the excavated crypt, which contains the tomb of the church's founder Alessandro Valignano and the bones of Japanese and Indochinese martyrs. Alongside is the **Museum of Sacred Art,** which contains statues, crucifixes, chalices, and other sacramental objects dating from the 17th–18th centuries and borrowed from local churches. The 17th-century paintings by exiled Japanese artists depict the crucified martyrs of Nagasaki and the Archangel Michael in the guise of a samurai. ⊠ *Rua de São Paulo, at Largo da Companhia.* 🖼 *Free.* ☉ *Daily 9–6.*

Restoration Macau

One of the most endearing aspects of Macau is the amount of imaginative restoration of old buildings, not as relics but as places where people live and work. Some are historic sites, while others are quite mundane, yet all are part of a unique heritage.

A Good Walk

Begin with a taxi ride to **Guia Hill** ⑬ for an overview of the city, then walk around the hill to the steps leading down to Flora Gardens and Avenida de Sidonio Pais. Turn left and stroll a block or so to the **Memorial Home of Dr. Sun Yat-sen** ⑭, between Rua de Antonio Basto and Rua de Leoncio Ferreira across from the police station. From here continue along the avenue and turn right on Estrada de Adolfo Loureiro. Follow it to the **Lou Lim loc Garden** ⑮ and explore this Suzhou-style garden. Upon leaving, turn left, and you'll be on Restoration Row, a section of Avenida do Conselheiro Ferreira de Almeida that has a series of restored ocher-and-red 1920s mansions, now housing the government archives, the national library, offices of the Open University, and the Health Department. The avenue becomes Rua do Campo, which leads to the Praia Grande and downtown.

TIMING

This walk should take a leisurely two hours.

Sights to See

⑬ **Guia Hill.** Studded with new homes, a convent, and a hospital, Guia (guide) hill is topped with a fort that dates from the 1630s, the oldest lighthouse on the China coast (built in 1865), and a small white-stone chapel built in 1707. Permission from the Macau Marine Department (☎ 573–409) is needed to enter the lighthouse, but the chapel is usually open and one of the guardhouses is a café and tourist information office. From the fort you can see all of Macau, its islands, the airport, and the surrounding Chinese seascape. ⊠ *Est. do Engenheiro Trigo.* ☉ *7–dusk.*

⑮ **Lou Lim loc Garden.** This classic Chinese garden, modeled on those of old Suzhou, was built in the 19th century by a wealthy Chinese merchant named Lou. With the decline of the Lou family fortunes early this century, the house was sold and became a school. The garden fell into ruin until it was taken over by the city in 1974 and totally restored. Enclosed by a wall, it is a miniaturized landscape, with miniforests of bamboo and flowering bushes, a mountain of sculpted concrete, and a small lake filled with lotuses and golden carp. A traditional nine-turn bridge zigzags (to deter evil spirits, which can move only in straight lines) across the lake to a colonial-style pavilion with a wide veranda. The pavilion is used for regular exhibitions and music concerts. ⊠ *Est. de Adolfo Loureiro at Av. do Conselheiro Ferreira de Almeida.* 🖼 *1 pataca.* ☉ *Daily dawn–dusk.*

⑭ **Memorial Home of Dr. Sun Yat-sen.** Sun, father of the 1911 Chinese revolution, worked as a physician in Macau from 1892 to 1894, and some of his family stayed here after his death. The memorial home, in a strange mock-Moorish style, was built in the mid-1930s. It contains some interesting photographs, books, and souvenirs of Sun and his long years of exile in different parts of the world. ⊠ *1 Rua Ferreira do Amaral, between Rua de Antonio Basto and Rua de Leoncio Ferreira.* ⊠ *Free.* ☾ *Mon.–Thurs. 10–1, weekends 10–1 and 3–5.*

On the Doorstep of China

The border of China lies at the north end of Macau, about 2 mi from the ferry terminal or downtown. The area has witnessed some dramatic history, symbolized by the Border Gate. It is also the home of dog racing and the site of a temple that has played a role in both American and Macanese history.

A Good Walk

Take any bus marked CERCO to the border and see something of Macau's bustling suburbs en route. At the border visit the attractive park built in front of the old gateway **Portas do Cerco** ⑯. Take the main road Avenida Artur Tamagnini Barbosa to the temple **Lin Fung Miu** ⑰, with its statue of the opium-burning Commissioner Lin. Across the road is the Canidrome, where greyhound dog races are run three or four nights a week. From here you should take a taxi to the **Kun Iam Temple** ⑱, on Avenida do Coronel Mesquita, where the first Sino-American treaty was signed.

TIMING

This walk should take about an hour, without stops for meals.

Sights to See

⑱ **Kun Iam Temple.** This Buddhist temple dedicated to the goddess of mercy was founded in the 13th century. The present 17th-century buildings are richly endowed with carvings, porcelain figurines, statues, old scrolls, antique furniture, and ritual objects. The temple is best known among Western visitors for the stone table in the right-hand courtyard, where, on July 3, 1844, the first Sino-American treaty was signed by the viceroy of Canton and the United States envoy, Caleb Cushing. The temple has a large number of funeral chapels, with offerings of paper cars, airplanes, luggage, and money burned so they will accompany the souls of the dead. ⊠ *Av. do Coronel Mesquita, at Rua do Almirante Costa Cabral.* ☾ *Daily dawn–dusk.*

⑰ **Lin Fung Miu.** This superb Temple of the Lotus, dedicated to both Buddhist and Taoist deities, was built in 1592 and used for overnight accommodations by mandarins traveling between Macau and Canton. It is famous for its facade's 19th-century clay bas-reliefs depicting mythological and historical scenes, and for an interior frieze of colorful writhing dragons. A statue of Commissioner Lin Zexu, who burned the foreign traders' opium in 1839, stands in the courtyard. ⊠ *Av. do Artur Tamagnini Barbosa at Est. do Arco.* ☾ *Daily dawn–dusk.*

⑯ **Portas do Cerco.** The Border Gate marks the traditional boundary of Macau. Beyond is the Chinese border town of Gongbei. The original gate, shaped like à triumphal arch, was built in 1870 and bears the arms of Portugal's navy and artillery along with a quotation from Camões that reads, in translation: "Honor your country for it looks after you." On either side of the gate the date 1849 is written to commemorate the year when Governor Ferreira do Amaral was assassinated by the Chinese. The local warlord planned to invade Macau but a Macanese colonel, Nicolau Mesquita, with 37 men, slipped across the border and captured the Chinese fort. Today the gate is part of a small park that features large panels of old maps and prints made in blue-and-white tiles. Modern immigration halls on the sides of the park handle a steady flow of vegetable farmers, businesspeople, and tourists who cross the border daily. ✉ *Av. Norte do Hipodromo, at Av. do Artur Tamagnini Barbosa.* ⊙ *Daily 7 AM–midnight.*

Peninsular Macau

The narrow, hilly peninsula is one of the oldest districts in the city and is full of colonial churches, landmark hotels, restaurants, and shopping streets. It's bordered on the east by the Rua da Praia Grande and the Avenida da República, both tree-shaded promenades beside a bay from which land is now being reclaimed to make way for new construction. This was once a favorite place for residents to stroll, fish, or play chess. On the west side, the Inner Harbour's Rua do Almirante Sergio and Rua das Lorchas still retain the bustle of an Asian port with their traditional Chinese shop houses—ground floors occupied by ship's chandlers, net makers, ironmongers, and shops selling spices and salted fish.

A Good Walk

Begin at the Leal Senado and take the steep Rua Dr. Soares, which climbs to the left of the senate. Branch left on Calçada Tronco Velho and arrive in the peaceful Largo Santo Agostinho. Visit the church of **St. Augustine** ⑲ and take a look at the **Dom Pedro V** ⑳ theater. The Seminary of St. Joseph's is also in the square, but its baroque chapel, with some fine religious art and sculpture, is closed awaiting renovation. The Rampo do Teatro will lead you down to Rua Central. Continue to the right and on the block-long Rua de São Lourenço find **St. Lawrence's Church** ㉑. Take the Travessa Padre Narciso down to the Praia Grande, and the **Government Palace** ㉒ will be on your left. Go right along the waterfront (trying to ignore the bay reclamation project) and make a detour up Calçada do Bom Parto to **Penha Hill** ㉓ for some great views. On the way back to the waterfront stop for a drink in the **Bela Vista Hotel** ㉔. Continue along Avenida da República to the landmark inn **Pousada de São Tiago** ㉕; its *Monument of Understanding,* celebrating Sino-Portuguese friendship, rises out of the nearby bay with massive granite arches. Walk around the tip of the peninsula to the **A-Ma Temple** ㉖ and finish with a visit to the unique **Maritime Museum** ㉗. It's worth a trip to Macau on its own but is closed on Tuesday.

TIMING

This should be a walk to last most of the day, with a leisurely lunch (at an Inner Harbour or Praia Grande restaurant), drinks in the landmark hotels, and plenty of time spent in the museum and temple. If you have less time, it can be done in three or four hours.

Sights to See

㉖ **A-Ma Temple.** Macau's oldest and most venerated place of worship stands on the site of the first Chinese settlement, which is also the landing place of the first Portuguese colonists. Built in the early 16th century, it is the territory's most picturesque temple, with ornate prayer halls and pavilions among the giant boulders of the waterfront hillside. The rocks are inscribed with red calligraphy telling the story of A-Ma (also known as Tin Hau). A favorite goddess of fishermen, she is purported to have saved a humble junk from a storm. One of the many Chinese names for the area was A-Ma Gau, the Bay of A-Ma, and when the Portuguese arrived, they took this name and transformed it into Macau. ✉ *Largo do Pagode da Barra, opposite the Maritime Museum.* ⊙ *Daily dawn–dusk. Lion dances held outside the temple 10 AM–10:30 AM Sun.*

㉔ Bela Vista Hotel. This century-old landmark reopened in 1992 as a luxury inn and restaurant, following restoration by the Mandarin Oriental Hotel Group (☞ Lodging, *below*). ⊠ *8 Rua do Comendador Kou Ho Neng.*

⑳ Dom Pedro V. This, the oldest Western theater on the China coast, was built in 1859 in the style of a European court theater and was in regular use until World War II. After a thorough renovation by the Orient Foundation, it is now in use again as a venue for concerts, plays, and recitals. In the square outside there is a craft market every Saturday afternoon 2–7 as well as performances of Portuguese and Chinese music on Friday and Saturday evenings 9–2. ⊠ *Largo do Sto. Agostinho, at Rampa do Teatro.*

㉒ Government Palace. This pink-and-white colonial mansion, with deep verandas and a handsome portico bearing the Portuguese coat of arms, is on the Praia Grande. It houses the offices of the governor and his cabinet and is Lisbon's seat of power in Macau. ⊠ *Av. de Praia Grande, between Travessa do Padre Narciso and Travessa da Paiva.*

㉗ Maritime Museum. This gem of a museum has been a consistent favorite since its doors opened at the end of 1987. It is ideally located on a waterfront site on **Barra Square.** The four-story building resembles a sailing ship and is considered one of the foremost maritime museums in Asia. The adjacent dock was restored to provide a pier for a tug, a dragon boat, a sampan, and working replicas of a South China trading junk and a 19th-century pirate-chasing *lorcha* (a type of wooden sailing ship). Inside the museum are displays of the local fishing industry, models of historic vessels, light-box charts of great voyages by Portuguese and Chinese explorers, a relief model of 17th-century Macau, the story in lantern-show style of the A-Ma Temple, navigational aids such as an original paraffin lamp once used in the Guia Lighthouse, along with all manner of touch screens and videos. The museum also operates 30-minute pleasure junk trips around the Inner and Outer harbours daily except Tuesday and the first Sunday of the month. ⊠ *Largo do Pagode da Barra, opposite A-Ma Temple.* ☎ *307–161.* ⊠ *8 patacas for museum, 10 patacas for boat trip.* ☉ *Wed.–Mon. 10–5:30.*

㉓ Penha Hill. Some of the best views of Macau are obtained from the courtyard of the **Bishop's Palace,** on Penha Hill, which overlooks the entire city and islands. The palace, built in 1935 on the site of the original 1622 structure, is always closed, but it contains a chapel, dedicated to the patroness of seafarers. ⊠ *Est. de D. João Paulino.* ☉ *Daily 10–4.*

㉕ Pousada de São Tiago. This Portuguese inn built into the ruined foundations of a 17th-century fort is as much a historic sight as a place to stay (☞ Lodging, *below*). ⊠ *Fortaleza de São Tiago da Barra, Av. da República.*

⑲ St. Augustine. This church, which dates from 1814, has a marble-clad high altar that contains the large statue of Our Lord of Passos that is carried through the streets on the first day of Lent. ⊠ *Largo do Sto. Agostinho, at Calçada do Tronco Velho.*

㉑ St. Lawrence's Church. Possibly the most elegant of Macau's churches stands in a pleasant garden, shaded by palm trees. It has always been a fashionable place and shows it with elegant wood carvings, an ornate baroque altar, and stunning crystal chandeliers. It is used for concerts during the Macau International Music Festival. ⊠ *Rua de São Lourenço, at Travessa do Padre Narciso.* ⊠ *Free.* ☉ *Daily 10–4.*

Taipa Island

With its neighbor Coloane, Taipa was ceded to Portugal in 1887 but remained a quiet rural retreat—and home for fireworks factories—until the 1970s, when it was linked to the city by a bridge. Since then it has developed into a substantial suburb, with the hillside Macau University, the Raceway of the Macau Jockey Club, resort hotels, a sports stadium and the Macau International Airport. At the same time its traditional temples, classic China coast village, and vast array of restaurants attract visitors.

A Good Walk

Take a bus or taxi over one of the bridges to **Taipa Village** ㉘ and explore the narrow lanes. Take the main Rua Direita Carlos Eugenio to Calçada do Carma and walk up to the small square in front of the Church of Our Lady of Carmel. Continue down to the old seafront to visit the **Taipa House Museum** ㉙. To see other aspects of Taipa, take a bus or taxi to the Hyatt Regency Hotel and walk around the back road, Estrada de Almirante Joaquim Marques Esparteiro, to the **Pou Tai Un Temple** ㉚. From here the road leads on to the Macau Jockey Club and Macau Stadium. Or take a trip to the Macau International Airport, which has one of the most attractive terminals you'll ever see, via the **United Chinese Cemetery** ㉛, which contains some colorful statuary. The **University of Macau** ㉜ is a short walk from the Hyatt Regency.

TIMING

The walk around Taipa Village and the house museum can take as little as 30 minutes, but a visit to Taipa isn't complete without lunch at one of its many restaurants.

Sights to See

㉘ **Taipa Village.** This tight maze of houses and shops has been changing, with new villa-style houses and modern conveniences like banks; however, it retains much of the appearance and atmosphere of a South China coast fishing village. The two- and three-story shop houses are kept fresh with new coats of white and pastel washes, the old wells are still in use, and fish are still placed out to dry in the sun. There are small well-kept temples, restored colonial buildings that house the Municipal Council for the Islands, and restaurants spilling out onto the sidewalks.

㉙ **Taipa House Museum.** This finely restored 1920s mansion contains authentic period furniture, decorations, and furnishings that recapture the atmosphere and lifestyle of a middle-class Macanese family in the early part of the century. ✉ *Taipa Praia off Largo do Carmo.* 💷 *Free.* ⊙ *Tues.–Sun. 9–1 and 3–5.*

㉚ **Pou Tai Un Temple.** This temple is famed for its vegetarian restaurant (the vegetables are grown in an adjoining garden). Thanks to donations from devotees, it has a series of prayer halls including a yellow-tile pavilion and a statue of the Buddhist goddess of mercy. ✉ *Est. de Almirante Joaquim Marques Esparteiro, behind the Hyatt Regency Hotel.*

㉛ **United Chinese Cemetery.** Buddhists, Taoists and Confucians have their last resting place in this cemetery, which covers the hillside overlooking the Macau International Airport. Some occupy elaborate graves while others are placed in ossuary walls. The cemetery is lavishly decorated with colored tiles and religious images. ✉ *Est. da Ponte da Cabrita.*

㉜ **University of Macau.** Compressed into a small area, this fully-accredited school has spacious lecture halls, sports grounds, and a theater. It

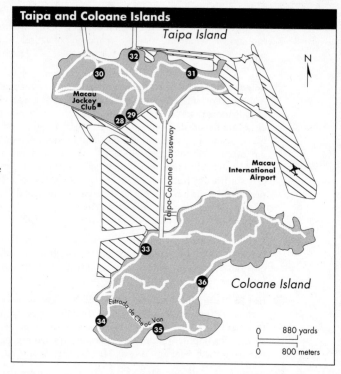

Taipa and Coloane Islands

Taipa Island

Macau Jockey Club ■

Taipa-Coloane Causeway

Macau International Airport

Coloane Island

Estrada de Cheoc Van

| 0 | 880 yards |
| 0 | 800 meters |

offers a wide range of graduate and postgraduate courses. ⊠ *Est. de Pak On, behind the New Century Hotel.*

Coloane Island

At the end of a 1½-mi causeway from Taipa, the larger, hillier island of Coloane, is a favorite destination for nature lovers, hikers, go-carters, windsurfers, sunbathers, and people who love good food. It does have some modern developments but remains basically rural.

A Good Walk

Take a bus or taxi to **Coloane Park** ㉝ any day but Monday and see the aviary, the forest, and the **Natural History Museum.** Continue by bus along Estrada de Seac Pai Van to Coloane Village and visit the **Chapel of St. Francis Xavier** ㉞. From here take the Ha Sa road to the **Pousada de Coloane** ㉟ and enjoy a drink on the terrace overlooking Cheoc Van Beach. Then continue on to **Hac Sa Beach** ㊱, a black-sand beach, from which you can spy on or actually continue on to investigate the marvelous bluff-side Westin Resort.

TIMING

Ideally you should try to spend a day on Coloane, taking it easy with the walk and stopping for a leisurely lunch, drinks, and snacks. The walk alone takes about three hours.

Sights to See

㉞ **Chapel of St. Francis Xavier.** This charming little chapel in the village, with its cream-and-white facade and bell tower, was built in 1928 to house a reliquary containing an arm bone of the eponymous saint, who died on an island 50 mi south of Macau while waiting to enter China. Since then the relic has been moved, as have the bones of Japanese and

Vietnamese martyrs once enshrined here. The square outside is paved with Portuguese colored tiles, landscaped with gardens, and has a monument commemorating the local defeat of a pirate band in 1910— Macau's last encounter with old-style buccaneers. ☒ *Largo do Sto. Francisco Xavier, Coloane Village.*

㉝ Coloane Park. On the west coast of the island, Coloane Park is one of Macau's most interesting natural preserves. It has a walk-in aviary containing more than 200 species of birds, including the rare Palawan peacock and the crested white pheasant. Nearby you'll find a pond with black swans, a playground, the Balichão restaurant, a picnic area, and a nature trail around the hillside. Its latest attraction is a small **Natural History Museum,** which contains traditional farm implements, clay statues illustrating rice growing, and displays of herbal medicines prepared by the laboratories of the Islands Municipal Council for the Islands. ☒ *Est. de Seac Pai Van.* ☒ *Aviary 5 patacas; free parking.* ☉ *Tues.–Sun. 10–6, museum Tues.–Sun. 10:30–4:30.*

Opposite the park is Coloane's newest attraction, the **Kartodromo** go-cart track, with interconnecting loops making seven different circuits and floodlights for night racing (☞ Outdoor Activities and Sports, *below*).

㊱ Hac Sa Beach. This black-sand beach is the biggest and best in Macau. Although it's an ocher color thanks to the silt carried by the Pearl River from the delta, the water is clean and safe for swimming and water sports. The popular restaurant **Fernando's** (☞ Dining, *below*) is a few feet from the beach. ☒ *Praia da Hac Sa, Est. de Hac Sa.*

㉟ Pousada de Coloane. About a 25-minute drive from the city, this 22-room inn is generally considered remote, which makes it a popular spot for relaxed holidays. There is a long beach below the *pousada,* along with casual open-air restaurants and water-sports facilities (☞ Lodging, *below*). ☒ *Praia de Cheoc Van.*

DINING

Portuguese cuisine favorites are regular menu items on most restaurants. Beloved *bacalhau* (codfish) is served baked, boiled, grilled, deep-fried with potato, and stewed with onion, garlic, and eggs. Portuguese sardines, country soups such as *caldo verde* and *sopa alentejana,* and dishes of rabbit are usually served at Macau eateries. Sharing the bill of fare are colonial favorites: from Brazil come *feijoadas,* stews of beans, pork, spicy sausage, and vegetables; from Mozambique, African chicken, baked or grilled in fiery *piri-piri* (a type of chili pepper). In addition, some kitchens prepare baked quail, curried crab, and the delectable Macau sole, which rivals its Dover cousin. And then there are the giant prawns in spicy sauce—one of Macau's special dining pleasures.

Not surprisingly, most restaurants that don't have Portuguese cuisine serve Chinese food, predominantly Cantonese and Chiu Chow, but quite a number feature authentic foods from elsewhere in Asia—Japanese, Thai, Korean, Indonesian, and even Burmese meals. Still others serve Italian, Continental, and British fare, and there are the inevitable fast-food restaurants. Prices are generally very reasonable, and restaurants are quite similar except for the most upscale and the most modest.

Wine has traditionally been a real bargain in Macau, and it still sells very cheaply in the stores. Some restaurants maintain a reasonable markup; others have taken advantage of Hong Kong's ever-increasing price hikes to raise their own. As a result Portuguese *vinho verde,* a slightly sparkling new wine, and table reds and whites, such as the Dao family of wines, can cost up to 100 patacas (for a bottle that would cost 30 patacas in a store). Except in hotels, beer and spirits—including some powerful Portuguese brandies—are very inexpensive.

Restaurants are open daily, with some closing for a few days after the Chinese New Year. In most cases they don't close for afternoon cleaning, and both lunch and dinner tend to be leisurely affairs, with no one urged to finish up and leave. Most people order wine, relax, look at the menu, note what other diners are eating, talk to the waiter, and then make their decision. Dress is informal, and jackets and ties are never required. The Department of Tourism's map brochure "Eating Out in Macau" is very useful.

CATEGORY	COST*
$$$	over 150 patacas (over US$19)
$$	70 patacas–150 patacas (US$9–US$19)
$	under 70 patacas (under US$9)

per person including service but excluding wine

Macanese-Portuguese

$$$ ✕ **Bela Vista.** Atop a winding staircase in the landmark hotel, this restau-
★ rant has it all—a nostalgically colonial setting, a romantic veranda, a cozy bar, friendly but efficient service, and a superb menu. The menu is regularly revamped and strikes a nice balance between Macanese and Continental. Fish and seafood dishes are particularly good, and desserts—such as the rice pudding with cinnamon—are irresistible. ⊠ *8 Rua do Comendador Kou Neng.* ☎ *965–333. Reservations essential. AE, DC, MC, V.*

$$$ ✕ **Os Gatos.** The setting would be reason enough to dine at this new restaurant in a traditional Portuguese inn, Pousada de São Tiago (☞ Lodging, *below*), which is in a 17th-century fortress. Os Gatos (the Cats) integrates the original bar, café, and large terrace into a casually smart restaurant, with inside and outside sections separated by sliding glass doors. The outdoor area sports huge linen umbrellas and patio furniture while the interior has hand-carved mahogany furniture, blue-and-white wall tiles, and terra-cotta tile floors. A vibrant, signature oil painting on the wall depicts Macau in the past, present, and future. The menu features dishes from Portugal, Spain, Provence, Italy, and Greece. Specialties include paella, clams, pork, chicken *piri-piri* and duck in port wine. ⊠ *Pousada de São Tiago, Av. da República.* ☎ *781–111. AE, DC, MC, V.*

$$$ ✕ **Military Club.** After the club, built in 1870, was beautifully restored to its former colonial elegance, the membership decided to share its restaurant with the general public. It has a marvelous old-world atmosphere and an extensive menu of Portuguese dishes. Specialties include partridge pie, cold stuffed crab, grilled venison, and a range of egg puddings. Members and other diners are usually local Portuguese, who tend to be a bit more formal than the Chinese; however, the dress code is as informal here as anywhere else in Macau. ⊠ *795 Av. Praia Grande,* ☎ *714–009. No credit cards.*

$$$ ✕ **O Porto Interior.** The menu at this restaurant, named for its location on the Inner Harbour but separated from the water by warehouses, is beautifully presented upmarket Macanese, but it's the design of the place that makes it so special. The architects created an elegant two-story facade with colonnades and Iberian arches. Inside, the walls are covered with blue-and-white tiles and intricately carved wooden grilles. Guests enter over a marble bridge. ⊠ *259 Rua Almirante Sergio,* ☎ *967–770. AE, MC, V.*

$$ ✕ **A Galera.** This elegant, handsomely decorated restaurant has blue-and-white tile panels, black-and-white tile floors, pearl gray table linen, Wedgwood china, a bar with high-back armchairs, and views of the São Francisco fortress. Try such main dishes as bacalhau *a bras*—cooked in a skillet with rice, olives, egg, and onion—and squid stuffed with spiced meat, any of the rich homemade soups, and the dessert soufflés. ☒ *Lisboa Hotel, 3rd floor of new wing,* ☎ *577–666, ext. 1103. AE, DC, MC, V.*

$$ ✕ **A Lorcha.** This restaurant in a converted shop house near the Mar-
★ itime Museum is believed by many locals to serve the best Portuguese food in town. It is also one of the most attractive dining places, with stone archways, white stucco, and terra-cotta tile floors. Among the most popular dishes are seafood rice, bread-based *açorda* casseroles, kidney beans, and codfish. Service is first rate, and prices are extremely reasonable. ☒ *289 Rua do Almirante Sergio,* ☎ *313–193. Reservations essential. MC, V. Closed Tues.*

$$ ✕ **Afonso III.** After some years at the Hyatt Regency (☞ *above*), Afonso decided to open his own place and cook food the way his grandmother did. The result is a simple café that is regularly packed with locals, in the heart of downtown. Most choose the specials of the day, which usually include codfish or braised pork and beef stew prepared like nowhere else in Macau. The wine list is equally unusual, and the prices are a real bargain. ☒ *11A Rua Central,* ☎ *586–272. No credit cards.*

$$ ✕ **Balichão.** This Macanese restaurant has a brilliant location in a spa-
★ cious pavilion in Coloane Park, between a swan lake and an aviary. The decor features birdcages—some with resident birds—brass pots, and rattan furniture. The owner's mother commands the kitchen, where she creates new dishes along with favorites such as casserole of pork and tamarind in *balichão* (the local shrimp paste), curry crab, and chicken Macau. This is also a great place for private parties. ☒ *Est. Seac Pai Van Granja, Coloane,* ☎ *870–098. AE, DC, MC, V.*

$$ ✕ **Fat Siu Lau.** Dating to 1903, this is the oldest European restaurant in Macau and still one of the most popular. Each of its three floors is elegantly furnished and decorated; the menu is tried and true. The restaurant was made famous by its roast pigeon and its African chicken, sardines, and ox breast with herbs are crowd pleasers, too. ☒ *64 Rua da Felicidade,* ☎ *573–580. No credit cards.*

$$ ✕ **Fernando's.** You have to look hard to find this great country-style
★ Portuguese restaurant, next to Hac Sa Beach, because the entrance looks like that of a typical Chinese café (though local cabbies usually know how to find it). There are also an open-sided bar and a courtyard in back overlooking a sandy beach. Clams in garlic are the best in town, and the bacalhau is hard to beat. Since the menu is only in Portuguese, you may need the aid of eccentric owner Fernando Gomes, who's always happy to translate and make suggestions. ☒ *Hac Sa Beach 9, Coloane Island,* ☎ *882–264. No credit cards.*

$$ ✕ **Flamingo.** Designed like a European pavilion, with verandas on three sides, this restaurant is ideally located in the gardens of the Taipa Island Resort. There are no flamingos, but there are some very well-fed ducks in the surrounding pond. At night there is music by a Filipino group in the air-conditioned main room. At all times there is a wonderfully carefree atmosphere. Flamingo has the greatest small crusty cottage loaves in Asia. The menu is varied and reasonable, with a selection of Portuguese dishes, such as seafood casseroles and baked chicken. ☒ *Taipa Island Resort, Hyatt Regency Hotel,* ☎ *831–234, ext. 1874. AE, DC, MC, V.*

$$ ✕ **Henri's Galley.** On the banyan-lined waterfront, with some tables on the sidewalk, this restaurant is a favorite with local residents and visitors from Hong Kong. The decor reflects owner Henri Wong's former career as a ship's steward: a coiled-blue-rope pattern on the ceiling, pictures of old ships on the walls, and red and green lights to keep passengers on an even keel. The food is consistently good, with probably the biggest and best spicy prawns in town, delicious African and Portuguese chicken, Portuguese soups, Macau sole, and fried rice, complete with hot Portuguese sausage. ⊠ *4 Av. da República,* ☎ *556–251. MC, V.*

$$ ✕ **Litoral.** As soon as it opened in late 1995, this Macanese restaurant
★ was a hit with local residents, and it has remained one of the top dining places. The menu has many unusual dishes, and the food is fresh and attractive at very reasonable prices and served by smiling staff. Although it occupies a modern, boxy building, it was designed to look like a traditional Portuguese restaurant installed in a Chinese shop house, all to brilliant effect. ⊠ *261 Rua Almirante Sergio,* ☎ *967–878. AE, MC, V.*

$$ ✕ **Montanha Russa.** In the northern suburbs of Macau is a quiet park, built on a hill shaped like a snail shell. It's a great retreat, and the perfect spot for Macau's only real outdoor restaurant, which accounts for its popularity among the people who work nearby. Operated by Filipino residents, it is very much a family-style place, with a daily choice of soups, fish, and meats. Service comes with a smile, and the cost will be a very pleasant surprise. ⊠ *Est. Ferreira de Amaral,* ☎ *302–731. No credit cards.*

$$ ✕ **Pinocchio's.** This was the first Macanese-Portuguese restaurant on Taipa, and it's still one of the best. It began with one room, then grew to fill a large covered courtyard. Now the owner has expanded again, to a neighboring modern block. Favorite dishes are curried crab, baked quail, grilled king prawns, and steamed shrimp. If you order ahead, you can have delectable roast lamb or suckling pig. ⊠ *4 Rua do Sol, Taipa Island,* ☎ *327–128 or 327–328. MC, V.*

$$ ✕ **Pousada de Coloane.** This restaurant is 20 minutes by car from the city, by Macau standards a long, long way to go for a meal, but many residents and Hong Kong regulars consider it well worth the trip. The setting is fine, with a large open terrace outside the restaurant. When the weather is good, an alfresco lunch overlooking the beach and water is marvelous. For indoor dining, the restaurant is reminiscent of many in Lisbon, with dark-wood panels, colorful tile floors, and folk art decorations. Service can be rather haphazard, but the food is usually excellent. Among the specialties are feijoadas, grilled sardines, and stuffed squid. ⊠ *Praia de Cheoc Van, Coloane Island,* ☎ *882–143. MC, V.*

$$ ✕ **Praia Grande.** Wonderfully situated on the Praia Grande, this classic Portuguese restaurant was cleverly created from an ordinary corner building. Decor is simple, with white arches, terra-cotta floors, and wrought-iron furniture. The menu has such imaginative items as Portuguese dim sum, and the not-so-unusual chocolate cake is terrific, too. ⊠ *10A Lobo d'Avila, Praia Grande,* ☎ *973–022. AE, MC, V.*

$$ ✕ **Sol Nascente.** Opened in late 1996, on the main road at the entrance to Taipa Village, this modest restaurant has proved a real winner. It is simply furnished, with homemade chairs and a nice mural to illustrate the name *Rising Sun,* but what's special is the menu, where you find clams in coriander sauce, mussels stuffed with bread crumbs, spring onions and garlic, Goan prawn curry, and beef rice with chestnuts, as well as the usual Macanese favorites, none more than 90 patacas. There's wine for as little as 60 patacas a bottle as well as service by helpful, friendly people. ⊠ *Av. Dr. Sun Yat-sen, Edificio Chun Leong Garden, ground floor, Taipa Island,* ☎ *836–288. MC, V.*

$$ ✕ **Solmar.** As long as most people can remember, the Solmar has been an unofficial club for local Portuguese and Macanese men, who gather here to drink strong coffee and gossip. In 1995 it was given a completely new Portuguese look, with tiled walls, wrought-iron lanterns, and Impressionist-style pictures. The most popular dishes are baked Portuguese chicken and spicy African chicken. ⊠ *11 Praia Grande, opposite the Metropole Hotel,* ☎ *574–391. No credit cards.*

Asian

$$ ✕ **Chiu Chau.** This is probably the best—certainly the most sumptuous—restaurant in Macau serving the Chiu Chow cuisine of Swatow. Many Hong Kong and Thai Chinese (and, therefore, many gambling visitors to Macau) are originally from the Chaozhou region of Guangdong province. Their food is richer and spicier than Cantonese food, with thick, strong shark's fin soup, chicken in hot *chinjew* sauce, and crabs in chicken sauce. ⊠ *Lisboa Hotel,* ☎ *577–666, ext. 83001. AE, DC, MC, V.*

$$ ✕ **Four Five Six.** Lovers of Shanghainese food flock to this restaurant, where the specialties are lacquered duck, braised eel, and chicken broiled in rice wine, plus steamed crabs during the winter. The atmosphere is generally cheerful, noisy, and welcoming. ⊠ *Lisboa Hotel, mezzanine of new wing,* ☎ *388–404. AE, DC, MC, V.*

$$ ✕ **Korean Restaurant.** This is the place for *bulgogi* (barbecued meat) and kimchi (spicy cabbage) as authentic as any in Seoul, made especially agreeable by efficient use of ventilation hoods over the tables. Other traditional dishes to be found here are *sinsollo* (meat grilled on braziers at the table) and *japchae* (cellophane noodles and vegetables). ⊠ *Hotel Presidente, Av. da Amizade,* ☎ *553–888. AE, DC, MC, V.*

$$ ✕ **Long Kei.** One of the oldest and most popular Cantonese restaurants in Macau, Long Kei has a huge menu. Daily specials are printed only in Chinese, so ask the waiter to translate. Like all good Chinese restaurants in this part of the world, it is noisy and apparently chaotic, with no attempt at glamour or sophistication. The focus is the food—few will be disappointed here. Be sure to sample the shrimp toast. ⊠ *7B Largo do Senado,* ☎ *573–970. No credit cards.*

$$ ✕ **Rasa Sayang.** In a new residential complex on Taipa, this agreeable restaurant serves a wide variety of dishes from Malaysia, Singapore, and Indonesia. The decor reflects the menu, with batik pictures, lots of potted plants, and summery furniture. ⊠ *Est. Noroeste da Taipa, Ocean Gardens, Plum Court,* ☎ *810–187. AE, MC, V.*

$$ ✕ **Royal Canton.** This large, attractively decorated Cantonese restaurant is very popular with locals and visiting groups, who use it for family parties and celebrations as well as for breakfast and morning dim sum. The menu is extensive and the service friendly and efficient. ⊠ *Royal Hotel,* ☎ *378–633. AE, DC, MC, V.*

LODGING

Characteristically, Macau offers a far more diverse variety of accommodations than other parts of the Far East. It has international hotels in the three- to five-star range carrying the names of the world's leading chains; a good choice of budget hotels, owned and managed by Chinese from Macau, Hong Kong, or China; and hostels and guest houses at real bargain prices.

In general, hotels listed in the $$$ category are of the highest international standard, with swimming pools and health clubs, meeting rooms for conferences and parties, fine restaurants, public areas that are design showcases, business centers, and guest rooms with all modern comforts and conveniences. Those in the $$ category are efficient, clean, and comfortable, with air-conditioning, color TV (with English and Chinese programs from Hong Kong as well as the local channel), room service, and restaurants. They cater primarily to gamblers, regular Hong Kong visitors, and budget tour groups. Hotels in the $ category tend to be old and spartan, but they are clean and safe. All the lodgings listed below have private baths.

CATEGORY	COST*
$$$$	1,800 patacas–2,700 patacas (US$230–US$350)
$$$	800 patacas–1,800 patacas (US$105–US$230)
$$	300 patacas–800 patacas (US$40–US$105)
$	under 300 patacas (under US$40)

per room, not including 10% service charge and 5% tax

$$$$ **Bela Vista.** Originally built in the 1880s on a hill overlooking Praia
★ Grande Bay, this landmark hotel has been extensively renovated and upgraded by its new managers, Mandarin Oriental Hotels, and is now a deluxe inn with suites. The Bela Vista veranda has been famous among visitors to Macau for decades, and a marble-floor open-air terrace is now available for private parties and barbecues. The clubby bar, with a working fireplace, is a great rendezvous. ⊠ *Rua do Comendador Kou Ho Neng 8,* ☎ *965–333 or 2881–1688 in Hong Kong, 800/526–6566 in the U.S.,* 𝔽𝔸𝕏 *965–588. 8 suites. Restaurant, bar. AE, DC, MC, V.*

$$$ **Grandeur.** Owned and operated by CTS (Hong Kong), this hotel in the Outer Harbour boasts Rotunda, Macau's first revolving restaurant, where dinner is served in the round, with great views and nightly entertainment. Other restaurants offer Chinese and Italian meals. There is an indoor pool and a health club. All the rooms have a window bay containing a table and chairs. The furnishings are brightly floral, and amenities include hair dryers. The hotel is an efficient, businesslike place, without the grand lobby favored by most other hotels. It caters to Japanese and Mainland tour groups, Hong Kong businesspeople, and Western tourists. ⊠ *Rua de Pequim,* ☎ *781–233 or 2857–2846 in Hong Kong,* 𝔽𝔸𝕏 *781–211. 350 rooms. 3 restaurants, bar, indoor pool, health club, business center. AE, DC, MC, V.*

$$$ **Grandview.** Opened in the summer of 1997, this upmarket hotel overlooks the Macau Jockey Club, is near the new stadium, and is just five minutes from the airport. It has an opulent marble-clad lobby with a spacious lounge, restaurants serving Cantonese and Western food, an outdoor pool, a health club, and possibly a casino (undecided as we went to press). Most impressive is the 18th-floor lounge, with bird's-eye views of the racetrack, which is part of the Executive Club floors. ⊠ *143 Est. Governador Albano de Oliveira, Taipa Island,* ☎ *837–788,* 𝔽𝔸𝕏 *837–777. 447 rooms, 41 suites. 2 restaurants, bar, pool, health club, business center. AE, DC, MC, V.*

$$$ **Holiday Inn.** Opened in 1993 and part of the international chain's superior Asia-Pacific brand, this hotel is the latest addition to the rapidly developing Outer Harbour area, minutes from the new ferry terminal and within walking distance of the town center. Each room has contemporary decor and a built-in window seat with a city or sea view. Dining choices include the glass-enclosed restaurant Frascati, serving Italian cuisine in an alfresco setting; the Dragon Court, for Cantonese specialties; and the VIP Café, with its harbor view. At street level is Macau's first sports pub, Oskar's, complete with a pool table and video games. ⊠ *Rua de Pequim,* ☎ *783–333, 2810–9628 in Hong*

Kong, or 800/465–4329 in the U.S., FAX *782–321 U.S. 450 rooms, 6 suites. 3 restaurants, bar, pool, hot tub, steam room, fitness center, casino. AE, DC, MC, V.*

$$$ 🏨 **Hotel Ritz.** This handsome hotel is a series of low-rise blocks built into the hillside opposite the Bela Vista, with many rooms having balconies that look out over the Praia Grande Bay to the bridge and Taipa Island. It has a huge marble-clad, chandelier-lighted lobby that opens onto a café, a French restaurant, and a large health center that contains two pools, a squash court, a gym, and a sauna. The Lijinxuan restaurant, which serves dishes from many parts of China, is over-the-top opulent, with enormous chandeliers and masses of gilded wood. Its guests include VIPs from the mainland and five-star tour groups from Japan. ⊠ *Rua Comendador Kou Ho Neng,* ☎ *339–955; 2739–6993, 2540–6333, or 2367–3043 in Hong Kong;* FAX *317–826. 162 rooms and suites. 3 restaurants, bar, 2 indoor pools, sauna, 2 tennis courts, health club, squash, business services. AE, DC, MC, V.*

$$$ 🏨 **Hyatt Regency and Taipa Island Resort.** Rooms here conform to Hyatt
★ Regency's high standards, with modern conveniences and attractive furnishings. The public areas were built in Macau from designs by Dale Keller, and they combine the best of Iberian architecture and Chinese decor. The foyer is a spacious lounge with white arches, masses of potted plants, and fabulous Chinese lacquer panels. Beyond is the aptly named Greenhouse, a glass-roof café; a bar; and a Chinese restaurant. A small casino is off the lobby. The Taipa Resort, which adjoins the hotel, has a complete health spa, with various baths and massage and beauty treatments, a running track, a botanical garden, and on the veranda, the marvelous Flamingo, serving Macanese cuisine (☞ Dining, *above*). The hotel is close to the racetrack and operates a shuttle-bus service to the wharf and to the Lisboa. It is particularly popular with Hong Kong families. ⊠ *Taipa Island,* ☎ *831–234, 2559–0168 in Hong Kong, 800/233–1234 in the U.S.,* FAX *830–195. 326 rooms. 5 restaurants, 2 bars, pool, barbershop, beauty salon, 4 tennis courts, health club, squash, casino. AE, DC, MC, V.*

$$$$ 🏨 **Mandarin Oriental.** This beautiful hotel built on the site of the old
★ Pan Am seaplane terminal has marvelous views of the Pearl River and nearby islands. Its lobby is furnished with reproductions of Portuguese art and antiques, and the Cafe Girassol could have been transported from the Algarve. The Italian restaurant, Mezzaluna, serves excellent pasta dishes and has a wood-burning pizza oven. The Bar da Guia is probably the most elegant drinking spot in town, and the casino is certainly the most exclusive. Recreation facilities overlook the outer harbor. The guest rooms have marble bathrooms and teak furniture. ⊠ *Av. da Amizade,* ☎ *567–888, 2881–1688 in Hong Kong, 800/526–6566 in the U.S.,* FAX *594–589. 438 rooms. 3 restaurants, bar, 2 outdoor pools, beauty salon, massage, sauna, 2 tennis courts, exercise room, squash, casino. AE, DC, MC, V.*

$$$ 🏨 **New Century.** Standing between the university and the Hyatt Regency, this sumptuously appointed hotel has quickly joined the industry leaders. The atrium lobby is breathtaking, and the huge pool terrace offers splendid views of the city and Taipa. Rooms are tastefully furnished, and there is a wide range of dining options, including a wooden deck with Caribbean-style cabanas for parties. The Prince Galaxie is an excellent entertainment center, with a pub, a disco, and karaoke rooms. A new casino was scheduled to open in 1997. ⊠ *Est. Almirante Marques Esparteiro, Taipa Island,* ☎ *831–111, 2581–9863 in Hong Kong,* FAX *832–222. 599 rooms. 4 restaurants, bar, pub, pool, 2 tennis courts, bowling, health club, squash, dance club. AE, DC, MC, V.*

$$$ 🏨 **Pousada de São Tiago.** This traditional Portuguese inn—as much
★ a leading tourist attraction as a place to stay—was built, with enormous imagination and dedication, into the ruins of a 17th-century
fortress. Ancient trees that had taken over the fort were incorporated
into the design; the positions of their roots, for example, dictate the
shape of the coffee shop and terrace, now a part of its casual Mediterranean restaurant, Os Gatos (☞ Dining, *above*). Furnishings, made to
order in Portugal, include mahogany period furniture, blue-and-white
tile walls, and crystal lamps, plus terra-cotta floor tiles from China and
carpets woven in Hong Kong. The entrance is the original entry to the
fort, and natural springs have been trained to flow down the rocky wall
in tile channels on either side of the staircase. Each room, complete
with a four-poster bed and a marble bathroom, has a balcony. Book
well in advance for weekends and holidays. ⊠ *Av. da República,* ☎
378–111, 2739–1216 in Hong Kong, FAX *552–170. 23 rooms. Restaurant, bar, pool, chapel. AE, DC, MC, V.*

$$$ 🏨 **Royal.** The Royal has an excellent location, with fine views of Guia,
the city, and the Inner Harbour. It has a marble-clad lobby with a marble fountain and lounge and some excellent shops. In the basement are
its sports facilities and a karaoke bar. Upstairs are the glass-roof swimming pool and four restaurants: the Royal Canton for Chinese food,
the Japanese Ginza, the Portuguese-Continental Vasco da Gama, and
a coffee shop. The hotel has shuttle bus service to the casinos. ⊠ *2Est.
da Vitoria,* ☎ *552–222, 2540–6333 in Hong Kong,* FAX *563–008. 380
rooms. 3 restaurants, bar, indoor pool, sauna, health club, squash, shops.
AE, DC, MC, V.*

$$$$ 🏨 **Westin Resort.** This marvelous facility opened in 1993 on a headland overlooking Hac Sa Beach on Coloane Island. Rooms are built
around the bluff and have great terrace views of the beach and water.
The Macau Golf and Country Club (☞ Outdoor Activities and Sports,
below) has a clubhouse in the building, with the course laid out behind it. ⊠ *Hac Sa Beach, Coloane Island,* ☎ *871–111, 2803–2015
in Hong Kong, 800/228–3000 in the U.S.,* FAX *871–122. 208 rooms.
4 restaurants, 2 bars, 2 pools, golf course, 8 tennis courts, health club,
squash, shops. AE, DC, MC, V.*

$$ 🏨 **Beverly Plaza.** In the new suburb behind the Lisboa, this hotel is
managed by the China Travel Service, which has offices in the building. The hotel's shop has bargain-priced stereos, television sets, microwave ovens, and other goods that local Chinese buy for their relatives
in China and provides a shipping service. This hotel is a fairly standard China-run hotel, with disco and karaoke, sauna and massage, large
Chinese banquet room and Western coffee shop. The rooms are clean,
air-conditioned, and equipped with television, minibar, and flasks of
hot water to make tea and coffee. However, mattresses are hard and
towels skimpy. ⊠ *Av. Dr. Rodrigo Rodrigues,* ☎ *782–288, 2739–9928
in Hong Kong,* FAX *780–684. 300 rooms. Restaurant, bar, coffee shop,
shop. AE, DC, MC, V.*

$$ 🏨 **Guia.** Situated on Guia Hill, this small, unpretentious hotel is an
excellent value, where guests feel very much at home. Rooms are simple and agreeable, and some have views of the residential area and hills.
⊠ *1Est. Engenheiro Trigo,* ☎ *513–888,* FAX *559–822. 89 rooms.
Restaurant, bar, coffee shop, dance club. AE, DC, MC, V.*

$$ 🏨 **Kingsway.** This moderately priced hotel on the Outer Harbour has
small rooms, but all have International Direct Dial telephones, minibars, and in-house movies. Its casino caters mostly to gambling junketeers from Southeast Asia. ⊠ *Rua Luis Gonzaga Gomes,* ☎ *702–888,
2571–1886 in Hong Kong,* FAX *702–828. 410 rooms. 2 restaurants,
sauna, casino. AE, DC, MC, V.*

$$ 🏨 **Lisboa.** Rising above a two-story casino, with walls of mustard-color tiles, frilly white window frames, and a roof shaped like a giant roulette wheel, this utterly bizarre building is a local landmark. The main tower of the Lisboa has, for better or worse, become one of the popular symbols of Macau. A second tower wing houses the *Crazy Paris Show,* the superb A Galera restaurant, a children's game room, and a billiards hall, plus an ostentatious collection of late Ching dynasty art objects in the small lobby-level exhibition area. The original tower has restaurants serving some of Macau's best food, featuring the cuisines of Chiu Chow province, Japan, and Shanghai. Also contained in the complex are a video arcade, a 24-hour coffee shop, a health spa, Macau's first Pizza Hut, some very good shops, and a pool terrace. ⊠ *Av. da Amizade,* ☎ *377–666, 2546–6944 in Hong Kong,* 🗚 *567– 193. 1,050 rooms. 12 restaurants, 3 bars, coffee shop, pizzeria, pool, sauna, bowling, casino, dance club, theater, video games. AE, DC, MC, V.*

$$ 🏨 **Metropole.** This centrally located hotel is managed by the China Travel Service. It has pleasant, comfortable rooms and restaurants serving Chinese and Western food. The hotel is frequented by business travelers and China-bound groups. ⊠ *63 Rua da Praia Grande,* ☎ *388–166, 2833–9300 in Hong Kong,* 🗚 *330–890. 109 rooms. Restaurant, coffee shop. AE, DC, MC, V.*

$$ 🏨 **Nam Yue.** This new, China-managed hotel is conveniently close to the ferry terminal, the Jai Alai casino and entertainment complex, and the Yaohan department store. It is a bright, welcoming place, with a popular Chinese restaurant and a coffee shop. ⊠ *International Centre, Av. do Dr. Rodrigo Rodrigues,* ☎ *726–288, 2559–0708 in Hong Kong,* 🗚 *726–726. 141 rooms. Restaurant, coffee shop, business services. AE, DC, MC, V.*

$$ 🏨 **New World Emperor.** This 1992 addition to the Outer Harbour district is close to casinos and the wharf and is a smart value. It has a fine Cantonese restaurant and a nightclub with disco and karaoke. The lobby bazaar sells name-brand clothes and accessories. Rooms are furnished with potted plants, desks and TV consoles, and pastel-color drapes and bedspreads. ⊠ *Rua de Xangai,* ☎ *781–888 or 2733–0399,* 🗚 *782– 287. 405 rooms. 2 restaurants, bar, sauna, dance club, nightclub. AE, DC, MC, V.*

$$ 🏨 **Pousada de Coloane.** Among the delights of this small resort inn is a huge terrace overlooking a good sandy beach, along with a pool and a superb restaurant serving Macanese and Portuguese food. Sunday buffets, held outdoors weather permitting, are popular with locals and tourists alike. The April in Portugal festival takes place here every year, with star performers flown in. The rooms have balconies, minibars, and roomy bathtubs. This is a place for lazy vacations, and in summer it's usually packed with families from Hong Kong as well as singles who want an inexpensive getaway. ⊠ *Praia de Cheoc Van, Coloane Island,* ☎ *882–143, 2523–5690 in Hong Kong,* 🗚 *882–251. 22 rooms. Restaurant, bar, pool. MC, V.*

$$ 🏨 **Presidente.** The Presidente has an excellent location a block from the Lisboa casino, on the Outer Harbour Road, between the ferry terminal and the bridge to Taipa Island. It's very popular with visitors from Hong Kong and has an agreeable lobby lounge, European and Chinese restaurants, the best Korean food in town, and a disco. ⊠ *Av. da Amizade,* ☎ *553–888, 2857–1533 in Hong Kong,* 🗚 *552–735. 340 rooms. 3 restaurants, sauna, dance club. AE, DC, MC, V.*

$$ 🏨 **Sintra.** The Sintra is both a sister hotel of and a contrast to the Lisboa; it's quiet, with few diversions apart from a sauna and a European restaurant with picture windows and Mediterranean decor. It has a handsome new facade and a chic Continental lobby and is ideally located, within easy walking distance of the Lisboa and downtown. ⊠ *Av. Dom Joã, IV,* ☎ *710–111, 2546–6944 in Hong Kong,* FAX *566–7749. 236 rooms. 2 restaurants, sauna. AE, DC, MC, V.*

$ ▦ Central. In the heart of town, this was once the home of Macau's only legal casino and its best brothel. Now it's a budget hotel with clean, basic rooms and an excellent Chinese restaurant. ⊠ *Av. Almeida Ribeiro,* ☎ *378–888,* FAX *332–275. 160 rooms. Restaurant. AE, MC, V.*

$ ▦ East Asia. This attractive small hotel is situated in an interesting old quarter off the main street. It has a restaurant serving Chinese and Western food, and it's close to many good restaurants. ⊠ *1A Rua da Madeira,* ☎ *922–433 or 2540–6333 in Hong Kong,* FAX *922–430. 98 rooms. Restaurant. AE, MC, V.*

$ ▦ Grande. A pre–World War II hotel geared for gamblers who frequent nearby casinos, the Grande has a European atmosphere and good restaurants. ⊠ *146 Av. Almeida Ribeiro,* ☎ *921–111,* FAX *922–397. 90 rooms. 4 restaurants, nightclub. AE, DC, MC, V.*

$ ▦ Holiday. This budget hotel is behind Monte Fort and St. Paul's. Rooms are basic one-star, with small, hard beds, TVs, telephones, air-conditioning, and bathrooms with tubs and showers. No English is spoken but the staff is friendly and helpful. ⊠ *36Est. de Repousa,* ☎ *361–696. 40 rooms. Restaurant, nightclub. AE, MC, V.*

$ ▦ Hou Kong. Built into a restored old building—its facade has Grecian columns and ornate balconies—this budget hotel has fifth-floor rooms with good views of the Inner Harbour. There is a simple Chinese restaurant on the lobby floor. Staff members don't speak English, but they do their best to please. ⊠ *1 Trav. das Virtudes,* ☎ *937–555,* FAX *338–884. 54 rooms. Restaurant. AE, MC, V.*

$ ▦ Ko Wah. In a modern building in the Felicidade entertainment district, this guest house is clean and comfortable. ⊠ *71 Rua Felicidade,* ☎ *554–993,* FAX *502–004. 30 rooms. No credit cards.*

$ ▦ London. This fairly new hotel on the Inner Harbour waterfront has no restaurant or recreation facilities, but many are close by. The rooms have summery furnishings, TVs, telephones and decent bathrooms. ⊠ *4 Praça Ponte de Horta,* ☎ *937–770. 46 rooms. No credit cards.*

There are some small, old hotels and boardinghouses (referred to as villas) in the $ category. They usually cater to Chinese visitors, so the staff generally speaks little English. However, they are clean and inexpensive, sometimes with private bath and TV. The Department of Tourism (☞ Macau A to Z, *below*) can provide details.

NIGHTLIFE

According to old movies and novels about the China coast, Macau was a city of opium dens, wild gambling, international spies, and slinky ladies of the night. For some Western visitors it might be a letdown to discover that these days the city's nightlife—apart from the casinos—is dominated by hostess nightclubs, karaoke lounges, and so-called sauna parlors that are all very much aimed at Asian men. A woman employed by a club or lounge may simply talk, drink, or dance a few hours away with a patron, but be wise to the fact that these establishments are also fronts for prostitution.

Mona Lisa Theater (Lisboa Hotel). *The Crazy Paris Show,* at the Lisboa, was first staged in the late 1970s and has become a popular fixture. The stripper-dancers are professional artists from Europe, Australia, and the Americas who put on a highly sophisticated and cleverly staged show. They shed their clothes, but there's nothing lewd or exploitative about the performance. In fact, half the audience is likely to be made up of female tourists. The acts change completely every few months, but one show-stopping act has become a regular: A woman, with apparently magical breath control, does Esther Williams–type routines in a huge tank of water on stage—but unlike the movie star, she wears no clothes. Tickets for this show are available at hotel desks, Hong Kong and Macau ferry terminals, and at the theater itself. ✉ *Lisboa Hotel, 2nd Floor, Av. da Amizade,* ☎ *377–666, ext. 1193.* 🎫 *HK$200–250.* ⏰ *Shows Sun.–Fri. 8 and 9:30, Sat. 8, 9:30, and 11.*

Discos and Nightclubs

Most nightspots are staffed with hostesses, usually from Thailand or the Philippines but occasionally from Europe or Russia. The girls drink and dance with customers, who can pay to take them out. Most clubs these days also offer karaoke rooms for private parties, complete with hostesses.

Among the best nightclubs are **China City** (☎ 726–633), in the Jai Alai casino complex, which employs 300 girls in a variety of sensual costumes; **Show Palace** (☎ 727–171), also in the Jai Alai building, where you pay for striptease shows and table dances in VIP rooms; the **Tonnochy** (☎ 372–211), in the downtown Si Toi Building, modeled on a turn-of-the-century Parisian bordello and featuring elegantly turned-out hostesses, marble statues, and luxurious boudoirs; and the **Skylight** (☎ 553–888), in the Presidente, a glass-roof nightclub with a floor show of European strippers. They have different admission prices and minimums, but all are open 6 PM–4 AM.

Pubs

In the last year both residents and visitors have welcomed some alternative nighttime entertainment with the opening of music pubs. Especially popular is **Talker's Pub** (✉ 102 Rua Pedro Coutinho, ☎ 528–975), with the latest rock on the jukebox. The latest "in" place is Carpenters, opposite the market in Taipa Village (☎ 825–586), with bar counters and tables on two levels. It's a cheerful, welcoming place, with mostly rock music on the jukebox. Regulars are local young professionals.

Casinos

There are 10 casinos in Macau: in the **Lisboa, Mandarin Oriental, New Century, Kingsway, Holiday Inn, and Hyatt Regency** hotels; and in the **Jai Alai Stadium,** the **Jockey Club,** the **Kam Pek,** and the **Palacio de Macau,** usually known as the Floating Casino. The busiest is the two-story operation in the Lisboa, where the games are roulette, blackjack, baccarat, *pacapio,* and the Chinese games fan-tan and big and small. There are also hundreds of slot machines, which the Chinese call hungry tigers.

There are few limitations to gambling in Macau. No one under 18 is allowed in, but identity cards are not checked. Although there are posted betting limits, high rollers are not discouraged by such things. A credit card can get you cash in patacas or HK dollars from the automatic teller machines and there are also 24-hour money exchanges. Bets are almost always in Hong Kong dollars.

The solid mass of players in the casinos might look rather unsophisticated, but they are as knowledgeable as any gamblers in the world. They are also more single-minded than most, eschewing alcohol and all but essential nourishment when at the tables. (Small bottles of chicken essence are much in evidence!) And they are extremely super-stitious, which leads to gambles that may confuse Westerners.

Baccarat has, in recent years, become a big status game for well-heeled gamblers from Hong Kong, who brag as much about losing a million as about winning one. An admiring, envying crowd usually surrounds the baccarat tables, which occupy their own special corners. Minimum bets are HK$1,000 to HK$30,000. In Macau the player cannot take the bank, and the fixed rules on drawing and standing are complex, making it completely a game of chance.

Big and small is a traditional game in which you bet on combinations of numbers for big or small totals determined by rolled dice. The minimum bet is HK$50.

Blackjack is enormously popular in Macau, and there are frequently dozens of people crowded around the players, often placing side bets. An uninitiated player might feel flattered to have others bet on his or her skill or luck—until you learn that by Macau rules anyone betting more than the player can call the hand! Otherwise, the rules are like American ones. The dealers, all women, must draw on 16 or less and stand on 17 or more. Minimum bets are HK$100–HK$1,000, depending on the casino. Many of the dealers are rude, surly, and greedy. In the Lisboa they take a cut of any winnings automatically, as a tip, and it's a battle to get it back. Players do, however, have a chance for revenge. No matter how bad a dealer's run of luck she has to stay through her hour's stint.

Fan-tan is an ancient Chinese game that surprisingly has survived Western competition—surprising because it is so boringly simple. A pile of porcelain buttons is placed on the table, and the croupier removes four at a time until one, two, three, or four are left. Players wager on the result, and some are so experienced they know the answer long before the game ends.

Pacapio has replaced keno, a game it resembles. Players choose 4 to 25 numbers from 1 to 80. Winning numbers are chosen by computer and appear every half hour or so on screens in the Lisboa and the Jai Alai Stadium.

Pai kao has been a popular Chinese game since the last century. It is played with dominoes and a revolving banker system, which make it all but impossible for novices to understand. The minimum bet is either HK$100 or HK$200.

Roulette is based on the European system, with a single zero but with some American touches. Players buy colored chips at an American-shape table, and bets are collected, rather than frozen, when the zero appears. It has been steadily losing popularity and is now played only in the Lisboa and Mandarin Oriental casinos. The minimum bet is HK$50.

Slot machines line the walls of all five Western casinos and seem in constant use. The biggest attraction is the Megabucks system, with computer links to all casinos and million-dollar payoff possibilities. As of press time, the record take to date is HK$13 million.

OUTDOOR ACTIVITIES AND SPORTS

For most regular visitors to Macau, the sporting life means playing the casinos, but there are plenty of other sports, albeit often including gambling on the side. The Macanese are keen on team sports and give creditable performances at soccer and field hockey matches. In addition to traditional annual events such as the Grand Prix auto race, there are international championships in volleyball and table tennis (ping-pong). Major indoor events, such as the World Volleyball Championships, are held in the **Macau Forum,** while the new venue for outdoor events is the **Taipa Stadium.** Participatory sports activities have increased, with some excellent routes for joggers and fitness facilities in hotels.

Dragon-Boat Racing

This newest of international sports derives from the ancient Chinese Dragon Boat Festival, during which fishing communities competed, paddling long, shallow boats with dragon heads and tails in honor of a poet who drowned himself to protest official corruption. At the time, about 2,000 years ago, his friends took boats into the water and pounded their oars and beat drums to scare away the fish who would have eaten the poet's body. The festival and races have been revived in many parts of Asia, with teams competing from Hong Kong, Nagasaki, Singapore, Thailand, Malaysia, and Macau, plus crews from Australia, the United States, Europe, and China's Guangdong province. The races are held alongside the waterfront, which provides a natural grandstand for spectators. The Dragon Boat Festival takes place on the fifth day of the fifth moon (usually sometime in June) and is attended by a flotilla of fishing junks decorated with silk banners and by fishing families beating drums and setting off firecrackers.

Go-Cart Racing

On reclaimed land opposite Coloane Park is the new go-cart racing track, the **Kartodromo**. It's basically headquarters for local carters and is usually open only on Sunday. There are floodlights for night racing. At press time no go-carts were for rent due to insurance problems. ⊠ *Seac Pai Van, Coalane,* ☏ *726–578.*

Golf

The **Macau Golf and Country Club** is part of the **Westin Resort** beside Hac Sa Beach. The 18-hole, par-71 course is built into the wooded headland above the hotel, in which the clubhouse occupies the upper floors, with a pro shop, a pool, a sauna, massage rooms, steam baths, and restaurants. The elevator leaves you a few yards from the first tee. Only members of affiliated clubs and hotel guests can play. ☏ *871–111.* 🖾 *Greens fees for 18 holes HK$1,100 weekdays, HK$1,500 weekends.*

Greyhound Racing

The dogs are very popular with residents and Hong Kong gamblers, who flock to races in the scenic, open-air **Macau Canidrome,** close to the old Chinese border. Most dogs are imported from Australia, with some from Ireland and the United States. The 10,000-seat stadium has rows and rows of betting windows and stalls for food and drink. Multimillion-dollar purses are not unheard of, and special events, such as Irish Nights, are held frequently. Races start at 8 PM (there are usually eight) and finish at about around 11 PM. ⊠ *Av. do Artur Tamagnini Barbosa at Av. General Castelo Branco.* 🖾 *2 patacas for public stands, 5 patacas for members' stand, 80 patacas for 6-seat box.* ☉ *Tues., Thurs. and weekends.*

Horse Racing

The **Macau Raceway,** originally built for Asia's first trotting track, is on 50 acres of reclaimed land close to the Hyatt Regency Hotel.

Trotting did not catch on with local gamblers, so the **Macau Jockey Club** was formed and the facility converted, with no expense spared, into a world-class racecourse, with grass and sand tracks, floodlighting, and the most sophisticated computerized betting system available. The five-story grandstand can accommodate 15,000 people, 6,000 of them in air-conditioned comfort; members have boxes where five-star meals can be catered. There are several public restaurants, bars, a small casino, and a huge electronic screen to show the odds, winnings, and races in progress. There is racing throughout the year on weekends (usually in the afternoon) and midweek (at night), timed not to clash with events at the Hong Kong Jockey Club. The Lisboa Hotel runs free bus service to the race course. For details check with your hotel desk. ⊠ *Est. Governador Albano de Oliveira.* ☏ *20 patacas.*

Ice Skating

The **Future Bright Amusement Park** has a rink that accommodates 300 skaters and has a highly qualified training staff. The park also houses a bowling alley, a food court, a video arcade, and a children's playground. ⊠ *Praça Luis de Camões,* ☏ *953–399.* ☏ *HK$40 weekdays, including skate rental for unlimited time.*

Motor Racing

The **Macau Grand Prix** takes place on the third or fourth weekend in November. From the beginning of the week, the city is pierced with the sound of supercharged engines testing the 4-mi (6-km) Guia Circuit, which follows the city roads along the Outer Harbour to Guia Hill and around the reservoir. The route is as challenging as that of Monaco, with rapid gear changes demanded at the right-angle Statue Corner, the Doña Maria bend, and the Melco hairpin.

The Grand Prix was first staged in 1953, and the standard of performance has now reached world class. Today cars achieve speeds of 140 mph (224 kph) on the straightaways, with the lap record approaching 2 minutes, 20 seconds. The premier event is the Formula Three Championship, with cars competing from around the world in what is now the official World Cup of Formula Three racing, where winners qualify for Formula One licenses. There are also races for motorcycles and production cars. Many internationally famous drivers have raced here, including the late Ayrton Senna, Michael Schumacher, Damon Hill, Ricardo Patrese, and Keke Rosberg.

Hotel bookings during the Grand Prix should be made well in advance, and the weekend should be avoided by anyone not interested in motor racing. Tickets are available from tourism offices or from agents in Macau and Hong Kong. Prices vary.

Running

The 26-mi (41.6-km) **Macau International Marathon** has been an annual event since 1980. Held in early December, it offers runners a challenging course that includes both of Macau's bridges, the airport, and a circuit of peninsular Macau. If you'd like a shorter challenge, the trails on Coloane are highly recommended. Guia Hill has an exercise trail. For further information contact the Sports Institute (☏ 580–762).

Stadium Sports

Since the opening of the **Macau Forum,** with its 4,000-seat multipurpose hall, it has been possible to stage a variety of sporting events in Macau. The world table tennis, volleyball, and roller hockey championships have been held here, as have regional basketball, soccer, and badminton matches. Interested visitors should check with their hotel's front-desk staff to find out if something special is on. The new, 15,000-seat **Taipa Stadium** (⊠ Av. Olimpica adjacent to the racetrack) opened in 1997, with facilities for soccer and track and field contests. Ask at your hotel desk about upcoming events.

Tennis and Squash

The Hyatt Regency, Mandarin Oriental, New Century, and Westin all have tennis and squash courts for use by guests only. At the Hyatt there is also a tennis coach.

SHOPPING

At first glance, Macau is a poor country cousin to Hong Kong when it comes to shopping. Most stores are small and open to the street, the clerks might be eating snacks at the counter, and the merchandise is likely to be haphazardly arranged. There is also very little for sale here that isn't available in far greater abundance and variety in Hong Kong.

So why shop in Macau? First, the shopping areas are much more compact. Second, the sales staff is in general more pleasant and relaxed (although the command of English might not be as good as in Hong Kong). And most important, many goods are cheaper. Like Hong Kong, Macau is a duty-free port for almost all items. But, unlike the former British territory, commercial rents are reasonable and wages low, which reduces the overhead.

Macau's shops are open every day of the year, except for family-run businesses, which take a short holiday after the Chinese New Year. Opening hours vary according to the type of shop but usually extend into midevening. Major credit cards are generally accepted, except on those items with the deepest discounts. Friendly bargaining is expected and is done by asking for the "best price," which produces discounts of 10% or more. Discounts larger than that on expensive items should be treated with suspicion. Macau has its share of phony antiques, fake name-brand watches, and other rip-offs. Be sure to shop around, check the guarantee on name brands (sometimes fakes come with misspellings), and get receipts for expensive items.

The major shopping districts of Macau are its main street, Avenida Almeida Ribeiro, commonly known by its Chinese name Sanmalo; Mercadores and its side streets; Cinco de Outubro; and Rua do Campo. Shop names reflect Macau's dual heritage; for example, Pastelarias Mei Mun (pastry shops), Relojoaria Tat On (watches and clocks), and Sapatarias João Leong (shoes).

Antiques

The days of discovering treasures from the Ming among the Ching chinoiserie in Macau's antiques shops are long gone, but there are still plenty of old and interesting pieces available. Collectors of old porcelain can find some well-preserved bowls and other simple Ming ware once used as ballast in trading ships. Prices for such genuine items run into the hundreds or thousands of dollars. Far cheaper are the ornate vases, stools, and dishes from the late Ching period—China's Victorian era—which are in vogue. This style of pottery is still very popular among the Chinese and a lot of so-called Ching is faithfully reproduced today in China, Hong Kong, and Macau. Many of these copies are excellent and hard to distinguish from their antique cousins.

Over the years dealers and collectors have made profitable trips to Macau. The standard answer to inquiries about where new supplies of antiques came from used to be "from an old Macau family" that was emigrating or had fallen on hard times. Today there is another explanation: They are brought out of China by legal and illegal immigrants in lieu of capital or foreign currency. Most of these smuggled items are small, but some are rare and precious. Among them are such things as 2,000-year-old bronze money shaped like knives, later types of coins with holes in the middle, jade *pi* (discs), ivory figurines, and old jewelry. In addition, you can still sometimes find Exportware porcelain, made for the European market in 19th-century China, and old bonds from the early 20th century.

Antique furniture was for many years almost impossible to find, until an English woman from Hong Kong opened **Asian Artefacts** on a side street in Coloane Village. The owner, a collector and connoisseur, has found suppliers in China and other parts of Asia, who keep her shop and its extension filled with valuable old tables, screens, chests and wardrobes, as well as some reproduction furniture that looks just like the original. ⊠ *25 Rua dos Negociantes, Coloane.* ☎ *881–022. Closed Wed.*

Other shops that have earned excellent reputations over the years include **Hong Hap** (⊠ 133 Av. Almeida Ribeiro), **Veng Meng** (⊠ 8 Trav. do Pagode), and **Wing Tai** (⊠ 1A Av. Almeida Ribeiro). There are good, reasonably priced reproduction ceramics and furniture on **Rua de São Paulo.**

Clothing

There are many shops in Macau that sell casual and sports clothes for men and women at bargain prices. Most are made in Macau and carry brand-name labels. In some cases these are fakes, but more often they are genuine overruns or rejects from local factories that are licensed manufacturers of garments for **Yves Saint Laurent, Cacharel, Van Heusen, Adidas, Gloria Vanderbilt,** and many others. Name-brand jeans cost about HK$150 and shirts HK$120. There are also padded jackets, sweaters, jogging suits, windbreakers, and a wide range of clothes for children and infants at very low prices. The best shopping areas are on **Rua do Campo** or around **Mercadores.** For the very best bargains you should visit the street markets of **São Domingos** (off Largo do Senado), on **Rua Cinco de Outubro,** and in **Rua da Palha.** There are also a growing number of name-brand boutiques, such as the two-story **Emporio Armani,** at 61 Sanmalo. Prices are usually much lower than in Hong Kong. Credit cards are accepted at most larger shops.

Crafts

Many traditional Chinese crafts are followed in Macau, and the best place to watch the craftspeople at work is along **Tercena** and **Estalagens.** These old streets are lined with three-story shop houses with open-front workshops on the ground floor (living quarters and offices are above). Some shops produce beautifully carved chests and furniture made of mahogany, camphor wood, and redwood, some inlaid with marble or mother-of-pearl. Other craftspeople make bamboo birdcages, with tiny porcelain bowls to go in them, family altars, and door plaques thought to bring luck. Macau also makes lacquer screens, modern and traditional Chinese pottery, and ceremonial items such as lion dance costumes, giant incense coils, and temple offerings.

Department Stores

In 1994 **Yaohan** opened Macau's first major department store, next door to the Jai Alai Casino, a one-stop arena for just about everything you could want, from linen tablecloths to a fully stocked food hall, clothing, jewelry, housewares, shoe repair, a bakery, and several dining options. The liquor store on the premises is a good place to buy Portuguese wine at low prices. Other popular stores are the two branches of **Nam Kwong,** on the main street, 95 Sanmalo, and next door to the Holiday Inn, at 8 Rua Pequim, which specialize in products made in China.

Gold and Jewelry

Macau's jewelry shops are not as lavish as those in downtown Hong Kong, but they offer much better prices. Each store displays the current price of gold per *tael* (1.2 troy ounces), which changes from day to day or even hour to hour according to the Hong Kong Gold Exchange. Some counters contain 14- and 18-carat jewelry, such as chains, earrings, pendants, brooches, rings, and bangles. There are also ornaments set with pearls or precious stones, as well as pieces of costume jewelry and fanciful traditional Chinese items. Most important, however, are the counters with 24-carat (pure) gold made into jewelry and in the form of coins and tiny bars, which come with assays from a Swiss bank. Pure gold is very popular with the Chinese as an investment and as a hedge against the vagaries of the stock exchange and currency fluctuations.

Prices for gold items are based on the day's price plus a small percentage profit, so only limited bargaining is possible.

Among the best-known shops are **Chow Sang Sang** (⊠ 58 Av. Almeida Ribeiro), **Pou Fong** (⊠ 91 Av. Almeida Ribeiro), **Sheong Hei** (⊠ 31 Av. Almeida Ribeiro), and **Tai Fung** (⊠ 36 Av. Almeida Ribeiro). Their salespeople speak English and are friendly and helpful.

MACAU A TO Z

Arriving and Departing

By Boat

The Hong Kong–Macau route is among the busiest international waterways in the world, with more than 13.5 million one-way passages a year and more than 25 million available seats. The crossing procedure is very efficient, and only on weekends and public holidays, when the Hong Kong gamblers travel en masse, are tickets sometimes hard to get. Of course, services are disrupted when typhoons are in the area.

The majority of ships to Macau leave Hong Kong from the Macau Terminal in the **Shun Tak Centre** (⊠ 200 Connaught Rd.), a 10-minute walk west of Central. In Macau ships use the modern three-story ferry terminal, which opened in 1994. There is also limited service to and from the China Hong Kong Terminal on the Kowloon side of Hong Kong Harbor.

The Macau Government Tourist Office, booking offices for all shipping companies, and offices of most Macau hotels, travel agents, and excursions to China are in the Shun Tak Centre.

There is a **departure tax** of HK$26 from Hong Kong and 22 patacas from Macau, which is included in the price of the ticket.

A fleet of Boeing Jetfoils operated by the **Far East Jetfoil Company** (✉ Shun Tak Centre, ☎ 2516–1268) provides the most popular service between Hong Kong and Macau. Carrying about 260 passengers, these craft ride comfortably on jet-propelled hulls at 40 knots and make the 40-mi (64-km) trip in about an hour. Beer, soft drinks, and snacks are available on board, as are telephones and Macau's instant lottery tickets. There is no smoking on board. Jetfoils depart every 15 minutes from 7 AM to 8 PM, with less frequent sailings between 8 PM and 7 AM. The top deck of each vessel is first-class. Two new craft, called **Foilcats,** were added to the fleet in 1995. They have three classes and are roomier, if a little less comfortable in bad weather, than the Jetfoils.

Jetfoil fares excluding tax for first-class are HK$110 on weekdays, HK$120 on weekends and public holidays, and HK$140 on the night service. Lower-deck fares are HK$97 weekdays, HK$108 weekends, and HK$126 at night.

The second-largest operator is **CTS-Parkview** (✉ Lai Chi Kok, ☎ 2789–1268), which has a fleet of sleek, spacious catamarans that depart every 30 minutes from Hong Kong and Macau between 8 and 5, with additional services in the evening. There are also six services between Kowloon and Macau. The journey takes about an hour. There are two different kinds of catamaran: the 266–303 seat **Turbo-cats** and **Tri-cats,** which have first-class and economy-class decks. Both have comfortable seats and counters selling drinks and snacks. Fares for first and economy class are the same as for Jetfoils. There are also VIP cabins on the two-deck vessels, which seat six and cost HK$1,180, HK$1,240, and HK$1,320. Rest assured that the Jetfoils' and 'cats' economy-class seats are perfectly comfortable, with the VIP cabins a definite extravagance.

There is also catamaran service by **HK Ferries** (✉ Shun Tak Centre, ☎ 2516–9581) from the China Terminal in Kowloon, with 12 round-trips a day. Fares are HK$85 weekdays, HK$100 weekends, and HK$118 nights. Call ☎ 726–301 in Macau.

TICKETS

Travel agents and most Hong Kong hotels can arrange for tickets. There are also 11 MTR Travel Service computer-booking outlets in Hong Kong that sell tickets up to 28 days in advance for the Jetfoils. They are found in major MTR stations. You can get your return ticket at the same time, although it's easy to get in Macau, except for very busy periods. If you decide to return earlier than your ticket says, you can go standby at the terminal. Jetfoil tickets can also be booked in Hong Kong by phone using credit cards (☎ 2859–6596; AE, DC, V) but must be picked up at least a half hour before the boat leaves. Tickets for CTS-Parkview vessels can be purchased from CTS offices throughout Hong Kong, from the terminals, and from the Hotel Grandeur in Macau. For information dial 2789–5421 in Hong Kong. Ticket prices include the departure tax.

By Helicopter
Helicopter service run by East Asia Airlines is available from the Macau Terminal, with departures every 30 minutes 9:30–5:30. The 20-minute flight costs HK$1,206 weekdays, HK$1,310 weekends from Hong Kong, and HK$1,202 and HK$1,306, respectively, from Macau, including taxes. Book through the Shun Tak Centre (☎ 2859–3359) or the terminal in Macau (☎ 790–7240).

By Plane

The **Macau International Airport** opened in late 1995 and has established itself as a busy regional hub. The airport itself, built on reclaimed land, is 15–20 minutes by road from downtown Macau and the Chinese border. The handsome glass-clad passenger terminal is connected by the gracefully arched Friendship Bridge to the Ferry Terminal and the Chinese border. At press time there were daily flights to and from Beijing, Shanghai, and Taiwan, with regular services from Singapore, Malaysia, Japan, Korea, Thailand, Vietnam, and Portugal, as well such cities in China as Xiamen, Qingdao, Xi'an, Tianjin, Wuhan, Dalian, and Shenyang. Air Macau is the local carrier. Departure tax for China destinations is 80 patacas, for others it is 150 patacas. ⊠ *Est. da Ponte da Cabrita,* ☎ *861–111 for Macau airport information or 396–5555 for Air Macau reservations.*

Currency

The pataca is tagged to the Hong Kong dollar, which is fixed to the U.S. dollar at approximately 8 Hong Kong dollars to the U.S. dollar, 6.52 to the Canadian dollar, and 12.5 to the pound sterling. The Hong Kong dollar is accepted in Macau, though having small change in patacas is handy for little purchases (also ☞ Money *in* the Gold Guide).

Getting Around

The old parts of town and shopping areas lend themselves to walking. Walking is the best method of getting around in the old parts of town and in shopping areas because the streets are narrow, often under repair, and invariably crowded with vehicles weaving between sidewalk vendors and parked cars. Otherwise transport is varied, convenient, and often fun.

By Bicycle

Rent bicycles for about 10 patacas an hour at shops near the Taipa bus station.

By Bus

Public buses in Macau are cheap—2.30 patacas within the city limits—and convenient. Services from the terminal are most useful for visitors: Itineraries are posted at bus stops. There are several services to Taipa, for 3 patacas, and Coloane, for 4 patacas. For 3.50 patacas, Minibus 1A provides service between the airport, the Lisboa Hotel, and the ferry terminal. All the other buses in town are chartered and are replicas of 1920s London buses, known as Tour Machines. Their depot is at the terminal, and they can be hired for parties of up to nine people for 200 patacas an hour. They are also often used to transfer groups to and from hotels.

By Hired Car

You can rent mokes, little jeeplike vehicles that are fun and ideal for touring. Drive on the *right* side of the road. International and most national driver's licenses are valid. Rental rates are HK$350 for 24 hours weekdays and HK$380 weekends, plus HK$50 insurance and a HK$1,000 deposit. Hotel packages often include special moke-rental deals. Contact **Happy Mokes,** ☎ 2523–5690 in Hong Kong, 831–212 or 439–393 in Macau). Large six-wheel mokes are available from Avis, which also has cars for rent, from HK$380 a day for a Cub 4 Pack to HK$2,500 for a Mercedes Benz 230. For details contact Avis Rent-a-Car (☎ 336–789 in Macau or 2541–2011 in Hong Kong).

By Pedicab

Tricycle-drawn two-seater carriages have been in business as long as there have been bicycles and paved roads in Macau. They cluster at the ferry terminal and near hotels around town, their drivers hustling for customers and usually offering guide services. In the past it was a pleasure to hire a pedicab, but heavy traffic and vast construction projects now detract from the experience. The city center is not a congenial place for pedicabs, and the hilly districts are impossible. If you decide to take one, you'll have to haggle, but don't pay more than HK$30 for a trip to a nearby hotel.

By Taxi

There are usually plenty of taxis at the terminal, outside hotels, and cruising the streets. All are metered, and most are air-conditioned and reasonably comfortable, but cabbies speak little English and probably won't know English or Portuguese names for places. It is highly recommended that you carry a bilingual map or name card in Chinese. The base charge is 8 patacas for the first 1,500 meters (about 1 mi) and 1 pataca for each additional 250 meters. Drivers don't expect more than small change as a tip. For trips to Taipa there is a 5-pataca surcharge; to Coloane, 10 patacas. Expect to pay about 10 patacas for a trip from the terminal to downtown.

Guided Tours

Traditional and customized tours for individuals and groups by bus or car are usually arranged before arriving in Macau.

There are two basic tours available. One covers mainland Macau, with stops at the Chinese border, Kun Iam Temple, St. Paul's, and Penha Hill. It lasts about 3½ hours. The other typical tour consists of a two-hour trip across the bridge to the islands to see old Chinese villages, temples, beaches, the Jockey Club, the University of East Asia, and the new airport. The tours are available by bus or car at prices that vary among tour operators.

The most comfortable way to tour is by chauffeur-driven luxury car. For a maximum of four passengers a car goes for HK$100 an hour. Regular taxis can also be rented for touring, although few drivers speak English or know the place well enough to be good guides. Depending on your bargaining powers, the cost will be HK$100 or more an hour.

Most people book tours with Macau agents while in Hong Kong or through travel agents before leaving home. If you do it this way, you will have transport from Hong Kong to Macau arranged for you with your guide waiting in the arrival hall. There are many licensed tour operators in Macau. Among those with offices in Hong Kong specializing in English-speaking visitors are **Able Tours** (✉ 5 Trav. do Pe. Narciso, ☎ 566–939; ✉ 128 Connaught Rd., Hong Kong, ☎ 2544–5656), **Estoril Tours** (✉ Lisboa Hotel, ☎ 710–461; ✉ Shun Tak Centre, Hong Kong, ☎ 2540–8028), **International Tourism** (✉ 9 Trav. do Pe. Narciso, ☎ 975–183; ✉ Shun Tak Centre, Hong Kong, ☎ 2541–2011), **Macau Tours** (✉ 35 Av. Dr. Mario Soares, ☎ 710–003; ✉ 91 Des Voeux Rd., Hong Kong, ☎ 2542–2338); and **Sintra Tours** (✉ Sintra Hotel, ☎ 710–361; ✉ Shun Tak Centre, Hong Kong, ☎ 2540–8028).

Visas

Visas are *not* required for Portuguese citizens or nationals of the United States, Canada, the United Kingdom, Australia, New Zealand, France,

Germany, Austria, Belgium, the Netherlands, Switzerland, Sweden, Denmark, Norway, Finland, Luxembourg, Italy, Greece, Spain, Japan, Thailand, the Philippines, Malaysia, South Korea, India, Ireland, Singapore, Mexico, and South Africa for up to 20 days, or for Brazil citizens for up to a six-month stay, or for Hong Kong residents for up to 90 days. Other nationals need visas, which can be obtained on arrival: 100 patacas for individuals, 200 patacas for family groups and 50 patacas for tour group members.

Important Addresses and Numbers

Visitor Information

In Macau, the **Department of Tourism** offers information, advice, maps, and brochures about the territory. It has offices at the ferry and airport terminals, which are open daily 9–6. The main office is in Largo do Senado (☎ 315–566).

Hong Kong has a **Macau Tourist Bureau** in Room 336 of the Shun Tak Centre (✉ 200 Connaught Rd., Central, ☎ 2540–8180), open Tuesday–Saturday 10–1 and 2–5, and at Hong Kong's Kai Tak Airport, just outside the Arrivals Hall (☎ 2769–7970), open daily, 8 AM–10 PM.

Business visitors to Macau can get trade information from the **Macau Trade and Investment Promotion Institute.** ✉ *Luso Bank Bldg., 1–2 Rua Dr. Pedro Lobo, 7th and 8th floors, Macau,* ☎ *712–660,* 𝖥𝖠𝖷 *590–309.*

9 Side Trips to South China

Althougth the Pearl River Delta region is best known as one of the new "little tigers" of Asia thanks to its booming economy, it preserves a heritage of traditional temples, arts, crafts, and the Cantonese cuisine that has become world famous.

WHEN CHINA OPENED ITS DOORS to foreign visitors in 1979, the response was overwhelming, and it was a rare first-time visitor to Hong Kong who didn't make a brief excursion across the border. Today Hong Kong is part of China and the rest of South China is wide open, but still the attraction of a one-day side trip from Hong Kong remains.

By Shann
Davies

Some of the most popular and convenient destinations for both tourists and business travelers are in the Pearl River Delta of Guangdong (Canton) Province. Both geographically and economically, Hong Kong and Macau are intrinsic parts of the delta, one of the richest agricultural regions of China. Here two annual rice crops and a superabundance of vegetables and fruit are produced, while coastal waters yield bountiful catches of fish and seafood.

Ever since the first foreign traders, probably from the Middle East, discovered the vast scope and possibilities of China, merchants have come to the "tradesmen's entrance" in the Pearl River Delta: the port city of Guangzhou (Canton), which was sheltered and close to suppliers from the south and conveniently distant from imperial authorities in the north. As a result, local merchants did not feel bound to obey the imperial ban on trade with Japan, imposed because the government declared that China needed nothing any foreign "barbarian" had to offer. In the mid-16th century, when Portuguese trading adventurers arrived off the coast and offered to act as intermediaries between Guangzhou and the merchants of southern Japan (whose government had similarly banned trade with China), Cantonese businessmen were delighted to accept.

With Guangzhou's approval, the tiny peninsula of Macau was settled by the Portuguese and quickly became a great international port, in time attracting traders from Britain, Europe, and America. By the early 19th century the Macau-based foreigners had gained a virtual monopoly on China's overseas trade.

Opium became the predominant commodity; this angered the Chinese government, and in the mid-19th century it placed restrictions on the opium trade, provoking the Opium War with Great Britain. Defeated by the British, the Chinese were forced to cede them Hong Kong, which rapidly became the dominant port city of the Pearl Delta.

In the 1980s China signed the agreements with Britain and Portugal that that established the return of Hong Kong to China in 1997 and will return Macau to China in 1999. During the same time period, investment poured across the borders into China, as industrialists and property developers from Hong Kong and Macau transformed the former farmland into booming new economic zones. So history comes full circle, as the two territories are once more bound up with that of South China.

In terms of travel, it has always made sense to treat the delta as a unified destination, and if you're in Hong Kong for at least a week, a Guangdong excursion of one to four days is practically a must to get a feel for the region. If you have less time, a day's excursion will at least give a flavor of the "new" China so vividly exemplified by the delta region.

Today Guangdong's cities are thoroughly modernized, as shown by their luxury hotels, good restaurants, reasonably reliable transportation, and efficient communications. At the same time they are in transition, with old buildings—however historic—succumbing to glass-and-steel skyscrapers, streets being dug up for new power lines, and pollution problems growing.

So what of the countryside, the "timeless China" promised in tour brochures? Sadly, a vast majority of the region has been converted into industrial suburbs, dormitory towns, and highways. However, you can still get an idea of the way it used to be, with glimpses of rural life off the main roads or in selected villages that are paid by the tour companies to preserve their traditional appearance and atmosphere.

This all combines to make a delta excursion the opportunity to see China's past, present, and future at one and the same time. This is also a chance to experience Cantonese cuisine at its most authentic and to visit the Shenzhen Bay theme parks that bring Chinese civilization into brilliant if somewhat idealized focus. Best of all, for golfers the delta is now home to a dozen new courses, which offer overseas visitors the chance to tee off in China.

Pleasures and Pastimes

Dining

When the rest of the world talks of Chinese food, they're usually referring to the cuisine of the Cantonese, who comprised the majority of migrants to the Americas, Australia, and Europe in the 19th and early 20th centuries.

Forced to use their ingenuity during centuries of feudal rule, to survive the Cantonese made use of roots, fungi, and every creature found on land and sea, developing what is arguably the most varied and imaginative cooking in the world. The results are to be found at their most authentic in Guangdong, where eating is the favorite activity and restaurants are prime hubs of society. It is possible to have a Cantonese meal for two or four people, but ideally you need 12 or at least 8, so everyone can share the traditional 8–10 courses.

The table is never empty, from the beginning courses of pickles, peanuts, and cold cuts to the fresh fruit signaling the end of the meal. In between you'll have mounds of steamed green vegetables (known rather vaguely as Chinese cabbage, spinach, and kale), braised or minced pigeon, bean curd that can be steamed or fried, luscious shrimp, mushrooms in countless forms, bird's nest or egg drop soup, fragrant pork or beef, and a large fish steamed in herbs, all accompanied by steamed rice, beer, soft drinks, and tea.

For the adventurous there are also sea cucumbers, duck's feet, fish maw, snake bile, and dishes of dog meat or endangered *pangolin* (spiny anteater). Or you can snack on dim sum, the little baskets of steamed shrimp dumplings, spring rolls, beef balls, and barbecued pork buns.

The restaurants of the Pearl Delta vary in price, decor, and atmosphere, but from the alleyway café to the banquet hall of a five-star hotel, all offer only the freshest of produce. Prices, of course, vary accordingly but generally are much lower than in Hong Kong. A six-course meal in one of the hotels used by tour operators will cost the equivalent of US$10 per person, including unlimited beer and soft drinks. At top-ranked Guangzhou hotels the cost is about US$20.

Golf

Because of the rapid industrialization of the Pearl Delta, many of its classically Chinese attractions have vanished. The development of first-class golf courses has given the area a new appeal. The first clubs were built by and for golfers, but their success has given developers visions of big profits from corporate memberships. How many will achieve this remains to be seen, but for now there is a wide choice of clubs that welcome guests as much as they do members.

Lodging

The majority of foreigners making excursions to destinations in the Pearl River Delta are on escorted tours and therefore have no say in the restaurants and hotels they visit. The growing number of independent travelers are usually businesspeople or golfers. If you are an independent traveler, you should be aware that although major hotels meet most international first-class standards, there is a shortage of English-speaking staff, so it's advisable to make reservations through travel agents or hotel offices in Hong Kong. All the hotels listed below have rooms with private baths. The best restaurants are generally found in hotels and resorts (☞ Dining and Lodging, *below*).

CATEGORY	COST*
$$$	over US$70
$$	US$40–US$70
$	under US$40

Rates are for double occupancy, not including 10% service charge.

EXPLORING

Numbers in the margin correspond to points of interest on the Pearl River Delta map.

Zhongshan

① **Zhongshan** is the county across the border from Macau that was known to the first Western visitors as Heungshan (Fragrant Mountain). The name was changed to Chung Shan (Central Mountain) in honor of Sun Yat-sen (Chung Shan was his pen name). Zhongshan is the pinyin transliteration of its name, the system now most commonly used to romanize Chinese ideograms. The county covers 687 sq mi (1,786 sq km) of the fertile Pearl River Delta and supports about 1.3 million people, many of whom are wealthy farmers who supply Macau with much of its fresh produce.

With substantial help from overseas Chinese investors, many new industries have been developed in recent years, mostly textiles, medicines, processed food, and electronic components. This prosperity contrasts starkly with the situation a century ago. At that time the mandarins benefited from nature's bounty, but the peasants who harvested it were kept in abject poverty. The same applied to much of China, but in Zhongshan the downtrodden had a way out—crossing the border to Macau and taking a coolie ship to the railroads of California and the gold mines of Australia.

Tens of thousands of peasants left. Zhongshan's city fathers boast of the half-million native sons now residing in lands around the globe. Quite a number came back, though, either from a sense of patriotism or the desire to show off their newly acquired wealth. Among them was Sun Yat-sen, born in Cuiheng, who led the movement to overthrow the Manchus and became known as the "father of the Chinese Republic."

Cuiheng, where Sun Yat-sen was born in 1866, is on every Zhongshan tour. Its major attractions are contained within a memorial park. One point of interest is the house that Sun built for his parents during a visit in 1892. It is a fine example of China coast architecture, with European-style verandas facing west. This is bad geomancy according to traditional Chinese, and it underscored Sun's reputation for rebellion. The interior, however, *is* traditional, with high-ceilinged rooms, ancestral

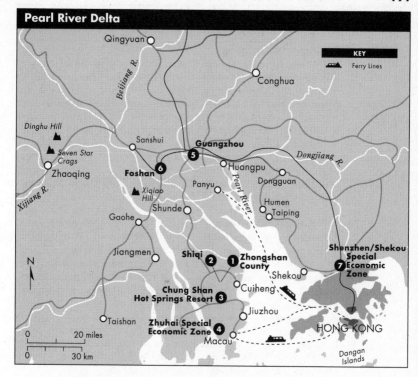

Pearl River Delta

plaques, gilded carvings, and heavy blackwood furniture that includes a roofed Chinese marriage bed. Next door to Cuiheng is the excellent **Sun Yat-sen Museum,** with rooms arranged around a patio, each showing the life and times of Sun as man and revolutionary. The exhibits are well chosen and displayed, with labels in English, Chinese, and Japanese. In addition, there are videos about Sun and Zhongshan.

Also in the park is the **Sun Yat-sen Memorial High School,** with splendid blue-tile roofs and a traditional Chinese gateway. It was built in 1934 and has about 700 students. Across from the park is the 242-room **Cuiheng Hotel,** a gracefully designed resort with a pool terrace and good Western and Chinese restaurants (☞ Dining and Lodging, *below*).

② **Shiqi** (formerly spelled Shekkei) is the capital of Zhongshan County, and for 800 years it has been an important market center and inland port. It's about 38 mi (61 km) from Macau and 49 mi (78 km) from Guangzhou and thus a convenient stopover on excursions to the delta area.

Until four or five years ago it was a picturesque port, where a cantilever bridge over the Qi River was raised twice a day to allow small freighters to pass, but the old town has been all but obliterated by modern highrises, and farms that used to surround it are now covered with factories. Nevertheless it can still be interesting to join the throngs who stroll along the riverbanks in the evening, and the **Sun Yat-sen Memorial Hall** and **Xishan Temple,** restored in 1994, are worth a visit. The dining here in Shiqi is exceptionally good.

③ **Chung Shan Hot Springs Resort** is more than a place to stay. Built by a Hong Kong millionaire, the complex is a tourist attraction in itself

(☞ Dining and Lodging, *below*). It is included as a stopover for lunch on many day tours, so visitors have a chance to explore the complex.

Dining and Lodging

$$ ✕🏨 **Chung Shan Hot Springs Resort.** This vast recreational complex consists of a charming compound of villas with pagoda roofs and Chinese antiques in some rooms, built around a traditional Chinese garden landscaped with classical pavilions beside willow-screened carp-and-lotus-filled ponds. The English-speaking staff is helpful, and there is a large Chinese restaurant (popular with tour groups) and a smaller Western restaurant. Outside, extensive grounds contain a swimming pool, shooting range, horseback-riding ring, and shopping center. There are also four baths fed by water from hot springs, piped from a neighboring valley. The hotel is 15 mi (24 km) from Macau. ⊠ *Zhongshan,* ☎ *760/668–3888,* 🇫🇦🇽 *760/668–3333. 350 rooms. 2 restaurants, pool, 36 holes of golf, 4 tennis courts, shops. AE, MC, V.*

$$ ✕🏨 **Fuhua Hotel.** Beside the river, this high-rise offers superb views. There are two Western restaurants and two Chinese; one of the latter is in its own pavilion, with stylishly furnished rooms and excellent food, particularly fish such as baked *garoupa* (grouper) and local pigeon, minced and eaten with plum sauce in lettuce leaves. ⊠ *Sunwen Xi Rd., Shiqi,* ☎ *760/886–1338,* 🇫🇦🇽 *760/886–1862. 420 rooms. 4 restaurants, pool, sauna, shops, bowling, dance club. AE, V.*

$$ ✕🏨 **Zhongshan International Hotel.** This 20-story tower, topped with a revolving restaurant, has become a landmark of downtown Shiqi. Its rooms, restaurants, and service are fairly standard. ⊠ *2 Zhongshan Rd., Shiqi,* ☎ *760/863–3388,* 🇫🇦🇽 *760/887–3368. 369 rooms. 4 restaurants, pool, sauna, bowling, billiards. AE, MC, V.*

$ 🏨 **Cuiheng Hotel.** Opposite the Sun Yat-sen Memorial Park, this hotel consists of low-rise wings and bungalows of contemporary and elegant design. It has gardens around the pool and a riding school next door. ⊠ *Cuiheng Village, Zhongshan,* ☎ *760/552–2668,* 🇫🇦🇽 *760/552–3333. 242 rooms. 2 restaurants, pool, dance club. AE, V.*

Outdoor Activities and Sports

GOLF

The **Chung Shan Golf Club** was the first and is still considered one of the best in China. Half an hour north of Macau, in Zhongshan County, it was designed by Arnold Palmer's company and opened in 1984, with Palmer among the first to try it out. It's a par-72, 5,991-meter course of rolling hills, streams, and tricky sand traps. Professionals who have competed in China's first international golf tournaments here declare it first class, and local youngsters who have been trained here now make up what amounts to China's national team. A second 18-hole course, designed by Jack Nicklaus, was added a few years ago, making this an ideal championship venue. The clubhouse, with gleaming mahogany paneling and elegant rattan furniture, has a bar, restaurant, sauna, and granite-walled pool, plus a pro shop with everything you'd expect to find in an American or Japanese club. Greens fees for visitors are HK$500 for 18 holes during the week, HK$1,200 on weekends. Caddies cost HK$160 a round, and club rentals cost HK$110. Bookings, transport (via Macau or Jiuzhou), and visas can be arranged through the club's office. ⊠ *38th Floor, Bank of China Bldg., 1 Garden Rd.* ☎ *2521–0377,* 🇫🇦🇽 *2868–4642.*

Zhuhai

❹ In 1980 **Zhuhai** was set up as one of the first Special Economic Zones, which have special liberal laws to encourage foreign investment. The zone has been extended from an original 5 sq mi (13 sq km) to 46 sq mi (121 sq km), complete with a long coastline and many small off-shore islands.

Zhuhai has the highest standard of living anywhere in China. It is also one of the most congenial and clean areas, thanks to its high-tech in-dustrial base, which includes factories producing electronics—Canon has its manufacturing headquarters here—textiles, glassware, TV parts, and computer discs. It is the place where pilots from all over Asia take Boeing simulator courses. Tourism is also important. Every day hun-dreds of Western visitors cross from Macau and observe hundreds of Chinese tourists, often from remote provinces, observing them in re-turn. Domestic tourists come to Zhongshan to pay their respects to Sun Yat-sen, and then they explore the shops and restaurants of Zhuhai, from which you can gaze across at Macau.

Dining and Lodging

$$$ ✗🏨 **Grand Bay View Hotel.** This handsome new hotel stands on the bay between the Macau border and the Zhuhai Ferry Terminal. It is sumptuously furnished and contains some of the zone's best nightlife and dining, as well as imaginative function areas that include a bal-cony overlooking the water and Macau. ⊠ *Shui Wan Rd., Gongbei,* ☎ *756/887–7998,* 🖷 *756/887–8998. 238 rooms. 4 restaurants, pool, 2 tennis courts, exercise room, billiards, nightclub. AE, DC, MC, V.*

$$$ ✗🏨 **Paradise Hill.** Looking like a Belle Epoch palace on the French Riv-iera, this new hotel replaced the modest little Shichingshan Resort. It has a stunning white-and-cream stone facade, with balconies overlooking a garden terraced around fountains. To one side are swimming pools beside a man-made lake, and at the back are tennis courts and six vil-las with guest rooms. The interior boasts a marble-clad atrium lobby and a marble grand staircase. The restaurants, serving Chinese, Con-tinental, Portuguese, and Japanese meals, are equally opulent, and the health center is state-of-the-art. The hotel is next door to the Zhuhai Resort and opposite the Zhuhai Convention Centre. ⊠ *Shichingshan, Zhuhai,* ☎ *756/333–7388,* 🖷 *756/333–3508 or 853/552–739 ext. 406 in Macau. 180 rooms. 8 restaurants, 2 pools, beauty salon, 2 ten-nis courts, health club. AE, DC, MC, V.*

$$ ✗🏨 **Zhuhai Resort.** This is a delightful reproduction of a Qing dynasty courtyard mansion. The Jade City restaurant serves excellent Cantonese food, which is also served in private dining rooms. ⊠ *Zhuhai,* ☎ *756/ 333–3718,* 🖷 *756/332–2339. 340 rooms. Restaurants, bar, 2 pools, 2 tennis courts, health club, conference rooms. AE, DC, V.*

Outdoor Activities and Sports

GOLF

Next to a proposed Formula 1 racing circuit in Zhuhai, the **Lakewood Golf Club** is about half an hour by car from Macau, 20 minutes from the Zhuhai Ferry Terminal. It opened its Mountain Course and club-house at the end of 1995 and the Lake Course in 1997. Managed by the Club Corporation of America, the club is a joint venture of Zhuhai and Malaysian companies. Greens fees for visitors are HK$600 week-days and HK$1,200 weekends, while caddies are HK$120 and golf carts HK$240. For details contact the Hong Kong office. ⊠ *Suite 1006, Cen-tral Plaza, 18 Harbour Rd., Hong Kong,* ☎ *2877–1128,* 🖷 *2877–8770.*

Guangzhou

⑤ **Guangzhou** is still better known as Canton, an English corruption of the Portuguese version of the Chinese name. With a strategic location on the South China coast, it has been a major trading port for almost

2,000 years. It received cargo from the Spice Islands, India, and the Middle East long before Europe knew China existed. It was also the port of export for silk, and centuries ago it began holding semiannual fairs at which silk was bartered for spices, silver, and sandalwood. From the time the Portuguese settled Macau, Guangzhou became the prime meeting place of East and West. During the 19th century it was a business home for British, American, and European traders.

Throughout its history Guangzhou has shown a rebellious character, and the Cantonese have frequently been at odds with the rulers in the north. Exposure to Western ideas made them more independent, and it is no surprise that the 1911 revolution and the organization of the Chinese Communist Party both started here.

The majority of current foreign visitors to Guangzhou attend trade fairs or are otherwise involved in business. Tourists rarely spend more than a day in the city. Although there are some interesting attractions, Guangzhou is best combined with tours of other parts of the delta.

Shamian Island appeals to those who know something of its history. This is where Western traders set up shop when the island was a sand spit in the Pearl River linked to the city by bridges that closed at night. The traders built fine mansions, churches, and even a cricket pitch. Most buildings have been renovated to house government and business offices, hotels, and shops.

Yuexiu Park is of general interest, with its array of Krupp cannons, and the 14th-century Zhenhai Tower, which contains the **Municipal Museum,** open daily 8:30–5:30. Nearby is a modern statue of five goats with sheaves of corn in their mouths. Legend has it the goats were sent from heaven with gifts of cereals; they have been adopted as the symbol of the city. Sun Yat-sen is, of course, honored in the city where he studied medicine and later celebrated the birth of the Chinese republic. The **Sun Yat-sen Memorial Hall,** built in 1925, contains a 5,000-seat auditorium.

The **Peasant Movement Institute** is a monument to an early Communist organization. In 1924 Mao Zedong and his comrades set up schools to teach their doctrine. The **Guangzhou Institute,** housed in a Ming dynasty Confucian temple, has been restored to recapture the atmosphere of a revolutionary's cell.

The **Chen Family Institute** has some magnificent porcelain friezes and stone carvings. The 11th-century Zen Buddhist **Temple of the Six Banyans,** which is open 8–5:30, has a 196-ft-high pagoda. The 7th-century **Huaisheng Mosque** (closed to tourists during services) was once a beacon for ships. The **Roman Catholic Cathedral** was built in the 1860s and is active again after years as a warehouse. Guangzhou's other attraction is its food (☞ Dining *in* Pleasures and Pastimes, *above*).

Dining and Lodging

$$$ ✕🏨 **China Hotel.** This vast complex of a hotel with office and apartment blocks and standing opposite the Trade Fair Exhibition Hall is greatly favored by business visitors because of its convenient location and multitude of restaurants, shops and entertainment possibilities. It is expertly managed by Hong Kong–based New World Hotels. ✉ *Liuhua Rd.* ☎ *8666–6888, 2724–4622 in Hong Kong,* 📠 *8667–7014, 2721–0741 in Hong Kong. 1,017 rooms. 6 restaurants, pool, bowling, health club, shops, theater, business services. AE, DC, MC, V.*

$$$ ✕🏨 **Dong Fang Hotel.** This luxury complex is across from Liuhua Park, which has the largest artificial lake in the city. There is an interesting selection of Chinese antiques and carpets in the shopping concourse,

and the complex includes an amusement park. Restaurants serve a variety of Chinese regional cuisines as well as Western and Southeast Asian dishes. ⊠ *120 Liuhua Rd., ☎ 8666–9900, 2575–5866 in Hong Kong, FAX 8666–2775, 2591–0335 in Hong Kong. 1,300 rooms. 5 restaurants, beauty salon, shops, recreation room, business services, meeting rooms. AE, DC, MC, V.*

$$$ ✕▦ **Garden Hotel.** In the eastern part of the city, this establishment has some spectacular gardens, including an artificial hill with a waterfall and pavilions. The hotel contains some fine antiques and modern artwork. ⊠ *368 Huanshi Dong, ☎ 8333–8989, FAX 8335–0467. 1,112 rooms. 8 restaurants, pool, health club, squash, shops, dance club, business services. AE, DC, MC, V.*

$$$ ✕▦ **GITIC Plaza Hotel.** The tallest hotel in China, this new landmark is part of a spectacular complex, built as a flagship property by GITIC, China's second-largest financial institution. The hotel occupies the top floors of the 63-story tower, next to a complex with 14 restaurants and lounges, shops, and banquet halls. There are also extensive recreation facilities. ⊠ *339 Huanshi Dong Rd., ☎ 8331–1888, FAX 8331–1666. 402 rooms, 300 suites. 14 restaurants, pool, health club, 2 tennis courts, shops, bowling, business services. AE, DC, MC, V.*

$$$ ✕▦ **Ramada Pearl.** In the eastern part of the city, this is a full-service deluxe hotel on the Pearl River with great views of the river traffic. It has also benefited from its proximity to the East Railway Station, a new terminus for Hong Kong trains. ⊠ *9 Ming Yue Yi Rd., ☎ 8777–2988, FAX 8776–7481. 394 rooms. 5 restaurants, pub, dance club, meeting rooms. AE, DC, MC, V.*

$$$ ✕▦ **White Swan.** The first international hotel in town, the White Swan occupies a marvelous site, on historic Shamian Island beside the Pearl River. It is a huge luxury complex surrounded by banyan trees and with a landscaped pool and a jogging track nearby. Many rooms have replicas of Chinese antique furniture and porcelain. Even if you don't stay here, visit the lobby to take a look at its spectacular indoor waterfall. ⊠ *Shamian Island, ☎ 8188–6968, 2524–0192 in Hong Kong FAX 8186–1188, 2877–0811 in Hong Kong. 843 rooms. 12 restaurants, pool, health club, shops, dance club, business services, meeting rooms, travel services. AE, DC, MC, V.*

$$ ✕▦ **Furama Hotel.** This modest hotel is well located beside the river downtown. Rooms are small but adequate, and the **Gourmet Court** restaurant serves excellent regional cuisine. ⊠ *316 Changdi Rd., ☎ 8186–3288, FAX 8186–3388. 360 rooms. 3 restaurants, bar, business services. AE, DC, MC, V.*

$$ ✕▦ **Holiday Inn City Centre.** Conveniently located in the financial district, this is a good, reliable place to stay in typical Holiday Inn style. There's an adjoining exhibition center and an 800-seat cinema. ⊠ *Huanshi Dong, Overseas Chinese Village 28, Guangming Rd., ☎ 8776–6999, FAX 8775–3126. 431 rooms. 3 restaurants, pool, health club, shops. AE, DC, MC, V.*

Outdoor Activities and Sports

GOLF

Opened in 1995, the **Guangzhou Luhu Golf & Country Club** (☎ 8350–4957 or 8359–5576 ext. 3282) occupies 180 acres of Luhu Park, one of the most convenient locations for golfing visitors—20 minutes from the Guangzhou train station and 30 minutes from Baiyun Airport. The 6,820-yard, 72-par course was designed by Dave Thomas. The club also offers a 75-bay driving range and fully equipped club house. Members' guests and those from affiliated clubs pay HK$500 greens fees for 18 holes on weekdays, HK$800 on weekends. The club is managed by Hong Kong–based CCA and is a member of the International Associate Club network.

Foshan

❻ Foshan (Buddha Mountain) is 12½ mi (20 km) southwest of Guangzhou on the main circuit of the delta region. The drive takes less than 30 minutes on the new expressway. The city's history goes back 1,200 years. At one time it was an important religious center with a population of a million. Today, after centuries of obscurity, it is again a prosperous town with numerous joint enterprises involving overseas cousins.

The legacy of the past is preserved in the city's **Ancestral Hall** (✉ Zumiao Lu St.), with its brilliantly decorated prayer halls and astonishing porcelain murals, all beautifully maintained. To fully appreciate the porcelain figurines, visit the suburban district of Siwan, which has been making porcelain for centuries, and watch the craftsmen at work. Some figurines are for sale.

Equally skilled workers are found in the **Folk Art Center,** where intricate paper cutouts are made by hand. Chinese lanterns, fish-bone carvings, and other handicrafts are also produced here. They are for sale at extremely reasonable prices. ✉ *Renmin Lu St.* ☉ *Daily 8–6.*

Shenzhen/Shekou

❼ Shenzhen (Shumchun in Cantonese) was just a farming village across the border from Hong Kong until, in the late 1970s, it was designated a Special Economic Zone and became the first "instant China" excursion for foreign tourists. Since then it has been transformed into a bustling industrial center, complete with one of the highest gross domestic products in China and the attendant pollution. Today most visitors to Shenzhen are Chinese from Hong Kong engaged in business or on family holidays, golfing and relaxing in lavish but moderately priced resorts. Foreign tourists are drawn to Shenzhen's series of theme parks, which provide a condensed tour of the great sights of China and an introduction to the country's culture and peoples. **Splendid China** replicates historical and scenic spots in other parts of the country, and the adjoining **China Folk Culture Village** shows the colorful customs and costumes of the country's ethnic minorities. Designed to appeal to Chinese tourists, the newest park, **Window of the World,** offers reduced-size representations of the world's most famous buildings and natural marvels. The other area of the Special Economic Zone that has developed into a city is Shekou, a major shipping port and headquarters for oil exploration companies.

Outdoor Activities and Sports

GOLF

Opened in late 1994, the **Honichi Golf Leisure Club** in Shenzhen's Baoan District was built primarily for Japanese who were either working in the area or visiting Hong Kong. It has proved popular, however, with many other golfers. One reason is its accessibility by high-speed catamaran service between Hong Kong and Shenzhen Airport. Another is the course design, which tests a player with the chance to use all 14 of his or her clubs during the round. There is a good clubhouse, with a sauna and restaurants. For visitors, greens fees are HK$500 weekdays. Weekends are for members only. Caddies are HK$100 and clubs HK$200. For bookings contact the club's Hong Kong office. ✉ *Room 1205, Mirror Tower, 61 Mody Rd., Kowloon,* ☎ *2312–1308,* FAX *2312–1726.*

Mission Hills Golf Club, in Shenzhen, scored a signal success when it hosted the World Cup of Golf in 1995. It has two 18–hole championship courses, with another 36 holes planned. Other facilities include a spectacular clubhouse and an adjoining 228-room resort, courts for basketball tournaments as well as tennis and squash courts, a variety of restaurants, and an indoor/outdoor pool around a stage for concerts or fashion shows. The courses are not open to nonmembers except for resort guests, for whom greens fees are HK$700 weekdays and HK$1,200 weekends; caddies are HK$100 and caddie carts HK$200. For more details contact their Hong Kong office. ⊠ *29/F, 9 Queen's Rd. Central,* ☎ *2973–0303,* FAX *2869–9632.*

Just across the border between Hong Kong and Shenzhen, the **Sand River Golf Club** can be the quickest to reach if there's no delay at immigration. Next door to Window of the World park, it offers courses—one is nine holes and floodlighted—all designed by Gary Player. There is also a large driving range, a fishing lake, and various resort facilities. Greens fees for visitors are HK$600 weekdays and HK$1,000 weekends. Caddies are HK$150. For details contact the Hong Kong office. ⊠ *19/F, SPA Centre, 55 Lockhart Rd., Wanchai,* ☎ *2520–2830,* FAX *2527–6885.*

SOUTH CHINA A TO Z

Arriving and Departing

Although there is no shortage of transportation options in and out of Guangdong, you may have trouble finding travel operators who speak English. Ask your hotel concierge for the latest schedules and prices or call the **China Travel Service** (CTS; ☎ 2853–3533).

Hong Kong–Zhuhai

Fast, modern catamaran ferries make eight round-trips daily to the **pier at Jiuzhou,** with five departures from the China Hong Kong City (CHKC) Terminal (⊠ Canton Rd., Kowloon) at 7:45 AM, 9:30 AM, 11 AM, 2:30 PM, and 5 PM) and three from the Macau Ferry Terminal (⊠ Shun Tak Centre, Connaught Rd., Central) at 8:40 AM, 12 PM, and 4 PM). The trip takes 90 minutes. 🚢 *HK$236 1st class, HK$211 2nd, HK$196 3rd.*

Hong Kong–Zhongshan

Catamarans make six round-trips daily to Zhongshan Harbor, close to Shiqi, with five departures from the **CHKC Terminal** and one from **Shun Tak Centre** on Hong Kong Island. The trip takes approximately 80 minutes. 🚢 *HK$251 1st class, HK$231 2nd class, HK$221 3rd class.*

Hong Kong–Guangzhou

There are five express trains daily, departing from **Kowloon Station** (⊠ Hong Chong Rd., Tsim Sha Tsui East) at 8:35 AM, 9:25 AM, 11:45 AM, 1:20 PM, and 2:45 PM. The trip takes about 55 minutes. The last train back to Hong Kong leaves at 6:00 PM. 🚆 *HK$280 1st class, HK$250 2nd class.*

A ferry makes the journey every day, departing **CHKC Terminal** at 9 PM; it arrives at dawn, and passengers disembark at 7 AM. There are cabins of different classes and restaurants. 🚢 *From HK$202 for a 4-berth cabin.*

There are two sailings by **Turbo Cat ferries,** departing CHKC Terminal at 7:15 AM and 1:30 PM. The journey takes about two hours. 🚢 *HK$370 1st class, HK$250 2nd class.*

CAAC, the Chinese airline has frequent flights between Hong Kong's Kai Tak Airport and Guangzhou Airport. The trip takes about 20 minutes. ✉ *HK$920 round-trip (plus a departure tax of HK$100 from Hong Kong, RMB90 from Guangzhou).*

Citybus (☎ 2873–0818) has five round-trips a day between Hong Kong and Guangzhou using new vehicles that have toilets, reclining seats, and individual air-conditioning and lighting controls and provide snacks and drinks. The trip takes 3½ hours and costs HK$180. Buses leave from CHKC and Shatin City One, in Hong Kong, and the Garden Hotel, in Guangzhou.

Among other bus services, **China Travel Service** (CTS) has 11 round-trips a day, with pickup and return at major Guangzhou hotels. The cost is HK$170. Following CTS's purchase of a stake in Citybus in 1997, there is likely to be a broader and coordinated service by 1998.

Hong Kong–Shenzhen

There's electric commuter train service throughout the day (first train at 6:08 AM; last train back to Hong Kong at 12:08 AM) from Kowloon Station to Lo Wu at the border. The trip takes about 40 minutes, but expect to spend up to an hour at border checkpoints. ✉ *HK$31 one-way.*

Citybus buses (☎ 2873–0818) make eight round-trips daily to Shenzhen, with six continuing on to the Shenzhen Bay theme parks. Buses depart Admiralty Station and the CHKC Terminal. Fares depend on the destination and day. ✉ *HK$65 one-way to Shenzhen City weekdays, HK$85 weekends; HK$75 one-way to Shenzhen Bay weekdays, HK$95 weekends.*

Fast ferries make a pleasant one-hour trip to Shekou, with five departures between 8:15 AM and 4:30 PM daily from the **Macau Ferry Terminal.** ✉ *HK$145 1st class, HK$110 economy class.*

Booking Your Trip

China Travel Service is the most convenient place to book tickets to China, although they add a service charge. In recent years customs and monetary declarations have rarely been checked, and those on group visas have had to ask to get a stamp in their passports. At the Chinese arrival points there are money-exchange counters and duty-free liquor and cigarettes at bargain prices.

Currency

You can easily change foreign currency at hotels and banks in Guangdong; the Hong Kong dollar is a very acceptable second currency here, however, so you probably won't need Chinese RMB.

Guided Tours

The vast majority of tourists on side trips to other parts of southern China take a guided tour ranging from one to four days. Although transportation in the region has greatly improved, it is still much easier for foreigners to get around this part of China with a guide. Tours offered by CTS and Hong Kong travel agents are designed to fit into any normal schedule.

By far the most popular is to **Zhongshan** via Macau, which provides a full and interestingly diverse if rather tiring daylong tour. All one-day Zhongshan tours begin with an early departure from Hong Kong to Macau and a bus transfer to the border at Gongbei, in the Zhuhai Special Economic Zone. From here tour itineraries vary, but all spend time in Cuiheng Village, to visit the house built by Sun Yat-sen, hero of the 1911 revolution, and an excellent museum devoted to his life and times. A six-course lunch, with free beer and soft drinks, is taken in Shiqi, an 800-year-old inland port that has become an industrial city, at the Chung Shan resort, or in one of the faux Ching dynasty hotels of Zhuhai. Completing the itinerary is a visit to a "typical" farming village, which is kept traditional for tourists. Tours return to Hong Kong in the late afternoon via Zhongshan Harbor. (This tour is often combined with a day and night in Macau, which makes for an excellent balance.) ☎ *Zhongshan tour: HK$880.*

The other established one-day China trip takes in the **Shenzhen Special Economic Zone,** immediately across the border from Hong Kong. This begins with a coach trip to Shenzhen and its prime tourist attraction, known as **Mini Kingdom** or **Splendid China,** a park containing 70 miniaturized historical or scenic wonders of China, complete with a population of thousands of porcelain figurines. ☎ *HK$680.*

An alternative is a visit to the adjoining theme park, **China Folk Culture Villages,** a superb collection of full-size buildings representing the different peoples of China, plus folk art and dance performances. The tour also includes visits to a Hakka village, a kindergarten, and a market. ☎ *HK$650.*

Thanks to the geographic and historic unity of the delta region, and the recent construction of bridges over the many Pearl tributaries and upgrade of major roads, multiday circular tours have become possible. The basic itinerary is a four-day tour (departs Tuesday, Thursday, or Saturday), beginning with a fast ferry to Macau. This is followed by a visit to Cuiheng, an overnight stay in Shiqi, a day in Foshan, a night in Zhaoqing, and a night and day in Guangzhou before a return by train to Hong Kong. ☎ *HK$2,520.*

The above examples represent the range of side trips available; other combinations exist. Ask for the "Guangdong Highlights" leaflet from CTS travel. Prices quoted apply per person, double occupancy. Most tours have daily or very frequent departures.

Reliable agents include **Able & Promotion Tours** (✉ 128 Connaught Rd., Central, ☎ 2544–5656, ℻ 2541–4413), **China Travel Service** (✉ 78 Connaught Rd., Central, ☎ 2853–3533, ℻ 2541–9777; 27 Nathan Rd., Kowloon, ☎ 2853–3534, ℻ 2721–7757), and **International Tourism** (✉ Shun Tak Centre, Sheung Wan, ☎ 2541–2011, ℻ 2541–3254). For a list of additional agents, call the Hong Kong Association of Travel Agents (☎ 2869–8624).

Visas

Travelers in groups of three or more can visit Shenzhen for up to 72 hours visa-free. However, to do so they must buy a package from one of the agents approved by the China Travel Service. Otherwise, visas are required to enter China. Cost depends on how quickly you have it issued. A single-entry visa with a two-day wait costs HK$160; a same-day visa costs between HK$310 and HK$560, depending on time of application. Visas are available from CTS offices and from most travel agents (all add a service charge). One passport-size photo is needed. For groups of 10 or more, travel agents get the visas; you need only supply your passport number to the agent the day before the tour.

10 Portraits of Hong Kong

IMPACTS AND IMAGES

HONG KONG IS in China, if not entirely of it, and after 150 years of British rule the background to all its wonders remains its Chineseness—98% if you reckon it by population, hardly less if you are thinking metaphysically.

It may not look like it from the deck of an arriving ship, or swooping into town on a jet, but geographically most of the territory is still rural. The empty hills that form the mass of the New Territories, the precipitous islets and rocks, even some of the bare slopes of Hong Kong Island itself, rising directly above the tumultuous harbor, are much as they were in the days of the Manchus, the Mings, or the neolithic Yaos. The last of the leopards has indeed been shot (1931), the last of the tigers spotted (1967, it is claimed), but that recondite newt flourishes still as *Paramesotriton hongkongensis,* there are still civets, pythons, barking deer and porcupines about and the marshlands abound with seabirds. The predominant country colors are Chinese colors, browns, grays, tawny colors. The generally opaque light is just the light one expects of China, and gives the whole territory the required suggestion of blur, surprise, and uncertainty. The very smells are Chinese smells—oily, laced with duck-mess and gasoline.

Thousands of Hong Kong people still live on board junks, cooking their meals in the hiss and flicker of pressure lamps among the riggings and the nets. Thousands more inhabit shantytowns, made of sticks, canvas and corrugated iron but bustling with the native vivacity. People are still growing fruit, breeding fish, running duck farms, tending oyster beds; a few still grow rice and a very few still plow their fields with water buffalo. Village life remains resiliently ancestral. The Tangs and the Pangs are influential. The geomancers are busy still. Half-moon graves speckle the high ground wherever *feng shui* decrees, sometimes attended still by the tall brown urns that contain family ashes. Temples to Tin Hau, the Queen of Heaven, or Hung Shing, God of the Southern Seas, still stand incense-swirled upon foreshores.

But the vast majority of Hong Kong residents live in towns, jam-packed on the flatter ground. They are mostly squeezed in gigantic tower-blocks, and they have surrounded themselves with all the standard manifestations of modern non-Communist chinoiserie: the garish merry signs, the clamorous shop-fronts, the thickets of TV aerials, the banners, the rows of shiny hanging ducks, the washing on its poles, the wavering bicycles, the potted plants massed on balconies, the canvas-canopied stalls selling herbs, or kitchenware, or antiques, or fruit, the bubbling caldrons of crab-claw soup boiling at eating stalls, the fantastic crimson-and-gold facades of restaurants, the flickering television screens in shop windows, the trays of sticky cakes in confectionery stores, the profusion of masts, poles and placards protruding from the fronts of buildings, the dragons carved or gilded, the huge elaborate posters, the tea shops with their gleaming pots, the smells of cooking, spice, incense, oil, the racket of radio music and amplified voices, the half-shouted conversation that is peculiar to Chinese meeting one another in the street, the ceaseless clatter of spoons, coins, mah-jongg counters, abaci, hammers, and electric drills.

It can appear exotic to visitors, but it is fundamentally a plain and practical style. Just as the Chinese consider a satisfactory year to be a year in which nothing much happens, so their genius seems to me fundamentally of a workaday kind, providing a stout and reliable foundation, mat and bamboo, so to speak, on which to build the structures of astonishment.

What the West has provided, originally through the medium of the British Empire, later by the agency of international finance, is a city-state in its own image, overlaying that resilient and homely Chinese style with an aesthetic far more aggressive. The capitalists of Hong Kong have been terrific builders, and have made of the great port, its hills and its harbors, one of the most thrilling of all metropolitan prospects—for my own tastes, the finest sight in Asia. More than 6 million people, nearly twice the population of New Zealand, live here in less than four hundred square miles of land, at least half of which is rough mountain country. They are necessarily packed tight, in urban forms as startling in the luminous light of Hong Kong as the upper-works of the clippers must have been when they first appeared along its waterways.

THE TANGS AND the Lius may still be in their villages, but they are invested on all sides by massive New Towns, started from scratch in starkly modernist manner. All over the mainland New Territories, wherever the hills allow, busy roads sweep here and there, clumps of tower-blocks punctuate the skyline, suburban estates develop and blue-tiled brick wilts before the advance of concrete. Even on the outlying islands, as Hong Kong calls the rest of the archipelago, apartment buildings and power stations rise above the moors. Flatland in most parts of Hong Kong being so hard to find, this dynamic urbanism has been created largely in linear patterns, weaving along shorelines, clambering up gullies or through narrow passes, and frequently compressed into almost inconceivable congestion. Some 80% of the people live on 8% of the land, and parts of Kowloon, with more than a quarter of a million people per square mile, are probably the most crowded places in all human history. An amazing tangle of streets complicates the topography; the architect I. M. Pei, commissioned to design a new Hong Kong office block in the 1980s, said it took nine months just to figure out access to the site.

There is not much shape to all this, except the shape of the place itself. Twin cities of the harbor are the vortex of all Hong Kong, and all that many strangers ever see of it. On the north, the mainland shore, the dense complex of districts called Kowloon presses away into the hills, projecting its force clean through them indeed by tunnel into the New Territories beyond. The southern shore, on the island of Hong Kong proper, is the site of the original British settlement, officially called Victoria but now usually known simply as Central; it is in effect the capital of Hong Kong, and contains most of its chief institutions, but it straggles inchoately all along the island's northern edge, following the track worn by the junk crews when, be-

fore the British came at all, adverse winds obliged them to drag their vessels through this strait. Around the two conglomerates the territory's being revolves: one talks of Kowloon–side or Hong Kong–side, and on an average day more than 115,000 vehicles pass through the underwater tunnels from one to the other.

Once the territory had a formal urban center. Sit with me now in the Botanical Gardens, those inescapable amenities of the British Empire that have defied progress even here, and still provide shady boulevards, flower beds, and a no more than usually nasty little zoo almost in the heart of Central. From this belvedere, fifty years ago, we could have looked down upon a ceremonial plaza of some dignity, Statue Square. It opened directly upon the harbor, rather like the Piazza d'Italia in Trieste, and to the west ran a waterfront esplanade, called the Praya after its Macau original. The steep green island hills rose directly behind the square, and it was surrounded by structures of consequence— Government House, where the Governor lived; Head Quarter House, where the General lived; a nobly classical City Hall; the Anglican cathedral; the Supreme Court; the Hongkong and Shanghai Bank. The effect was sealed by the spectacle of the ships passing to and fro at the north end of the square, and by the presence of four emblematically imperial prerequisites: a dockyard of the Royal Navy, a cricket field, the Hong Kong Club and a statue of Queen Victoria.

It has all been thrown away. Today Statue Square is blocked altogether out of our sight by office buildings, and anyway only the specter of a plaza remains down there, loomed over, fragmented by commercialism. Even the waterfront has been pushed back by land reclamation. The surviving promenade is all bits and pieces of piers, and a three-story car park obstructs the harbor view. The cricket ground has been prettified into a municipal garden, with turtles in a pond. Government House and the cathedral are hardly visible through the skyscrapers, the Hong Kong Club occupies four floors of a twenty-four-story office block. Queen Victoria has gone (well prior to the handover).

This is the way of urban Hong Kong. It is cramped by the force of nature, but it is irresistibly restless by instinct. Except for the harbor, it possesses no real center now. The territory as a whole has lately become a stupendous exercise in social design, but no master plan for the harbor cities has ever succeeded—Sir Patrick Abercrombie offered one in the heyday of British town planning after the Second World War, but like so many of his schemes it never came to anything. Proposals to extend that promenade were repeatedly frustrated down the years, notably by the military, who would not get their barracks and dockyards out of the way; all that is left of the idea is the howling expressway that runs on stilts along the foreshore.

Today beyond Statue Square, all along the shoreline, across the harbor, far up the mountain slopes, tall concrete buildings extend without evident pattern or logic. There seems to be no perspective to them either, so that when we shift our viewpoint one building does not move with any grace against another—just a clump here, a splodge there, sometimes a solitary pillar of glass or concrete. Across the water they loom monotonously behind the Kowloon waterfront, square and Stalinesque; they are limited to a height of twelve stories there, because the Kai Tak airport is nearby. On the sides of distant mountains you may see them protruding from declining ridges like sudden outcrops of white chalk. Many are still meshed in bamboo scaffolding, many more are doomed to imminent demolition. If we look down the hill again, behind the former governor's palace immolated in its gardens, we may see the encampment of blue-and-white awnings, interspersed with

bulldozers and scattered with the laboring straw-hatted figures of construction workers, which shows where the foundations of yet another skyscraper, still bigger, more splendid and more extravagant no doubt than the one before, are even now being laid.

The fundamentals, then, are plain and practical, the design is inchoate, the architecture of a somewhat mixed character; yet Hong Kong is astonishingly beautiful. It is made so partly by its setting, land and sea so exquisitely interacting, but chiefly by its impression of irresistible activity. It is like a cauldron, seething, hissing, hooting, arguing, enmeshed in a labyrinth of tunnels and overpasses, with those skyscrapers erupting everywhere into view, with ferries churning and hovercraft splashing and great jets flying in, with fleets of ships lying always offshore, with double-decker buses and clanging tramcars, with a car it seems for every square foot of roadway, with a pedestrian for every square inch of sidewalk, and funicular trains crawling up and down the mountainside, and small scrubbed-faced policemen scudding about on motorbikes—all in all, with a pace of life so unremitting, a sense of movement and enterprise so challenging, that one's senses are overwhelmed by the sheer glory of human animation.

— By Jan Morris

Jan Morris is the author of more than 20 books, including such best sellers as Journeys, Destinations, *and* Manhattan '45. *This excerpt comes from her book on Hong Kong.*

FOOD AND DRINK IN HONG KONG AND MACAU

IF YOU ARE COMING to Hong Kong for the first time, there are certain misconceptions that you must leave at home. First, Hong Kong doesn't just have some of the better Chinese food in the world; it has the best.

Such a statement may not find immediate acceptance in Taiwan or the People's Republic of China, but the proof of the pudding is in the eating, as they say in the West, and those Taiwanese and mainland Chinese who can afford it come to Hong Kong to eat. It is historical fact that chefs were brought from Canton to Peking to serve in the Chinese emperors' kitchens, and that for many centuries the Cantonese were acknowledged as the Middle Kingdom's finest cooks.

There is an old Chinese maxim that tells listeners where to find the prettiest girls, where to get married, where to die, where to eat, and so forth; the answer to "where to eat" is Canton (now called Guangzhou in the approved official romanization of Chinese names that also changes Peking to Beijing).

Hong Kong's 6-million-plus population is 98% Chinese, and the vast majority of that number are Cantonese (that includes a significant group of Chiu Chow people, whose families originated around the port city of Swatow). Food is a subject of overriding importance to the Cantonese, and it can be claimed of them as it is of the French, that they live to eat rather than eat to live. Find out how true that statement is on a culinary tour of Hong Kong.

There's no such thing as a fortune cookie in a Hong Kong restaurant; it was the overseas Chinese who came up with that novelty. Chop suey was invented overseas, too. The exact origin is disputed: Some people say it began on the California goldfields; others give credit (or blame) to Australian gold miners.

The Cantonese made an art out of a necessity, and, during times of hardship, used every part of an animal, fish, or vegetable. Some dishes on a typical Hong Kong menu will sound strange, even un-

appetizing—goose webs, for example, or cockerels' testicles, cows' innards, snakes (in season), pigs' shanks, and other things that may not be served at McDonald's. But why not succumb to new taste experiences? Who scorns the French for eating snails and frogs, or the Japanese for eating raw fish, or the Scots for stuffing a sheep's stomach lining?

Visit a daytime dim-sum palace. Served from before dawn to around 5 or 6 PM, the Cantonese daytime snacks of dim-sum are miniature works of art. There are about 2,000 types in the Cantonese repertoire. Most dim-sum restaurants prepare 100 varieties daily. Generally served steaming in bamboo baskets, the buns, crepes, and cakes are among the world's finest hors d'oeuvres. Many are works of culinary engineering—such as a soup with prawns served in a translucent rice pastry shell, or a thousand-layer cake, or the ubiquitous spring roll.

There are hundreds of dim-sum restaurants. The Hong Kong Tourist Association (HKTA) publishes a listing of some of the better ones that welcome tourists. The publication also provides color illustrations of the main dim-sum favorites. Many of the top-rated Chinese restaurants in hotels, and some of the better restaurants, provide (somewhat incongruously) elegant settings for lunchtime dim sum—with bilingual check sheets, waiter service, and private tables. Such class costs about HK$15 or more per basket. History-minded snackers will prefer, preferably in the company of Cantonese colleagues, to visit the culinary shrine of the Luk Yu Teahouse in Central (24 Stanley St.).

Luk Yu is more than a restaurant. It is one of Hong Kong's few historical monuments. It's fitting that a restaurant should be an unofficially preserved monument in this culinary capital of the world. It opened in the early 20th century as a wood-beamed, black-fanned, brass-edged place for Chinese gentlemen to partake of tea, dim sum, and gossip. When it was forced to relocate over a decade ago, everything was kept intact—marble-back chairs, floor spittoons, kettle warmers, brass coat hooks, lock-up liquor cabinets for regular patrons, and a Sikh doorman. Despite the modern air-conditioning, fans still decorate a plain ceiling that looks down on elaborately framed scrolls, carved-wood booth partitions, and colored-glass panels. The ancient wood staircase still creaks as Hong Kong's gentlemen ascend to the upper floors to discuss the territory's government and business.

Modernity has brought the English language, bilingual menus (but not for the individually served dim-sum items), and some good manners to Luk Yu. And so the adventurous tourist will seek out daytime dim-sum palaces where such modern affectations do not exist—as in the authentic teahouses of Mongkok, where local customers still "walk the bird" at dawn (the Chinese tradition—considered very "masculine"—of taking one's caged bird out for a morning stroll).

Birds are also to be eaten, of course. As far as the Cantonese are concerned, anything that "keeps its back to heaven" is fit for cooking. Bird-tasting experiences in Hong Kong should include a feast of quails; smooth, salted chicken; sweet roasted chicken in lemon sauce; and minced pigeon served in lettuce leaf "bowls" (that are rolled up with a plum sauce "adhesive"). Pigeons in dozens of different forms can best be enjoyed in the New Territories, around the new city of Shatin.

Fish can be enjoyed anywhere. Hong Kong is a major port with numerous fishing communities—something easily forgotten by the city-centered visitor. Go to the islands, to **Lamma** especially, for fine seafood feasts. Or take the bus and ferry trip to **Leiyuemun,** where you can choose your dinner from the massive fish tanks, haggle over its price, and take it into any restaurant for cooking and an alfresco feast.

At Causeway Bay, a small fleet of sampans turns dining out into a memorable experience. Your private floating restaurant table bobs past other craft selling shellfish, fresh fruit and vegetables, beer and spirits. There is even a floating Cantonese Opera minitroupe that can be hired to serenade you.

The prime floating experience is, of course, the **Jumbo restaurant** at Aberdeen. It is moored to another floating home of seafood and gaudy multicolored carvings and murals that are a sight worth seeing. The Jumbo, a 2,000-seat three-decker, is a marvel of outrageous ostentatiousness.

THERE'S IS NO SUCH thing as "Chinese" cooking in China. Every good "Chinese" cook has his (or sometimes her) own repertoire that will reflect his clan's origin. Most Hong Kong restaurants are Cantonese. Others concentrate on Pekingese or northern styles, Shanghai specialties, or the other regional styles of Szechuan or Chiu Chow cooking. There are a few spots that offer Hakka-style food, some Mongolian specialty restaurants (featuring hot pots), a Hunanese restaurant, and even a Taiwanese café on Food Street.

Food Street, in Causeway Bay, is a good place for a first-timer to start discovering the variety of food available in Hong Kong. There are now two covered and fountained arcades of relatively well-managed restaurants to suit most tastes and budgets. All around them, in an area that's generally named after the Daimaru department store, are literally hundreds of other cafés and restaurants.

Other favored eating places are in **Wanchai,** once the fictional home of Suzie Wong and now a struggling nightlife area that has run out of sailors. Restaurants have appeared instead, alongside the topless bars, hostess-filled nightclubs, and dance halls that are expensive ways to get a drink in Hong Kong.

In "old" **Tsim Sha Tsui,** on both sides of Nathan Road, from the Peninsula Hotel up to the Jordan Road junction, there is another batch of good, long-established restaurants. And Tsim Sha Tsui East has skyscrapers bursting with a wide variety of eating spots—from grand Cantonese restaurants to cheerful little cafés. There, as everywhere, you'll find not only Cantonese fare but Korean barbecues, Singaporean satays, Peking duck, Shanghainese breads and eel dishes, fine Western cuisine—and junk food, of course.

The **Harbour City** complex, along Canton Road, has many fine spots tucked into shopping arcades or courtyards. **Central,** once morguelike at night, is now a bustling dining district with a warren of trendy bistros and good Indian restaurants up the hillside lanes, on and off Wyndham Street and Lan Kwai Fong. All are much favored by resident expatriates.

Then there are the hotels, culinary competitors full of stylish salons—so stylish it's now hard to find a simple, old-fashioned coffee shop. Travel away from downtown districts and you find more temptations. Every housing estate and community center now boasts at least one brass-and-chrome home of good Cantonese cuisine, often as chic as it is wholesome.

Deciding what and where to eat can be a headache in Hong Kong. There is an embarrassment of riches. This guidebook's restaurant listings will help. Once in Hong Kong, get the HKTA's guide to dining and nightlife. It is free and gives a useful introduction to Chinese regional cuisines, chopstick wielding, dim-sum selecting, and other topics that can confuse a novice.

IN SIMPLE TERMS, the Northern or Peking cuisine is designed to fill and warm—noodles, dumplings, and breads of various types are more evident than rice. Mongolian or Manchurian hot pots (a sort of fondue-cum-barbecue) are specialties, and firm flavors (garlic, ginger, leek, etc.) are popular. Desserts, of little interest to Cantonese, are heavy and sweet. Feasts have long been favored in the north, and not just by emperors composing week-long banquets with elaborate centerpieces such as Peking duck (a three-course marvel of skin slices, sautéed meat, a rich soup of duck bones, and Tien Tsin cabbage). Beggar's chicken, about which you'll hear varying legendary origins, is another culinary ceremony, in which a stuffed, seasoned, lotus-leaf-wrapped, and clay-baked bird releases heavenly aromas when its clay is cracked open.

Farther south, the Shanghai region (including Hangzhou) developed tastes similar to Peking's but with an oilier, sweeter style that favored preserved meats, fish, and vegetables. In Hong Kong, the Shanghainese cafés are generally just that—unostentatious cafés with massive "buffet" displays of preserved or fresh snacks that are popular with late-nighters.

The phenomenal development of a middle class in Hong Kong in recent years has prompted the appearance of grander, glitzier restaurants, for Shanghainese and all other major regional cuisines. Those run by the Maxim's group are always reliable, moderately priced, and welcoming.

The territory's Chiu Chow restaurants also come alive late at night—especially in the Chiu Chow–populated areas of the Western District (on Hong Kong Island) or in parts of western Kowloon. As with Shanghainese and Cantonese cuisine, the Chiu Chow repertoire emphasizes its homeland's marine traditions, especially for shellfish. The exotic-sounding "bird's nest" is the great Chiu Chow delicacy. It's the refined, congealed saliva of nest-building swallows (mainly gathered from Gulf of Siam cliff-face nests). Although it may sound terrible, it is often exquisitely flavored. The dish is also deemed to be an aphrodisiac, as are many of China's most expensive luxury food items. That's why a visit to a Chinese department store should include a shocked glance at the "medicine" counter's natural foods. The prices of top-grade bird's nest, shark's fins, deer horns, ginseng roots, and other time-tested fortifications are staggering. The laws of supply and demand are very apparent on the price tags.

The roughest, simplest fare can appear to be that of the Szechuan region. At first tasting, the fiery peppercorned dishes, akin to both Thai and Indian cuisines, can be tongue-searing. After a while, when the taste buds have blossomed again, the subtleties of Szechuan spices will be apparent—particularly in the classic smoked duck specialty, where camphor wood chips and red tea leaves add magical tinges to a finely seasoned, daylong marinated duck.

Other regional variations (such as those of Hunan or the Hakka people) are not as distinctive as the major regional cuisines and are rarely found in Hong Kong. But any visitor who wants a taste of adventure can find a host of alternatives.

Chinese-influenced Asian cuisines are well represented. Even before the exodus of ethnic Chinese from Vietnam, that nation's exciting blend of native, French, and Chinese cooking styles was popular in Hong Kong. Now there are many cafés and a few smart restaurants specializing in prawns on sugar cane, mint-leaved meals, Vietnamese-style (labeled "VN") salamis, omelets, and fondues. Look, too, for Burmese restaurants.

The most ubiquitous Asian cuisine is the multiethnic "Malaysian," a budget diner's culinary United Nations that includes native Malay, Indian, and Straits Chinese dishes, as well as "European" meals and the Sino-Malay culinary cross-culture of the *nonya* cooking (developed by Malay wives to satisfy Chinese spouses).

Indian restaurants are also popular, and not just with Hong Kong's population of immigrants from the subcontinent. Usually the Indian kitchens concentrate on the northern Moghul styles of cooking, with reliable tandoori dishes. Vegetarians also find pleasures at Indian cafés. Thailand has not been forgotten, and the territory sports more than 24 spicy Thai restaurants.

Northeast Asia is also well represented. Some observers claim that Hong Kong has some of the world's finest Japanese restaurants, which thrive on local seafood catches and still tempt big spenders with their imports of the highly prized Kobe or Matsukaya beef (marbled slices of fine flavor produced by beer-massaged and pampered steers). Smaller spenders welcome the many local Korean cafés, whose inexpensive *bulgogi* (barbecues) provide that country's distinctive, garlicky, marinated meats and the minibuffet of preserved kimchee selections.

Then there's Indonesia, which has given Hong Kong another host of inexpensive, nourishing cafés. From Europe, there is a culinary wonderland of fine French restaurants (mostly in the top hotels), British pubs, German wining-and-dining havens, deli delights, and a sprinkling of delightfully offbeat eating experiences—from Mexican to Austrian, Spanish-Filipino, and Californian.

Although the Cantonese are the world's finest cooks, they are among the least polite waiters and waitresses in the world.

The Cantonese are proud, some say arrogant, and their dialect has a belligerent tone and abruptness that translates poorly into English. Don't expect smiles or obsequiousness: Hong Kong isn't Bangkok or Manila. It's friendly in its own abrupt way, and it's certainly efficient, and if you meet smiles as well, count yourself lucky. And give the extra percentage on the tip that the pleasant waiter deserves.

Don't tip at local corner cafés or the few remaining roadside food stalls, since it's not expected. And wherever you eat, at the top or lower ends of the culinary scale, always check prices beforehand, especially for fresh fish, which is now a luxury in Hong Kong. "Seasonal" prices apply to many dishes and can be steep. And note that there are various categories of prized Chinese delicacies on menus—shark's fin, abalone, bird's nest, and bamboo fungus, for example—which can cost an emperor's ransom. Although few Hong Kong restaurants set out to rip off tourists (certainly not those that are sign-bearing members of the HKTA), waiters will of course try to "sell up."

Also, don't settle for the safe standbys for tourists. Sweet and sour pork, chop suey, and fried rice can be marvelous in Hong Kong. But the best dishes are off the menu, on table cards, written in Chinese, advertising seasonal specialties. Ask for translations, ask for interesting recommendations, try new items—show that you are adventurous and the captains will respond, giving you the respect and fine dishes you deserve.

— Barry Girling

A food, travel, and entertainment columnist, Barry Girling has lived in Hong Kong since 1977.

DOING BUSINESS IN HONG KONG

IN MORE WAYS than one, Hong Kong is returning to its roots. The most obvious transition came at midnight on June 30, 1997, when the Union Jack was lowered from the Government House flagpole in the Central District of Hong Kong Island for the last time. At that moment, China regained sovereignty over the island for the first time since 1842, when Britain officially assumed control.

Indirectly related to Hong Kong's becoming again a part of China is a more subtle change: An ongoing economic transformation that is seeing the one-time colony become closely integrated with the mainland and especially with Guangdong Province, the part of China Hong Kong abuts.

China's opening to world commerce under Deng Xiaoping in the late 1970s came at the perfect time for Hong Kong. Though its population was growing, the territory had nevertheless reached its peak as a manufacturing center. But soon, Hong Kong factories were being shuttered up and moved to Guangdong Province, where labor costs were much cheaper. Hong Kong became the principal gateway to China, benefiting by the more than 20% annual growth of the southern mainland. And its economy shifted to embrace a clean and lucrative set of industries that revolved around trade and financial services.

Hong Kong and China began to merge economically even before the political day of destiny arrived. China's influence grew while Britain's weakened. The decision in 1996 by Swire Pacific, an old-line British trading hong, to sell major parts of its Cathay Pacific Airways and sister company Dragonair to mainland interests typified the transition. The Royal Hong Kong Jockey Club, long the essence of colonial British rule, dropped "Royal" from its name and British-influenced place names and street names in Hong Kong—Victoria Park and Queen's Road are two of the more obvious examples—may also change under pressure.

Cosmetic name changes are one thing, but will the essence of Hong Kong—its business culture—also be transformed? Hard to say. But if it does change, it's not hard to guess which habits will be the first to go. Business dress in Hong Kong, formal as ever, seems much closer to a British tradition than to the more laid-back styles in other Southeast Asian business centers such as Singapore and Kuala Lumpur. True, those cities are intensely hot and humid year-round, but a sultry summer day in Hong Kong is more than muggy enough to make you wonder whether a suit is really warranted. Business fashion in China is generally less formal, but it remains to be seen whether China will begin dressing up or Hong Kong dressing down.

Until Hong Kong fashion changes substantially, be sure to wear the lightest possible suit materials you can afford, and always carry an extra supply of handkerchiefs—you'll need them to towel off the sweat. Also, in the summer have an umbrella handy. And keep one eye out for typhoon warning flags in the lobbies of hotels and office buildings. When the No. 8 flag is hoisted, time is running out. Cabs are likely to be few and far between, and the ones you can find will be charging a steep premium. You aren't likely to miss much anyway, since many businesses shut down when the No. 8 shows.

Harder to gauge than the impact of the changeover on fashion will be the effect on language requirements in business. For decades in mainland China, Beijing has sought to make Mandarin the official language in deed as well as in word. But southern Chinese, especially in Guangdong Province, have insisted on retaining their Cantonese dialect, which is as different from the official language as French is from Spanish. Despite the resistance, Mandarin, or *putonghua*—the people's language—has made inroads. Television newscasts in Guangdong today come in both flavors. Hong Kong is likely to be even more resistant to Mandarin. It's true that Mandarin classes are ubiquitous among the downtown Hong Kong high-rises, but some Hong Kongers still are loath to admit they understand the mainland language even when they do. Travelers to France will be familiar with the expressions of feigned lingual bewilderment.

Surprisingly, the changeover is not apt to have an impact on the use of English in Hong Kong. Even Malaysia, the former British colony that bitterly rejected the English language after the nation was formed from a polyglot of British colonies and outposts in 1957, has returned to it on purely utilitarian grounds. With ethnic Chinese holding strong economic influence throughout the region, various Chinese dialects are unquestionably useful, but English remains, arguably, the language of business in Asia.

One Hong Kong trait that is unlikely to change anytime soon is its citizens' single-minded devotion to making money. An American businessman remarked: "I'm from Minnesota. When I wake up in the morning, I'm thinking about fishing. When a Chinese person wakes up, he's thinking about ways to make money." That's an important characteristic to keep in mind, whether you're considering how much *laisee* money to give staff at the Chinese New Year or contemplating gifts for a new business partner. Resist the temptation to skimp.

But don't assume that understanding Hong Kong's lust for money is enough to overcome all cultural differences. For example, Hong Kongers have a keen sense of hierarchy in the office. Egalitarianism may be admired in the U.S., but it is often insulting in Hong Kong. Let the tea lady get the tea and coffee—that's what she's there for. Your assistant or Chinese colleague has better things to do than make copies or deliver messages. You'll only engender animosity if you assign such tasks without appreciating whether they fit with job descriptions. And if you do the jobs yourself, you may be sending the message that the person assigned is incompetent—it's easy to offend unwittingly.

Hong Kong's attraction to business cards is easily explained. Status and hierarchy go hand in hand, and business cards are the tangible evidence of both. For your part, have plenty of cards available. Preferably, they should be printed in English on one side and Chinese on the other. Exchange cards by proffering yours with both hands and a slight bow. Receive a card in the same way. It is polite to examine the card you

get immediately upon receiving it, still holding it with two hands, and comment on some aspect of it: your colleague's title is impressive, or the card itself is of high quality. Such a response gives the person you're greeting face: His or her prestige and personal dignity have been publicly acknowledged.

DON'T BE SURPRISED, no matter how late in the day it may be, if you are invited to a meal after you're done making a suitably impressive showing on your first meeting with a business associate. Hong Kongers work late, and they often don't get around to eating dinner until well into the evening. A full day of meetings followed by dinner at 10 PM is not unusual, and it's a good idea to make dinner reservations even when it seems you're unlikely to find a restaurant of any sort still open. The fact is, they are open, and they're probably busy.

It won't hurt to brush up on your use of chopsticks. Silverware is common in Hong Kong, but it might be seen as another face-giving gesture if you try your hand at chopsticks. After all, the conversation is probably in English, and learning to use chopsticks is a fairly easy way to reciprocate a cultural interest.

Of course, all of these things—dress, language, business cards, chopsticks—pale next to some of the meaty questions surrounding the changeover. As uncertain as the impact the transition will have on Hong Kong's business culture may be, the effect on weightier issues is even less clear. For instance, the Hong Kong currency has been pegged to the U.S. dollar since 1982 at a rate that fluctuates in a narrow range near 7.8 Hong Kong dollars to $1 U.S. Publicly, Chinese officials say the peg won't change after 1997. But it is undeniable that the peg has been responsible for a good portion of Hong Kong's inflation, which has fluctuated between 7% and 10% for most of the '90s. In large part that's because the U.S. dollar has lost so much ground to the Japanese yen in the last decade, though the dollar regained strength in 1996. For the time being, the Chinese government already has more on its plate than it can easily swallow, which makes it unlikely that the peg will change soon. But the long run is a different story.

As for taxes, China has pledged not to change Hong Kong's reputation as a tax haven for business. The territory has been able to keep its flat tax rate to just below 15%, partly because it hasn't had to pay for its defense (the British garrison provided protection) and because it hasn't chosen to spend much on social welfare. Beijing made it clear before the handover that China does not want to inherit an expanding welfare state.

Of all the questions hanging over the transition, none is likely to have a bigger impact on business than what becomes of the rule of law. Unquestionably, mainland China is moving in Hong Kong's direction on this issue—attempting to establish a legal framework in which laws are written and contracts enforced in a way that is quite new to the world's oldest culture. Today, Hong Kong is southern Asia's regional headquarters of choice for a variety of multinational American, European, and Asian firms. By itself, that's a powerful incentive for China to want to leave Hong Kong alone—don't tinker with success. But there are those who wonder whether Beijing will be able to keep its hands totally off its expensive new toy, and whether, just by handling, the toy might be damaged.

In other ways, will Hong Kong become more like the mainland, or vice-versa? It will be interesting to see how, to take just one for-instance, Hong Kong's zoning laws will fare under Chinese rule. China essentially has no tradition of zoning.

How will a mainland developer feel when told he can't build in Hong Kong because a law prohibits it? Such a case may go a long way toward describing whether Hong Kong is ultimately ruled by laws or by people.

In spite of the questions, it would be short-sighted not to see the Chinese takeover of Hong Kong as, at least in an economic sense, precisely what the city needs. There is no question that China's growth has fueled Hong Kong's economy since the early 1980s. At the time China opened up to the outside world, nearly half of Hong Kong's workers were employed in manufacturing. Today, the fraction is barely one-sixth. In the same period, employment in trade, tourism, and services has gone from 30% to 55%.

Clearly, if Hong Kong is to continue its strong economic performance, it will be on the back of China—providing financial and insurance services, advice, and investment. Hong Kong will most assuredly change. The big remaining question is whether Hong Kong will continue to be an international city that caters to foreign interests looking for a comfortable conduit to China, or whether it will be swallowed by the mainland.

— Tim Healy

Tim Healy has reported, written, and edited business news for more than 10 years. He currently writes for Asiaweek, a weekly newsmagazine published in Hong Kong.

A SHOPPER'S PARADISE

WHATEVER YOUR reason for coming to Hong Kong, and whether or not you are a shopper by nature, it is very unlikely that you will leave the place without having bought *something*. Indeed, there's a roaring trade in bargain-priced luggage because so many visitors run out of space in the suitcases they arrived with.

There are several good reasons why Hong Kong is such an extraordinary shopping mecca. The first is its status as a free port, whereby everything, other than alcohol, tobacco, perfumes, cosmetics, cars, and some petroleum products, comes in without import duty. The second is the fact that Hong Kong has a skilled and still relatively inexpensive labor force. Goods made here are considerably cheaper than they will be by the time they reach shop shelves anywhere else in the world. The third factor is the highly competitive nature of the retail business—the result of a local policy of free trade, which encourages everyone to try to undercut his neighbor. To this end, many shops, with the exception of those in the Western and Central districts, stay open until 10 PM. Shops are also humming on Sundays and on all holidays apart from Chinese New Year, when everything closes for at least three days.

What else is special about Hong Kong? For a start, consider the geography of the place. It is very small, and very heavily populated. It has had to grow upward and downward rather than outward, which means that there are shops and small businesses in all sorts of unexpected places. You'll find a trendy fashion designer tucked away on the third floor of a scruffy alleyway building, a picture framer operating out of the basement of a lighting shop, a tailor snipping and stitching in the back room of a shoe shop. Many of the buildings will appear dingy and dirty, and you will be convinced that no self-respecting business can be carried on there. But it can be and it is. And these are the places where Hong Kong residents do much of their shopping. Also disconcerting for people who come expecting to find the streets lined with bargains is the discovery that prices for the same goods vary from sky-high to rock-bottom within a 100-yard stretch of shops. But this is the land of free trade. And it is why shopping around and sticking to reputable establishments are prerequisites to any successful purchase, particularly an expensive one.

By reputable establishments we mean ones that have been recommended by a friend who lives or shops regularly in Hong Kong, by this guidebook, or by the Hong Kong Tourist Association (HKTA) via its invaluable shopping brochure.

All shops bearing the HKTA's red junk logo in their window are supposed to provide good value for money, accurate representation of products sold, and prompt rectification of justified complaints, but if you have problems, call the HKTA (☎ 2801–7177). For complaints about non-HKTA shops, call the Consumer Council (☎ 2736–3322).

The law of the jungle is alive and well in Hong Kong, so be prepared for lots of shoving and pushing on the sidewalks, little respect for taxi lines, a limited amount in the way of gallantry, and an overwhelming urge on the part of sales staff to sell you something, no matter what!

Contrary to popular belief, not everyone speaks English. In the main tourist shopping areas you can probably count on most shop staff speaking some English—but do not assume that they understand all you say, even if they nod their heads confidently. Many of the taxi drivers' English is limited, too, and it can make life easier if you get your destination written down in Chinese by the hotel concierge before you set off. Most taxis now carry a radio microphone that lets you speak to their headquarters, where someone will translate.

Once on the right road, shopping around and bargaining are your golden rules. The pressure from sales staff can be exasperating. If you are just browsing, make this very clear. Don't be pushed into a purchase. Note the details of items and prices on the shop's business card. Always ask about discounts—sizable ones for multiple purchases. You should be able to get a discount just about everywhere except in Japanese department stores and some of the larger boutiques, which sell on a fixed-price basis. When other shops try to convince you that everything is fixed price, don't believe them. You should get a discount of at least 10%, and more likely 40%, from jewelers and furriers.

EQUALLY, **DO NOT** necessarily believe a salesman when he assures you that his price is his "very best" unless you have done enough shopping around to know that he is offering you a good deal. Never be bashful about asking for a discount. It is the accepted and expected way of conducting business all over Asia.

After checking out the prices in several different shops, you'll have a good idea of how much you should pay. Don't imagine that you will get the very best price (you won't know what it is, anyway); these are generally given only to local Chinese customers. Your best bet is to compare the price with what you might have to pay for such an item back home.

If you are planning to shop in markets, alleys, or market stalls, it's best not to go very dressed up; this will not help your bargaining position. Make sure to inspect the goods you buy very carefully; many of them are seconds. Look closely at lengths of fabric; they may have faults. When you buy clothing, inspect the actual item handed to you. You may have chosen it on the strength of a sample hanging up, but what you are given could be different. It may not be the same size, and it could have more serious flaws.

At the other end of the scale, if you are intending to shop for something important like jewelry or a fur coat, it can work in your favor to dress smartly. It is amazing how much more seriously you are taken if you look the part.

If you do not know much about the commodity you are buying, do not hesitate to ask the salesperson to explain or to show you the difference between, say, a HK$30,000 diamond and a HK$10,000

one of the same size, or the difference between the two mink coats that look similar to you but carry vastly different price tags. Any reputable dealer in these specialist items should be happy to show you what you are getting for the extra money, and how it compares to the less expensive item. The understanding of such factors can help you to make up your mind about which is really the better buy.

Having satisfied yourself that you really want the item and have struck the right price for it, you are ready for the exchange of money. (Although credit cards and traveler's checks are widely accepted, the best prices are offered for cash purchases.) An appropriate guarantee and a fully itemized receipt should be provided by the shop for any major purchase. Such details as the model number and serial number of manufactured goods such as cameras, VCRs, or electronic equipment, or the description of gems and precious metal content in jewelry and watches, should be noted.

Make sure you get a worldwide/international guarantee that carries the name or logo of the relevant sole agent in Hong Kong and that there is a service center in your home town or country. And if you are having something shipped home for you (many shops are geared up for this), make sure that the insurance covers not only loss, but also damage, in transit.

So much for the nuts and bolts. But forewarned is forearmed, which, we hope, will make the experience of shopping in Hong Kong all the more fun. Because fun it certainly is. Whether you are drifting about in the comfort of the air-conditioned shopping malls, exploring the factory outlets of Hung Hom, or poking about in the alleys and backstreets, you are getting a look at the life and guts of Hong Kong. It's as much a cultural experience as a shopping expedition. In a way, that can be the most unexpected bargain of all.

— Patricia Davis

A freelance writer based in Hong Kong, Trish Davis specializes in the arts and consumer affairs. Her shopping columns appear regularly, and her background includes extensive experience with women's magazines and newspapers.

BOOKS AND PERIODICALS

JAMES CLAVELL'S *Taipan* and *Noble House* are blockbuster novels covering the early history of the British colony and the multifaceted life found there around the 1950s. Both books provide insights, sometimes sensationalized, sometimes accurate. Robert S. Elegant's *Dynasty* is another epic novel tracing the development of a powerful Eurasian family. It has some simplified history, but it does reveal a lot about the way locals think. Another best-seller set in Hong Kong is John LeCarre's *The Honorable Schoolboy*, a superb spy thriller. On a smaller scale is Han Suyin's *A Many Splendoured Thing*. Another classic novel is Richard Mason's *The World of Suzie Wong*, which covers an American's adventures with a young woman in the Wanchai bar area. Austin Coates's *Myself a Mandarin* is a lively and humorous account of a European magistrate handling Chinese society, and his *City of Broken Promises* is a rags-to-riches biography of an 18th-century woman from Macau.

Maurice Collis's beautifully written classic, *Foreign Mud,* covers the early opium trade and China wars. Colin N. Criswell's *The Taipans: Hong Kong's Merchant Princes* describes the historical inspiration for novels exploring that era. G. B. Endicott's *History of Hong Kong* traces Hong Kong from its beginnings to the riot-wracked 1960s. Trea Wiltshire's *Hong Kong: Improbable Journey* focuses exclusively on recent times. Richard Hughes's *Borrowed Time, Borrowed Place* looks at Hong Kong immediately before the signing of the 1984 Sino-British Agreement that returned Hong Kong to the People's Republic of China in 1997. David Bonavia's *Hong Kong 1997: The Final Settlement* provides history and analysis of the agreement.

Jan Morris's *Hong Kong: Social Life and Customs* is a current primer on the region's daily interpersonal interactions. For younger readers, try Nancy P. McKenna's *A Family in Hong Kong,* part of a series describing families all over the world. G. S. Heywood's *Rambles in Hong Kong* is a personal reflection on the former colony. T. Wing Lo's *Corruption and Politics in Hong Kong and China,* published by Taylor & Francis, is an intriguing current criminology study. *Born to Shop Hong Kong: The Insider's Guide to Name-Brand, Designer, & Bargain Shopping in Hong Kong,* by Suzy Gershman, is great for die-hard bargain hunters. And Kevin Rafferty's *City on the Rocks: Hong Kong's Uncertain Future* looks at the break from colonialism.

There are many publications available for businesspeople. Most banks and major realty companies publish economic newsletters for their customers. The American Chamber of Commerce publishes books on Hong Kong and China, including *Living in Hong Kong, Doing Business in Hong Kong,* and *Establishing an Office in Hong Kong,* available to members and nonmembers. The *Far Eastern Economic Review Yearbook* and the Hong Kong Government *Yearbook* are essential reference books; the *Monthly Digest* from the government's Census and Statistics Department may also be useful. *Hong Kong Tax Planning* is, as the name implies, a useful book to cut through the legalese of Hong Kong's tax codes. The China Phone Book Co. publishes a slew of useful publications on China in addition to its telephone and telex directories.

Newspapers

Newspapers and magazines from all over the world are readily available in Hong Kong. The *Asian Wall Street Journal,* the *Eastern Express, International Herald Tribune,* and *USA Today International* print international editions in Hong Kong to supplement the two English-language daily newspapers, the *South China Morning Post* and the *Hongkong Standard.* The *Far Eastern Economic Review* leads the pack in business publications. *Time* and *Newsweek* both print in Hong Kong, and the news weekly *Asiaweek* is published here.

INDEX

WHEREVER YOU TRAVEL, *H*ELP IS NEVER FAR AWAY.

From planning your trip to providing travel assistance along the way, American Express® Travel Service Offices are always there to help you do more.

Hong Kong

American Express Travel Service
25 Kimberley Road
Tsimshatsui, Kowloon
2/2732-7327

http://www.americanexpress.com/travel

American Express Travel Service Offices are located throughout Hong Kong. For the office nearest you, call 1-800-AXP-3429.